Lecture Notes in Computer Science 14714

The series Lecture Notes in Computer Science (LNCS), including its subseries Lecture Notes in Artificial Intelligence (LNAI) and Lecture Notes in Bioinformatics (LNBI), has established itself as a medium for the publication of new developments in computer science and information technology research, teaching, and education.

LNCS enjoys close cooperation with the computer science R & D community, the series counts many renowned academics among its volume editors and paper authors, and collaborates with prestigious societies. Its mission is to serve this international community by providing an invaluable service, mainly focused on the publication of conference and workshop proceedings and postproceedings. LNCS commenced publication in 1973.

Aaron Marcus · Elizabeth Rosenzweig ·
Marcelo M. Soares
Editors

Design, User Experience, and Usability

13th International Conference, DUXU 2024
Held as Part of the 26th HCI International Conference, HCII 2024
Washington, DC, USA, June 29 – July 4, 2024
Proceedings, Part III

Springer

Editors
Aaron Marcus
Principal
Aaron Marcus and Associates
Berkeley, CA, USA

Elizabeth Rosenzweig
World Usability Day and Bubble Mountain
Newton Center, MA, USA

Marcelo M. Soares
Federal University of Pernambuco
Recife, Pernambuco, Brazil

ISSN 0302-9743 ISSN 1611-3349 (electronic)
Lecture Notes in Computer Science
ISBN 978-3-031-61355-5 ISBN 978-3-031-61356-2 (eBook)
https://doi.org/10.1007/978-3-031-61356-2

This Springer imprint is published by the registered company Springer Nature Switzerland AG
The registered company address is: Gewerbestrasse 11, 6330 Cham, Switzerland

Foreword

This year we celebrate 40 years since the establishment of the HCI International (HCII) Conference, which has been a hub for presenting groundbreaking research and novel ideas and collaboration for people from all over the world.

The HCII conference was founded in 1984 by Prof. Gavriel Salvendy (Purdue University, USA, Tsinghua University, P.R. China, and University of Central Florida, USA) and the first event of the series, "1st USA-Japan Conference on Human-Computer Interaction", was held in Honolulu, Hawaii, USA, 18–20 August. Since then, HCI International is held jointly with several Thematic Areas and Affiliated Conferences, with each one under the auspices of a distinguished international Program Board and under one management and one registration. Twenty-six HCI International Conferences have been organized so far (every two years until 2013, and annually thereafter).

Over the years, this conference has served as a platform for scholars, researchers, industry experts and students to exchange ideas, connect, and address challenges in the ever-evolving HCI field. Throughout these 40 years, the conference has evolved itself, adapting to new technologies and emerging trends, while staying committed to its core mission of advancing knowledge and driving change.

As we celebrate this milestone anniversary, we reflect on the contributions of its founding members and appreciate the commitment of its current and past Affiliated Conference Program Board Chairs and members. We are also thankful to all past conference attendees who have shaped this community into what it is today.

The 26th International Conference on Human-Computer Interaction, HCI International 2024 (HCII 2024), was held as a 'hybrid' event at the Washington Hilton Hotel, Washington, DC, USA, during 29 June – 4 July 2024. It incorporated the 21 thematic areas and affiliated conferences listed below.

A total of 5108 individuals from academia, research institutes, industry, and government agencies from 85 countries submitted contributions, and 1271 papers and 309 posters were included in the volumes of the proceedings that were published just before the start of the conference, these are listed below. The contributions thoroughly cover the entire field of human-computer interaction, addressing major advances in knowledge and effective use of computers in a variety of application areas. These papers provide academics, researchers, engineers, scientists, practitioners and students with state-of-the-art information on the most recent advances in HCI.

The HCI International (HCII) conference also offers the option of presenting 'Late Breaking Work', and this applies both for papers and posters, with corresponding volumes of proceedings that will be published after the conference. Full papers will be included in the 'HCII 2024 - Late Breaking Papers' volumes of the proceedings to be published in the Springer LNCS series, while 'Poster Extended Abstracts' will be included as short research papers in the 'HCII 2024 - Late Breaking Posters' volumes to be published in the Springer CCIS series.

I would like to thank the Program Board Chairs and the members of the Program Boards of all thematic areas and affiliated conferences for their contribution towards the high scientific quality and overall success of the HCI International 2024 conference. Their manifold support in terms of paper reviewing (single-blind review process, with a minimum of two reviews per submission), session organization and their willingness to act as goodwill ambassadors for the conference is most highly appreciated.

This conference would not have been possible without the continuous and unwavering support and advice of Gavriel Salvendy, founder, General Chair Emeritus, and Scientific Advisor. For his outstanding efforts, I would like to express my sincere appreciation to Abbas Moallem, Communications Chair and Editor of HCI International News.

July 2024 Constantine Stephanidis

HCI International 2024 Thematic Areas and Affiliated Conferences

- HCI: Human-Computer Interaction Thematic Area
- HIMI: Human Interface and the Management of Information Thematic Area
- EPCE: 21st International Conference on Engineering Psychology and Cognitive Ergonomics
- AC: 18th International Conference on Augmented Cognition
- UAHCI: 18th International Conference on Universal Access in Human-Computer Interaction
- CCD: 16th International Conference on Cross-Cultural Design
- SCSM: 16th International Conference on Social Computing and Social Media
- VAMR: 16th International Conference on Virtual, Augmented and Mixed Reality
- DHM: 15th International Conference on Digital Human Modeling & Applications in Health, Safety, Ergonomics & Risk Management
- DUXU: 13th International Conference on Design, User Experience and Usability
- C&C: 12th International Conference on Culture and Computing
- DAPI: 12th International Conference on Distributed, Ambient and Pervasive Interactions
- HCIBGO: 11th International Conference on HCI in Business, Government and Organizations
- LCT: 11th International Conference on Learning and Collaboration Technologies
- ITAP: 10th International Conference on Human Aspects of IT for the Aged Population
- AIS: 6th International Conference on Adaptive Instructional Systems
- HCI-CPT: 6th International Conference on HCI for Cybersecurity, Privacy and Trust
- HCI-Games: 6th International Conference on HCI in Games
- MobiTAS: 6th International Conference on HCI in Mobility, Transport and Automotive Systems
- AI-HCI: 5th International Conference on Artificial Intelligence in HCI
- MOBILE: 5th International Conference on Human-Centered Design, Operation and Evaluation of Mobile Communications

List of Conference Proceedings Volumes Appearing Before the Conference

1. LNCS 14684, Human-Computer Interaction: Part I, edited by Masaaki Kurosu and Ayako Hashizume
2. LNCS 14685, Human-Computer Interaction: Part II, edited by Masaaki Kurosu and Ayako Hashizume
3. LNCS 14686, Human-Computer Interaction: Part III, edited by Masaaki Kurosu and Ayako Hashizume
4. LNCS 14687, Human-Computer Interaction: Part IV, edited by Masaaki Kurosu and Ayako Hashizume
5. LNCS 14688, Human-Computer Interaction: Part V, edited by Masaaki Kurosu and Ayako Hashizume
6. LNCS 14689, Human Interface and the Management of Information: Part I, edited by Hirohiko Mori and Yumi Asahi
7. LNCS 14690, Human Interface and the Management of Information: Part II, edited by Hirohiko Mori and Yumi Asahi
8. LNCS 14691, Human Interface and the Management of Information: Part III, edited by Hirohiko Mori and Yumi Asahi
9. LNAI 14692, Engineering Psychology and Cognitive Ergonomics: Part I, edited by Don Harris and Wen-Chin Li
10. LNAI 14693, Engineering Psychology and Cognitive Ergonomics: Part II, edited by Don Harris and Wen-Chin Li
11. LNAI 14694, Augmented Cognition, Part I, edited by Dylan D. Schmorrow and Cali M. Fidopiastis
12. LNAI 14695, Augmented Cognition, Part II, edited by Dylan D. Schmorrow and Cali M. Fidopiastis
13. LNCS 14696, Universal Access in Human-Computer Interaction: Part I, edited by Margherita Antona and Constantine Stephanidis
14. LNCS 14697, Universal Access in Human-Computer Interaction: Part II, edited by Margherita Antona and Constantine Stephanidis
15. LNCS 14698, Universal Access in Human-Computer Interaction: Part III, edited by Margherita Antona and Constantine Stephanidis
16. LNCS 14699, Cross-Cultural Design: Part I, edited by Pei-Luen Patrick Rau
17. LNCS 14700, Cross-Cultural Design: Part II, edited by Pei-Luen Patrick Rau
18. LNCS 14701, Cross-Cultural Design: Part III, edited by Pei-Luen Patrick Rau
19. LNCS 14702, Cross-Cultural Design: Part IV, edited by Pei-Luen Patrick Rau
20. LNCS 14703, Social Computing and Social Media: Part I, edited by Adela Coman and Simona Vasilache
21. LNCS 14704, Social Computing and Social Media: Part II, edited by Adela Coman and Simona Vasilache
22. LNCS 14705, Social Computing and Social Media: Part III, edited by Adela Coman and Simona Vasilache

23. LNCS 14706, Virtual, Augmented and Mixed Reality: Part I, edited by Jessie Y. C. Chen and Gino Fragomeni
24. LNCS 14707, Virtual, Augmented and Mixed Reality: Part II, edited by Jessie Y. C. Chen and Gino Fragomeni
25. LNCS 14708, Virtual, Augmented and Mixed Reality: Part III, edited by Jessie Y. C. Chen and Gino Fragomeni
26. LNCS 14709, Digital Human Modeling and Applications in Health, Safety, Ergonomics and Risk Management: Part I, edited by Vincent G. Duffy
27. LNCS 14710, Digital Human Modeling and Applications in Health, Safety, Ergonomics and Risk Management: Part II, edited by Vincent G. Duffy
28. LNCS 14711, Digital Human Modeling and Applications in Health, Safety, Ergonomics and Risk Management: Part III, edited by Vincent G. Duffy
29. LNCS 14712, Design, User Experience, and Usability: Part I, edited by Aaron Marcus, Elizabeth Rosenzweig and Marcelo M. Soares
30. LNCS 14713, Design, User Experience, and Usability: Part II, edited by Aaron Marcus, Elizabeth Rosenzweig and Marcelo M. Soares
31. LNCS 14714, Design, User Experience, and Usability: Part III, edited by Aaron Marcus, Elizabeth Rosenzweig and Marcelo M. Soares
32. LNCS 14715, Design, User Experience, and Usability: Part IV, edited by Aaron Marcus, Elizabeth Rosenzweig and Marcelo M. Soares
33. LNCS 14716, Design, User Experience, and Usability: Part V, edited by Aaron Marcus, Elizabeth Rosenzweig and Marcelo M. Soares
34. LNCS 14717, Culture and Computing, edited by Matthias Rauterberg
35. LNCS 14718, Distributed, Ambient and Pervasive Interactions: Part I, edited by Norbert A. Streitz and Shin'ichi Konomi
36. LNCS 14719, Distributed, Ambient and Pervasive Interactions: Part II, edited by Norbert A. Streitz and Shin'ichi Konomi
37. LNCS 14720, HCI in Business, Government and Organizations: Part I, edited by Fiona Fui-Hoon Nah and Keng Leng Siau
38. LNCS 14721, HCI in Business, Government and Organizations: Part II, edited by Fiona Fui-Hoon Nah and Keng Leng Siau
39. LNCS 14722, Learning and Collaboration Technologies: Part I, edited by Panayiotis Zaphiris and Andri Ioannou
40. LNCS 14723, Learning and Collaboration Technologies: Part II, edited by Panayiotis Zaphiris and Andri Ioannou
41. LNCS 14724, Learning and Collaboration Technologies: Part III, edited by Panayiotis Zaphiris and Andri Ioannou
42. LNCS 14725, Human Aspects of IT for the Aged Population: Part I, edited by Qin Gao and Jia Zhou
43. LNCS 14726, Human Aspects of IT for the Aged Population: Part II, edited by Qin Gao and Jia Zhou
44. LNCS 14727, Adaptive Instructional System, edited by Robert A. Sottilare and Jessica Schwarz
45. LNCS 14728, HCI for Cybersecurity, Privacy and Trust: Part I, edited by Abbas Moallem
46. LNCS 14729, HCI for Cybersecurity, Privacy and Trust: Part II, edited by Abbas Moallem

47. LNCS 14730, HCI in Games: Part I, edited by Xiaowen Fang
48. LNCS 14731, HCI in Games: Part II, edited by Xiaowen Fang
49. LNCS 14732, HCI in Mobility, Transport and Automotive Systems: Part I, edited by Heidi Krömker
50. LNCS 14733, HCI in Mobility, Transport and Automotive Systems: Part II, edited by Heidi Krömker
51. LNAI 14734, Artificial Intelligence in HCI: Part I, edited by Helmut Degen and Stavroula Ntoa
52. LNAI 14735, Artificial Intelligence in HCI: Part II, edited by Helmut Degen and Stavroula Ntoa
53. LNAI 14736, Artificial Intelligence in HCI: Part III, edited by Helmut Degen and Stavroula Ntoa
54. LNCS 14737, Design, Operation and Evaluation of Mobile Communications: Part I, edited by June Wei and George Margetis
55. LNCS 14738, Design, Operation and Evaluation of Mobile Communications: Part II, edited by June Wei and George Margetis
56. CCIS 2114, HCI International 2024 Posters - Part I, edited by Constantine Stephanidis, Margherita Antona, Stavroula Ntoa and Gavriel Salvendy
57. CCIS 2115, HCI International 2024 Posters - Part II, edited by Constantine Stephanidis, Margherita Antona, Stavroula Ntoa and Gavriel Salvendy
58. CCIS 2116, HCI International 2024 Posters - Part III, edited by Constantine Stephanidis, Margherita Antona, Stavroula Ntoa and Gavriel Salvendy
59. CCIS 2117, HCI International 2024 Posters - Part IV, edited by Constantine Stephanidis, Margherita Antona, Stavroula Ntoa and Gavriel Salvendy
60. CCIS 2118, HCI International 2024 Posters - Part V, edited by Constantine Stephanidis, Margherita Antona, Stavroula Ntoa and Gavriel Salvendy
61. CCIS 2119, HCI International 2024 Posters - Part VI, edited by Constantine Stephanidis, Margherita Antona, Stavroula Ntoa and Gavriel Salvendy
62. CCIS 2120, HCI International 2024 Posters - Part VII, edited by Constantine Stephanidis, Margherita Antona, Stavroula Ntoa and Gavriel Salvendy

https://2024.hci.international/proceedings

Preface

User experience (UX) refers to a person's thoughts, feelings, and behavior when using interactive systems. UX design becomes fundamentally important for new and emerging mobile, ubiquitous, and omnipresent computer-based contexts. The scope of design, user experience, and usability (DUXU) extends to all aspects of the user's interaction with a product or service, how it is perceived, learned, and used. DUXU also addresses design knowledge, methods, and practices, with a focus on deeply human-centered processes. Usability, usefulness, and appeal are fundamental requirements for effective user-experience design.

The 13th Design, User Experience, and Usability Conference (DUXU 2024), an affiliated conference of the HCI International conference, encouraged papers from professionals, academics, and researchers that report results and cover a broad range of research and development activities on a variety of related topics. Professionals include designers, software engineers, scientists, marketers, business leaders, and practitioners in fields such as AI, architecture, financial and wealth management, game design, graphic design, finance, healthcare, industrial design, mobile, psychology, travel, and vehicles.

This year's submissions covered a wide range of content across the spectrum of design, user-experience, and usability. The latest trends and technologies are represented, as well as contributions from professionals, academics, and researchers across the globe. The breadth of their work is indicated in the following topics covered in the proceedings, encompassing theoretical work, applied research across diverse application domains, UX studies, as well as discussions on contemporary technologies that reshape our interactions with computational products and services.

Five volumes of the HCII 2024 proceedings are dedicated to this year's edition of the DUXU Conference, covering topics related to:

- Information Visualization and Interaction Design, as well as Usability Testing and User Experience Evaluation;
- Designing Interactions for Intelligent Environments; Automotive Interactions and Smart Mobility Solutions; Speculative Design and Creativity;
- User Experience Design for Inclusion and Diversity; Human-Centered Design for Social Impact.
- Designing Immersive Experiences Across Contexts; Technology, Design, and Learner Engagement; User Experience in Tangible and Intangible Cultural Heritage;
- Innovative Design for Enhanced User Experience; Innovations in Product and Service Design.

The papers in these volumes were accepted for publication after a minimum of two single-blind reviews from the members of the DUXU Program Board or, in some cases, from Preface members of the Program Boards of other affiliated conferences. We would like to thank all of them for their invaluable contribution, support, and efforts.

July 2024

Aaron Marcus
Elizabeth Rosenzweig
Marcelo M. Soares

13th International Conference on Design, User Experience and Usability (DUXU 2024)

Program Board Chairs: **Aaron Marcus,** *Aaron Marcus and Associates, USA,* **Elizabeth Rosenzweig,** *World Usability Day and Bubble Mountain Consulting, USA* and **Marcelo M. Soares,** *Federal University of Pernambuco, Recife, Pernambuco, Brazil*

- Sisira Adikari, *University of Canberra, Australia*
- Ahmad Alhuwwari, *Orange Jordan, Jordan*
- Claire Ancient, *University of Winchester, UK*
- Eric Brangier, *Université de Lorraine, France*
- Lorenzo Cantoni, *USI - Università della Svizzera italiana, Switzerland*
- Silvia De los Rios, *Indra, Spain*
- Romi Dey, *Solved by Design, India*
- Marc Fabri, *Leeds Beckett University, UK*
- Michael R. Gibson, *The University of North Texas, USA*
- Zaiyan Gong, *Tongji University, P.R. China*
- Hao He, *Central Academy of Fine Arts, P.R. China*
- Ao Jiang, *Nanjing University of Aeronautics and Astronautics, P.R. China*
- Hannu Karvonen, *VTT Technical Research Centre of Finland Ltd., Finland*
- Zhen Liu, *South China University of Technology, P.R. China*
- Wei Liu, *Beijing Normal University, P.R. China*
- Ricardo Gregorio Lugo, *Tallinn University of Technology, Estonia*
- Keith Owens, *University of North Texas, USA*
- Francisco Rebelo, *University of Lisbon, Portugal*
- Christine Riedmann-Streitz, *MarkenFactory GmbH, Germany*
- Patricia Search, *Rensselaer Polytechnic Institute, USA*
- Dorothy Shamonsky, *Brandeis University, USA*
- Qi Tan, *Central Academy of Fine Arts, P.R. China*
- Ana Velhinho, *University of Aveiro - Digimedia, Portugal*
- Elisangela Vilar, *University of Lisbon, Portugal*
- Wei Wang, *Hunan University, P.R. China*

The full list with the Program Board Chairs and the members of the Program Boards of all thematic areas and affiliated conferences of HCII 2024 is available online at:

http://www.hci.international/board-members-2024.php

HCI International 2025 Conference

The 27th International Conference on Human-Computer Interaction, HCI International 2025, will be held jointly with the affiliated conferences at the Swedish Exhibition & Congress Centre and Gothia Towers Hotel, Gothenburg, Sweden, June 22–27, 2025. It will cover a broad spectrum of themes related to Human-Computer Interaction, including theoretical issues, methods, tools, processes, and case studies in HCI design, as well as novel interaction techniques, interfaces, and applications. The proceedings will be published by Springer. More information will become available on the conference website: https://2025.hci.international/.

General Chair
Prof. Constantine Stephanidis
University of Crete and ICS-FORTH
Heraklion, Crete, Greece
Email: general_chair@2025.hci.international

https://2025.hci.international/

Contents – Part III

User Experience Design for Inclusion and Diversity

Using the Technology Acceptance Model to Explore the User Experience of Smart Kitchen Use Among Older Adult Women

Cristina Perdomo Delgado[1], Jacquie Ripat[1](✉), Shauna Mallory-Hill[2], and Sarah Bohunicky[3]

[1] College of Rehabilitation Sciences, University of Manitoba, Winnipeg R3E 0W2, Canada
jacquie.ripat@umanitoba.ca

[2] Faculty of Architecture, University of Manitoba, Winnipeg R3E 0W2, Canada

[3] Faculty of Kinesiology and Recreation Management, University of Manitoba, Winnipeg R3E 0W2, Canada

Abstract. Smart kitchens can facilitate aging in place, improve older adults' autonomy in cooking, and reduce household injuries. Understanding the experiences of older adults can improve smart kitchen accessibility, acceptance, usability, and design. In this qualitative descriptive study, a Technology Acceptance Model (TAM) describes the user experience of thirteen older adult women in a smart kitchen. Participants prepared a standardized recipe in a smart kitchen and were interviewed with semi-structured questions afterward. Data was analyzed according to TAM, and four themes were identified: ease-of-use, perceived usefulness, attitude towards use, and intention-to-use. Ease-of-use was hindered by the participants' technological competence and the smart kitchen's innovative design, leading to challenges in physical and cognitive accessibility. However, participants perceived the smart kitchen to be easy to use. Regarding perceived usefulness, notable benefits included preventing ergonomic risks and enhancing usability for individuals using wheelchairs. However, there was a common belief that smart kitchens are more suited for younger individuals than for older adults. Regarding attitudes towards use, there was a perceived interest in using technological devices in the kitchen, provided they are not overly complex. The intention to use smart kitchens is influenced by a lack of knowledge regarding their existence and usability. It is important to implement training and awareness so clients can correctly use smart kitchens and perceive their benefits to improve adoption.

Keywords: Usability · Smart kitchen · older adults · Aging in place

1 Introduction

The term "Aging in place" refers to the ability to live comfortably and independently in one's own home rather than moving into an assisted living facility as one age. For many people, aging in place is associated with empowerment and dignity [1]. Several studies affirm that older adults prefer to age in place, surrounded by their family environment

A. Marcus et al. (Eds.): HCII 2024, LNCS 14714, pp. 3–12, 2024.
https://doi.org/10.1007/978-3-031-61356-2_1

[2, 3]. Other researchers have suggested that aging in place allows older adults to retain autonomy and independence in daily activities by delaying the option of institutional care [4, 5].

Home technology devices such as monitors, sensors, apps, and robotics can help older adults continue to live independently at home as they age. Smart homes equipped with technological devices have been designed to address the needs of older adults who wish to age in place. These homes aim to provide enhanced security, promote independence, offer better control over health-related aspects, and facilitate caregiving activities [6, 7]. Smart homes are made up of technologies that operate household appliances such as washing machines, ovens, and stoves and control daily routines, such as turning lights on and off, and opening and closing doors and windows. Telepresence robots are also sometimes introduced to reduce social isolation and to maintain contact with family remotely through video calls. Other technologies, such as apps and websites, have also been used to help guide and remind people of daily activities, such as taking medication, alerting them to meal and personal hygiene times, and choosing clothing based on the weather [8, 9].

The kitchen is one of the spaces in the home where older adults are at greater risk of accidents during cooking activities [10]. For this reason, different studies are committed to developing and designing smart kitchens that can improve usability for older adults and quality of life while aging in place [11, 12]. The descriptive article by Ceccacci et al. [13] introduced an accessible smart kitchen design, where the researchers demonstrated that older adults using this specific kitchen design improved the usability of appliances, such as the oven and dishwasher, compared to a traditional kitchen. It also highlighted how the placement of technological devices in the kitchen improved usability for older adults, even if they initially resisted or hesitated to adopt such technologies.

Understanding older adults' usability experiences with smart kitchens and their integrated technological devices can improve their accessibility, acceptability, and adoption [14, 15]. The older adult user experience (UX) with smart kitchen relates to usability, usefulness, function, and satisfaction with the technology. It focuses on the user's overall experience, including their perceptions and emotions. Different UX studies have recommended smart kitchen designs for older adults. However, more knowledge is needed about the usability and user experience of the smart kitchen among older adults aging in place [16, 17].

Features such as height-adjustable kitchen cabinets and user-friendly appliances are important features for older adults. However, the acceptance and usability of these devices among older adults remains uncertain. Research is needed to better understand how older adults can effectively use smart kitchens in order to design to their specific needs. The aim of this study was to qualitatively explore older women's experiences regarding the usability of a smart kitchen. Our research questions included: How do older women use smart kitchens? How usable is the smart kitchen? And how do usability experiences influence participants' intention to use the smart kitchen?

We used the Technology Acceptance Model (TAM) [18] as our analytic framework to examine and conceptualize our findings. This allowed us to qualitatively describe the user experience and intention to use the smart kitchen among older adult women.

1.1 Technology Acceptance Model (TAM).

The technology acceptance model (TAM) shapes how users accept and use technology. The model proposes that when users use a technology, different factors influence the decision about how and when they use it. The model analyzes perceived ease of use, which refers to when the person believes that the use of technology can reduce effort; perceived usefulness, which refers to when the person thinks that the use of technology can improve their performance; and perceived enjoyment, when the person enjoys using the technology [19].

1.2 Smart Kitchen

The University of Manitoba's L-shaped smart kitchen (Fig. 1) features height-adjustable kitchen cabinets and appliances controlled through custom-designed tablet software. The kitchen includes touchless sensors to turn the sink faucet on and off. Appliance controls and outlets are front-located for ease of access and visibility. Lower cabinets offer fully extendable drawer storage, with removable options provided at the cooktop and preparation areas and under sink clear space. Undercabinet task and toe-kick lighting is also provided. These design elements aim to enhance older adults' performance of cooking tasks. The intent is to improve the ergonomic positioning of older adults while cooking, facilitate manipulation of kitchen elements, and prevent possible risk situations.

Fig. 1. Smart kitchen

2 Method

2.1 Study Design

The study design was qualitative, descriptive, and exploratory based on subjective experiences of older women performing a standardized cooking task in the smart kitchen [20]. This study is one component of a mixed methods investigation examining ergonomic kitchen design to support aging in place. After completing the cooking task participants completed a semi-structured recorded interview that allowed them to delve deeper into their interactions with the smart kitchen. The multidisciplinary research team developed the interview guides, which included researchers with professional and research experience in design, architecture, occupational therapy, and kinesiology.

2.2 Participants

Participants were selected according to the following inclusion criteria: women, over 65 years old, right-hand dominant, generally healthy for the last six months, regularly prepare meals in their home kitchen, able to read and follow the steps of a recipe written in English, and able to participate in an interview of approximately one-hour duration. Participants received full written and verbal details of the experimental procedures and potential risks involved in the study before providing written consent. Study procedures were approved by the Research Ethics Board of the University of Manitoba in the spirit of the Declaration of Helsinki.

2.3 Data Collection

Participants attended an experimental session where they prepared the standardized recipe in the smart kitchen at the University of Manitoba. The standardized recipe required participants to cook a quiche, which was selected because it required participants to use all kitchen task zones. All participants used the same kitchen utensils the research assistants set up before each session.

In the smart kitchen, the heights of the kitchen counters and upper cabinets are adjustable using custom tablet software and lifting mechanisms. Initially, this adjustment was based on industry standards for the individual's anthropometry. During the preparation of the recipes, each task area was re-adjusted to the participants' preferred height. After completing the standardized cooking task, participants completed a semi-structured interview detailing their experiences of kitchen usability. Sample questions included: When you were gathering the ingredients, did you find anything to be difficult or anything that stood out? Did you find cooking difficult at any time? Was this kitchen easier to work in than the one you have at home? Did you enjoy cooking in this kitchen?

2.4 Data Analysis

A theoretical approach based on the Technology Acceptance Model (TAM) [18] was used to capture the opinions and experiences of older women. The analysis was completed by a postdoctoral-level researcher with expertise in conducting qualitative studies. The interviews were transcribed verbatim into a MS Word document and reviewed inductively by the authors. For initial coding, TAM-based theoretical codes (e.g., user intention, use behaviour, usefulness, and ease-of-use) were used to capture participants' experiences of use intention and user experience of the smart kitchen.

Reliability was calculated for all transcripts. Coding modelled on the initial codes was then used to identify patterns in responses among participants related to ease-of-use, perceived usefulness, attitude to use, and intention to use. These patterns were then used to develop the thematic findings.

2.5 Study Team

The multidisciplinary research team developed the interview guides, which included researchers with professional and research experience in design, architecture, occupational therapy, and kinesiology.

3 Results

Older women participants (n = 13) had a mean age of 73.9 years. Most participants reported spending between one and two hours daily on cooking activities. The participants used "traditional" kitchens in their homes, and for all participants, this was the first time they used a smart kitchen.

3.1 Description of the Technology Acceptance Model for Smart Kitchen

Figure 2 presents the findings from the interviews regarding the usability of the smart kitchen, user experience, usage intention, and usage attitude.

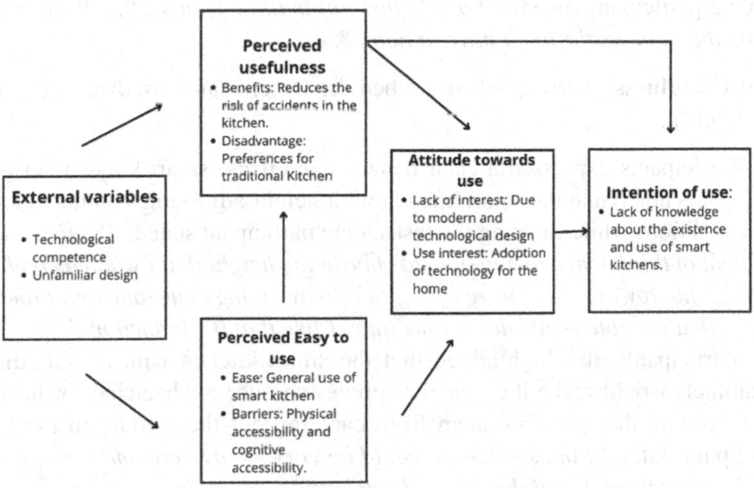

Fig. 2. Description of the TAM as applied in the Smart Kitchen

Perceived Ease-of-Use

Participants acknowledged that the smart kitchen, equipped with height-adjustable counters, facilitated cooking activities. However, participants quickly identified design challenges related to appliance placement, kitchen space, and cognitive accessibility issues. These included concerns about the usability of household appliances and physical accessibility problems, such as issues with faucet sensors. Some participants expressed the need to learn how to program the temperature when using the stove. Additionally, even those who could operate it needed help understanding its usability. One participant stated:

"Well, it's a new kitchen to me...so, the, the newness, um, and trying to figure out a. You know, like how to put the minutes on or on the stove? Yeah. Newness, I would say".

Some participants reported that using the faucet with sensors was complicated since they had to be mindful of the sensor's location to ensure water flow. Despite some barriers to using the smart kitchen, most participants thought it was generally easy to use. The perceived ease-of-use, however, was influenced by technological competence and the unfamiliar design of the smart kitchen.

External Variables

Technological competence. The participants expressed problems with technological competence, defined as the skills and knowledge that allow the usability of everyday technological devices. This manifested in specific difficulties in using the smart kitchen devices. As one participant said: *"Gosh, what was hard? Well, just cuz I'm unfamiliar with the cooktop trying to figure out the temperature".*

Unfamiliar Design of the Smart Kitchen. Participants indicated that the smart kitchen was unfamiliar to them and needed guidance for its usability. Some participants experienced disorientation, particularly when using various appliances or navigating different kitchen areas, such as the sink or drawers. This aspect influenced the ease-of-use of the kitchen. One participant stated: *"No, it's just unfamiliar. That's all... Well, it's never going to be the same as the one I have at home".*

Perceived Usefulness. Participants described the benefits and disadvantages of using the smart kitchen.

Benefits. Participants expressed a clear benefit from using smart kitchens in general. The participants noted that the smart kitchen with height-adjustable counters facilitated ergonomic positions while carrying out tasks. One participant stated: *"So that would've been a benefit of this kitchen, being able to choose the height that I wanted. Yeah.... It's especially the microwave cuz you're lifting hot, heavy things out sometimes and, um, I think that's, that's a potentially dangerous time. I like that it's induction."*

Other participants also highlighted that the smart kitchen with height-adjustable kitchen cabinets would make it easier for people who use a wheelchair or have some physical limitation that prevents them from carrying out the activity in the kitchen. One participant stated: *"I think someone could be very happy here and the open space, openness here for them, like if they're a wheelchair".*

Disadvantages. Most participants expressed that they perceived the smart kitchen would be useful for young or middle-aged people but did not find it useful for older adults because the devices they found in the smart kitchen were not considered useful. One participant stated, *"For older people, I don't see this being a really useful kitchen...probably because it's different."*

Attitude Towards Use

Lack of interest. Some participants showed a lack of interest in using a smart kitchen. The technological features of smart kitchen devices and their modern design influenced their attitude towards possible use in the home. One participant stated: *"I'm so used to mine. I know what needs to be done, where and how to put it. And this is, if the question is, would I like a kitchen like this? No".*

Interest of use. However, other participants highlighted that the experience with the smart kitchen gave them ideas to install drawers in their homes' kitchens that were adjustable according to height and the placement of lighting in different kitchen areas to facilitate the activity. One participant stated: *"Well, certainly the having one section of it at a lower height for doing those things that you like rolling out the dough or if I were kneading bread or I was doing something where I wanted a lower height, that is certainly something that I would appreciate in my kitchen, and I don't have".*

Intention of Use
Lack of knowledge. The intention to use was influenced by the participant's need for knowledge about the functions of the different smart kitchen devices (e.g., oven, microwave, stove). Most participants were not aware of the specific usability features of the devices. They did not know how to use them correctly, as one participant stated: *"Um, the, uh, the height or, or the timer on it is, um, it works, but it's, um, it doesn't show you the time counting down, which would be preferable because sometimes you, you wanna see how much time is left and you can't see how much time is left on this oven."*

4 Discussion

This study used the TAM to qualitatively explore the connections between ease-of- use, perceived usefulness, attitude toward use, and intention to use when using a smart kitchen with height-adjustable kitchen cabinets among older adult women.

According to the TAM framework, several external variables influence smart kitchens' usability and ease-of-use. The older adult participants in the study identified two external variables: technological competence and unfamiliar kitchen design. Specific training for using a smart kitchen can help older adults learn to use kitchen technology devices properly and reduce technology-related stress or anxiety episodes. Several studies refer to the fact that two of the barriers to the adoption of technological devices are the lack of training and the lack of training on the part of the companies that market the devices [21, 22]. The importance of a smart kitchen design is also underscored by its potential resemblance to traditional and intuitive kitchen layouts, aiming to streamline preparation activities for improved ease and orientation among older adults. Designing environments that are both interactive and easy to use is crucial. Older adults can rely on technological systems that are easy to use. An accessible design in technological devices is decisive in facilitating usability for older adults and positively impacting users' perception of technology [23].

The usability of height-adjustable kitchen cabinets in the smart kitchen was perceived as useful and easy to use. It is easier for participants to perform kitchen tasks when the drawers are at an appropriate height, considering the preferences and needs of the users. Physical and cognitive accessibility difficulties were also perceived when using smart kitchen technological devices. These difficulties influenced their overall evaluation of the ease-of-use. Our results align with previous studies suggesting that technology adoption is determined by perceived ease-of-use [24]. Older adults are unlikely to accept technological devices with complicated user systems. Therefore, technological devices for smart homes should seek feedback from older adults on the user experience and usability of interfaces during the development of new devices [25].

Physical and cognitive accessibility difficulties were also perceived when using smart kitchen technological devices, influencing the participants during the ease-of-use evaluation.

The preference for traditional kitchens poses a challenge to the willingness to adopt and use smart kitchens among older adults. This inclination acts as a barrier, affecting their intention to embrace smart kitchen technologies. To address this, designers of smart kitchens should consider the appeal of traditional kitchen designs. Incorporating features and technological devices that align with the familiar aspects of conventional kitchens may encourage older adults to consider and install these modern kitchen setups in their homes. For instance, when developing smart homes tailored for older adults who aim to age in place, it is crucial for designers to deeply understand the individual's needs, considering them in detail rather than solely relying on the designer's perspective [26].

Understanding the preferences and needs of older adults is necessary to design a smart home that meets the expectations of future users. The design of smart homes should also be based on the daily habits of older adults [27]. Older adults' lifestyles interfere with the needs and use of technological devices so that they may require different design solutions depending on their interests. Depending on the characteristics of the older adult, the desire to grow old at home and confidence in technological devices are important for positive technological acceptance at home [28].

Regardless of preference, older adults' interactions with assistive devices and hardware to allow for greater adjustability in the kitchen are increasing in use. Addressing user experience challenges and promoting perceived benefits can improve the use and acceptance of these types of technological devices in the homes of older adults aging in place.

4.1 Limitations

Although this study analyzed the perceptions of older adult women with a smart kitchen, the ease-of-use may differ between different smart kitchen designs. We used a qualitative descriptive approach to understand the user experience with the smart kitchen, their attitude and intention of use, and semi-structured interviews for data collection. Study results may have been enhanced using other data sources, such as usability and observation questionnaires. The small sample size may have led to limitations in the quantity of feedback.

5 Conclusion

Older adults increasingly use technological devices in their homes to improve their quality of life and promote their ability to age in place. There is an opportunity to involve older adults in the design and usability of smart kitchens. However, key considerations that promote ease-of-use, usefulness, attitude, and intention-to-use must be considered. Implementing training is crucial so that older adults, family members, and caregivers can effectively use a smart kitchen. This training is essential for enhancing understanding and awareness of the benefits of smart kitchens, ultimately fostering greater adoption among older adults.

Research on smart kitchens spans a transdisciplinary domain, drawing from disciplines such as architecture, engineering, and health, including occupational therapy. This study emphasizes the imperative of sharing knowledge and fostering collaboration in these interconnected fields. It supports the need for an integrated approach to smart homes, specifically tailored to address the unique needs of older adults who aim to age in place.

Acknowledgments. This study was funded by Mitacs and industry partner Decor Cabinet Company. Student research assistance was provided by Antoinette Baquiran, Keerthana Kalliat, Alandra Barairo, Valentina Lizcano Caballero, Reyhane Aliakbari, Taravat Nourian and Hussein Agoushi.

References

1. Maurenn, A.: Aging in Place. Home Healthc. Now **39**(6), 301 (2021)
2. Marshall, K., Hale, D.: Aging in Place. Home Healthc. Now **38**(3), 163–164 (2020)
3. Vanleerberghe, P., De Witte, N., Claes, C., Schalock, R.L., Verté, D.: The quality of life of older people aging in place: a literature review. Qual. Life Res. Int. J. Qual. Life Aspects Treatment Care Rehabil. **26**(11), 2899–2907 (2017)
4. Morley, J.E.: Aging successfully: the key to aging in place. J. Am. Med. Directors Assoc. **16**(12), 1005–1007 (2015)
5. Owusu, B., Bivins, B., Marseille, B.R., Baptiste, D.L.: Aging in place: programs, challenges and opportunities for promoting healthy aging for older adults. Nurs. Open **10**(9), 5784–5786 (2023)
6. Becker, S.A., Webbe, F.M.: The potential of hand-held assistive technology to improve safety for elder adults aging in place. In: Henriksen, K., (Eds.) et. al., Advances in Patient Safety: New Directions and Alternative Approaches (vol. 4: Technology and Medication Safety). Agency for Healthcare Research and Quality (US) (2008)
7. Peek, S.T., et al.: Older adults' reasons for using technology while aging in place. Gerontology **62**(2), 226–237 (2016)
8. McMurray, J., et al.: The importance of trust in the adoption and use of intelligent assistive technology by older adults to support aging in place: scoping review protocol. JMIR Res. Protoc. **6**(11), e218 (2017)
9. Sapci, A.H., Sapci, H.A.: Innovative assisted living tools, remote monitoring technologies, artificial intelligence-driven solutions, and robotic systems for aging societies: systematic review. JMIR Aging **2**(2), e15429 (2019)
10. Fisher, G.S., et al.: Home modification outcomes in the residences of older people as a result of cougar home safety assessment (version 4.0) recommendations. Californian J. Health Promot. **6**(1), 87–110 (2008)
11. Blasco, R., Marco, Á., Casas, R., Cirujano, D., Picking, R.: Una cocina inteligente para una vida asistida por el ambiente. Sensores (Basilea, Suiza) **14**(1), 1629–1653 (2014)
12. Perotti, L., Strutz, N.: Evaluation and intention to use the interactive robotic kitchen system AuRorA in older adults. Bewertung und Nutzungsbereitschaft des interaktiven Küchenroboters AuRorA bei älteren Erwachsenen. Zeitschrift fur Gerontologie und Geriatrie, **56**(7), 580–586 (2023)

13. Ceccacci, S., Menghi, R., Germani, M.: Example of a new smart kitchen model for energy efficiency and usability. In: Fourth International Conference on Smart Systems, Devices and Technologies, pp. 12–18 (2015)
14. Chung, J., Demiris, G., Thompson, H.J.: Ethical considerations regarding the use of smart home technologies for older adults: an integrative review. Ann. Rev. Nurs. Res. **34**, 155–181 (2016)
15. Zhou, C., Zhan, W., Huang, T., Zhao, H., Kaner, J.: An empirical study on the collaborative usability of age-appropriate smart home interface design. Front. Psychol. **14**, 1097834 (2023)
16. Li, L., Li, F.Y., Liu, Z.: Emotional social system design of smart kitchen for aging population. In: Rebelo, F. (eds.) Advances in Ergonomics in Design. AHFE 2021. Lecture Notes in Networks and Systems, vol. 261 (2021)
17. Zeiner, K.M., Henschel, J., Schippert, K., Haasler, K., Laib, M., Burmester, M.: Experience categories in specific contexts – creating positive experiences in smart kitchens. In: Marcus, A., Wang, W. (eds.) Design, User Experience, and Usability: Theory and Practice. DUXU 2018. Lecture Notes in Computer Science, vol. 10918 (2018)
18. Davis, F.D.: Technology acceptance model: TAM. Al-Suqri, MN, Al-Aufi, AS: Inf. Seek. Behav. Technol. Adoption 205–219 (1989)
19. Silva, P.: Davis' technology acceptance model (TAM)(1989). Inf. Seek. Behav. Technol. Adoption Theories Trends, pp. 205–219 (2015)
20. Carvalho, L., Scott, L., Jeffery, R.: An exploratory study into the use of qualitative research methods in descriptive process modelling. Inf. Softw. Technol. **47**(2), 113–127 (2005)
21. Martín-García, A.V., Redolat, R., Pinazo-Hernandis, S.: Factors influencing intention to technological use in older adults. The TAM Model Application. Res. Aging, **44**(7–8), 573–588 (2022)
22. Yusif, S., Soar, J., Hafeez-Baig, A.: Older people, assistive technologies, and the barriers to adoption: a systematic review. Int. J. Med. Inform. **94**, 112–116 (2016)
23. Pirzada, P., Wilde, A., Doherty, G.H., Harris-Birtill, D.: Ethics and acceptance of smart homes for older adults. Inform. Health Soc. Care, **47**(1), 10–37 (2022)
24. Berkowsky, R.W., Sharit, J., Czaja, S.J.: Factors predicting decisions about technology adoption among older adults. Innov. Aging **1**(3), 1–12 (2017)
25. Koskela, T., Väänänen-Vainio-Mattila, K.: Evolution towards smart home environments: empirical evaluation of three user interfaces. Pers. Ubiquit. Comput. **8**, 234–240 (2004)
26. Orpwood, R., Gibbs, C., Adlam, T., Faulkner, R., Meegahawatte, D.: The design of smart homes for people with dementia—user-interface aspects. Univer. Access Inform. Soc. **4**, 156–164 (2005)
27. Crabtree, A., Rodden, T.: Domestic routines and design for the home **13**, 191–220 (2004)
28. Peek, S.T., Wouters, E.J., Van Hoof, J., Luijkx, K.G., Boeije, H.R., Vrijhoef, H.J.: Factors influencing acceptance of technology for aging in place: a systematic review. Int. J. Med. Inform. **83**(4), 235–248 (2014)

Empowering Older Adults: A User-Centered Approach Combining iTV and Voice Assistants to Promote Social Interactions

Juliana Duarte de Camargo(✉), Telmo Silva, and Jorge Ferraz de Abreu

Department of Communication and Art (DeCA), University of Aveiro, Aveiro, Portugal
{julianacamargo,tsilva,jfa}@ua.pt

Abstract. Low digital literacy is classified by the United Nations (UN) and the World Health Organization (WHO) as one of the main factors in the social exclusion of seniors. Faced with this scenario, the two institutions put digital inclusion initiatives at the center of the debate. Projects and activities developed in this area are seen as ways of reducing isolation indicators and feelings of loneliness. To fill this gap, this study seeks to use smart speakers and televisions to empower older adults. The aim is for them to be able to contact their family and friends more easily, through a system that offers a simplified User experience (UX). The aim of this study is to help increase intergenerational connections through a system consisting of an application that sends notifications to the TV and a smart speaker. The whole process of devising the solution was based on the opinions/perceptions of the target audience. Firstly, 20 interviews were carried out with a group of older adults. Then, a focus group with six individuals helped clarify some perceptions and identify potential scenarios. This information supported the development of the web supporting platform, which was tested with a group of six older adults for 44 days in a real-life context. A gerontologist was subsequently interviewed so that she could evaluate the system before starting the final tests. The expert's perceptions were evaluated and changes were made so that the solution was as suitable as possible for the target audience. Next, an 82-year-old Portuguese man was invited to validate the process. The aim was to assess whether the testing procedure was the most appropriate before moving on to the final field tests. All the perceptions of the beta tester and the gerontologist are described throughout this paper. This experience has shown that the system's proactivity is a way of stimulating social interactions, as well as the ease of using voice commands to make calls and send messages.

Keywords: iTV · smart speaker · voice assistants · older adults · social isolation · social connections · loneliness · voice commands

1 Introduction

"*Older people don't like technology*". "*They are less inclined to learn*". "*They no longer care about new things*". These are some of the phrases commonly uttered when the subject comes up. But do they accurately reflect reality? This study brings several pieces

A. Marcus et al. (Eds.): HCII 2024, LNCS 14714, pp. 13–25, 2024.
https://doi.org/10.1007/978-3-031-61356-2_2

of evidence that show exactly the opposite. An analysis of previous research, such as [1–3] e [4], shows that this group does recognize the importance and usefulness of digital tools. However, they are aware that there are still many barriers between them and technology. Some of the main ones are: i) older adults don't always receive the most appropriate guidance on how to use digital resources; ii) they hardly have access to devices/systems that have been designed for senior citizens, considering their specificities.

Previous experiences show that putting the user at the center of the development process is essential if the use and, above all, the adoption of technological resources is to be real and effective among older people [5–8]. When this happens, the chances of having a result that meets senior expectations tend to increase.

Based on this perspective, this study shows the stages of an investigation that consists of always putting the elderly at the center, listening carefully to their wishes, desires and needs. The central aim is to devise a system capable of empowering the elderly to make calls and send messages to the people they love. All in a simpler, more practical and natural way, showing that they are capable of anything.

This paper begins with a summary of recent work in this area. It then presents how the solution that will be studied with older adults was devised. It follows to shows the initial test carried out with an expert, namely a gerontologist with extensive knowledge in this area. Finally, the results of a pre-field trial carried out with an 82-year-old man, who made phone calls and sent messages using voice commands for three months, are presented. The paper ends with a conclusion and a presentation of future work.

2 Related Work

Technology acts as an important link between generations, stimulating connections between older adults and geographically dispersed family/friends. However, just as digital resources have the capacity to strengthen bonds, they can also result in exclusion - and this has become evident in the wake of the Covid-19 pandemic [9]. It was clear from the social experiments carried out during this period that not knowing how to use devices and platforms can widen the gap between generations.

In the study [10], for example, the researchers carried out a survey of 37 older adults from Canada and found that the use of social networks and social technologies made the elderly maintain a greater bond with their children and grandchildren, especially those living in other countries. The results showed that families separated by geography can feel united if they use technology to keep in touch, especially platforms that allow them to call and send messages, as well as social networks.

In the study [11], 15 older adults Nigerians aged between 60 and 88 have shown that they recognize the importance of technology in connecting generations. However, they are aware that there are some barriers that can get in the way of these interactions: i) anxiety about using new platforms; and ii) difficulties of use. Different studies show, however, that these problems can be alleviated if there is more exchange/connection between the generations. In other words, younger people have an important role to play in passing on knowledge and guiding older people to use technological tools that promote social connection. During the pandemic, for example, the study [12] showed the experience of 115 postgraduate students who took part in a project in which they made 2 to 5 calls a week to older adults over a six-week period. The results included improvements in the quality of life in both groups of participants - and an increase in the digital literacy of the elderly participants.

In addition to the exchange of knowledge between the generations, the choice of device also makes a difference in boosting intergenerational connections. In this study [13], an experiment carried out with a tablet specially designed for older adults showed that the device can be useful for stimulating social interactions (if it has an interface specifically designed for this audience). In this other study [14], the researchers highlighted that television is an easy device to adopt precisely because of the familiarity seniors already have with it - they generally feel less anxious when the interface is similar to the TV. Regarding smartphones, although they are used by this audience, it is common for the elderly to have difficulties while interacting with it. These problems mean that various tasks are not completed, leading to frustration [15]. According to [16], the low levels of acceptance of smartphones by the elderly are related to the poor design of the interface, mainly because it is not suitable for this audience. Finally, interactions using voice commands have also been important in this context since they eliminate the typing barrier. This study [17] found that voice assistants, used through smart speakers, can reduce the barrier to accessing technology due to the ease of use of the interface. The potential of this type of technology with the senior audience has also been detected in [18–22].

These specificities show that the adoption of technology by the older adults depends on a combination of factors. The main ones are: the exchange of knowledge with individuals from other generations and the use of a suitable device. Therefore, solutions designed especially for this audience, which consider their perceptions at the development stage, tend to be more accepted by older individuals. These analyses were fundamental in guiding this study. There was a special concern to listen to the elderly at all stages so that the proposed solution would be appropriate to the reality - and the needs - of this audience.

3 The Solution

This study aims to propose a solution capable of facilitating and motivating intergenerational interactions (e.g. between grandparents and grandchildren or uncles and nephews). It was therefore necessary to think of a combination of resources so that older people could make calls, send messages and exchange information (in general) with younger people.

To achieve the desired result, it was decided to divide the study into phases, always placing the user at the center of the process so that it would be possible to understand their perceptions and desires. First, a literature review was carried out to identify communication needs of senior citizens and clarify key concepts for the study. This analysis showed that using television as a central element would be an interesting way forward, due to the familiarity of the elderly with the device. In addition, proactivity had also been shown to be a promising choice for motivating older people to use technology more often. The results of this analysis were published in [removed for blind review].

This review led to the creation of a semi-structured interview script, which was applied to 20 older adults aged between 60 and 95 to identify their preferences, their experience of using technology and their television content consumption habits (also available at [removed for blind review]).

The interviews made it possible to identify three scenarios related to sending notifications to television, presented in a focus group in which six elderly people took part (aged between 64 and 80). The results were published in [removed for blind review].

These initial stages were fundamental in choosing one of the technologies that would be part of the proposed solution: a platform for sending notifications to the TV, created by members of [removed for blind review]. The platform was developed and tested by six older adults in a real-life context for 44 days (the results were presented [removed for blind review].

In the next stage, to allow interactions to be made by voice commands, it was decided to incorporate a virtual assistant into the system. Six Brazilians used this combination of functionalities for a week in a pre-test, the aim of which was to verify the relevance of the chosen technologies. The results were published in [removed for blind review]. These steps allowed the final solution, called [removed for blind review]., to be structured. The prototype is therefore a mix of different technologies/devices (Fig. 1).

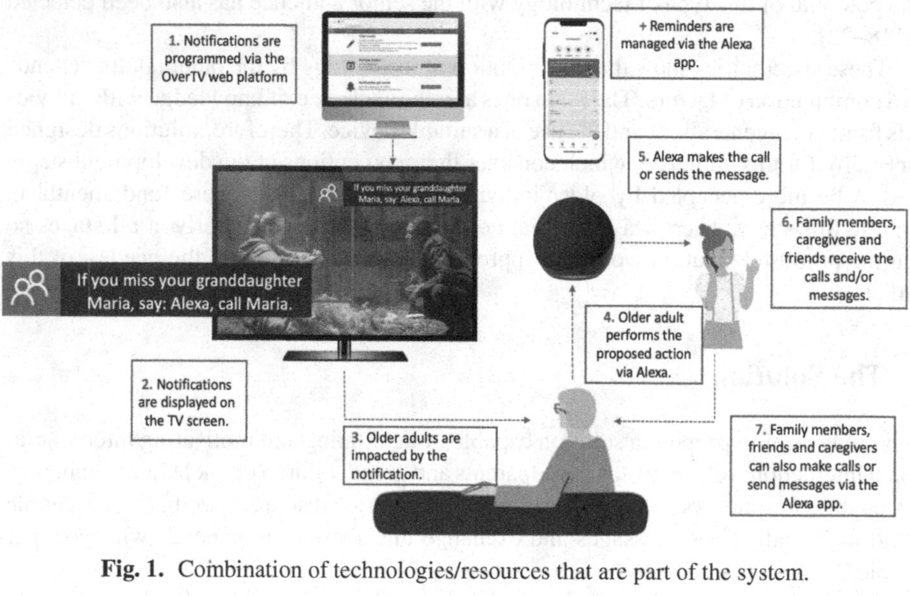

Fig. 1. Combination of technologies/resources that are part of the system.

As shown in Fig. 1, the operation of the system consists of:

- Schedule proactive messages sent via a web platform (1);
- Messages are displayed on the TV screen suggesting actions, such as “Dona Ana, if you miss your granddaughter Maria say: Alexa, call Maria”, “Dona Ana, ask me to send a message to Maria”, “Today is Maria’s birthday! Ask me to congratulate her” (2);

- The elderly person is impacted by the message sent proactively (3);
- The proposed action is carried out via Alexa by voice commands, eliminating the need to type. This provides an alternative to simplify the challenges associated with using technology for interacting with people (4);
- Alexa makes the calls or sends the messages (5);
- Family members and caregivers receive the contacts made by the elderly (6);
- Family members and caregivers also make calls via the app, which can be answered via the smart speaker (7).

In short, the users' perceptions have been the driving force behind this study. Figure 2 summarizes the methodology used, with all its phases.

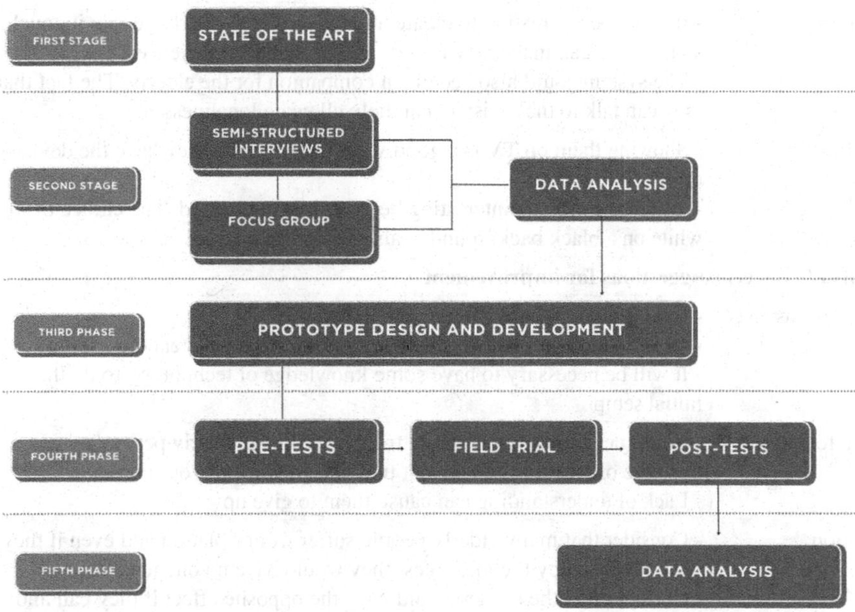

Fig. 2. Methodology defined for the study

4 Expert Opinion

Once the technologies that make up the solution had been defined, a gerontologist was invited to test it in a controlled environment. The session took place in December 2022 in the [removed for blind review] and lasted 42 min. Initially, when she was introduced to the project, she pointed out that, in general, technology has great potential to connect people. However, she emphasized that everything depends on how the resources are presented to this audience.

"You have to understand the profile of each elderly person. There are people who really aren't consumers of technology. That's why it's a plus to use the TV, since it's a

device that's already open to them", she said. Regarding the relevance of the proposed solution, the specialist made some specific observations, which are systematized in Table 1 (Table 2).

Table 1. The expert's opinions on the proposed system.

Theme	Expert opinion
Positive feedback	
Voice features	- It's an excellent resource for elderly people with visual impairments. Many people don't call because they can't see the keys on the phone - not having to type is a very interesting possibility
Isolation	- It could be interesting to create a network to put elderly people in touch, so that they can make new friends and exchange experiences; - The system could also become a companion for the elderly. The fact that they can talk to the assistant can help alleviate loneliness
Notifications	- Showing them on TV is a good way to go because they have the device on for a long time; - The font chosen is interesting because it is not serifed. The choice of white on a black background is also a good way to go
Points of concern/suggestions for improvement	
Cognitive aspects	- Not all older people will be able to use it; - Older adults with dementia, for example, will have great difficulty; - It will be necessary to have some knowledge of technology to do the initial setup
Voice features	- You'll need to do some initial training with the elderly person's voice, as this type of technology may not understand some of your commands; - Lack of understanding can cause them to give up
Isolation	- Consider that many elderly people suffer from isolation and even if they were impacted by the messages, they would have no one to call; - Consider that the system could have the opposite effect if they call and send messages and don't hear back from their relatives; - It's interesting to think about notifications that help to provide physical encounters, such as event suggestions, for example
Notifications	- Many elderly people can't read or have difficulty seeing. Therefore, having only the text can be a problem. It would be interesting to have audio support; - Consider adding a sound signal to attract the attention of the elderly; - The display time of 20 s is too short. I think it needs to be extended
Training	- Prior training on how to use the system is essential; - Leave a manual with them, especially with drawings that help guide use (but be careful not to infantilize the illustrations)

Overall, the expert expressed interest in the proposed solution for potentially mitigating loneliness and addressing social isolation. However, one we need to be aware that

Table 2. Opinion of the expert consulted and the respective corrections.

Expert's opinion	Corrections
The display time of 20 s is too short. I think it needs to be extended	The notification time has been increased from 20 to 40 s
Consider that the system could have the opposite effect if they call and send messages and don't hear back from their relatives	The content of the notifications has been revised so as not to generate adverse effects
It's interesting to think about notifications that help to provide physical encounters, such as event suggestions, for example	Messages encouraging face-to-face contact were included
Consider that the system could have the opposite effect if they call and send messages and don't hear back from their relatives	A volume of notifications was set (one per day) so as not to overdo it, thus avoiding possible frustrations
Consider that the system could have the opposite effect if they call and send messages and don't hear back from their relatives	It was decided that before the tests the UCLA loneliness scale would be applied to identify the profile of the elderly and thus plan suitable content for the notifications
Leave a manual with them, especially with drawings that help guide use	An imagery user manual (leaflet) was developed to guide the elderly during the usage of the system, without infantilizing them
Lack of understanding can cause them to give up	The voice assistant was changed - from Google Home to Alexa - as it allows calls to be made and messages to be sent more easily and has a greater capacity to understand the Portuguese language
You'll need to do some initial training with the elderly person's voice, as this type of technology may not understand some of your commands	Initial training has been planned to guide the elderly

this problem can be much deeper in some cases than simply not knowing how to use digital resources to connect. Hence the importance of applying a validated loneliness scale for the Portuguese language before starting the tests - in this way, it will be possible to understand the profile of the participants.

Another suggestion she emphasized was to include notifications that encourage physical contact with other people. Some examples: "*It's a beautiful day today. How about a walk*?"; "*The afternoon calls for warm bread! How about going to the bakery*?"; "*Have you talked to your neighbor today? Why don't you go and give her a hug*?".

In general, the gerontologist recognized the potential of proactivity and voice resources to encourage social contacts. Another point is that the simplicity of using a virtual assistant empowers the elderly - it makes them feel more at ease with technology, losing their fear and anxiety. He also pointed out that the system itself can become a companion for the elderly.

5 Pre-Field Trial

After the interview with the gerontologist, the system was revised based on the opinions collected. Some of the changes put into practice:

With the adjustments made, a Portuguese 82-year-old man was invited to test the solution. The experiment took place in a real-life context and lasted 3 months (90 days).

Regarding characterization, the participant (Fig. 3) has a master's degree, lives with his partner and has children and grandchildren. He also said that he has vision difficulties, although it doesn't hinder his usual activities. Regarding the use of devices, he has a cell phone, tablet and computer and consults one of her daughters when she has difficulty using them.

Fig. 3. Pre-field trial participant.

Regarding the use of TV, he said that he usually watches TV shows with family members or alone, more than once a day. He leaves the television on between 2.5 and 4 h a day. He usually watches news, documentaries, films and series, soap operas and entertainment programs. He considers television to be his daily companion.

Regarding the feeling of loneliness, on a scale of 0 to 6, where 0 meant "totally accompanied" and 6 "totally alone", the participant answered that he feels "quite accompanied – 1″. The user also reported that he usually communicates with family members via phone calls and voice messages.

The tests began in October/23 and ended in December/23, totaling three months. On the first day, the participant was introduced to the system and invited to try out a few phrases to interact with the Alexa virtual assistant. His daughter was also present, as she would be the point of contact for the tests. In other words, she was also invited to interact with her father via Alexa. An explanatory leaflet was given to both and some tests were carried out.

Proactive notifications were programmed via the platform so that the user was impacted and encouraged to take the proposed actions. Some examples: "*Do you miss your daughter Helena? Ask me to make a call to her*"; "*Today is Mafalda's birthday. Ask me to send a message to say happy birthday*!"; and "*Say: Alexa, send Helena a hug*". In addition to these messages aimed to improve social interactions, complementary notifications were also programmed, such as encouragement to exercise, reminders to take medication and music suggestions. In this way, the participant could interact and become more familiar with the system.

6 Results and Discussion

In total, 180 notifications sent by the TV were programmed, averaging to 2 per day. Of these, 94 were not received - this problem happens when the user's box is not turned on. Therefore, the message is not delivered. To detect why the messages weren't arriving, the participant was contacted frequently (around four times a week) - these conversations were also important for understanding their fears, anxieties and difficulties. Some notification schedules were adjusted based on these informal chats, which increased the incidence of messages being received.

Of the 180 scheduled notifications, 90 had content aimed at social interaction. In other words, they suggested some kind of action that encouraged people to make calls or exchange messages. The participant pointed out that these messages "are an interesting resource to remind him of his tasks and also to encourage him to get in touch with his family". However, of the 90 messages sent during the 90 days, 56 were received. There is no evidence that the proposed actions were carried out immediately after the notifications were sent. The user pointed out that he "often thought about doing the proposed activity but was distracted by the television content and hardly did it". However, he said that he felt more encouraged to do it at other times of the day. The most effective messages, according to him, were those containing birthday reminders or commemorative dates.

In parallel to sending messages to the TV, the researcher also programmed similar reminders transmitted via Alexa. The messages were delivered to the participant in audio only via the smart speaker. The inclusion of the messages via Alexa took place a month after the start of the tests after the researcher detected that he wasn't seeing all the messages sent to the TV.

In order not to tire the participant out, 2 notifications a week were delivered over a period of 60 days, giving a total of 16 social messages. Of this total, 10 actions were carried out immediately afterwards (as shown in Table 3).

When asked about the usefulness/effectiveness of the two types of notification (textual-television and Audio-Alexa), the participant preferred those issued by the smart speaker because: "the audible warning and the audio drew more attention than the textual message on the television". Another important factor is that the times of the notifications sent to the TV were adjusted according to his favorite programs so that the messages

Table 3. Notifications sent and actions taken.

	Time when notification is sent	Suggested action	Time of the proposed action	Interval between notifications and the action taken by the participant
1	9:45 a.m	Audio call	9:46 a.m	1 min
2	3:55 p.m	Audio call	3:58 p.m	3 min
3	2:27 p.m	Audio call	2:32 p.m	5 min
4	9:07 a.m	Sending a message	9:07 a.m	10 s
5	4:46 p.m	Audio call	4:47 p.m	1 min
6	4:46 p.m	Audio call	4:47 p.m	1 min
7	9:32 a.m	Sending a message	2:05 p.m	4 h and 30 min
8	2:45 p.m	Sending a message	2:45 p.m	20 s
9	2:16 p.m	Sending a message	2:17 p.m	1 min
10	3:21 p.m	Sending a message	3: 22 p.m	1 min

were viewed more frequently. In other words, such content can often be considered an interruption. Notifications on Alexa, on the other hand, were programmed in the morning or afternoon, at alternative times when the user pointed out that they have more free time. Thus, the tasks suggested by Alexa were considered a pastime.

Another discovery made during this testing period was the smart speaker's potential to empower the elderly to use technology. The voice commands enabled the elderly participant to do various tasks that require digital skills just by using spoken resources, without the need to type, which, according to him, gave him more "courage and desire to test new possibilities".

Table 4 shows the interactions made by the participant during the 90 days of testing. Only the fields marked with an "X" had proactive notifications encouraging the elderly person to do the proposed task. In other words, the rest were autonomous activities, carried out based on their own interests.

Table 4 shows that there was a good variety of queries/uses of the virtual assistant during the test period. The functionalities most used by the participant were "queries on specific topics on the internet" (60), "audio calls" (44), "music requests" (36), "everyday conversations" (34) and "sending a message" (28).

Table 4. Interactions carried out by Alexa.

Category of interaction	Number of interactions	Notifications
Consultation of specific topics on the internet	60	
Audio call	44	X
Music requests	36	
Everyday conversations with Alexa	34	
Message sending	28	X
Listen to the news	24	
Consult weather conditions	22	
Checking for new messages	15	X
Integration of another device (a smart gate)	9	
Set alarm	5	
Schedule reminder	2	
Timetable consultation	1	
Radio station	1	
Religious content	1	
Include items on the shopping list	1	

7 Conclusion

The stages described here were extremely important for preparing the final field trial for this study, which began in December 2023 and are scheduled to end in May 2024. The results obtained in the initial phases described here show that putting the user at the center of the process is extremely important for the development of solutions aimed at the elderly.

The opinion of an expert, namely the gerontologist who was consulted for the study, was crucial in making relevant adjustments. Some examples: i) increasing the time notifications are displayed on the screen; and ii) not overloading the participants with so many social messages. According to her, the important thing would be to show older adults that there is a simpler way of contacting the people they love. What's more, it would be possible to do this without stress or anxiety, two feelings that tend to put the elderly off using technological resources. According to the expert, the important thing was to empower them to use these resources only when they felt like it. No pressure. No demands or judgments. These perceptions, especially the social/emotional ones, were fundamental in guiding the field pre-test period.

During this period, an 82-year-old man was invited to use the solution for 90 days, an experience that resulted in several discoveries. The notifications sent to the TV were not as efficient as imagined in terms of numbers - there was no evidence that the actions were done in sequence. However, the user stated that he felt more motivated to call or send messages when he was impacted by the notifications on the TV. Messages programmed via Alexa, on the other hand, were more effective in the sense that they culminated in immediate actions. Of the 16 sent during the period, 10 were reproduced by the participant. This leads to three indications: i) audible warnings may be more relevant to the senior audience; and ii) alternative times may be more efficient; and iii) messages on TV may visually interrupt programs they are watching, which has an impact on carrying out the proposed actions. It is important to note that the specialist consulted (a gerontologist) warned of the relevance of sound warnings, but they were not integrated into the system due to technical limitations of the platform.

Another relevant finding is that Alexa herself was considered a companion for the elderly during the testing period. The category "everyday conversations with Alexa" ranked fourth among the most recurrent interactions, behind music requests, audio calls and queries on specific topics on the internet, Table 4, which lists the interactions made by the user, shows that the virtual assistant was used most frequently for social activities, whether calling, sending messages or simply chatting with the assistant.

For future tests, therefore, the aim is to assess whether these perceptions are valid for a wider group with less digital literacy. In general, we would like to use more audio notifications and vary the times when messages are sent to the TV to identify how useful this feature is with other older adults.

Acknowledgments. [removed for blind review].

References

1. Morrow-Howell, N., Galucia, N., Swinford, E.: Recovering from the COVID-19 pandemic: a focus on older adults. J. Aging Soc. Policy **32**(4–5), 526–535 (2020). https://doi.org/10.1080/08959420.2020.1759758
2. Talukder, M.S., Sorwar, G., Bao, Y., Ahmed, J.U., Palash, M.A.S.: Predicting antecedents of wearable healthcare technology acceptance by elderly: a combined SEM-neural network approach. Technol Forecast Soc. Change **150** (2020). https://doi.org/10.1016/j.techfore.2019.119793
3. Naudé, B., Rigaud, A.S., Pino, M.: Video calls for older adults: a narrative review of experiments involving older adults in elderly care institutions. Front. Public Health **9**. Frontiers Media S.A. (2022). https://doi.org/10.3389/fpubh.2021.751150
4. Jin, B., Kim, J., Baumgartner, L.M.: Informal learning of older adults in using mobile devices: a review of the literature. Adult Educ. Q. **69**(2), 120–141 (2019). https://doi.org/10.1177/0741713619834726
5. Mannheim, I., et al.: Inclusion of older adults in the research and design of digital technology. Int. J. Environ. Res. Public Health **16**(19) (2019). https://doi.org/10.3390/ijerph16193718
6. Pappas, M.A., Demertzi, E., Papagerasimou, Y., Koukianakis, L., Voukelatos, N., Drigas, A.: Cognitive-based E-learning design for older adults. Soc. Sci. **8**(1) (2019). https://doi.org/10.3390/socsci8010006
7. Taylor, J.R., Milne, A.J., Macritchie, J.: New musical interfaces for older adults in residential care: assessing a user-centred design approach. Disabil. Rehabil. Assist. Technol. **18**(5), 519–531 (2023). https://doi.org/10.1080/17483107.2021.1881172
8. Howes, S.C., Charles, D., Pedlow, K., Wilson, I., Holmes, D., McDonough, S.: User-centred design of an active computer gaming system for strength and balance exercises for older adults. J Enabling Technol **13**(2), 101–111 (2019). https://doi.org/10.1108/JET-12-2018-0057

9. Seifert, A., Cotten, S.R., Xie, B.: A double burden of exclusion? digital and social exclusion of older adults in times of COVID-19. J. Gerontol. Ser. B Psychol. Sci. Soc. Sci. **76**(3), E99–E103 (2021). https://doi.org/10.1093/geronb/gbaa098
10. Freeman, S., et al.: Intergenerational effects on the impacts of technology use in later life: Insights from an international, multi-site study. Int. J. Environ. Res. Public Health **17**(16), 1–14 (2020). https://doi.org/10.3390/ijerph17165711
11. Ojembe, B.U., Kalu, M.E.: Television, radio, and telephone: tools for reducing loneliness among older adults in Nigeria. Gerontechnology **18**(1), 36–46 (2019). https://doi.org/10.4017/gt.2019.18.1.004.00
12. Joosten-Hagye, D., Katz, A., Sivers-Teixeira, T., Yonshiro-Cho, J.: Age-friendly student senior connection: students' experience in an interprofessional pilot program to combat loneliness and isolation among older adults during the COVID-19 pandemic. J. Interprof. Care **34**(5), 668–671 (2020). https://doi.org/10.1080/13561820.2020.1822308
13. Barbosa Neves, B., Franz, R., Judges, R., Beermann, C., Baecker, R.: Can digital technology enhance social connectedness among older adults? a feasibility study. J. Appl. Gerontol. **38**(1), 49–72 (2019). https://doi.org/10.1177/0733464817741369
14. Wang, C.H., Wu, C.L.: Bridging the digital divide: the smart TV as a platform for digital literacy among the elderly. Behav. Inf. Technol. **41**(12), 2546–2559 (2022). https://doi.org/10.1080/0144929X.2021.1934732
15. Salman, H.M., Wan Ahmad, W.F., Sulaiman, S.: A design framework of a smartphone user interface for elderly users. Univers. Access Inf. Soc. **22**(2), 489–509 (2023). https://doi.org/10.1007/s10209-021-00856-6
16. Balata, J., Mikovec, Z., Slavicek, T.: KoalaPhone: touchscreen mobile phone UI for active seniors. J. Multimodal User Interfaces **9**(4), 263–273 (2015). https://doi.org/10.1007/s12193-015-0188-1
17. Pradhan, A., Lazar, A., Findlater, L.: Use of intelligent voice assistants by older adults with low technology use. ACM Trans. Comput.-Hum. Inter. (2020). https://doi.org/10.1145/3373759
18. Kim, S., Choudhury, A.: Exploring older adults' perception and use of smart speaker-based voice assistants: a longitudinal study. Comput. Hum. Behav. **124** (2021). https://doi.org/10.1016/j.chb.2021.106914
19. O'Brien, K., Liggett, A., Ramirez-Zohfeld, V., Sunkara, P., Lindquist, L.A.: Voice-controlled intelligent personal assistants to support aging in place. J. Am. Geriatr. Soc. (2020). https://doi.org/10.1111/jgs.16217
20. Hanley, M., Azenkot, S.: Understanding the Use of Voice Assistants by Older Adults, Cornell Tech (2019)
21. Stigall, B., Waycott, J., Baker, S., Caine, K.: Older adults' perception and use of voice user interfaces: a preliminary review of the computing literature. In: ACM International Conference Proceeding Series (2019).https://doi.org/10.1145/3369457.3369506
22. Orlofsky, S., Wozniak, K.: Older adults experiences using Alexa. Geriatr. Nurs. (Minneap) **48**, 240–250 (2022). https://doi.org/10.1016/j.gerinurse.2022.09.017

UX Design Curriculum: Intersectionality, Race and Ethnicity in Persona Construction

Guy-Serge Emmanuel(✉)

Quinnipiac University, Hamden, CT 06518, USA
gsestudio@gmail.com

Abstract. In UX Design, personas function as representations of typical users showing empathy for their unique needs while maintaining focus on a product. Personas help designers and engineering teams find a balance between user values, constraints, and limitations. Students and practitioners who lack a background in intersectionality will, understandably, demonstrate a limited understanding of the role of race and ethnicity in the persona creation process. In fact, previous research shows that UX designers create personas closely related to themselves, rather than focusing on the needs of the user, especially when it comes to race and ethnicity. Race and racism have played a role in UX design, so there must be a move toward educating design students and professionals on the impact of race and ethnicity when creating personas.

This research paper proposes to extend previously constructed teaching modules, focused on gender and Human-Computer Interaction, to extrapolate a more nuanced intersectional lens emphasizing the importance of race and ethnicity in persona creation. Students are introduced to theories of intersectionality, specifically regarding race and ethnicity, through various readings. Students apply what they learn by practicing, evaluating, and applying theories of intersectionality through group projects and case studies covering various topics such as consumerism, body, and medicine. Group interactions allow them to share their ideas, echoing the real-world scenario of UX Design practitioners, potentially leading to the creation of less racist products. Having educational modules on intersectionality and race and ethnicity is needed if we want UX designers to create inclusive technology.

Keywords: UXD Pedagogy · Intersectionality · HCI Curriculum · Persona Pedagogy

1 Introduction

This research paper is meant to introduce Intersectionality into the User Experience Design (UXD) educational process for the workforce of the future and will hopefully inform and educate the reader on the importance of inclusive design. UXD is the process employed by designers to create products whose goals are to make purposeful and significant experiences for users. A review of 15 graduate programs in UXD and HCI found most programs lack an Ethics course and thus are most likely not introducing

A. Marcus et al. (Eds.): HCII 2024, LNCS 14714, pp. 26–47, 2024.
https://doi.org/10.1007/978-3-031-61356-2_3

intersectionality to their students. This research paper investigates how Intersectionality might be introduced into graduate HCI and UXD curriculums.

The first wave of HCI focused on engineering and the second on cognitive science and psychology, whereas the third wave, UXD, focuses on the user's experience and their socio-cultural context. This paper proposes that a gap remains in HCI curricula: attention to intersectionality as an aspect of user identity creation in the design process. According to Don Norman, "no product is an island. A product is more than the product. It is a cohesive, integrated set of experiences". If HCI can be operationalized as user experience design, a term coined by Norman, then research is needed on the interactions between different groups of people and computer technology, especially those groups who hold non-majority identities. Building on Norman's work, the current International Organization for Standardization (ISO) defines the user experience as "a person's perceptions and responses that result from the use or anticipated use of a product, system or service" [1]. However, the term "person" in this definition has not been questioned other than to assume that it represents a typical user. This paper proposes that such generic terminology excludes some populations from the UXD process, as pictured in Fig. 1.

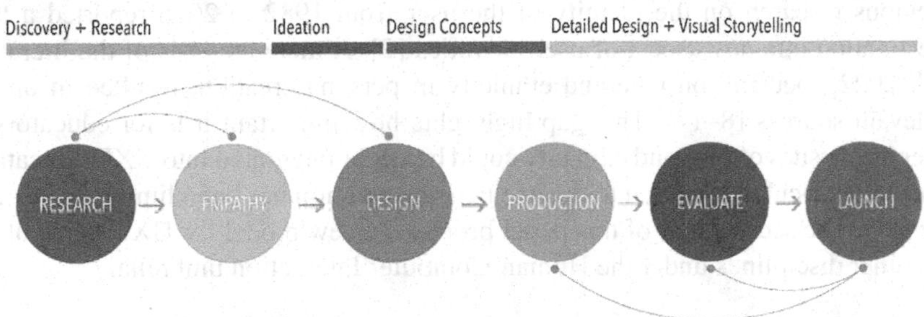

Fig. 1. UXD Design Process

This paper proposes an intervention into the teaching of UXD with the introduction of intersectionality into graduate-level curricula as a first step in addressing the profession's inadequate attention to this topic. Intersectionality, which was defined by legal scholar Kimberlé Crenshaw, involves "understanding the ways that multiple forms of inequality or disadvantage sometimes compound themselves and create obstacles that often are not understood in conventional ways of thinking" [2]. A survey of graduate-level courses in UXD curricula at fifteen (15) schools showed that few programs require a course on ethics or similar topics where intersectionality might be included. Instead, the focus is often on technology and innovation. In addition to highlighting this problem, this paper will provide a workable solution in the form of learning modules that will not only introduce intersectionality via a social constructivist learning framework but also provide assignments on how intersectionality can be assessed when it comes to race and ethnicity.

Oftentimes, the first representation of future users is during persona creation in the empathy stage of the process. Personas, first proposed by Alan Cooper [3], are tools that assist in analyzing user needs and design objects. In the world of UXD, personas are a tool used widely across many industries to represent what designers learned through their research. In healthcare, for example, personas are used to create a representation of the diversity of a population. The Nielsen Norman Group, a leader in UXD, defines three types of personas: Lightweight, Qualitative, and Statistical [4]. Lightweight personas are mostly taught in UXD programs and used by UXD students to create their portfolios so they may enter the workforce. They are also frequently used in the industry by UXD practitioners. Unfortunately, the hypothetical nature of the persona leaves its content dependent on what the designer of the persona chooses to highlight as well as the archetype the designer wishes to portray.

Previous research on this process has shown that UX designers create personas closely related to themselves when it comes to race and ethnicity [5]. This is also a pattern for UX designers of color, i.e. people who identify as Asian, Latinx, or Black, typically design personas that are more diverse than counterparts who identify as white [5]. Research looking at a small sample of Black UX designers shows that they design the most diverse personas. Given that only 3.5–5% of UX Designers are Black/African American [6, 7] and a mere 12% identify as LGBT [6], these trends are unlikely to change unless future generations of UX design students are trained to consider the importance of intersectional identities in the persona creation process.

Previous research on the identity of the user from 1982 to 2016 reported a lack of investigation into any aspect of user identities [2]. A meta-analysis of the literature through 2022, focusing on race and ethnicity in persona creation, resulted in only a few relevant sources [8–10]. This gap highlights how important it is for educators to consider how issues of race and ethnicity could be better integrated into UXD education. The current curricular approach to diverse persona creation has been limited to sex and gender [11]. The second half of this paper proposes a new model for UXD curricula as well as other disciplines under the Human-Computer Interaction umbrella.

2 Review of UXD Graduate Programs

2.1 Selection Process

The selected sample for the UXD program population was obtained via a Google search utilizing keywords that included "best UXD graduate program", "UXD master's program", and "best HCI graduate programs". Even when searching specifically for UXD results, most queries returned programs still named under the HCI umbrella. However, all results contained the UXD components necessary for this research. In particular, six websites were chosen to identify the best UXD graduate programs.

Note: The 10 Best Affordable HCI Masters Programs [12], *The Top 50 Best UX Design Graduate Programs* [13], *The College Rank* [14] *The Top 10 Best UX Design Graduate Programs in 2023* [15], *Top 10 Masters in UX Design programs* by the Career Foundry [16], and the *Best Universities for Human-Computer Interaction (HCI) in the World* [17] webpages are all supported by advertisement.

These websites provided a comprehensive search list of graduate programs. One website had an international focus, naming 100 institutions offering UXD programs. The other five websites focused solely on programs in the United States; one website gave a listing of their five best higher education institutions, two other sites gave their top 10 institutions, one their top 20, and the last named 50 institutions. Institutions and

RANKING						INSTITUTION	CARNEGIE	ONLINE	ON-GROUND
9	1	1	15	2	1	CARNEGIE MELLON	R1	No	Yes
7	2	NR	18	50	NR	DEPAUL UNIVERSITY	R2	No	Yes
14	8	9	14	48	NR	DREXEL UNIVERSITY	R1	No	Yes
1	5	3	5	8	3	GEORGIA INSTITUTE OF TECHNOLOGY	R1	Yes	No
2	NR	NR	3	31	NR	IOWA STATE UNIVERSITY	R1	Yes	Yes
NR	NR	NR	17	1	2	MASSACHUSSET INSTITUTE OF TECHNOLOGY	R1	No	Yes
NR	7	NR	NR	5	37	PURDUE UNIVERSITY	R1	No	Yes
NR	NR	2	13	4	4	STANFORD UNIVERSITY	R1	No	Yes
15	NR	10	20	13	NR	ROCHESTER INSTITUTE OF TECHNOLOGY	R1	Yes	Yes
NR	NR	6	NR	6	7	UNIVERSITY OF CALIFORNIA - BERKELEY	R1	No	Yes
4	4	NR	9	3	34	UNIVERSITY OF CALIFORNIA - IRVINE	R1	Yes	No
8	18	NR	4	25	30	INDIANA UNIVERSITY - BLOOMINGTON	R1	No	Yes
5	NR	NR	2	20	6	UNIVERSITY OF MARYLAND	R1	No	Yes
NR	NR	NR	7	17	11	UNIVERSITY OF MICHIGAN	R1	No	Yes
13	3	5	1	27	5	UNIVERSITY OF WASHINGTON	R1	No	Yes

15 Best Affordable HCI Masters Programs | 10 Best UX Design Graduate Programs | 10 Masters in UX Design programs

20 Best Master's in HCI | 50 Best UX Design Graduate Programs | Best Universities for HCI in the World

Fig. 2. Ranking, Institutions, Carnegie Classification, and Delivery Mode

programs were ranked by both academics and the monetary value of the UXD education. To be selected, a program had to appear on at least three of the six lists and offer a graduate degree in either HCI, UXD, or User Experience (UX). At the end of this process, a list of 15 programs were selected for further analysis.

2.2 Curriculum Review

A concern when selecting programs for review is students' inability to understand the concepts proposed by Crenshaw in their early college years. Similarly, in her book Intersectional Pedagogy, author Kim Case argues that undergraduate students struggle with the concept of intersectionality [18]. Therefore, this study focuses on graduate programs as the best vehicle for delivery of this content. The selected graduate programs all offer a variety of Master of Science (M.S.) degrees ranging from Design, Information, Computer Graphics Technology, Information Experience Design, to an M.S. without specification (as well as the same degree with the option of two designations, including the HCI and HCI-Design). The majority of these programs are housed at Research 1 (R1) institutions, following the Carnegie Classification of Institutions of Higher Education [19]. Most are public institutions, offering on-ground education in various concentrations such as Media Arts and Sciences, Media Technology, Design Core, UX Design, Information Visualization, and Industrial Design.

The course catalogs and program pages of each institution were analyzed, with a focus on the program curriculum, course descriptions in the program, required core courses, and sequence of course offerings. Further analysis determined whether these

DEGREE	FOCUS AREAS	INSTITUTION
MHCI		CARNEGIE MELLON
M.S in HCI		DEPAUL UNIVERSITY
M.S in Information - HCI & UX		DREXEL UNIVERSITY
M.S in HCI	Industrial Design, Interactive Computing	GEORGIA INSTITUTE OF TECHNOLOGY
M.S in HCI		IOWA STATE UNIVERSITY
MS	Media Arts and Sciences, Interactive Computing	MASSACHUSSET INSTITUTE OF TECHNOLOGY
M.S in Computer Graphics Techonology	UX Design	PURDUE UNIVERSITY
MS in Design	Design Core, Method, Domain	STANFORD UNIVERSITY
M.S in HCI	e-Learning, GIS, Smart Device, Web Development	ROCHESTER INSTITUTE OF TECHNOLOGY
Master of Information Management and Systems		UNIVERSITY OF CALIFORNIA - BERKELEY
MHCI and Design		UNIVERSITY OF CALIFORNIA - IRVINE
M.S in HCI		INDIANA UNIVERSITY - BLOOMINGTON
M.S in HCI		UNIVERSITY OF MARYLAND
M.S in Information		UNIVERSITY OF MICHIGAN
MHCI and Design		UNIVERSITY OF WASHINGTON

Fig. 3. Degree, Focus Area, and Institution

programs required a course in ethics as well as where intersectionality could be introduced in the UXD education process. The program pages were also used to obtain contact information of the directors and/or coordinators of the academic degree programs. All programs were contacted via email. The institutions (n = 15) were selected based on rankings and prominence of the program: Carnegie Mellon, DePaul University, Drexel University, Georgia Tech, Iowa State University home institution, MIT, Purdue University, Stanford University, Rochester Institute of Technology, University of California – Berkeley and Irvine, University of Indiana – Bloomington, University of Maryland, University of Michigan, and the University of Washington. These institutions were sent an email and asked if their curriculum included an ethics course or another course where race and ethnicity are taught as dimensions of the user experience. Of the 15 higher education institutions, 13 replied. Depending on their initial response, follow-up questions were sent so more data could be collected (Fig. 4).

An inventory of the syllabi from the University of Maryland determined that, "although they do not have an HCI course that focuses solely and primarily on race and ethnicity, several courses likely include some discussion of the topic including Inclusive Design in HCI, Interaction Design Studio, and Fundamentals of HCI". They also cover ethics in several courses that HCI master's students could take as electives, including Information Ethics, Privacy & Security for a Networked World, and Diverse Populations, Inclusion, and Information, a course in their Master's in Library Science program.

At Carnegie Mellon, the MHCI program does not have a required course in ethics as part of its curriculum. The program, however, has a "pro-seminar in which many topics (including ethics) are discussed. Faculty have given guest lectures and led discussions for the pro-seminar on topics including unconscious bias, justice through design, and

# of COURSES	ETHICS CLASS	required	INSTITUTION
7 core-4 elective	No		CARNEGIE MELLON
6 core - 5 elective	No		DEPAUL UNIVERSITY
8 core - 5 elective	Yes	No	DREXEL UNIVERSITY
	No		GEORGIA INSTITUTE OF TECHNOLOGY
4 core/6 elective	Yes	No	IOWA STATE UNIVERSITY
7 core/4 elective	No		MASSACHUSSET INSTITUTE OF TECHNOLOGY
1 core-2 methodology-7 elective	No		PURDUE UNIVERSITY
	Yes	No	STANFORD UNIVERSITY
4 core/6 elective	No		ROCHESTER INSTITUTE OF TECHNOLOGY
6 core - 3 elective	No		UNIVERSITY OF CALIFORNIA - BERKELEY
12 core	No		UNIVERSITY OF CALIFORNIA - IRVINE
7 core/6 elective	Yes	No	INDIANA UNIVERSITY - BLOOMINGTON
3 core/6 elective	Yes	No	UNIVERSITY OF MARYLAND
7 core/2 elective	Yes	No	UNIVERSITY OF MICHIGAN
8 core - 5 elective	No		UNIVERSITY OF WASHINGTON

Fig. 4. Degree, Focus Area, and Institution

algorithmic bias". Their HCI curriculum includes several electives that touch on concerns related to ethics, including two courses that ground students' design work in methods of inclusive or justice-oriented design: Justice through Design and Persuasive Design.

UC Berkeley Master of Information Management and Systems is an interdisciplinary program, of which HCI is a track students can take. They do not offer "any Ethics courses, but they integrate ethics throughout their program courses". A follow up on if Race and Ethnicity along with intersectionality was sent but remained unanswered at the time of publication. UC Irvine informed the research that they did not have an Ethics course for their MHCI and Design program. The University of Washington does not have a formal ethics class, however issues of DEIAB are addressed throughout their curriculum.

University of Michigan offers "several classes on ethics, plus ethics interleaved in many of our classes with other topic names". While most of the courses shared by the program were undergraduate courses, Information Ethics is a graduate course. An analysis of the syllabus indicated that during week four of the semester topics covering Race and Ethnicity such as Decolonization and Critical Race Theory are addressed. Anthony Dunbar's Introducing Critical Race Theory to Archival Discourse [20] is on the reading list. Decolonial AI: Decolonial Theory as Sociotechnical Foresight in Artificial Intelligence [21] is another assigned reading. However, without confirmation from the faculty member teaching the course, it is unclear how the readings were assessed and if intersectionality is covered.

DePaul requires four introductory courses before taking their three foundational courses. In a response to the querying email, they indicated that they did not have a "course that is focused specifically on race or ethics in HCI in their curriculum". Students are required to take at least one elective course focused on a diverse audience. That includes courses on accessibility which focus on people with disabilities, global user research with a focus on people of varying ethnicities and cultures worldwide, learner-centered design which focuses on children, and behavioral economics. The current instructor of record for the global user research course shared the syllabus but indicated that it was a version that left significant room to maneuver, as they "like to modify it as necessary" and stated that the course did not cover race and ethnicity. Further correspondence with a faculty who has taught the class for the past five years clarified that race and ethnicity is indirectly covered and assessed. For example, one of the assignments is to design a research project which takes place in Korea. Students are asked to use the Hofstede model to guide some of the interactions. Hofstede's cultural dimensions theory is a framework for cross-cultural communication which indicates the effects of a society's culture on the values of its members [22]. Intersectionality is not directly covered or assessed in the course.

The Iowa State University M.S in HCI requires students to choose any four courses, one from each of the Design, Implementation, Phenomena, and Evaluation categories. The degree also requires a minimum of three research credits and students must take a one credit course named Responsible Conduct of Research. There is a Design and Ethics course listed in the Phenomena category; the syllabus does not directly mention race and ethnicity, but a follow up with the faculty who teaches the course divulged that race and ethnicity is discussed in the class. "Students are assigned reading chapters from Race After Technology [23] by Ruha Benjamin and are asked to respond to the chapters". Intersectionality is not mentioned or discussed.

Interestingly, MIT mentioned they probably should not be on the list, "as they are not an HCI/UX department to the same degree as the others. They do not have a course on UX or even standard HCI. Their program focuses more on the frontier concepts in tangible interaction. They do have a few classes that are often offered that involve ethics and race - some of the classes by Ekene Ijeoma (more race issues and art) and Danielle Wood (underrepresented people and remote sensing, and identity in performance) cross into this". However, they were clear that these classes have nothing to do with HCI/UX.

Drexel University informed the study that they were in the process "of changing their HCI/UX degree to be a standalone degree starting in the fall of 2023 and all the requirements will change"; currently it is in the same degree program with Library and Information Science. Currently, an Information Professions and Ethics course, which focuses on the ethics of information science, is required. For their new HCI/UX degree they utilize a totally different approach. The faculty have integrated ethics topics throughout the following required courses in the new curriculum. In the Design Thinking (Design and Values) course, students read Critical Race Theory for HCI [24] and depending on the faculty of record, they may watch the documentary Coded Bias [25]. In Social and Collaborative Computing (Antisocial Computing, Ethical Challenges in Online Research), students read Decolonizing Tactics as Collective Resilience: Identity Work of AAPI Communities on Reddit [26]. The syllabus for Accessible and Inclusive Design (Feminist HCI, Ethics and History of Inclusive Design, Social Issues and Design i.e., hate speech, etc.) was not shared but the course will be taught for the first time Fall 2023 with race and ethnicity as a topic.

At Purdue University, no program requires a course in ethics. Instead, "they integrate ethics-related concerns into many of their HCI/UX courses (e.g., into projects, class discussions, readings, etc.)". For their degree, students must complete one core course, two methodology courses, and additional courses in their chosen focus area and electives. Since students can take up to two electives across the institution, it is possible that some might take Ethics or another course which introduces them to the concept of intersectionality. However, that scenario is unlikely unless they are advised to do so or are inclined towards focusing on justice and social change. At RIT, "there is not an ethics course at the grad level. They have one at the undergrad level that addresses race and ethnicity, but not specific to user design".

Two institutions did not respond to inquiries for further information about their program requirements around the teaching of race and ethnicity in design. A review of the public information about the program yielded some useful information. Georgia Tech offers an M.S in HCI. Two of their four interdisciplinary programs fit the selection criteria for this research: Industrial Design (ID) and Interactive Computing (IC). In ID, one of their elective courses is focused on Universal Design. Universal Design is the method used to design a product and an environment that can be understood, used, and accessed by everyone. The IC program at Georgia Tech lacked an ethics course. Stanford University M.S centers both a Design Core and a Methods Focus Area, while also offering an elective focus area to gain added knowledge in a student's field of interest. The Design Core does provide a Design Ethics course.

Of the 15 selected institutions, six have an ethics course in their curriculum but it is not a required course in any program. Stanford, who did not reply, offers Tinkering with Inequity in Emerging Tech. The course description states that "throughout history, innovations in science and technology, while bold and visionary, have often resulted in catastrophic consequences for Indigenous and Black communities, immigrants and the environment". From an in-depth analysis of the surveyed programs, most of the courses offered were related to technology and its deployment.

One example of intersectionality being taught at the graduate level was found at Indiana University - Purdue University Indianapolis (IUPUI) campus, an institution based on the collaboration between Indiana University and Purdue University. The faculty who taught the UXD Ethics course taught in the spring of 2022 mentions "Race shows up a lot in the design ethics syllabus. We explicitly talk about intersectionality, critical race theory, etc. Race plays a role in multiple lectures based on the readings; however, some of the readings are less clearly about race if you are unfamiliar with the cannon. E.g., Richmond Wong's paper is about race as are the readings on "community participation, revisited" is equally about race". According to the shared syllabus, intersectionality is introduced in week five of the syllabus. Students read An intersectional approach to designing in the margins [27], Critical Race Theory for HCI [24], and Straighten up and fly right: rethinking intersectionality in HCI research [28]. No chosen assignments are listed on how intersectionality is assessed in the course but a Position Statement, which resembles the Autobiographical Diagrams assignment in the Intersectional Pedagogy [18], is listed among the listed graded assignments in the syllabus.

From the faculty at IUPUI, the research was informed of another example of intersectionality being taught in a HCI graduate program. The University of California Santa Cruz offers an Ethics and Activism in Tech and Design course, a core course in their Professional Master's in HCI. The faculty respondent, who designed and taught the course twice, explained that "We primarily talk about race, ethnicity, and intersectionality at various points, interweaving it within the different topics, rather than as a standalone unit. For example, in our unit on AI ethics, we talk about how various racial and gender biases show up in training data sets. We did have one day devoted exclusively to these types of issues."

While the aforementioned syllabi provide evidence for how intersectionality might be introduced in graduate level UXD programs, they lack the social constructivist framework which would allow UX designers to build on the knowledge they gain and be able to further develop the empathy required for the UXD process. While intersectionality can be both addressed and assessed using the proposed educational module without the addition of programs creating an ethics course, the overall lack of an ethics requirement should still be addressed in all UXD and HCI programs at the graduate level.

2.3 Ethics in Healthcare and Implications for HCI Curricula

According to Kim Case, "intersectionality reinforces teaching about social justice" [18]. Ethics courses in healthcare graduate programs often cover inequalities as the field of health care is known for their unethical behaviors in the past. One can look at the Tuskegee experiment, a medical study conducted by the U.S government on Black men lead to the Belmont Report and subsequently the creation of the Institutional Review Board to omit future repeat research [29]. Furthermore, the similarities between UXD and healthcare are grounded due to their use of technology and impact on human beings. Unethical, racist healthcare behaviors have been further enabled and compounded by technology. Medical professionals have been aware of the issue of oxygen readers failing to provide accurate readings for patients with darker skin tones since 1976. The bias baked into these technologies can endanger the life of people of color [30].

According to the Current Trends in Teaching Ethics in Healthcare Practices [31] which conducted a systematic literature review, "Healthcare Ethics education has become a basic requirement for any training programme for health professionals" [31]. As a strategy to repair the previous ills done in healthcare, programs have begun introducing Ethics in their curriculum [30, 32]. Catholic universities such as Duquesne and Saint Louis University have doctoral programs in healthcare ethics. Other institutions, such as the University of Louisville, University of Missouri, and Wayne State University, have created one-year graduate certificates in healthcare Ethics. This research aims to extrapolate how race and ethnicity can be introduced in UXD instruction by finding parallels in healthcare curricula.

2.4 Proposed Curriculum

The module proposed in this paper uses the pre-made intersectional personas and scenarios model case studies from the Intersectional Design Card, a series of cards with 12 intersectional factors and case studies that introduce designers to the "intersecting factors that interact to shape a person's or a group's experience and social opportunities as a starting point for a more inclusive design approach" according to new research from Schiebinger et al. [16]. The focus is on creating a ripple effect during the empathy phase of the UXD process. This phase can be seen as the most important step in understanding the users of the proposed product. Introducing intersectionality during the empathy phase, which begins with persona creation, would impact every step in the design process thereafter. Most educational UXD models utilize a similar methodology and the empathy phase of understanding the user is emphasized. From there, UX designers move onto Empathy Mapping, a stage where they visualize the user's attitudes and behaviors towards the product, followed by the creation of scenarios for the users. Journey Mapping, as defined by the Nielsen Group, is the visualization of the process the user goes through to accomplish a goal [4].

The final step in the design process is User-Story Mapping, where UX designers consider interactions they believe the user will go through to complete their goal. While practical, hands-on information is valuable for UX designers, the failure to introduce ethics to the future generation of UXD practitioners is compounded by a lack of education around the multiple facets of identity and experience that shape the user's needs.

3 Literature Review

In their article Intersectionality: a means for centering power and oppression in research, Wyatt et al. explain how the theory of intersectionality "examines how matrices of power and interlocking structures of oppression shape and influence people's multiple identities. It reminds us that people's lives cannot be explained by taking into account single categories, such as gender, race, sexuality, or socio-economic status. Rather, human lives are multidimensional and complex, and people's lived realities are shaped by different factors and social dynamics operating together" [17]. The literature on the topic is also lacking as most of the research on identifying the user in UXD research with an intersectional lens has been focused on gender [18]. Schlesinger et al.'s research explains that "manuscripts about race and ethnicity accounted for a small number of publications in the corpus" [2].

UXD faculty are in a unique position to impact the next generation of UX designers. They are often the first introduction future UXD practitioners will have to the UXD process. Even though persona creation is a small part of that process (see Fig. 2), it often influences the direction of the final product. Faculty also have the opportunity to introduce social change into their curriculum. For example, Constructivism Learning Theory (CLT), developed by John Dewey, Jean Piaget, and Lev Vygotsky claims learners construct Knowledge rather than just passively taking in information. The focal point of their theory was that solving problems will enhance the student's thinking, learning, and development. Problem solving allows students to employ their own experiences and skills to find a solution [19]. As UX designers experience the world and reflect on those experiences, they build their own representations and incorporate new information into their pre-existing knowledge. Cate Thomas argues that self-reflection can be used to "challenge internal assumptions and impact on a change of behaviour, values, and practice to practice in a socially just way" [20]. It is imperative students be introduced to intersectionality when they are creating personas. In their paper Bridging Designers' Intentions to Outcomes with Constructivism, researchers Kevin Muise and Ron Wakkary mention that oftentimes "design intentions for user experiences were expressed in terms similar to constructivist ideas" [21]. Vanessa Burgar, influenced by the book Technology Education for Teachers [22] writes in a journal article titled HCI and UX Design Education, that UXD educational activities such as collaboration align well with constructivism [23] (Fig. 5).

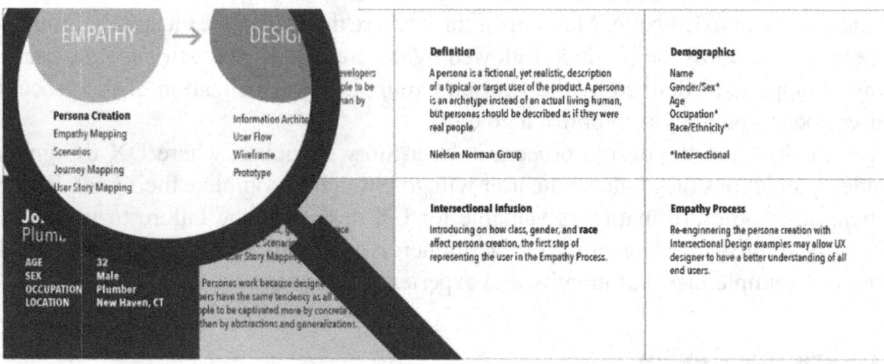

Fig. 5. The Persona Creation Process

CLT proves particularly useful in UXD education when we consider studio pedagogy, a practice in which expertise is developed through learning by doing and reflecting on those activities via critique. Constructivist pedagogy emphasizes learning through experience, while critique provides the social sharing value of design education and acts as a formative feedback mechanism [24].

In their article, Advancing UX education: A model for integrated studio pedagogy, the authors note that "the integration of studio approaches such as critique and constructivist-oriented learning in UX pedagogy have built on third-paradigm approaches to HCI scholarship that bring increased focus on design and criticality" [24]. Other theories have been used to teach UXD. For example, B. Alenjung et al. cite the use of theories of situated and embodied cognition. They mention "emphasis is placed on the interaction between brain, body, and the material and social environment where cognition is seen as something more than what happens inside the brain, in contrast to cognitivist theories on human cognition" [25]. While it may not be immediately apparent how this learning theory would align with the teaching of intersectionality to UXD students, situated learning activities such as social interactions with other people would certainly prove beneficial for learning.

In her book, Intersectional Pedagogy, the author Kim Case mentions that "the lack of effective pedagogical tools for teaching and learning about intersections of identity persists" [12], especially when it comes to addressing the intersectional identities of the user in UXD education. This gap provides an opportunity to assemble a new pedagogy for introducing personas to UXD students through the lens of intersectionality. Persona pedagogy, a term coined by Catherine (Cate) Thomas, is a pedagogy used to enhance empathy. It is considered a critical pedagogy meant to challenge and change exclusionary behavior. The author articulates that "persona pedagogy involves developing personas with a range of intersecting identities and applying them to oneself with a range of scenarios to make a positive difference to inclusion practices" [20]. In their research training, persona pedagogy is used to deconstruct power imbalances while modeling diversity using real-world scenarios. Persona pedagogy methods are impactful training for thinking about intersectionality. The author mentions two methods that are particularly promising: scenario-based personas and tailored personas. The author refers to the research work of AlSabban et al. to operationalize scenario-based personas which "introduce individuals to personal stories that are outside their own experience" [26]. This allows the student to critically reflect on another person's lived experience while considering their own positionality. As for tailored personas, Thomas articulates that they "are relevant for the context of training, with evidence-informed reasoning as to why the training is taking place, and with critical reflection that will lead to transformational social change" [20].

In Towards a Gender HCI Curriculum [11], the researchers focused their teaching module on gender; the authors of New Directions for Teaching and Learning argue that "Attending to multiple, intersecting identities can inhibit students from understanding concepts such as social power and privilege" [27]. It is therefore important to introduce examples that give students space to consider one facet of intersectionality at a time to ensure depth of understanding. A broad range of examples ensures that they consider these issues from multiple standpoints and gradually develop an understanding of how different aspects of identity complicate and inform each other and the persona creation process. With this in mind, even though the literature on identity of the user focuses on gender, it does provide a model off of which it is possible to extrapolate the construction of a module on race and ethnicity by incorporating and adapting core topics, learning outcomes, and assessments.

In the book Mismatch, How Inclusion Shapes Design, Kat Holmes introduces the persona spectrum as an inclusive design method. According to Holmes, "it is a design method that solves for one person and then extends to many. Holmes' persona spectra are based on physical human, cognitive, emotional and social abilities [28]. Yet again, the focus is not on race and ethnicity but Holmes' creation of the persona spectrum. However, Logan Williams expanded on Holmes' framework by classifying race as marked, hidden, or unmarked. For example, encountering a scenario where the student explores the experiences of a light-skinned Black person who, "due to lighter skin color" can "hide their race to pass as white" thereby attaining "higher status and concurrent benefits" [29], can help students begin to develop a more nuanced understanding of the way marginalized people navigate the world around them.

Understanding that race and ethnicity are social constructs will allow UX designers to better frame their personas. Race is not a biological reality, but a social, cultural, and political reality [30]. The authors Markus and Moya define race as being "groups according to perceived physical and behavioral human characteristics that are often imagined to be negative, innate, and shared". Ethnicity has been identified by language, region of origin, ancestry, and others. The authors explain that ethnicity, "when claimed, provides a sense of belonging, pride and motivation" [31]. Understanding these constructs will allow UX designers to be better prepared when creating new innovative products [1, 3].

4 Position Statement

The reasons for only creating a module on race and ethnicity for UXD students can be defined by three factors: the gap in the literature, pedagogical literature on intersectionality, and the author's positionality. As for the author's positionality, the epistemology that is applied to the work acknowledges the context in which he is working and both the privileges and limitations that come with it. The epistemology is guided by his upbringing and his exposure to higher education; as an educated French Canadian Black man, a doctoral candidate, and faculty at a Higher Education institution, he has been exposed to and has the access to resources he needs. As for his intersectional perspective of race and ethnicity, the author identifies as Black man with French Caribbean ethnicity, which is distinct from the perspective of a Black African-American man [32]. E. Seaton et al. argue that Caribbean Blacks "may have a have diminished awareness and expectations of encountering racial discrimination" in comparison to African Americans [33]. As a result, this may impede African Americans in their desire for upward mobility in comparison to Caribbean Blacks who do not carry this burden. That said, as a minority of color, most educational resources and technologies are not designed with the author in mind. He respects how his position in the academy frames his presence and value in his discipline, granting privileges and opportunities to provide scholarly perspective and data on graphic and UX design. Concentrating only on race and ethnicity when it comes to intersectionality and persona creation may seem incomplete as the researcher fails to incorporate gender and class, however the intention is to address this specific gap in the literature [2].

5 Methodology and Module Design

Oftentimes, persona examples shared in instruction do not reflect all the facets of the user, as most persona instruction follows the method derived from Nielsen and Norman [34]. Persona pedagogy has been used as a pedagogy to expand an individual's worldview and increase inclusion [20]. This approach aims to address the issue that UXD often focuses on creating products for a user without understanding all the facets of the users. The proposed module design introduces UXD students to intersectional personas in three steps: the social construct of race and ethnicity; intersectional perspectives on race and ethnicity; as well as race and ethnicity, knowledge, and methodology in science, technology, and design (see Fig. 3) (Fig. 6).

Step one starts with readings about the experiences of others and asks students to consider new perspectives before they create their personas. This approach allows them to understand how and why choices about gender, class, race, and ethnicity in their

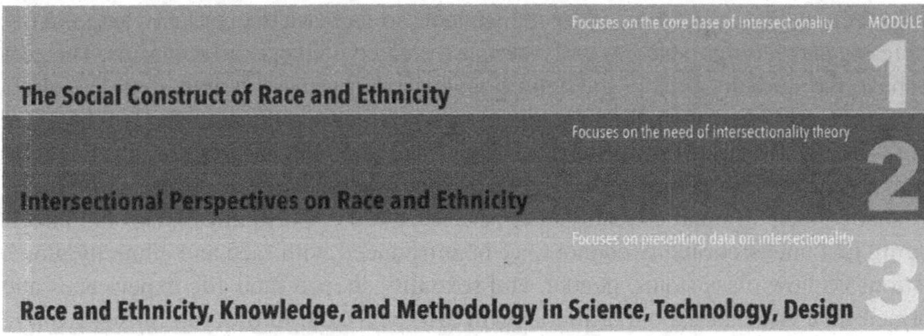

Fig. 6. Proposed Module Design

personas may impact the usefulness of the personas and also introduce them to unfamiliar segments of the population. Specifically, students will be introduced to theories and concepts around intersectionality and scenarios including personas whose intersectional identities are made clear.

In the second step, instructors will use prompts to guide UXD students' discussion of their personas and individual scenarios with their partner(s). Usually, personas are just glanced over in the classroom without a true study of all the facets of the users. UXD students are only introduced to their classmates' personas during presentation and critique. The exchange of personas between a small group of students will foster security as it is sometimes easier to share with one other person than with a whole group. This exchange also follows the process of critique that UXD students will be familiar with. Together, they familiarize themselves with the theory and foundation of intersectionality. Afterwards, students are asked to individually reflect on their intersectional persona and how that persona would engage with the product, which provides opportunities for students to construct knowledge on class, gender, as well as race and ethnicity in practice.

According to Cate Thomas: "co-designing of personas with key participants of training sessions who have diverse lived experiences is a powerful tool to address any key issues or areas of challenge within an organization [20]. In step three, students will be paired with rotating partners so they can discuss their personas with peers who may potentially have a broader set of identities and experiences, thereby potentially empathizing with a wider range of potential users. A cyclical approach to creating, sharing, and reflecting on the decision-making process for persona selection will deepen insights into the process that can be further extended through peer input and introduce issues previously not considered or unfamiliar to the individual designer.

The proposed educational module will cover three core topics: the social construct of race and ethnicity; intersectional perspectives on race and ethnicity; as well as race and ethnicity, knowledge, and methodology in science, technology, design. The module on the social construct of race and ethnicity will focus on introducing more recent understandings that emphasize race as a social, cultural, and political reality and not a biological truth [30]. In the U.S, racial attributes are focused primarily on skin color and tone. Students will be asked to select two or three readings from a selection of intersectional research articles on race and ethnicity written by a wide range of authors theorizing on intersectionality, which will allow the students to gather a deeper knowledge. After completing the readings, students will examine a created persona and scenarios. The goal is to have the students explore the definitions by gaining insights into someone else's lived experience. Finally, to conclude the first part of the module, students will be given prompts in order to guide their reflections, which will include questions focused on their own experiences. For example, they will be asked to consider how race and ethnicity have shaped their life and educational experiences and opportunities. With the understanding that intersectionality cannot only be introduced with race and ethnicity alone, questions on how class status, gender, and sexuality shaped their life experiences and informed their educational opportunities will also be asked. In order to further explore the constructed nature of race, students will consider that a man could be considered Black in the United States, white in Brazil, and multi-racial in another part of the world and the implications that this additional complexity holds for their persona design.

Students should be able to discuss race and ethnicity explicitly and clearly after completing this module, an outcome which will be assessed through the evaluation of their design of a persona utilizing a richly descriptive scenario. According to Thomas, "in aligning realistic personas that encompass a range of diversity with scenarios, a story or a lived-experience of that persona emerges which is powerful in training for inclusion and intersectionality" [20]. Alsabban et al. argues that "scenario-based personas introduce individuals to personal stories that are outside their own experience" [26]. The persona and scenarios will be constructed so that the vocabulary, definitions, and theories relating to race and ethnicities and their significance in relation to understanding and designing technologies [11] are clarified for students. The application of persona methodology and the information contained within the scenarios will allow the students to individually reflect on their character's experience. Thomas et al. argue that "critical thinking and reflection coupled with persona pedagogy forms the basis for insightful empathy and understanding to progress inclusion and social change via inclusion and intersectionality training design" [35]. To further reinforce their understanding, students will be paired to discuss their intersectional persona and scenario by sharing what they experience through a Think-Pair-Share activity, which is a CTL cooperative learning strategy [36] that accentuates collaborative learning. The collaboration between students allows them to discuss and reflect on the new vocabulary, definitions, and theories they just have been exposed to, which allows for information to be retained at a higher level. After students complete the Think-Pair-Share activity, faculty will follow up with some prompts for classroom discussion. In the event the instructor is not comfortable or knowledgeable enough to lead the discussion, students can move- on to self-directed reflection on their and their partner's experience. The writing will reinforce the student capability for self-reflection and empathy, an important trait for UX design students entering a world facing issues such as climate change, pollution, lack of drinkable water, and violence.

Students should be able to analyze race scripts embedded in particular technologies; for example, how facial recognition [37] and soap dispensers fail to recognize people with darker skin [38]. Additionally, medical professionals have been aware of the issue of oxygen readers with darker skin tones since 1976. The bias baked into these technologies can endanger the life of people of color [29] and it is crucial we educate future designers in such a way as to ensure their practices are not harmful. The hope of this paper is to proactively bring awareness of the race and ethnicity of the user into the UXD process before the test prototype is built. To create a just world and workforce, it is important that we teach designers to consider their biases before designing new products, rather than attempting to address errors after BIPOC have had to suffer harm and raise awareness around the issue in their own defense [40]. To assess this outcome, students will be asked to construct their persona using Counter-Story Telling, an intersectional pedagogy learning method, which is used to introduce and teach intersectionality by giving a voice to multiple marginalized groups [12]. In their research article Critical Race Methodology: Counter-Storytelling as an Analytical Framework for Education Research, the authors articulate the five elements that make a counter-story: "intercentricity of race/racism with other forms of subordination; challenges the dominant ideology; commitment to social justice; centrality of experiential knowledge; and transdisciplinary perspective" [40]. This framework will give guidance to students when co-designing their persona and ensure they learn to make conscientious and inclusive decisions from the outset.

Often UXD students might have been introduced to what a persona is before learning about them in class. For example, the majority of UX designers come from the design field and as a result are familiar with personas. Unfortunately, what is often lacking is a true understanding of the intersecting factors that define a user. According to the Nielsen Norman Group, "the value of personas is that they make implicit assumptions about the users explicit" [4]. Being informed on gender, class, and race and ethnicity will allow students and UX designers to view all the facets of the users thus developing a better understanding of how to create inclusive and representative personas.

Critique and reflections will be used to discuss the learning outcome of how different facets of identity shape people's lives and experiences. The critique of the personas will resemble the design critique students are familiar with. In their article A systematic literature review of the Design Critique method, the authors mention how "collecting feedback is an integral part of any design process" [41]. To guide the critique, the faculty will adapt course content from Intersectional Pedagogy [12]. UXD students will be asked to identify how the dimensions of their persona differ from those of another student's persona, the hierarchy of the dimensions they have chosen, and how these dimensions can be used to make judgments about their persona. The goal of the critique will be for students to examine their own identity, implicit biases, and stereotypes they may need to unpack, all of which are important and often forgotten elements in UXD when it comes to building empathy through persona creation for the end-user. The feedback generated during the critique will be shared with all the students so that they can learn from each other's exploration of these themes.

For the final individual reflection, students will be given questions that help them reexamine their personas, and the reflections will be assessed for three criteria: personal growth, civic learning, and academic enhancement. To start their reflections, students will be asked to share what assumptions they have around intersectionality and therefore bring to the identity of the user for their persona. Writing on the positives and negatives of interacting with others and co-designing their persona will help them chart their personal growth over time. Civic learning will be fostered through their reflection on how privilege and power emerged during their critiques. Finally, academic enhancement will be assessed by asking students to elucidate how the concepts and the theories of intersectionality when it comes to race and ethnicity are reflected in their design process.

This approach aims to address the issue that UXD often focuses on creating products for a user without understanding all the facets of the users. After this first individual introduction to intersectional personas, UXD students will be paired in teams of two and discuss their personas and individual scenarios with their partners. Prompts will be given to lead the discussion between students. Usually, personas are glanced over in the classroom without an in-depth study of all the facets of the users and UXD students are only introduced to their classmates' personas during presentation and critique. The exchange of personas between a small group of students will not only foster security and openness of discussion but also improve their peers' ability to offer constructive and conscientious critiques. This exchange also follows the process of critique that UXD students will be familiar with. Together, they familiarize themselves with the theory and foundation of intersectionality. Afterwards, students will be asked to individually reflect on their intersectional persona and how the persona will be able to use the product they have been tasked to create, which will provide opportunities for students to construct knowledge on class, gender, as well as race and ethnicity.

6 Limitations

This research and teaching module will have no impact on the statistical personas, which are best known for creating complex personas utilizing large amounts of data. Qualitative personas, often the solution for UXD teams, require interviewing at least five to 30 users to create personas. Intersectionality may help educate UX designers in creating their interviews thus getting intersectional information so they may create more informed personas. The data received from the interviews might be used to reengineer these modules.

We must also consider how UXD is being taught. The growth of undergraduate and graduate degree programs in UXD has been slow [42]. Countless new UXD bootcamp schools have been created to fill this gap in supply and demand. Students in bootcamps are meant to learn UXD in a short amount of time with the goal of becoming employed. Due to the short duration of bootcamps and their online delivery method, it is possible that educators in these programs may struggle to integrate these theories and concepts or will fail to address them in sufficient depth. Working in pairs might work best when the students are face to face co-designing their persona as online critiques are not as successful as an on-ground class critique. Similarly, UXD content and pedagogies might differ between programs due to a lack of centralized UXD certification and unevenness of educator preparation.

The limitations of introducing intersectionality into the UXD curriculum are plenty and range from the faculty lack of knowledge to the comparative difficulty of introducing these topics to undergraduate students in comparison to graduate students. In her book, Intersectional Pedagogy, Kim Case writes of the challenges of introducing intersectionality to undergraduate students and how "educators must critically reflect on their own social location within the classroom" [12]. Is the faculty the know-it-all master or are they willing to enhance their knowledge by positioning themselves as learners alongside their students? As there is limited literature on the intersectionality of the user, UXD faculty will potentially have limited knowledge on how to introduce the topic to their students regardless of supportive materials. Additionally, some instructors may feel discomfort over engaging with a subject outside of their field of expertise or even recognize the importance of intersectionality but choose to continue to teach in the ways they are accustomed or required to.

The lack of incorporation on class and gender in the proposed teaching module is an additional limitation when it comes to introducing intersectionality to UXD students. Race, gender, and class are facets that affect the identity of the user. Modules on gender already exist but literature and educational modules do not exist when it comes to class. For UX designers to have a better grasp on intersectionality, gender and class should also be addressed when it comes to persona creation. Given the complexity of tackling an in-depth understanding of any one facet of the intersectional experience, it is understandable that other researchers have also consistently focused on only one aspect of identity when developing a matrix or educational module for persona creation. Relatedly, introducing more than one facet of identity in an undergraduate course would prove to be catastrophic for both the faculty and students unless the students had taken or were concurrently enrolled in another course where intersectionality was introduced to provide space for them to explore these themes in more depth. As for the faculty, they would also need to possess a deep understanding of how gender, race, and class affect each other; this knowledge is often deemed more valuable to sociologists and psychologists than UX designers. While this paper seeks to fill the gap in resources around race and ethnicity in UXD education, a truly intersectional design process will need to not only address all aspects of the user's identity, but also the complex interplay between the axes of their experience.

7 Future Research

Intersectional design is a method that is slowly gaining momentum and recognition as it supports social justice and inclusivity in design. Further research on how intersectional design can be used to guide UX designers on creating more inclusive personas should be conducted. UXD educators and practitioners should investigate the use of this new methodology for the UXD process and persona creation. The expanding representation in emoji design, for example the development of a pregnant man emoji, can be seen as one future path toward a more nuanced persona creation process and understanding of inclusivity in technology and UXD.

Future research should also look at this and other pedagogical research models so that intersectionality can be introduced into UXD education. This could be accomplished by compiling a list of the few researchers who work in the HCI and UXD sphere and their research on intersectional curriculum in HCI and UXD. Future research might be able to provide students and practitioners a road map to creating inclusive personas and provide the foundation for them to create more just products. New teaching methods should also be investigated; for example, Digital Game Based Learning has been used to introduce and improve the empathy of students.

Finally, the construction of qualitative personas, based on small-sample qualitative research, such as interviews and usability tests and statistical personas based on large amounts of data and a mix of qualitative research, should be researched so they can be leveraged to represent all users. As qualitative personas are often considered the best fit for UXD teams [4], it is important that UX designers are at least introduced to intersectionality so they may understand their own positionality and intersectionality during the UX process. For statistical personas, my hope is that with intersectionality, UX designers might be able spot bias in the sea of data. Most importantly, future research should aim to increasingly center inclusivity and social justice in UXD and HCI.

References

1. What is User Experience (UX) Design? Interaction Design Foundation. https://www.interaction-design.org/literature/topics/ux-design
2. Schlesinger, A., et al.: Intersectional HCI: engaging identity through gender, race, and class. In: Proceedings of the 2017 CHI Conference on Human Factors in Computing Systems, pp. 5412–5427 (2017). https://doi.org/10.1145/3025453.3025766
3. Cooper, A.: The Inmates are Running the Asylum: Why High Tech Products Drive Us Crazy and How to Restore the Sanity. Pearson Higher Education (2004). https://dl.acm.org/doi/ https://doi.org/10.5555/984201
4. Persona Types: Lightweight, Qualitative, and Statistical. Nielsen Norman Group. https://www.nngroup.com/articles/persona-types/
5. Emmanuel, G-S., Polito, F.: How related are designers to the personas they create?. In: Lecture Notes in Computer Science: Design, User Experience, and Usability: Design Thinking and Practice in Contemporary and Emerging Technologies, vol. 13323, pp. 3–13 (2022).https://doi.org/10.1007/978-3-031-05906-3_1
6. User Experience Designer Demographics and Statistics In The Us. Zippia. https://www.zippia.com/user-experience-designer-jobs/demographics/
7. UX designer demographics in the United States. Career Explorer. https://www.careerexplorer.com/careers/ux-designer/demographics/
8. Chen, Y.T., et al.: Collecting and reporting race and ethnicity data in HCI. In: Conference on Human Factors in Computing Systems – Proceedings, vol. 1, issue 1. Association for Computing Machinery (2022). https://doi.org/10.1145/3491101.3519685
9. Rankin, Y.A., Henderson, K.K.: Resisting racism in tech design: centering the experiences of black youth. In: Proceedings of the ACM on Human-Computer Interaction, 5(CSCW1) (2021). https://doi.org/10.1145/3449291
10. Abebe, V., et al.: Anti-Racist HCI: notes on an emerging critical technical practice. In: Conference on Human Factors in Computing Systems – Proceedings (2022).https://doi.org/10.1145/3491101.3516382
11. Breslin, S., Wadhwa, B.: Towards a gender HCI curriculum. In: Conference on Human Factors in Computing Systems - Proceedings, vol. 18, pp. 1091–1096(2015). https://doi.org/10.1145/2702613.2732923
12. Templeton, M., Kacey Reynolds, S.: 10 Best Affordable HCI Masters Programs. Scribbr (2022). https://www.mastersprogramsguide.com/rankings/human-computer-interaction-masters/
13. Best Value Colleges: Online tools and rankings to help you find your perfect value college. Value Colleges. https://www.valuecolleges.com/
14. The Best Master's in Human Computer Interaction Degree. College Rank. https://www.collegerank.net/best-masters-human-computer-interaction-hcim/
15. Marlin, L.: Top 10 Best UX Design Graduate Programs in 2023. The GradCafe (2022). https://blog.thegradcafe.com/best-ux-design-graduate-programs/#carnegie-mellon-univ-nrfo

16. John, C.: The Best Masters in UX Design Programs: 2023 Guide (2022). https://careerfoundry.com/en/blog/ux-design/masters-in-ux-design/
17. Best Universities for Human-Computer Interaction (HCI) in the World. EduRank. https://edurank.org/cs/hci/
18. Case, K.A. (Ed.). Intersectional Pedagogy: Complicating Identity and Social Justice. Routledge/Taylor & Francis Group (2017)
19. Basic Classification. Carnegie Classifications of Institutions of Higher Education (2021). https://carnegieclassifications.acenet.edu/carnegie-classification/classification-methodology/basic-classification/
20. Dunbar, A.W.: Introducing critical race theory to archival discourse: getting the conversation started. Arch. Sci. **6**(1), 109–129 (2006). https://doi.org/10.1007/s10502-006-9022-6
21. Mohamed, S., Png, M.T., Isaac, W.: Decolonial AI: decolonial theory as sociotechnical foresight in artificial intelligence. Philos. Technol. **33**, 659–684 (2020). https://doi.org/10.1007/s10502-006-9022-6
22. Dewiyanti, S.: Hofstede's Cultural Dimensions of Theory. Binus University School of Accounting (2021). https://accounting.binus.ac.id/2021/11/15/hofstedes-cultural-dimensions-theory/#:~:text=Hofstede's%20cultural%20dimensions%20theory%20is,structure%20derived%20from%20factor%20analysis
23. Benjamin, R.: Race after technology: Abolitionist tools for the new Jim code. Polity (2019)
24. Ogbonnaya-Ogburu, I.F., Smith, A.D., To, A., Toyama, K.: Critical race theory for HCI. In: Conference on Human Factors in Computing Systems - Proceedings, pp. 1–16 (2020).https://doi.org/10.1145/3313831.3376392
25. Coded Bias. 7th Empire Media (2020). https://www.codedbias.com/
26. Dosono, B., Semaan, B.: Decolonizing tactics as collective resilience: identity work of AAPI communities on reddit. In: Proceedings of the ACM on Human-Computer Interaction, vol. 4(CSCW1), pp. 1–20(2020). https://doi.org/10.1145/3392881
27. Erete, S., et al.: An intersectional approach to designing in the margins. Interactions **25**(3), 66–69 (2018). https://doi.org/10.1145/3194349
28. Rankin, Y.A., Thomas, J.O.: Straighten up and fly right: rethinking intersectionality in HCI research. Interactions **26**(6), 64–68 (2019). Association for Computing Machinery. https://doi.org/10.1145/3363033
29. Cabanas, A.M., et al.: Skin pigmentation influence on pulse oximetry accuracy: a systematic review and bibliometric analysis. Sensors **22**(9), 1–20 (2022). https://doi.org/10.3390/s22093402
30. Hattab, A.S.: Current trends in teaching ethics of healthcare practices. Dev. World Bioeth. **4**, 160–172 (2004). https://doi.org/10.1111/j.1471-8731.2004.00091.x
31. Nicolaides, A.: The critical role of ethics training in medical education. Afr. J. Hospitality Tourism Leisure **3**(1), 1–12 (2014). https://uir.unisa.ac.za/handle/10500/20272
32. Schiebinger, L., et al.: Intersectional Design Cards (1st ed.). Intersectional Design (2021)
33. Wyatt, T.R., et al.: Intersectionality: a means for centering power and oppression in research. Adv. Health Sci. Educ. **27**, 863–875 (2022). https://doi.org/10.1007/s10459-022-10110-0
34. Marsden, N., et al.: Developing personas, considering gender: a case study. In: ACM International Conference Proceeding Series, pp. 392–396 (2017). https://doi.org/10.1145/3152771.3156143
35. Alzahrani, I., Woollard, J.: The role of the constructivist learning theory and collaborative learning environment on wiki classroom , and the relationship between them. In: ELI: 3rd International Conference, pp. 2–8 (2013). https://eric.ed.gov/?id=ED539416
36. Thomas, C.: Overcoming identity threat: using persona pedagogy in intersectionality and inclusion training. Soc. Sci. **11**(6) (2022). https://doi.org/10.3390/socsci11060249

37. Muise, K., Wakkary, R.: Bridging designers' intentions to outcomes with constructivism. In: DIS 2010 - Proceedings of the 8th ACM Conference on Designing Interactive Systems, pp. 320–329 (2010). https://doi.org/10.1145/1858171.1858229
38. Williams, J.P.: Technology Education for Teachers. Sense Publishers (2012)
39. Burgar, V.: HCI and UX Design Education (2017). https://www.researchgate.net/publication/338121833
40. Vorvoreanu, M., et al.: Advancing UX education: A model for integrated studio pedagogy. In: Conference on Human Factors in Computing Systems - Proceedings, May 2017, pp. 1441–1446 (2017). https://doi.org/10.1145/3025453.3025726
41. Alenljung, B., et al.: The user experience design program: applying situated and embodied cognition together with reflective teaching. Front. Comput. Sci. **4**, 1–9 (2022). https://doi.org/10.3389/fcomp.2022.794400
42. AlSabban, M., Karim, A., Sun, V.H., Hashim, J., AlSayed, O.: Co-design of color identification applications using scenario-based personas for people with impaired color vision. In: Stephanidis, C., Antona, M., Gao, Q., Zhou, J. (eds.) HCI International 2020 – Late Breaking Papers: Universal Access and Inclusive Design. HCII 2020. Lecture Notes in Computer Science, vol. 12426, pp. 171–83. Springer, Cham (2020). https://doi.org/10.1007/978-3-030-60149-2_14
43. Fink, L.D.: Editorial. New Dir. Teach. Learn. **119**, 1–7 (2009). https://doi.org/10.1002/tl
44. Holmes, M.: Mismatch: How Inclusion Shapes Design. The MIT Press (2018)
45. Williams, L.D.A. Design, Feminism, and The Persona Spectrum: Introducing The Intersectional Persona Matrix. https://www.inclusiveresearchbydesign.com/news/design-feminism-and-the-persona-spectrum-introducing-the-intersectional-persona-matrix
46. Sano-Franchini, J.: What can Asian eyelids teach us about user experience de-sign? a culturally reflective framework for UX/I design. Rhetoric. Prof. Commun. Globalization **10**(1), 27–53 (2017). https://docs.lib.purdue.edu/rpcg/vol10/iss1/3
47. Moya, Paula M.L., Markus, H.R.: 2010 Moya Markus doing race - an introduction.pdf. In: Doing Race: 21 Essays for the 21st Century, pp. 1–102 (2010). https://web.stanford.edu/~hazelm/publications/2010%20Moya%20Markus%20Doing%20Race%20-%20An%20Introduction.pdf
48. Fullwood, Sam III. COLUMN ONE : U.S. Blacks: A Divided Experience : Animosity clouds relations between Caribbean immigrants, native-born African Americans. Competition for jobs, differences in their dealings with whites are at the heart of the split. LA Times. https://www.latimes.com/archives/la-xpm-1995-11-25-mn-6855-story.html
49. Seaton, E.K., et al.: An intersectional approach for understanding perceived discrimination and psychological well-being among African American and Caribbean black youth. Dev. Psychol. **46**(5), 1372–1379 (2010). https://doi.org/10.1037/a0019869
50. Harley, A.: Personas Make Users Memorable for Product Team Members. Nielsen Norman Group. https://www.nngroup.com/articles/persona/. Accessed 10 Jan 2023
51. Cate, T., et al.: Seeing and overcoming the complexities of intersectionality. Challenges **12**, 5 (2021). https://doi.org/10.3390/challe12010005
52. Bamiro, A.O.: Effects of guided discovery and think-pair-share strategies on secondary school students' achievement in chemistry. SAGE Open **5**(1) (2015). https://doi.org/10.1177/2158244014564754
53. Breslin, S., Wadhwa, B.: Towards a gender HCI curriculum. In: Conference on Human Factors in Computing Systems - Proceedings, vol. 18, pp. 1091–1096.https://doi.org/10.1145/2702613.2732923
54. Hankerson, D., et al.: Does technology have race?. In: Conference on Human Factors in Computing Systems - Proceedings, 07–12-May-, pp. 473–485 (2016). https://doi.org/10.1145/2851581.2892578

55. Solórzano, D.G., Yosso, T.J.: Critical race methodology: counter-storytelling as an analytical framework for education research. Qual. Inq. **8**(1), 23–44 (2002). https://doi.org/10.1177/107780040200800103
56. Alabood, L., et al.: A systematic literature review of the design critique method. Inf. Softw. Technol. **153**(December 2021), 107081 (2023). https://doi.org/10.1016/j.infsof.2022.107081
57. Getto, G., Beecher, F.: Toward a Model of UX education: training UX designers within the academy. IEEE Trans. Prof. Commun. **59**(2), 153–164 (2016). https://doi.org/10.1109/TPC.2016.2561139

Intersectionality in UX Design and HCI Research and Curriculum Development: Bringing Race and Ethnicity into Focus

Guy-Serge Emmanuel[1] (✉) and Francesca Polito[2]

[1] Quinnipiac University, Hamden, CT 06518, USA
gsestudio@gmail.com
[2] University of Maryland, College Park, MD 20742, USA

Abstract. Reating personas in UX Design (UXD), the process used by designers to create purposeful products and significant experiences for users, becomes increasingly complicated when UX Designers creating inclusive personas must take greater responsibility for designing evolved and iterated products tailored to the circumstances and environments of their respective audiences; this can be achieved using an intersectional framework to capture the complexity of user identities to better inform the persona creation process.

Intersectionality, defined by Professor Kimberlé Crenshaw, involves Understanding the ways that multiple forms of inequality or disadvantage sometimes compound themselves and create obstacles that often are not understood in conventional ways of thinking [3]. In Human-Computer Interaction (HCI), the interdisciplinary field that studies the dynamics of communications between humans, there is lack of attention to race and ethnicity in the current body of research. According to Schlesinger et al., previous "research on ethnicity and race lags behind research on gender and socio-economic class" [3] which indicates that researchers in the field of UX Design must rethink their approach to applying an intersectional lens to the study of the persona creation process to fill this gap in the literature.

Through a literature review of the identity of the user in HCI, this study examines how the emerging literature sees, or fails to see, the user and the intersectionality of their identity when it comes to race and ethnicity. Schlesinger et al.'s research, whose goal is to understand how the user is represented in the literature using intersectionality as a framework, did not provide more insight than previous research; they explain that "Manuscripts about race and ethnicity accounted for a small number of publications in the corpus" [3]. It became clear that gender is instead overwhelmingly centered as the focal aspect of user identity in UX Design research [4].

To address these issues for the future generation of designers, this study asked how the emerging literature on race and ethnicity in UXD and HCI might be applied to educate the future generation of UX designers on the common design errors found in technology in relation to the race and ethnicity of the user. This work led to the development of a syllabus that will lead future designers to develop more inclusive personas by gaining greater insights of intersectional identity representation.

A. Marcus et al. (Eds.): HCII 2024, LNCS 14714, pp. 48–69, 2024.
https://doi.org/10.1007/978-3-031-61356-2_4

Great care has been taken to examine the function of gender when it comes to the HCI curriculum [5] with race and ethnicity lagging. With the use of the literature, this study addresses this issue and provides a pathway for UXD faculty to implement a series of three modules which educates UX designers and the HCI community on the importance of intersectionality when representing the user.

Keywords: UXD Pedagogy · Intersectionality · HCI Research · Race and Ethnicity

1 Introduction

The categories of race and ethnicity are becoming more prevalent considerations in User Experience Design (UXD) due to the increasing importance of representing a variety of identities when developing technologies for users. A famous example of the importance of creating safe, equitable, and inclusive technologies is the failure of oxygen readers on measuring the blood oxygen level for darker skinned individuals, an issue that medical professionals have been aware of since 1976 [1]. The issue of race and technology is not only limited to skin color, but other prejudices about racial differences. The spirometer, a device meant to measure lung capacity, was designed with a race button that would change the device settings to be more favorable to white patients [2] due to eugenic policies of the 1920's when most studies found that "whites had higher lung capacity than blacks, Chinese or Indians" [3]. In contemporary discourses on UX design, the focus is on developing a deeper understanding of how users interact and experience products by exploring their needs, values, abilities, and limitations. This can, in turn, prove a helpful jumping off point for rectifying implicit bias, a form of bias that affects judgment and decisions, in design. While this focus has expanded the range of concerns that UX designers engage for the better, race and ethnicity remain outside of the mainstream in terms of the criteria that the field employs, which needs to be addressed given the increased visibility of racial and other forms of bias in society.

This paper focuses on UXD, which is defined as the process employed by designers to create purposeful products and significant experiences for users. Personas are fictional characters used to represent the user. They are tools that assist UX designers in analyzing user needs and design objects. A study titled "How Related Designers Are To The Persona They Create?" showed that UX designers created personas closely related to themselves [4]. Alan Cooper was the first to propose personas as fictional characters who could represent different versions of users [5]. Personas are often the starting point for UX designers when it comes to envisioning their future users. Given the disproportionate number of white UX designers [6], implicit bias can impact the end results of a product, as research shows many designers create personas closely related to their race [4].

UXD is considered part of the third wave of Human-Computer Interaction (HCI) which focuses on the user's experience and their socio-cultural context. The first wave of HCI centered on engineering and the second on cognitive science and psychology. With an understanding that there is not enough literature and curricula on race and ethnicity in HCI, this research asks how the emerging literature on race and ethnicity in UXD and HCI might be applied to educate the future generation of UX designers on the common design errors found in technology in relation to the race and ethnicity of the user. The results are used to develop a pedagogical approach that will lead future designers to develop more inclusive personas.

According to the literature review conducted by the authors of the journal article, "Intersectional HCI: Engaging Identity through Gender, Race, and Class," [7] between the three keyword search terms of race, gender, and class, "race had the largest number of keywords that ultimately produced no results in the final corpus" [7] confirming that most of the literature on the intersectional representation of the user in HCI is focused on gender, with class appearing but lagging behind. This research argues that, without the implementation of an intersectional teaching module the race and ethnicity problem in UXD, user personas created by these designers will not meet the diverse needs of users. One proposed solution, discussed further in the later sections of this paper, is to require UXD students to learn about race and ethnicity in the context of their professional education. The paper has two objectives: first, to survey the literature in Human-Computer Interaction (HCI) when it comes to the teaching of intersectionality in HCI and UXD; and second, to research how the user is represented in terms of race and ethnicity in HCI and UXD.

With the creation of a syllabus to address the lack of intersectional representation of the user, this paper proposes UXD pedagogies and teaching strategies required by students to understand the function of race and ethnicity in UX design. This intervention is meant to address an issue which is embedded in UXD professional practice due to the lack of diversity of personas shown by designers when attempting to represent users in persona creation. Through repeated exposure to these concepts through discussion and reflection, the goal of this module is to ensure they will feel comfortable sharing their intersectional knowledge when creating personas to represent a broad range of potential users.

Kimberlé Crenshaw defined intersectionality as "understanding the ways that multiple forms of inequality or disadvantage sometimes compound themselves and createobstacles that often are not understood in conventional ways of thinking" [7]. The birth of intersectionality can be found in the feminist movement. While both Black and White women face unfairness due to their gender, discrimination against Black women is compounded by racial discrimination. Intersectionality asserts that, race, gender, class, and other factors all impact each other when it comes to the representation of the user in HCI and UXD (see Fig. 1).

The definitions and theories of intersectionality are needed UXD process (see Fig. 2) second phase, empathy which consist of persona creation, empathy mapping, scenarios, journey mapping, and user story mapping. Intersectional educational to give UX designers more information on the representation of the user. Approaches to teaching about gender and sexism can be used to build a framework for instructions on race and ethnicity.

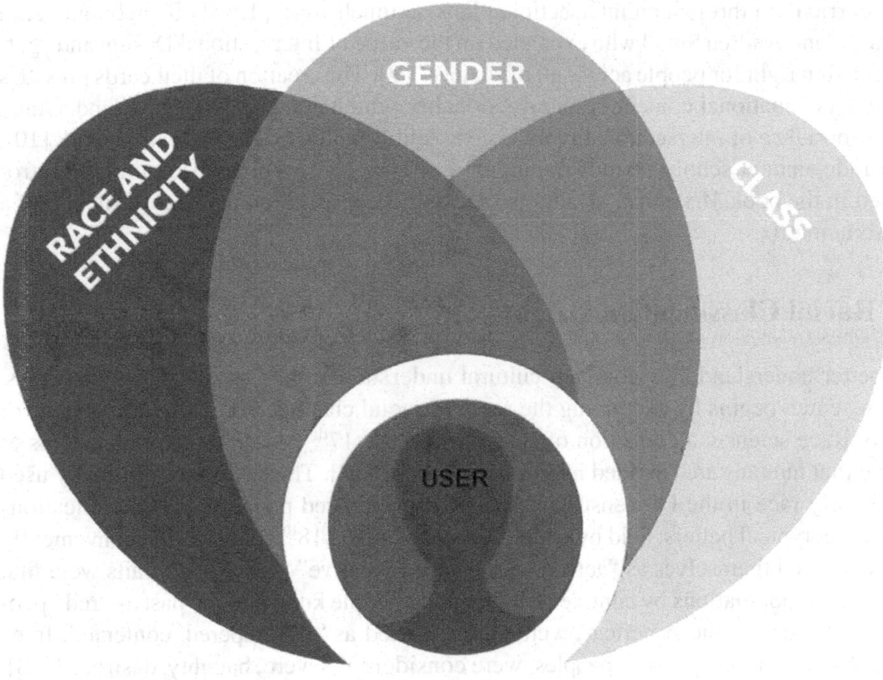

Fig. 1. Intersectionality – Race & Ethnicity, Gender, Class, and the User. Graphic adaptation sourced from Just Associate - Big Ideas: Intersectionality

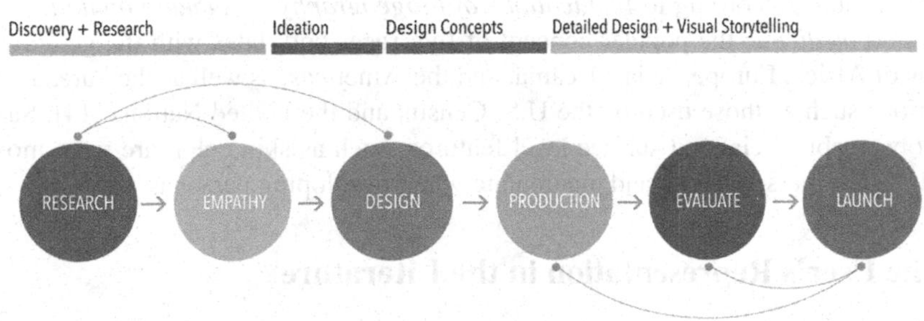

Fig. 2. UXD Process and Stages

2 Literature Review

In order to build a sufficient understanding of the applications that intersectionality may hold for more inclusive design pedagogy, it is crucial to first identify how the race and ethnicity of users is represented in HCI [8]. Additionally, it is important to examine how intersectional concepts of user identities are incorporated into HCI curricula. This research aims to build on the knowledge provided by authors such as Samantha Breslin and Bimlesh Wadhwa when it comes to implementing intersectionality in HCI curriculum. The authors article advances the integration of gender in HCI education and curriculum through an intersectional lens. Hannah Jones, Londa Schiebinger, Ann Grimes, and Andrea Small who expanded on the value of Intersectional Design and "getting design right for people across all of society" [9]. The creation of their cards provides designers situational content on intersectionality which allows designers to understand the importance of intersectionality in design. Additionally, Logan Williams' work [10], and independent scholar, builds on author Kat Holmes' persona spectrum [11] introduced in the book *Mismatch*, by adding race to the conversation in the construction of a persona matrix.

3 Racial Classification Origins

To better understand how common cultural understandings of race elicit implicit bias, this research begins by examining the roots of racial characterization in the Science of Race. Race science, a collection of studies from the 17th and 18th centuries, claims to prove that humans are "divided into unequal races" [12]. The categories originally used to classify race in the US census are based on prejudiced phenotypical classifications and stereotypical beliefs, held by white Europeans in the 18th century, who conveniently characterized themselves as "active, very smart, inventive" [13]. Racial traits were first assigned to populations by continent. Indigenous people known in the past as "red" peoples, representing the Americas, were characterized as "ill-tempered, contented, free" [13]. Asians, or the "yellow" peoples, were considered "severe, haughty, desirous" [13]. Africans, or the "black" peoples, were portrayed as "crafty, slow, foolish" [13]. While these racialized worldviews and imperfect racial categories are no longer considered acceptable, they are mentioned to prove that the foundation of race is based on continental location. According to *Implications of biogeography of human populations for 'race' and medicine*, the popular concept of five races correlates with the geographic regions of Africa, Europe, Asia, Oceania, and the Americas, as well as the bureaucratic definitions such as those used by the U.S. Census and the United Nations [14]. Sadly, these observable facial and surface level features, such as skin color, are what mostly what UX designers consider and manipulate when developing personas.

4 The User's Representation in the Literature

Intersectionality informs the UX designer that race is a social construct [16]. Race is not a biological reality, but a social, cultural, and political reality [16]. In her article, *What Can Asian Eyelids Teach Us About User Experience Design?* [16], Jennifer Sano-Franchini, argues "UX designers need to look beyond traditional UX methods in order to better understand race and user experience, as these methods have evidently been limited for addressing such issues". Through a case study centered on videos about Asians double eyelid surgery, the author intends to help "UX designers better understand and consider how culturally biased representations are constructed in subtle ways." Sano-Franchini's work provides insight into the racial aspects of intersectionality, explaining that "examining the rhetorical construction of race in this context—keeping in mind that race is not a biological reality but a social, cultural, and political one—can help us to see with greater clarity the significance of race in UX, particularly in contexts that may not have an inherent or apparent connection to race." [16] The author informs this research by setting these three tenets: "1) the idea that both designers and users are always already culturally situated; 2) the idea that user experiences are shaped by culturally contingent and ideologically laden symbolic representations; and 3) the understanding that because technology design contributes to the articulation of cultural values, logics, and perspectives, designers need to consider issues of social impact and potential harm to users [16]."

"Intersectional HCI: Engaging Identity through Gender, Race, and Class" [7] is the first article to survey how the intersectional representation of the user is addressed in the HCI and UXD literature. It offers the first glimpse of how the user is represented in the Association for Computing Machinery in Human Factors in Computing Systems (CHI) conference proceedings from 1982 to 2016, the premier international conference of HCI. The authors are the first to mention how an intersectional lens is needed to adequately represent the user in HCI. Their study found that the racial classifications in the literature are based on the U.S. census racial classifications demographics: White, Black or African American, American Indian or Alaska Native, Asian, and Native Hawaiian or Other Pacific Islander. The failures to classify race in HCI are illustrated by the fact Schlesinger, A. et al. utilized a keyword list to describe race that failed to include the terms: Asian American, Chicanx and Latinx, First Nations, Alaskan Native, Pacific Islander, Middle Eastern, Native American, American Indian, and Hispanic when analyzing the final 140 corpus their research selected.

An important factor in creating equitable products for all users is using a diverse pool of participants in HCI research. To understand how race and ethnicity of the participants is addressed in HCI research, this study surveyed *Collecting and Reporting Race and Ethnicity Data in HCI* [15], which investigates the racial and ethnic makeup of study participants in HCI research. Building on the work of Schlesinger et al. [7], the authors ask, "Who are the study participants in HCI and when are their race and ethnicity information reported?" and "What are some considerations that speak for and against collecting this information?" Their research found that "for studies published in CHI between 2016 and 2021, less than 3% included detailed race and ethnicity information about their study participants." Intersectionality is only addressed in a passing reference to Schlesinger et al. [7]. Their research stated that the race and the ethnicity of the participants is not adequately reported. The paper also mentioned the WEIRD bias found in the literature, explaining that "the paper and existing work surveyed within are based on the racial and ethnic context of the United States [15]". Furthermore, the authors state that "depending on the nature of the study, categories used in the U.S. Census such as Asian Americans and Pacific Islanders do not necessarily capture the underlying diversity of the group" [15].

To gain a greater understanding of how race and technology are intertwined, this study looked at the article *Does Technology Have Race* [17] the authors of which use case studies and contextualize them with intersectional theories. The article mentions how The Nikon Coolpix S360 camera kept asking an Asian family "Did someone blink?" when they tried taking family pictures. Most of the technologies analyzed by their research focused on facial recognition software technologies such as sensors of automatic faucets and Apple iWatches. Both the faucet and soap dispenser failed to recognize darker skin tones. Similarly, the iWatch was unsuccessful in measuring blood oxygen levels via pulse sensor for dark skinned users. Due to the malfunction, Apple removed the oxygen meter, opting to keep only the pulse reader. While this study and syllabus are not meant to resolve the skin recognition technological issues, the implementation of these cases studies can be used to illustrate technological limitation that should not have made it into a final software and/or product. These case studies are meant to guide the syllabus when it comes to the adaptation Intersectional Design [9], a framework meant to introduce designers to the intersectional facets of user identities. Beside UXD, the researchers cover instances of algorithms gone wrong, such as Flickr and Google categorizing pictures of Black faces as gorillas and apes. For video games, the authors cited a study which found "one study found over two- thirds of the main characters were white (68%), followed by Latino (15%), and black (8%)" [17]. This lack of representation is also seen in the HCI workforce where there are discrepancies in terms of scientists and engineers by race. Out of 5.6 million, 70% are White and 51% are White male, 4.7 are Black or African American, 6% are LatinX or Hispanic, and 17% are Asians. The researchers concluded that "technologies can have race, and as such we as HCI practitioners must go beyond Universal Design and explicitly question the role of race in our technological creations and in our corporate organizations" [17].

To aid UX designers in better understanding the difference between race and ethnicity, this paper turns to Hannah Jones, et al.'s article *Intersectional Design Cards* [9]. The card creators attempt to provide a roadmap for how an intersectional representation of the user can be deployed during the persona creation process by providing pre-made intersectional personas and scenarios model case studies to serve as practical applications for classroom discussions and assignments. A series of cards with 12 intersectional factors and case studies introduce designers to the "intersecting factors that interact to shape a person's or a group's experience and social opportunities as a starting point for a more inclusive design approach" [9]. The card's creators acknowledge that in the U.S skin tone used to define race and that the terminology of race may differ across countries" [9]. For race, the cards realize that racial attributes such as skin tones are important to developing technologies. When it comes to ethnicity, the cards prioritize "groups that share a common identity-based ancestry, language or culture", which may extend to religion, customs, beliefs, and memories of migration or colonization.

One core tenet of intersectional design is social justice. The goal is, from the start of the project, as mentioned by the authors "getting design right for people across all of society". The cards are "designed to help teams explore, analyze, and develop intersectional design solutions." The proposed syllabus will follow an adaptation of the six steps proposed by the cards. The first step consists of introducing the intersectional design methodology which can make some team members uncomfortable with new definitions for race and ethnicity, gender, class, and other demographic categories. The focus of the syllabus is on race and ethnicity within an intersectional lens; to accomplish this task through the comprehensive representation of the user, intersectional characteristics such as gender, class, and others will also be mentioned. The importance of step two cannot be minimized, as it allows the team to establish ground rules to make all members comfortable and ensure all will be treated with care and respect. Only a fraction of the card's methodology is deployed for the proposed syllabus, with a focus on the case studies. Specifically, Hannah et al. propose three ways to use the cards: start a conversation, critique your work, brainstorm ideas, quoting Stanford University school designer and educator Louie Montoya's on the importance of reflection during the design process, explaining that "Most design malpractice happens when people are acting and not reflecting" [9].

In *What Can Asian Eyelids Teach Us About User Experience Design?* [16], a Culturally Reflexive Framework (CRF) is proposed. The author explains that the CRF framework is not used "just to produce more culturally reflexive designs, but also to open up conversations about the social and material consequences of design, and to encourage UX designers to be increasingly deliberate with their strategies of representation, keeping issues of race and culture in mind" [16]. CRF will assist UX designers in their "conversations about the representation of race and culture in UXD". This will hopefully allow incoming UX designers to join the workforce and use those skills without feeling self-conscious about it. The author mentions that "CRF focuses on creating more culturally reflexive UX designers, as opposed to singular instances of culturally reflexive technology," [16] another framework which will be implemented in the syllabus.

5 Modules

While this research acknowledges that intersectionality is needed for UX designers and HCI practitioners, this syllabus emphasizes the introduction of intersectionality mainly for the persona creation process. Persona creation, the first of the five steps of the empathy process in UXD (see Fig. 3.), often represents the first stage in product creation where UX designers consider the user explicitly.

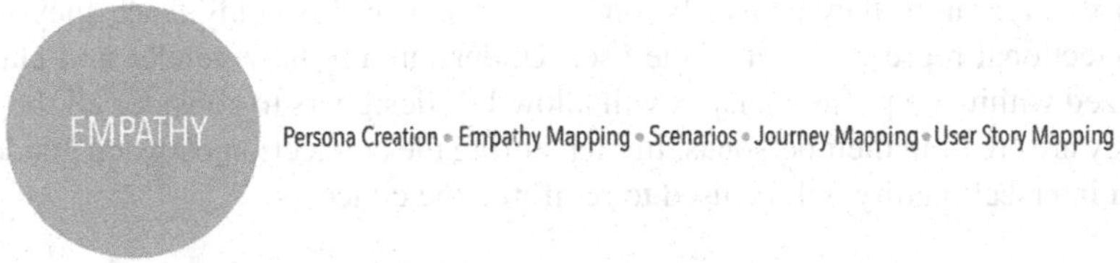

Fig. 3. Empathy Phase of the UXD process

In theory, personas allow design teams to gain a better understanding of their users' needs, experiences, and goals as well as build empathy for users. As such, it is the best time to introduce the diverse intersectional facets of the user's identity when it comes to race and ethnicity. This research, along with researchers such as Logan Williams and Kat Holmes does not believe in the current format of using design thinking to generate empathy for the implementation of personas. UX designers use design thinking as a problem-solving methodology deployed to create innovative solutions. While the first stage of the process is empathy, the methodology often fails to represent the user within an intersection spectrum. The Nielsen Norman Group, leaders in UXD, provides a study guide [18] to aspiring UX designers to learn how to create a persona. At the time of this paper, their study guide failed to mention intersectionality.

6 Influences

Towards *a Gender HCI Curriculum* by Samantha Breslin and Bimlesh Wadhwa, provides a suggested outline for a module that "should cover three core topics that will provide students with a solid foundation in gender HCI" [8]. Their core topics will be adapted for the proposed syllabus to reflect the integration of race and ethnicity in the persona creation process. The first core topic, the Social Construction of Gender and Sex, examines "the vocabulary, definitions, and theories relating to gender and sex and how these are significant in relation to understanding and designing technologies" and will be adapted as the Social Construct of Race and Ethnicity. Intersectional Perspectives on Gender and Feminism, as well as the Gender and Knowledge lesson suggested by the authors, cover the history of feminist theory and provide an intersectional viewpoint when it comes to gender, which will be adapted to aid future designers while considering race and ethnicity. The final core topic, Intersectional Perspectives on Gender and Feminism, and Gender, Knowledge, and Methodology in Science, Technology, and Design "focuses on critically exploring design practices and methodologies in relation to the significance of gender and to feminist approaches and critiques to defining knowledge, knowledge production, and expertise" [8]. The authors explain that "students should be introduced to critiques and scientific objectivity developed in science and technology studies and feminist technology studies" [8]. This article provided the syllabus with suggested readings and learning outcomes. In the proposed syllabus, race and ethnicity technology studies will be covered in the lesson also as they intersect with gender and class. Additional topics will include race and work; race, beauty, consumerism, and the body; and race and medicine.

Finally, it is also important for UX designers to understand how gender and class are viewed both within the persona matrix and intersectionality. While they are not the focus of this research, they cannot be omitted as part of this study since they impact the intersectional representation of the user. Understanding how gender and class are categorized within the persona matrix will allow UX designers to consider all the facets when they are creating their personas. Implementing the connection between gender and class via intersectionality will be used to reinforce the concepts.

7 Faculty

Viewing the user through an intersectional lens might be new for most UXD instructors. Besides being new, it could become a hindrance to some faculty if asked to impart this information. Understanding that UXD practitioners often become instructors, like the demographic base of UXD practitioners, is largely comprised of White practitioners [39]. Instructors may question the need for these materials and discussions but might also feel uncomfortable teaching such a topic due to a plethora of reasons including but not limited to their own positionality, personal beliefs, and lack of knowledge, among others. While this research will not convince every UXD instructor teaching persona creation that the implementation of this module is needed, it does provide a roadmap for those who are interested in making a difference. This research created modules provides learning outcomes, assignments, and assessments.

This module focuses on ways we can teach the future generation of UX designers to better understand, discuss, and apply the intersectional facets of the user in the persona creation process. This is achieved by investigating on how the authors in *Towards a Gender HCI Curriculum* [8] addressed gender in their curriculum, by what other fields, especially healthcare, have done to address race in their curricula. This will result in the creation of a proposed module which will include a reading list and adequate information which will prepare instructors to deliver the material in a confident manner.

The following sub-modules are designed to be taught to students in graduate programs. Kim Case, the author of *Intersectional Pedagogy,* mentions the challenges of introducing intersectionality to undergraduate students and how "educators must critically reflect on their own social location within the classroom" [19]. As to where faculty can best introduce future designers to intersectionality, it is clear that there are a number of options available outside of undergraduate educational programs. The vocational nature of UXD bootcamp programs, LinkedIn, Nielsen Group, and Google UX Design mean they rarely offer courses on race, technology, and design. The purpose of these programs is to impart employable skills. Therefore, social issues such as race, gender, and class might be a concern but may not fit with their curriculum even though they should be a core part of their curriculum.

Currently, intersectionality is being introduced at the graduate level in UXD programs, but not in connection to the persona creation. For example, shared syllabi from another study on the subject confirmed that the topic of intersectionality is mostly covered during an ethics course. Faculty from Indiana University - Purdue University Indianapolis (UIUIP) and University of California Santa Cruz shared syllabi and lesson plans on how intersectionality is introduced, covered, assessed in their courses. At Iowa State University, Anna Slavina's article describes a course she created focusing on encouraging students to "explore HCI activities through traditionally ignored lenses" [20] by providing students an alternative method to be introduced to the theories of intersectionality. Further discussions with the author and shared syllabus and slide presentations by Lynn Dombrowski of UIUIP also provided guidance on the proposed module.

8 Module Breakdown

The purpose of the module outlined in this paper is not to create an eight- or 15-week course but to assist UX designers with seeing the user through an intersectional lens. Adopting the core topics found in *Towards a Gender HCI Curriculum* [8], the proposed module is divided into three sub-modules: the social construct of race and ethnicity; intersectional perspectives on race and ethnicity; as well as race and ethnicity, knowledge, and methodology in science, technology, and design. This teaching guide is constructed to guide UXD faculty.

Module One
(See Fig. 4)

Overview. This sub-module focuses on the introduction of the core base of intersectionality using the prevention framework [21], which utilizes classroom content in a manner that goes beyond supplying information and adds the dimension of questioning

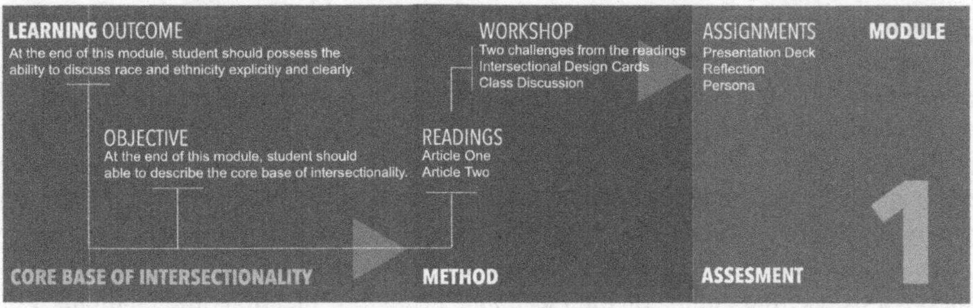

Fig. 4. Module One Learning Outcome, Objective, and Assessment

students' perspectives, preconceived assumptions, and attitudes that might be preventive in nature.

Learning Outcome. When creating a persona, UX designers have demonstrated a bias when it comes to the persona they create [4]. This learning module aims to explore how important issues of race and ethnicity present challenges when creating personas among UX and HCI practitioners who lack personal experience and knowledge of the nuanced dimensions of race. This sub-module assesses the students' knowledge on race and ethnicity via an intersectional lens.

Through the Intersection Design card model [9], readings and class activities, students will be introduced to important key issues within the intersectionality domain. The module highlights sensitive issues around race and underserved populations and aims to enable students to be immersed in the lived experience beyond demonstrating competence in content. With this knowledge, students will comprehend how intersectional factors can influence the representation of the user's identities.

Readings. *An Intersectional Approach to Designing in the Margins* [22] and *Straighten Up and Fly Right: Rethinking Intersectionality in HCI Research* [23] introduces students to intersectionality within the HCI context. The Axis of Oppression (see Fig. 5) assists students in deepening their understanding of how the way they experience the world relates to their social categories and experiences.

Assignment. The Intersectional Design Cards introduced intersectionality in the design context. The article An Intersectional Approach to Designing in the Margins [22] and Straighten Up and Fly Right: Rethinking Intersectionality in HCI Research [23] discussed two main issues that HCI and UX professionals frequently encounter with working with underserved populations in various stages of the product development lifecycle, most notably research. These challenges include:

1. The need and difficulties of adapting appropriate design and research methods to support underserved populations.
2. Methods for responsibly engaging UX designer in research and design through time and trust.

Method. Divide the class into three student groups. Distribute Intersectional Design Cards [9] case studies and assign each group one of the two challenges. Using case studies with a focus on race and ethnicity, gender, and class found in the Intersectional Design

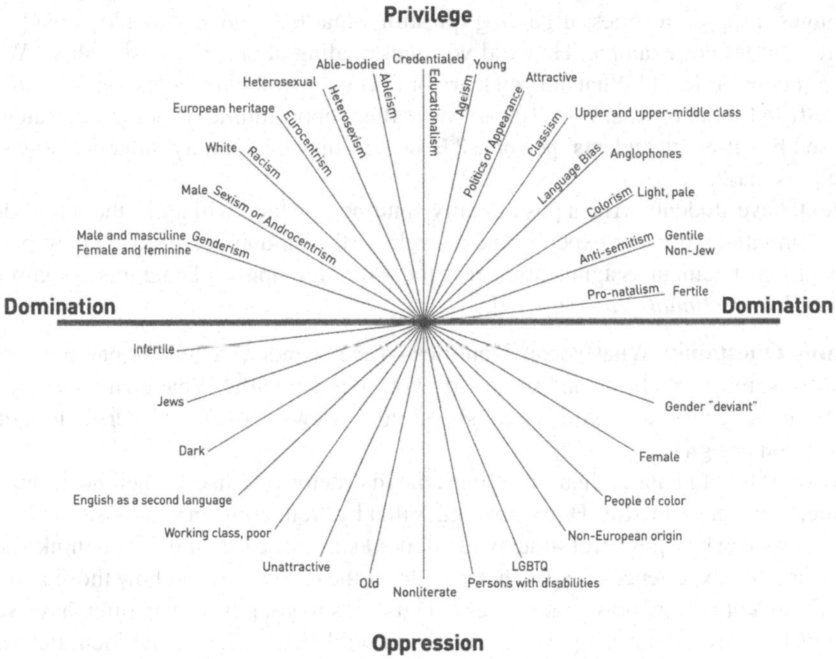

Fig. 5. Axis of Oppression. Sourced from the ACM: Digital Library: interactions

Cards [9], ask the students to highlight the technology failure focused on dimensions of race and underrepresented populations found in the case studies. Have students discuss strategies they would utilize to overcome the challenge they were assigned.

Submission. Each student should submit a presentation deck that illustrates how the impact of race and ethnicity can influence the representation of the user during the creation of a product. Students should also provide a detailed overview of how the failures to represent the user through an intersectional lens impacted the end user in the case study and develop a strategy to rectify the problem discussed.

In-Class Workshop. Begin the class with a brief presentation reviewing the key takeaways from the papers, the cards, and intersectional definitions. Next, create breakout discussion groups organized by the challenge themes. Have the students present their presentations to the group and discuss challenges, insights, and ideas. Instruct students to capture ideas, concerns, and suggested improvements to the strategies during the workshop.

Online Class Modification. For an online course, set up an online whiteboard, a learning space for the instructor and students, with activity areas for each group and instruct students to post their presentations on their group activity board. Students can then post ideas and challenges in the board with stickies under each respective presentation.

Reflections. Have students reflect on the workshop activity and the insights, ideas, and issues gathered from other students during the workshop activity. Based on their challenges, propose a series of guiding questions that the students should consider in their reflection. For example: How did you feel reading about intersectionality? What was your comfort level? What did you learn or find interesting in the readings? What are you confused about or what wasn't clear? Were there opportunities to combine strategies proposed by different students' personas? How will intersectionality influence how you create personas?

Next, have students write a positionality statement, which will assist them to reflect on the limitations of their experiences, as well as the unique perspectives they bring. The position statement assignment mirrors the Autobiographical Diagrams assignment found in *Intersectional Pedagogy* [19].

Guiding Questions. What social identities—race, gender, sexual orientation, age, social class, religion, ability and so on—do you identify with? What elements of your identity, experiences, and worldviews shape your views on UXD? Intersectionality? How do you design?

To assist the students in their reflections, the instructor will discuss their positionality with their students. Christine Harrigton argues that by "reflecting on your positionality as an instructor can be a powerful strategy for student success, especially if you think about how your lived experiences shape what you do in the classroom and how those actions may or may not be supporting the success of students in your class who often have very different lived experiences." [24]. Instructors should share what social identities they identify with and how significant is each identity to how they teach and design, their epistemology and role in UXD and HCI. The type of training and experiences they had and how those shaped who they are as practitioners and influenced their teaching style and philosophy.

In Class Presentation. Student groups present their presentations in class and discuss takeaways, ideas and challenges with the class. This will allow opportunity for deeper discussion and broader insights on the definitions and theories of intersectionality. Students will gain new perspectives and ideas from other students.

Module Two
(See Fig. 6)

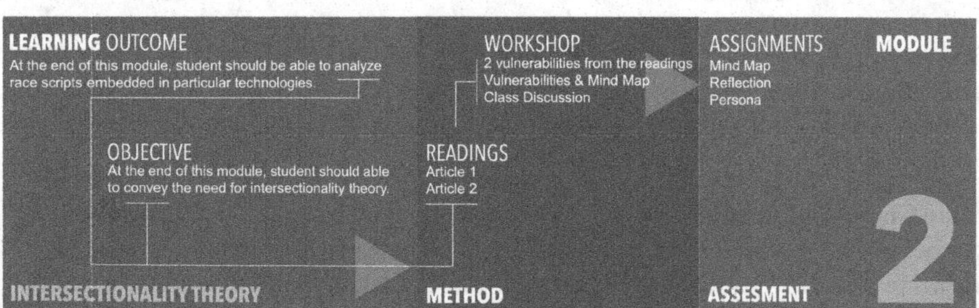

Fig. 6. Module Two Learning Outcome, Objective, and Assessment

Overview. This sub-module focuses on the need of intersectionality theory by exploring the dimensions of power in a vulnerability framework [25]. This framework guides practitioners to explore multiple dimensions of vulnerability and how they can be accounted for in the UXD process.

Learning Outcome. At the end of this sub-module, students should be able to analyze race scripts embedded in particular technologies. To achieve this task, students will explore examples of power inside UXD, robotics, aesthetics, and healthcare, and their manifestations and impact to highlight conditions of vulnerability. Through understanding of these conditions and vulnerabilities, students are better able to identify vulnerability points in persona and product design and devise opportunities to safeguard and mitigate these vulnerabilities ahead of time.

The intersectionality theory investigates how power matrices and interlocking structures of oppression shape and influence the multiple identities of individuals. UX designers typically explore dimensions of needs, wants, pains, gains, and values in research to best understand how these underlying forces impact the personas they create and thus shape product features and drive overall product design. This framework introduces a new dimension to these commonly used matrices, vulnerabilities by which to understand users. Through exploration of the multiple facets of vulnerability that manifest as a result of power and oppression, UXD practitioners can deepen their knowledge of user perspectives and broaden their research focus to include areas that warrant attention and understanding.

Readings. The first chapter of *Race after technology* [2] which focuses on *Engineered Inequity* and *Does technology have a race?* [17] introduces students to inequalities and how they manifest in UXD and HCI. The readings illustrate histories of racial injustice and power, and oppression that exist in areas of human development such as beauty (aesthetics), hygiene, and healthcare. Designers are increasingly expected to tackle some of the issues through design.

Assignment. Ask students to identify a product that they wish to investigate in one of the following sectors: education, robotics, jobs, hygiene, or healthcare. You can expand on this list or students may also consider products outside of this. Create a mind map including the following:

Histories. Identify histories of power and prejudice inside these industries that may relate to the chosen product.

Vulnerabilities. To explore and identify possible areas vulnerable to power that may manifest in their product design or features, as students to consider opportunities that may manifest through the following lenses. These lenses guide the students through considering a new perspective of the features and system from a position of vulnerability adding another dimension to the common, needs, wants, values, and pain point perspectives UX designers are familiar with considering in product design.

Rights. Identify areas of vulnerability where the product may nudge, coerce, oppress, exclude, marginalize, manipulate, harm, control, or oppress.

- Thought

- Speech
- Action
- Live, exist
- Family
- Property
- Safety from violence
- Equality
- Citizenship
- Recognized as a person
- Expression
- Vote
- Religion
- Health
- Language
- Safety
- Love
- Work
- Marriage
- Liberty

Methods. Consider methods of power used to oppress

- Moral - people to people
- Political - governing on behalf of people - policy
- Economic - through money

Ecosystem. Consider vulnerabilities in the ecosystem of the end user and the product.

- People
- Technology
- Process
- Goals
- Culture - language, customs, beliefs, fears
- Physiological
- Social
- Beliefs

Mitigation Principles. Consider how you might mitigate vulnerabilities and points of control through the following ethical guidelines at each phase in the UXD process.

Congruence. Ensures that the process/feature/ system matches the objective and goals values of the end user.

Minimize Control. Matches system and product goals to user goals and gives users the freedom to decide how to achieve them.

Local Control. Options, personalization.

Flexibility. Give users fair, easy-to-execute decision capabilities, and choices.

Transparency. Transparency of information first to those it affects. Protect privacy, protect rights.

Evolution. Consider vulnerabilities over the short and long terms.

Support. Human needs through justice, freedom, and autonomy.

Method. Divide the class into three student groups. Ask students to create a mind map focused on the vulnerabilities of the user. Have students explore how UX practitioners can anticipate, diagnose and remedy potential control points that emerge in research, design, and development.

Submission. Each student should submit a mind map that illustrates how the impact of dimensions of power can influence the representation of the user during the creation of a product. Students should also provide a detailed overview of how the failures to implement intersectional theories impacted the end user in the mind map. They should develop a strategy to rectify the problem discussed.

In-Class Workshop. Begin the class with a brief presentation reviewing the key takeaways from the papers, mind map elements, and intersectional theories. Next, create breakout discussion groups organized by the sectors. Have the students present their mind maps to the group and discuss challenges, insights, and ideas. Instruct students to capture ideas, concerns, and suggested improvements to the strategies during the workshop.

Online Class Modification. For an online course, set up an online whiteboard, a learning space for the instructor and students, with activity areas for each group and instruct students to post their presentations on their group activity board. Students can then post ideas and challenges in the board with stickies under each respective presentation.

In Class Presentation. Student groups present their mind map in class and discuss takeaways, ideas and mitigation principles with the class. This will allow opportunity for deeper discussion and broader insights as students gain new perspectives and ideas from other students as well as enable them to address and discuss challenges to the issues that other groups reported.

Guiding Questions. Describe mechanisms, strategies, and design policies to safeguard freedoms, inclusivity, and justice around critical issues faced by designers today and how UX designers play a critical role in driving sustainable futures? Discuss any limitations and challenges you feel would still exist and why when it comes to enabling mitigation principles in the workplace?

Follow-up Workshop. Instructors will have students participate in two follow-up group activities to further refine a mitigation strategy and reinforce the theories covered in module one by bringing them further into the UXD process. Students will be asked to identify vulnerabilities, asked to brainstorm safeguard and mitigation strategies for each vulnerability they identified including the area of the UXD process where the vulnerability exists. These can be added to the mind map and later used in the creation of personas, empathy maps, journey maps, and user stories. Students will also be shown images of individuals from different ethnic groups or different physical locations, such as different urban environments or country locations, before they are asked to create their own personas. Research in cognitive science has demonstrated that racial biases can be lessened through practices of seeing [26]. The exercise will be used to address the students' own-race bias, which is demonstrated by difficulty in identifying faces from other races [27]. Own-race bias is detrimental to the creation persona process. Understanding intersectionality theories will enhance UX designers own-race bias.

Post Assignment. Based on the first workshop, ask students to select one of the safeguard and mitigation strategies proposed in the first workshop that they would like to further develop as a group. Students should then define the merit of the strategy they propose and identify areas for improvement and challenges. Next, they can discuss ideas and concerns they presented through group discussion during the first workshop. Of the vulnerabilities and concerns presented, the group should identify which safeguard and mitigation strategies they would like to research further and then refine.

Submission. Students should present a new mind map highlighting their vulnerabilities, original strategy, why they chose it, discuss the safeguard and mitigation strategy selected, ideas and challenges identified, and a detailed instruction of their new strategy including references. The mind map should also address any limitations and challenges that they envision with their proposal. This method includes a follow up assignment, recreating personas that addresses the vulnerabilities found in the student selected research and in class workshop.

Module Three
(See Fig. 7)

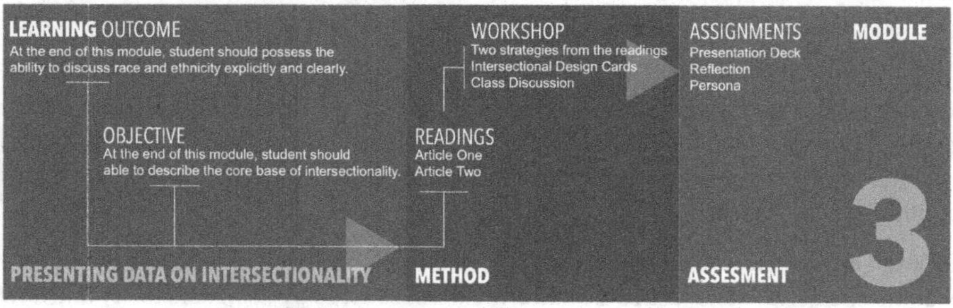

Fig. 7. Module Three Learning Outcome, Objective, and Assessment

Overview. This sub-module focuses on presenting data on intersectionality using the prevention framework [21], similar to sub-module one. The framework utilizes classroom content in a manner that goes beyond supplying information and adds the dimension of questioning students' perspectives, preconceived assumptions, and attitudes that might be preventive in nature.

Learning Outcome. At the end of this sub-module, students will be able to discuss how different facets of identity shape people's lives and experiences. Before creating a product, UX designers frequently have goals, assumptions, and even calculated project outcomes. This learning module focuses on how while, as students, future UX designers should first understand the user for the product they create through an intersectional lens. Additionally, having the ability while in school to develop a vocabulary and be able to discuss how intersecting factors shape the end user will benefit the students when they enter the UXD workforce.

Through an exploration of how important the issues of race and ethnicity are in UXD and HCI, the last module focuses on examples of racism found in UXD technologies. This learning module offers a pathway for research and co-designing activities among UX and HCI practitioners. Via research, readings and class activities, students will be introduced to important key issues within the intersectionality domain. The module highlights sensitive issues around race and aims to enable students to be immersed in the lived experience beyond demonstrating competence in content.

Readings. Anti-Racist HCI: notes on an emerging critical technical practice [28] and My manifesto towards changing the conversation around race, equity and bias in design [29] provide first an understanding of the lack of trust of some user due to race and then strategies for students on eliminating race bias within the HCI and UXD context, valuable knowledge for students to possess when they create personas.

Assignment. Anti-Racist HCI: notes on an emerging critical technical practice [28] and My manifesto towards changing the conversation around race, equity and bias in design [29] article discussed two main challenges that HCI and UX professionals may encounter when attempting to utilize some of the strategies they mentioned. These challenges include:

1. The need to shift the power as anti-racist systems should address instead of neglecting racial inequalities.
2. Methods for responsibly engaging UX designers and HCI practitioners in flagging systems that are misused for racial discrimination and providing solutions to remedy those issues.

Method. Divide the class into three student groups. Distribute A Designer's Critical Alphabet [30] cards and the Critical Alphabet repository [31], both created by Leslie-Ann Noel, the author of the My manifesto towards changing the conversation around race, equity and bias in design [29] article. Ask the students to find an article that highlights a technology failure focused on dimensions of race. Have students research methods, strategies, and workshops utilized by other practitioners in the field to overcome the challenge they were assigned.

Submission. Each student should submit a presentation deck that illustrates what research strategy they found, why they chose it, and how it addresses their challenge. Students should also provide a detailed overview of the method, and strategy used, insights on the strategies' success, challenges the practitioners faced, challenges they envision with the method, and ideas on how to overcome those issues. It is important to highlight the importance of an informational presentation deck over a research report and the need to illustrate key points in the presentation for effective group discussion.

In-Class Workshop. Begin the class with a brief presentation reviewing the key takeaways from the papers, the cards and repository. Next, create breakout discussion groups organized by the challenge themes. Have the students present their presentations to the group and discuss challenges, insights, and ideas. Instruct students to capture ideas, concerns, and suggested improvements to the strategies during the workshop.

Online Class Modification. For an online course, set up an online whiteboard, a learning space for the instructor and students, with activity areas for each group and instruct students to post their presentations on their group activity board. Students can then post ideas and challenges in the board with stickies under each respective presentation.

Reflections. While the authors of *Anti-Racist HCI: notes on an emerging critical technical practice* [28] mentioned that reflection is not enough in anti-racist design. Have students reflect on the workshop activity and the insights, ideas, and issues gathered from other students during the workshop activity. Based on their challenges, propose a series of guiding questions that the students should consider in their reflection. For example: What were the key takeaways from the group discussion? What additional challenges were raised? What were some suggestions that can be further explored? Were there opportunities to combine strategies proposed by different students' research?

Next, have students redesign their strategy incorporating ideas and suggestions gathered from the group discussion for improvement. Second, have students design personas which will rectify the failures found in the students research. Last, have students rewrite their positionality statement as mentioned by the authors of *Anti-Racist HCI: notes on an emerging critical technical practice* [28], "both designers and users must be pluralistically identified, with intersectional identities front and center throughout the design and persona process". Positionality is also the first point mentioned in the *My manifesto towards changing the conversation around race, equity and bias in design* [29] article.

In Class Presentation. Student groups present their presentations in class and discuss takeaways, ideas and challenges with the class. This will allow opportunity for deeper discussion and broader insights as students gain new perspectives and ideas from other students as well as enable them to address and discuss challenges to the issues that other groups reported.

Guiding Questions. Describe methods you would use to strengthen your anti-racist insight when it comes to persona creation? Discuss any limitations and challenges you feel would still exist and why when it comes to enabling anti-racist theories in the workplace?

Follow-up Workshop. Instructors will have students participate in a follow-up group activity to further refine a strategy in a workshop. This method includes a follow up assignment, recreating personas that addresses the deficiency found in the student selected research and in class workshop.

Post Assignment. Based on the first workshop, ask students to select one of the methods proposed in the first workshop that they would like to further develop as a group. This might be one that they felt was too weak or possibly one they collectively ideated novel ideas for. Students should then define the merit of the original strategy they propose to redesign and identify areas for improvement and challenges. Next, they can discuss ideas and concerns they presented through group discussion during the first workshop. Of the ideas and concerns presented, the group should identify which ideas challenges they would like to research further and then refine.

Submission. Students should present a new presentation deck highlighting their challenge, original strategy, why they chose it, discuss the technology failure associated with the strategy, ideas and challenges identified, and a detailed instruction of their new strategy including references. The deck should also address any limitations and challenges that they envision with their proposal. Students should also redesign a persona that address the failure to properly represent the user found in their research.

Review and Reflection. Review and reflect on what went well and areas that present opportunity for improvement. Did the module help students understand how dimensions of race and its underrepresentation in the product design lifecycle impact the products and further marginalize these populations? What worked and what did not?

9 Discussion

10 Limitations

Due the fact the representation of the user within an intersectional lens is an emerging literature in HCI and UXD, a limited number of articles are available. On the topic of race and ethnicity, the literature is lagging since most of the research on identifying the user in UXD research with an intersectional lens has been focused on gender [7]. Another limitation is seen the lack of input in the literature from non-WEIRD (Western, Educated, Industrialized, Rich, Democratic) articles. Chen mentions that "a majority (>90%) of the articles that report participants' race and ethnicity are conducted in the United States" [15]. Future research should investigate how the user is represented in non-WEIRD literature. In terms of education, the pedagogical literature is scarce and emerging. Kim Case Intersectional Pedagogy is the "first academic text to extend intersectionality into the domain of pedagogical praxis" [19]. Even then, introducing the definitions and theories of intersectionality to students is usually reserved for the cognitive sciences. The author mentions how bringing together fields such as psychology, sociology, social work, and gender studies are utilized to "advance an education agenda that dismantle the dominant categorical approach which treats social identity as mutually exclusive" [9].

Also, this study does not entirely focus on persona creation but hopes to utilize the information it gathered it its literature review to better inform the representation of user during the persona creation. Case studies on the persona creation process regarding gender [32] could have been included in this study.

11 Future Research

Future research should investigate Intersectional Design, which acknowledge the "intersecting factors such as gender, ethnicity, age, geographic location, etc. that interact to shape a person's or a group's experience and social opportunities as a starting point for a more inclusive design approach" [9] can be reengineered and become Intersectional UXD. In addition, future research should consider how A Designer's Critical Alphabets [30] cards can become part of the UXD student and practitioner lexicon and took kit. The merge of with A Designer's Critical Alphabets and Intersectional Design could provide a foundation for Intersectional UXD. Future research should continue investigating race and ethnicity in person creation. Again, the focus has been mostly on gender [32].

At last, to test their validity, these teaching modules need to be implemented and assessed in the classroom. Further studies will explore the introduction of intersectionality to undergraduate students. As noted by Kim Case, the integration of intersectionality usually occurs in diversity courses [19], not in UXD courses.

References

1. Cabanas, A.M., Fuentes-Guajardo, M., Latorre, K., León, D., Martín-Escudero, P.: Skin pigmentation influence on pulse oximetry accuracy: a systematic review and bibliometric analysis. Sensors **22**(9), 1–20 (2022). https://doi.org/10.3390/s22093402
2. Benjamin, R.: Race After Technology: Abolitionist Tools for the New Jim Code. Polity (2019)
3. Braun, L.: Race, ethnicity and lung function: a brief history. Can. J. Respir. Therapy **51**(4), 99–101 (2015)
4. Emmanuel, G-S., Polito, F.: How related are designers to the personas they create?. In: Lecture Notes in Computer Science: Design, User Experience, and Usability: Design Thinking and Practice in Contemporary and Emerging Technologies, vol. 13323, pp. 3–13 (2022).https://doi.org/10.1007/978-3-031-05906-3_1
5. Cooper, A.: The Inmates are Running the Asylum: Why High Tech Products Drive Us Crazy and How to Restore the Sanity. Pearson Higher Education (2004). https://dl.acm.org/doi/https://doi.org/10.5555/984201
6. https://www.zippia.com/user-experience-designer-jobs/demographics/
7. Schlesinger, A., et al.: Intersectional HCI: engaging identity through gender, race, and class. In: Proceedings of the 2017 CHI Conference on Human Factors in Computing Systems, pp. 5412–5427 (2017). https://doi.org/10.1145/3025453.3025766
8. Breslin, S., Wadhwa, B.: Towards a gender HCI curriculum. In: Conference on Human Factors in Computing Systems - Proceedings, vol. 18, pp. 1091–1096 (2015). https://doi.org/10.1145/2702613.2732923
9. Schiebinger, L., et al.: Intersectional Design Cards (1st ed.). Intersectional Design (2021)
10. Williams, L.D.A.: Design, Feminism, And The Persona Spectrum: Introducing The Intersectional Persona Matrix. https://www.inclusiveresearchbydesign.com/news/design-feminism-and-the-persona-spectrum-introducing-the-intersectional-persona-matrix
11. Holmes, K.: Mismatch: How Inclusion Shapes Design. Markets, Globalization & Development Review, vol. 04, no. 02 (2018). https://doi.org/10.23860/mgdr-2019-04-02-09
12. Facing History & Ourselves, The Science of Race, last updated November 15 (2017)
13. The Atlantic Monthly; The Genetic Archaeology of Race - 01.04; volume 287, no. 4, 69–80 (2001)
14. United States Census Bureau. Quick Facts: Race. https://www.census.gov/quickfacts/fact/note/US/RHI625221#:~:text=OMB%20requires%20five%20minimum%20categories,report%20more%20than%20one%20race
15. Chen, Y.T., Smith, A.D.R., Reinecke, K., To, A.: Collecting and reporting race and ethnicity data in HCI. In: Conference on Human Factors in Computing Systems – Proceedings, vol. 1, Issue 1. Association for Computing Machinery (2022). https://doi.org/10.1145/3491101.3519685

16. Sano-Franchini, J.: What can asian eyelids teach us about user experience design? a culturally reflexive framework for UX/I design. Rhetoric Prof. Commun. Globalization **10**(1), 27–53 (2017)
17. Hankerson, D., et al.: Does technology have race?. In: Conference on Human Factors in Computing Systems - Proceedings, 07–12-May-, pp. 473–485 (2016). https://doi.org/10.1145/2851581.2892578
18. Kaplan, K.: Personas: Study Guide. https://www.nngroup.com/articles/personas-study-guide/
19. Case, K.A.: (Ed.). Intersectional Pedagogy: Complicating Identity and Social Justice. Routledge/Taylor & Francis Group (2017)
20. Slavina, A., Gilbert, S.B.: Perspectives in HCI: a course integrating diverse viewpoints. In: EduCHI 2021: 3rd Annual Symposium on HCI Education (2021)
21. Reppucci, N.D., Britner, P.A., Woolard, J.L.: Preventing Child Abuse and Neglect Through Parent Education. Baltimore, MD: Brookes (1997)
22. Erete, S., Israni, A., Dillahunt, T.: An intersectional approach to designing in the margins. Interactions **25**(3), 66–69 (2018). https://doi.org/10.1145/3194349
23. Rankin, Y., Thomas, J.: Straighten up and fly right: rethinking intersectionality in HCI research. Interactions **26**, 64–68 (2019). https://doi.org/10.1145/3363033
24. https://www.queensu.ca/ctl/resources/equity-diversity-inclusivity/positionality-statement#:~:text=Positionality%20Statement%20(syllabus)%3A&text=Here%20are%20some%20prompts%20that,identity%20to%20how%20I%20teach%3F
25. Rogers, W., Lange, M.M.: Rethinking the vulnerability of minority populations in research. Am. J. Public Health. **103**(12), 2141–2146 (2013). https://doi.org/10.2105/AJPH.2012.301200. Epub 2013 Oct 17. PMID: 24134375; PMCID: PMC3828952
26. Lebrecht, S., Pierce, L.J., Tarr, M.J., Tanaka, J.W.: Perceptual other-race training reduces implicit racial bias. Plos One **4**(1) (2009). https://doi.org/10.1371/journal.pone.0004215
27. Meissner, C.A., Brigham, J.C.: Thirty years of investigating the own-race bias in memory for faces: a meta-analytic review. Psychol. Public Policy Law **7**(1), 3–35 (2001). https://doi.org/10.1037/1076-8971.7.1.3
28. Abebe, V., et al.: Anti-Racist HCI: notes on an emerging critical technical practice. In: Conference on Human Factors in Computing Systems – Proceedings (2022). https://doi.org/10.1145/3491101.3516382
29. https://medium.com/future-of-design-in-higher-education/9-steps-towards-changing-the-conversation-around-race-equity-and-bias-in-design-304242194116
30. https://design.ncsu.edu/blog/2022/01/07/from-a-to-z-lesley-ann-noel-and-decolonizing-design/
31. https://criticalalphabet.com/
32. Marsden, N., et al.: Developing personas, considering gender: a case study. In: ACM International Conference Proceeding Series, pp. 392–396 (2017)

Proactive TV Gamification: Engaging Older Adults Socially

Gabriel Faria(✉), Telmo Silva, and Jorge Ferraz de Abreu

DigiMedia, Department of Communication and Art, University of Aveiro, Aveiro, Portugal
{g.martinsfaria,tsilva,jfa}@ua.pt

Abstract. This study explores the capabilities of television as a tool to promote social relationships among older adults, considering that these relationships are vital for an active and healthy ageing process. Physical changes, encompassing sensory and locomotor decline, alongside cognitive deterioration, underscore the need for robust social networks to support older adults. Social relationships play a crucial role in determining the quality of life for older adults. Furthermore, television holds significance in the lives of older adults, serving as an information source and a catalyst for social interactions. Acknowledging the importance of leveraging television's potential, the ProSeniorTV system was developed. This gamified proactive system, seamlessly integrated into television, informs older adults about local events through notifications on the TV-set display and encourages active participation in those events. Through mini-games and a player ranking, the system motivates engagement to support social connections among older adults. This article presents initial results from the ongoing field trial conducted in the homes of four individuals aged between 60 and 80, with an average age of 67.5 years, over one month. Participants were given daily notifications through their television displays, encouraging them to play the minigames and access four social events. The results demonstrate that the proposed system facilitates easy access to information about social events, motivating participation and raising awareness among older adults about the importance of maintaining social relationships and ensuring an active and healthy ageing process. Specifically, on average, participants accessed half of the suggested events, and all said they gained access to information about events through the ProSeniorTV system.

Keywords: Gamification System · Interactive Television · Local Community · Older Adults · Proactivity · Social Agenda · Social Engagement

1 Introduction

In contemporary times, the global population is experiencing a rapid ageing phenomenon. This is occurring concurrently with declining birth rates, while in stark contrast, scientific advancements have consistently improved the overall quality of life, subsequently leading to increased life expectancy. For instance, between 2011 and 2022, Portugal witnessed a decline in the percentage of the active population (aged between 15 and 64) from 65.8% to 63.1%. In the same period, there was also a notable increase in the percentage of the elderly population, which rose from 19.2% to 24% [1].

A. Marcus et al. (Eds.): HCII 2024, LNCS 14714, pp. 70–85, 2024.
https://doi.org/10.1007/978-3-031-61356-2_5

As individuals age, they undergo diverse physical and cognitive transformations that can pose challenges when interacting with their environment. Physically, for instance, there is a decline in visual, auditory, and locomotor capabilities [2, 3]. Cognitive changes are also evident, including deteriorating memory and concentration abilities [2, 4].

In response to the aforementioned biological limitations stemming from the ageing process, there is a heightened emphasis on the significance of the social networks of older adults. As these limitations increase their level of dependence, it becomes essential for older adults to have access to a robust support network to assist them in their daily lives. In this context, social relationships, particularly with family members, play a pivotal role in determining the quality of life for older adults. According to Lucca [5], the primary source of support for elderly individuals comes from their families. Consequently, the social activities most meaningful to older adults involve interaction with their relatives. Furthermore, existing literature underscores that meaningful social interactions in which older adults can engage are associated with several benefits, including: *i)* maintaining good cognitive health; *ii)* enhancing life satisfaction; *iii)* promoting emotional stability; and *iv)* improving physical well-being [6–10].

In addition to the crucial socialisation factor, numerous other factors are vital for older adults' overall well-being in their daily lives. Television is essential in older adults' lives, as it is often their primary source of information and entertainment. This is especially true for older adults in Portugal, where individuals aged 64 and above are the most frequent consumers of television content since they are the ones who watch TV for an average period of about 5 h per day [11], comprising approximately 30% of the total television audience [12–15].

Simultaneously, in a social context, television also assumes a significant role in the well-being of the elderly population. Television often catalyses social interactions, prompting discussions and conversations revolving around content multiple individuals have watched [16]. Hence, it becomes imperative to develop innovative technological solutions that leverage the social potential of television, mainly when directed at older adults. This approach makes it more feasible to stimulate social engagement among older adults and sustain their relationships with others, whether family members, friends, or acquaintances.

Considering the topics mentioned above, in the next section, we present the *ProSeniorTV* system, a proactive gamified system seamlessly integrated into television to inform older adults about upcoming social events organised in their local community and encourage active involvement in these activities. The third section presents the strategy adopted to run a field trial to test the developed prototype in authentic contexts and with real users. Consequently, we show the preliminary results of this field trial in the fourth section. Finally, in the fifth section, we refer to the conclusion and next steps of the investigation.

2 Proposal of a Proactive Gamified System Integrated on Television

This chapter introduces the *ProSeniorTV* prototype. The primary objective of this system is to promote active ageing among older adults through a proactive gamified approach integrated into an Internet Protocol Television (IPTV) solution.

Regarding its operation, the developed prototype relies on proactively displaying notifications on the TV. These notifications inform the viewer about specific events and allow navigation to a gamified interface developed in Unity. This interface is hosted on a Raspberry Pi 4, connected to the viewer's TV via HDMI, as illustrated in Fig. 1. The OverTV[1] service, created by the Social iTV Group[2], was used to enable the presentation of notifications on the TV screen. To access the system's interface, the user only needs to select a specific notification (using the OK button on their remote control). This triggers an HDMI-CEC command sent to the TV from a Node.js server integrated into the Raspberry Pi, automatically switching the HDMI source to the one to which the Raspberry Pi is connected.

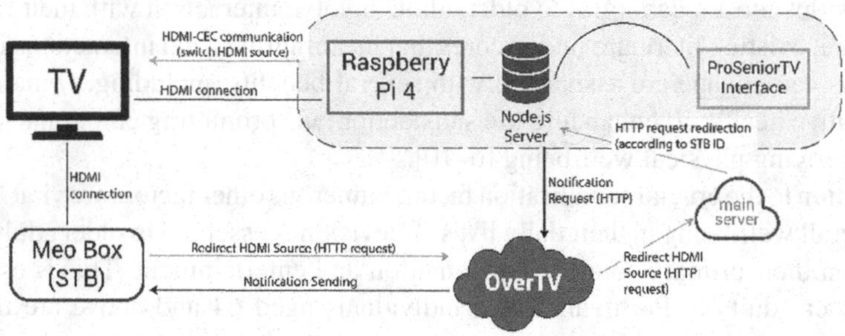

Fig. 1. ProSeniorTV system architecture.

In the *ProSeniorTV* interface, the user has the option to explore three main functionalities: *i)* access one of the three cognitive stimulation minigames displayed in the interface; *ii)* enter participation codes personally delivered to the user when attending a specific event suggested through the TV; and *iii)* check their position in the user ranking, which is directly influenced by the number of participations in social events and the score obtained while playing minigames. Users occupying the top three positions receive podium medals, aiming to encourage participation in events suggested through TV notifications.

Considering those above, in the following figure (on the left), the types of notifications that the user can receive on their TV set are highlighted, including: *i)* notification encouraging the user to explore the ProSeniorTV interface, including the minigames within it; and *ii)* notification informing the user about upcoming events in their residential area (Fig. 2).

It was established that the mini-games integrated into the interface should focus on cognitive stimulation. The power of video games in this regard is well-known, as they serve as a potent tool for rehabilitating and enhancing cognitive abilities in older individuals [17]. This aspect is crucial for an active and healthy ageing process, emphasising the importance of incorporating cognitive stimulation into the ProSeniorTV system. The

[1] https://socialitv.web.ua.pt/index.php/portfolio/overtv/.
[2] https://socialitv.web.ua.pt/.

Fig. 2. ProSeniorTV system notification examples (left) and its interface (right).

minigames, whose interfaces are shown in Figs. 3, 4 and 5, stimulate various specific cognitive abilities: i) memory capacity, ii) attention direction capacity, and *iii)* visuospatial capacity.

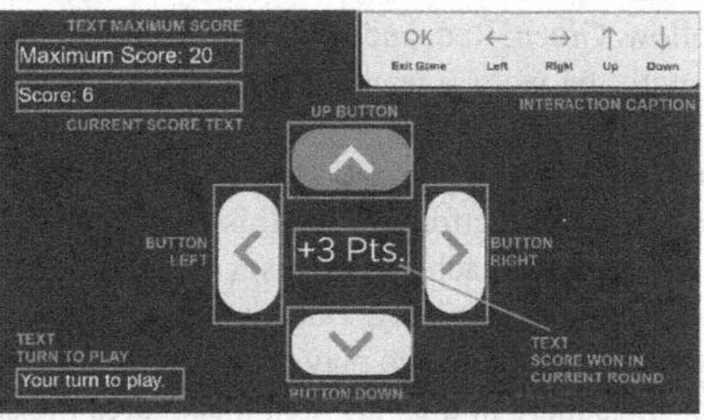

Fig. 3. Graphical elements that compose minigames 1.

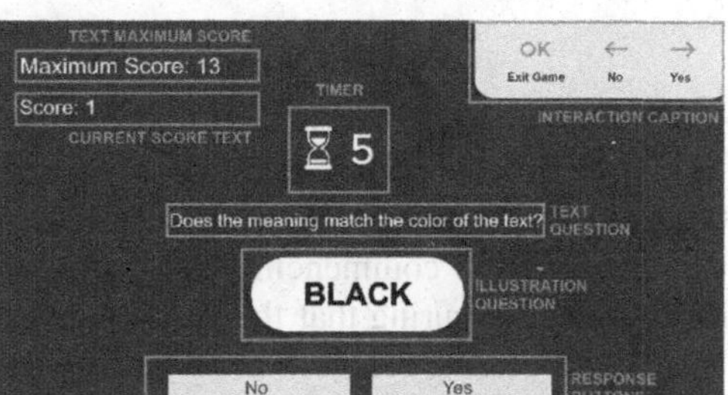

Fig. 4. Graphical elements that compose minigames 2.

The first minigame (memory test) is a game where the user has four directional buttons on their remote control (up, down, left, and right) to create sequences. At the beginning of the game, a specific sequence is presented to the user, which they must replicate. Whenever the user enters the correct sequence, the game generates a new sequence, almost identical to the previous one but adding a new element. For example, if the first sequence is *down*, the second could be, for instance, *down; right*. Whenever the user makes a mistake in the sequence, the game ends.

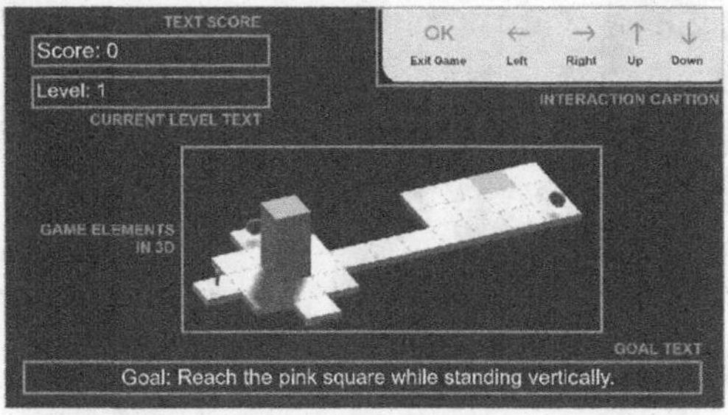

Fig. 5. Graphical elements that compose minigames 3.

In the case of the second minigame (attention direction test), a specific word is presented to the user. This word can be one of the following options: *"Black"; "Yellow"; "Green"; "Red"*; or *"Blue"*. Furthermore, the word may be written in one of the following colours: Black, Yellow, Green, Red, and Blue. The user's goal is to identify whether the colour associated with the word (meaning) matches or does not match the colour with which the word is written.

Finally, in the third (visuospatial perception test), the user is challenged to move a parallelepiped on a specific game platform. To do this, they must use the directional keys (up, down, left, and right), where each click causes the parallelepiped to rotate in the direction corresponding to the pressed key. During the game, the user must be careful not to let the parallelepiped fall out of the play area. The main objective is to position the parallelepiped over the square in the play area that shares the same colour, keeping the game character in the vertical position.

3 Methods

After conceptualising and prototyping the ProSeniorTV system, it was time to test the developed product in a real-world context to determine whether the proposed system effectively motivated older individuals to participate in social contexts (crucial for active and healthy ageing). However, before commencing this test, it was also vital for the research team to devise a strategy ensuring that the system and the conducted testing and evaluation would yield the necessary results to ascertain whether the conceptualised system fulfilled its primary objective of encouraging sociabilisation among older adults.

Considering what has been mentioned, it was initially defined that this field trial should be conducted with the participation of 20 individuals ($n = 20$) who should have characteristics equal or similar to those of the target audience aimed at, specifically individuals aged 60 or older who use the television in a daily basis.

It was also decided that before and after the field test, participants should respond to a questionnaire during a semi-structured interview. By comparing the results obtained at these two points, it would be possible to assess the effectiveness of the usefulness the participants attributed to the proposed system. Figure 6 outlines a representative scheme of the devised field test strategy.

Specifically, at the beginning of the test, each participant responded to a questionnaire aimed at obtaining their characterisation concerning sociodemographic data and daily habits, including:

- their habits of using new technologies (usage frequency; purposes; owned technological devices);
- their TV consumption habits;
- their social interaction habits; and
- their habits of using cognitive stimulation games (including digital games).

Additionally, the UCLA Loneliness Scale (version 3) [18] was used to assess the participants' level of loneliness, and the Lubben Social Network Scale [19] was used to measure the level of social integration and the risk of social isolation associated with each participant. Participants were also asked about their initial impressions and expectations regarding the ProSeniorTV system.

In the post-test phase, participants will be asked about their final impressions regarding the use of the ProSeniorTV system, and the UCLA Loneliness Scale (version 3) [18] and the Lubben Social Network Scale [19] were administered again. Several scales were also applied to evaluate the system prototype regarding usability and user experience in this context. The scales used included: *i)* the Self-Assessment Manikin (SAM) [18]; *ii)* the ATTRACKDIFF scale[3]; and *iii)* the System Usability Scale (SUS) [20, 21].

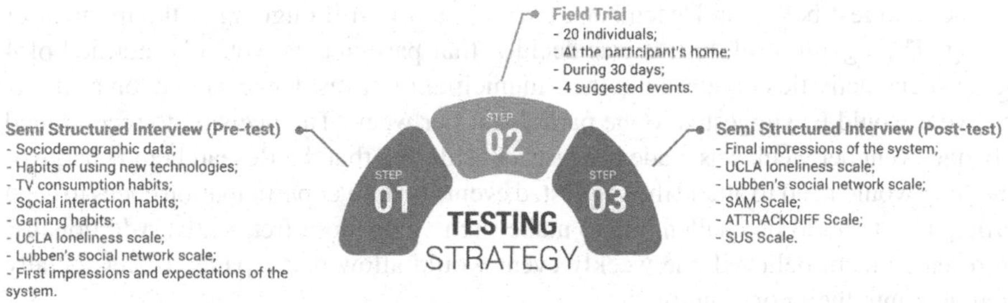

Fig. 6. Representative diagram of the adopted field trial strategy.

In order to start the field trial, installing the system in each participant's home was necessary before conducting the test. It's worth noting that each test should last for 30 days. After a discussion among the research team members, it was considered that this would be the minimum period to obtain reliable data reflecting the participants' daily use of the system.

It is also noteworthy that during the system installation at each participant's home, typically occurring on the start dates of each test, the participant was required to perform a series of actions using the *ProSeniorTV* interface (in the presence of the investigator). This ensured that participants were already minimally familiar with the system at the beginning of each test, allowing them to interact with it throughout the testing period without hesitation (which could compromise the obtained results). Specifically, participants were asked to perform the following actions during their first interaction:

[3] https://www.attrakdiff.de/index-en.html.

- View details regarding an event suggestion notification;
- Access the *ProSeniorTV* interface through a game suggestion notification;
- Enter a participation code for an event – in this case, participants immediately received a welcome code to earn 25 points. The following image shows the welcome code given to each participant, similar to the participation codes provided at each event;
- Access one of the mini-games offered by the interface;
- Access the player ranking; and
- Exit the game interface (Fig. 7).

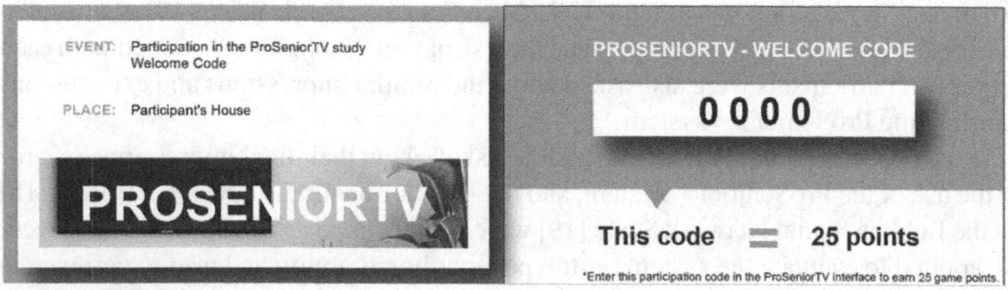

Fig. 7. Welcome code given to each participant at the beginning of the field test.

The field test began on December 22, 2023, and is still ongoing at the moment of writing. Throughout each test, it was decided that participants would be notified of 4 events/social activities organised in their municipality of residence so that, on average, one event would be suggested to the participant per week. The decision to recommend only one event per week was made because, considering that the Researcher in charge of this study would need to attend the suggested events to deliver participation codes to each participant, it would be challenging to make such visits more frequently. Additionally, the research team believed one weekly event would allow participants to feel socially integrated into their community.

Until now four individuals have participated in the field trial since, due to technical restrictions, it is impossible to address this trial with 20 participants simultaneously. Therefore, in the next chapter, preliminary results achieved up to this point through the test with these four individuals are presented.

4 Preliminary Results of the Field Trial

Regarding the sociodemographic data of individuals who have participated in the field trial so far (a sample of 4 individuals), they ranged in age from 60 to 86 years of age, with an average age of 67.5 years ($\bar{x} = 67.5$). Regarding gender, three were female (75%), and one was male (25%). Regarding their educational background, two had completed primary education (1st to 4th grade), and the other two had completed primary education (5th to 9th grade).

Concerning the place of residence, all participants lived in the same municipality, namely, in the city of Albergaria-a-Velha, belonging to the district of Aveiro (Portugal).

Similarly, for all participants (4 individuals, corresponding to 100% of the individuals), the size of their household averaged between 2 and 3 members. Regarding occupation, 50% (n = 2) were employed, and the remaining 50% (n = 2) were retired.

Through the questionnaire answered by each participant in the form of a semi-structured interview during the pre-test moments, it was also possible to assess the sample's characteristics regarding their habits, namely: *i)* social interaction habits; *ii)* TV consumption habits; *iii)* technology usage habits; and *iv)* cognitive stimulation game usage habits.

4.1 Social Interaction Habits

Regarding social interaction habits, it was observed that all individuals in the sample (n = 4) interacted daily with friends or family members and similarly used technology daily for this purpose (interacting with friends/family). In this context, all individuals in the sample (n = 4) admitted using voice calls on mobile phones/landlines or video calls on mobile phones to contact friends/family. Additionally, 75% of the sample (n = 3) acknowledged communicating with friends/family through mobile phone text messages/chat applications. Regarding participation in events/social activities organised in the participants' residential area, it was found that 50% of the sample (n = 2) did not habitually attend such events/activities. In comparison, the remaining 50% admitted that they occasionally participated – stating that they did so quarterly. Among the participants, 75% (n = 3) mentioned that they did not find it easy to access information about events/social activities in their residential area. Only 1 participant (25% of the sample) said he occasionally became aware of these events/activities through friends/family or the municipality's newspaper. Despite the low attendance at events/social activities by the individuals in the sample, most individuals (n = 3) answered *Yes* to the question, "*Do you consider these events important for maintaining social relationships?*". Only one individual responded to the same question with a *Maybe*, demonstrating that, in general, the individuals in the sample recognise the importance of events/social activities in their lives.

4.2 TV Consumption Habits

Regarding TV consumption habits, it was found that, for all participants, TV plays a crucial role in their daily lives, with 50% of individuals (n = 2) acknowledging that they use the TV for more than 5 h per day. The other half of the sample admitted to using the TV for a period between 2 and 3 h per day. The content was diverse, including news, soap operas, talk shows, documentaries, and movies/series. Concerning the times of TV usage, all participants (n = 4) mentioned watching TV after dinner. 75% (n = 3) stated that they watched television in the afternoon, 50% (n = 2) watched TV during breakfast, 50% watched during lunch, and 50% watched during dinner. Notably, one participant (Participant Two – P2) admitted that, depending on the day, he could access TV almost any time.

4.3 Technology Usage Habits

Regarding technology usage habits, all participants (n = 4) owned a smartphone and a TV and used these devices for a set of primary actions such as: *i)* talking to friends/family (4 individuals); *ii)* accessing leisure content (3 individuals); *iii)* accessing information/news (3 individuals); *iv)* checking weather forecasts (1 individual); *v)* accessing email (1 individual); and *vi)* accessing online social networks (1 individual). When asked, "*How often do you use new technologies and the internet?*" all participants (n = 4) answered that they use them daily. Notably, 50% of the sample (n = 2) had difficulty using new technologies, while the remaining 50% did not encounter problems. Of the participants who faced challenges in using technology (P1 and P2), one of them attributed the difficulty to much of the information found on the Internet being in a foreign language (P1), and the other found it challenging to memorise how to perform non-routine actions (P2). However, these two participants (P1 and P2) considered that these difficulties did not prevent them from accessing important information.

4.4 Cognitive Stimulation Games Usage Habits

Concerning the characterisation of the participant sample, how the participants used cognitive stimulation games was also investigated. In this context, it was identified that three individuals (75% of the sample) had played cognitive stimulation games at some point. Among these participants, 66.7% (n = 2) mentioned doing so only once or twice a year, and none of these games were accessed through digital devices. The remaining 33.3% (n = 1) admitted playing them once or twice a week, and they also mentioned that more than 50% of these games were accessed through technological devices, specifically smartphones. When asked about the importance they attributed to cognitive stimulation games in maintaining good mental health, 50% (n = 2) of the participants admitted that this type of game is *very relevant*, 25% (n = 1) said it is *relevant*, and 25% (n = 1) considered it to be of *little relevance*.

4.5 Interface Interaction

Throughout the 30-day test period, four participants were notified, at least once per day, through their TV sets about the occurrence of 4 different social events/activities in their area during the testing period. To ensure that the senior had access to notifications and were not sent when the user was not in front of their television, notifications were transmitted when the user performed the channel-changing action.

The first suggested event was a Photography Exhibition attended by only one individual (P1 – 25% of the sample). The second suggested event was a Christmas Show attended by all participants (n = 4). In the third week of testing, participants were advised to participate in a Water Aerobics Class, but none attended. Lastly, a Three Kings' Day Walk was suggested, and three individuals participated (P1, P2, and P3–75% of the sample). The figure below (on the left) shows the participants' attendance at each suggested event. Additionally, on the right side of the figure, the leaderboard obtained at the end of the testing period (composed of game points and participation points) is displayed. It shows that, in addition to the 25 Event points each participant received as a welcome prize, P1 earned 75 points (25 for each event attended), P3 and P2 earned 50 points, and P4 earned only 25 points. Considering what was mentioned, on average, participants took part in half of the suggested events, indicating a satisfactory level of participation.

Similarly, participants also received daily suggestions throughout the testing period to access the minigames offered by the *ProSeniorTV* interface. In the figure below (on the right), one can see that P1 obtained a total of 246 points (of which 146 were earned with the minigames), P3 and P2 obtained a total of 219 points (of which 144 were earned with the minigames), and P4 obtained a total of 104 points (of which 54 were earned with the minigames) (Fig. 8).

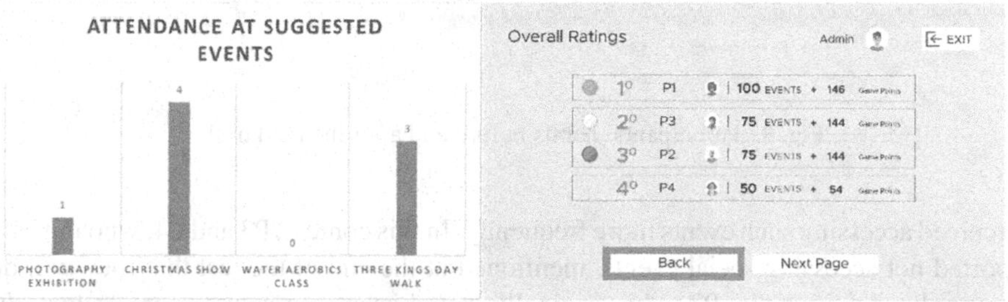

Fig. 8. Attendance graph for suggested events (left) and participants' ranking with points earned in events and points gained by playing (right).

The values presented above demonstrate that, in general, the participants were quite willing to use the *ProSeniorTV* interface, and the attendance at the events was also entirely satisfactory.

4.6 Changes in Participant's Habits

By comparing the data collected before and after the test, some changes in participants' habits or perceptions regarding specific questions were observed (resumed in Fig. 9). Specifically, regarding the habits of using cognitive stimulation games, the individual who had initially reported never using this type of game (P4) was now engaging with such games once a day through the *ProSeniorTV* interface (since all participants were notified for it once a day). As for the other participants, those who had initially mentioned using these games only once or twice a year (P2 and P3) were now doing so once or twice a week. Even the participants who initially used cognitive stimulation games more frequently (P1) started using them more regularly (once a day), which occurred only once or twice a week before the test. At the end of the test, all participants ($n = 4$) attributed high importance to this type of game (cognitive stimulation games). When asked, *"How relevant do you consider cognitive stimulation games to maintaining a healthy lifestyle?"* P1 and P3 maintained their response (*very relevant*), P2 stated they were *relevant* (a response that corresponded to *not very relevant* at the beginning of the test), and P4 also declared they were *very relevant* (a response that corresponded to *relevant* at the start of the test).

Regarding social interaction habits, participants' perceptions changed regarding the frequency of participation in social events in their residential area, as they generally

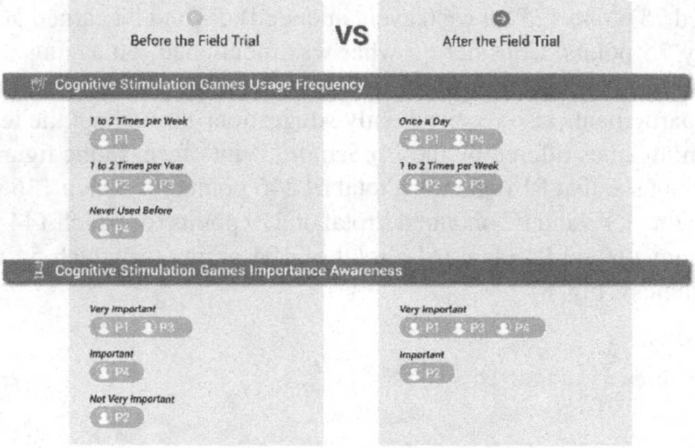

Fig. 9. Participants' habits before and after the field trial.

perceived accessing such events more frequently. In this context, P3 and P4, who initially reported not accessing social events, mentioned at the end of the test that they will do it *annually*. Additionally, P2, who originally stated accessing social events *quarterly*, reported he will do it *monthly* after the end of the test. Only P1 maintained the opinion that he accessed social events *every quarter*. It is noteworthy that participants began to have easier access to information about social events in their residential area because, in response to the question, "*Do you have easy access to information about social events in your residential area?*" 75% of the participant sample (n = 3) answered *Yes*, and only one participant (P2) answered *Sometimes*. According to the participants, this was due to the availability of the *ProSeniorTV* system at their homes.

4.7 Loneliness and Isolation

As mentioned earlier, the UCLA Loneliness Scale [18] and the Lubben Social Network Scale [19] were also used to understand whether participants felt loneliness and social isolation and to determine any correlation between the values obtained before and after the test.

Regarding the UCLA Loneliness Scale, it was observed that the values obtained by each participant at the beginning of the test (P1 – 35 points; P2 – 30 points; P3 – 47 points; P4 – 31 points) corresponded to a moderate level of loneliness, as they ranged between 30 to 50 points. At the end of the test, after a new application of the UCLA Loneliness Scale, the values underwent slight changes (P1 – 30 points; P2 – 35 points; P3 – 42 points; P4 – 30 points). Although, in most cases, these values decreased (indicating a reduced level of loneliness for most people), it was found that there was no correlation between the values obtained before and after the test, as the obtained significance level was 0.201 (above 0.05) as we can see through the Table 1.

As for the Lubben Social Network Scale, following the same procedure – applying the scale before and after the test – it was initially observed that none of the participants scored below 12 points (P1 – 22 points; P2 – 24 points; P3 – 20 points; P4 – 17 points),

Table 1. Correlation test between UCLA Scale results before and after the field trial.

Correlações

		UCLA SCALE (pre-test)	UCLA SCALE (post-test)
UCLA SCALE (pre-test)	Pearson's Correlation	1	,799
	Sig. (2 extremities)		,201
	N	4	4
UCLA SCALE (post-test)	Pearson's Correlation	,799	1
	Sig. (2 extremities)	,201	
	N	4	4

indicating that none of the participants suffered from social isolation. In the second application of the Lubben scale, the values remained above 12 (P1 – 24 points; P2 – 22 points; P3 – 13 points; P4 – 22 points), and the hypothesis of social isolation remained distant. Once again, there was no correlation between the values obtained at the two moments, as the significance value obtained was 0.790 (above 0.05), as shown in Table 2.

Table 2. Correlation test between Lubben Scale results before and after the field trial.

Correlações

		Lubben Scale (pre-test)	Lubben Scale (post-test)
Lubben Scale (pre-test)	Pearson's Correlation	1	,210
	Sig. (2 extremities)		,790
	N	4	4
Lubben Scale (post-test)	Pearson's Correlation	,210	1
	Sig. (2 extremities)	,790	
	N	4	4

Although there is currently no apparent relationship between the values obtained before and after the test, the research team is confident that, with more participants and more time, these values may become related, as the scores received by the participants demonstrate their solid adherence to the proposed system.

4.8 Final Participants' Impressions Regarding System Usage

At the end of the test, participants were also asked about their feelings regarding using the *ProSeniorTV* system. Before the test, to the question, "*Do you find it easy to get information about events and social activities taking place in your residence?*" all participants answered *Yes* (n = 4). Considering the statement, "*The system I tested facilitates access to information about social events in my area of residence*", three individuals (75% of the participant sample) *fully agreed*, and one individual (25% of the sample) *agreed*. It is considered that the proposed system contributed significantly to improving access to information about social events in the elderly participants' area of residence. This conclusion is further supported by the fact that, at the beginning of the test, 75% of the participants (n = 3) considered that they did not have easy access to such information, and only one individual mentioned having access sometimes.

Regarding access to cognitive stimulation games, 75% of the participants (n = 3) considered that the proposed system considerably facilitates access to such games. Similarly, 75% of the participants fully agreed with the statements "*The system I tested promotes a more active and regular participation in social events in my area of residence*" and "*The system I tested promotes a more regular performance of mental exercise games*".

Participants were also asked about the difficulty they experienced during interactions with the interface. Only P4 admitted to having some difficulty in this context. The remaining participants (n = 3) considered having no difficulty interacting with the interface.

It is noteworthy that, in the general opinion of the participants, this system helped them develop their mental abilities (through cognitive stimulation games) and encouraged them to leave home to participate in social events, thus increasing their social interactions. According to P3, the *ProSeniorTV* system has a vital leisure component resulting from its gamified nature, which he finds very interesting, especially, in his opinion, for people who live alone. As for P4, the oldest participant (86 years old), despite recognising that his motor difficulties often prevented him from leaving home to access the suggested events, acknowledged the importance of knowing what was happening in his area of residence (in terms of events/social activities).

From the participant's perspective, it is noteworthy that the gamification strategy devised is exciting and an excellent motivator to participate in suggested events. Participants highlighted that the player ranking is fascinating because it allows them to know the scores of other players, motivating them to earn more points to surpass others. P1 even mentioned that he "*(...) always wanted more points to move ahead of other people*".

4.9 Usability and User Experience of the ProSeniorTV System

As mentioned earlier, the SAM, SUS, and ATTRACKDIFF scales were used for participants to evaluate the *ProSeniorTV* system interface regarding usability and UX in this domain. Although the testing phase is still very early (where it is impossible to obtain results with the ATTRACKDIFF scale - as it needs to be applied to 20 individuals), preliminary results have already been received regarding the SAM and SUS scales.

Regarding the SAM scale, it was possible to determine that the developed prototype received a good rating in terms of UX, with a score of 4 points - 80% in the *valence criterion*, 4,25 points - 85% in the *arousal criterion*, and 4 points - 80% in the *dominance criterion* (shown in Table 3 and 4). As seen in the table below, these values were entirely satisfactory. Regarding the SUS scale, it was also observed that, in terms of usability, the prototype was rated satisfactorily by the 4 participants, as it obtained a SUS score of 80% (shown in Table 4), which, according to the Nielsen Norman Group[4], corresponds to an A- rating.

[4] https://www.youtube.com/watch?v=UMv_OW9__qY.

Table 3. Global scores of field trial – SUS and SAM.

Instrumental Qualities	Emotional Impact		
SUS (0 to 100)	SAM (1 to 5)		
	Valence	Arousal	Dominance
80	4	4,25	4

Table 4. Normalised scores of field trial.

normalised values at 100%	SUS	SAM		
		Valence	Arousal	Dominance
	80%	80%	85%	80%

5 Conclusion and Future Work

As discussed in the previous chapter, the *ProSeniorTV* system appears to be a platform that can motivate seniors to leave their homes and actively participate in social events and activities, fostering connections with familiar faces, friends, or family. These social bonds are crucial, making a significant difference between experiencing an active and healthy ageing process or facing a period of elderly life marked by loneliness and social isolation. Notably, the gamified approach adopted to encourage participation in social events made perfect sense to the participants, effectively motivating them to engage in these activities.

A significant outcome of this test is the participants' enhanced accessibility to information about events and activities in their local communities by deploying the *ProSeniorTV* system at their homes. According to the participants, this marked a paradigm shift, as they found it challenging to obtain such information under normal circumstances.

Regarding future work, the plan is to conduct a field trial with 16 new users. The results obtained from this test aim to conclusively demonstrate that the proposed system effectively contributes to the social well-being of older individuals. The promising preliminary results obtained thus far provide optimism for achieving this goal.

In the long term, there are plans to further enhance the system's robustness, potentially paving the way for its commercial release. In this context, establishing partnerships with third parties is envisioned, where the points earned in the game could translate into discounts at specific stores or services of significant interest to the senior audience.

Acknowledgements. The Fundação para a Ciência e a Tecnologia (FCT) funded this study through a PhD research grant. It is also being conducted in partnership with ALTICE LABS.

Disclosure of Interests.. The authors have no competing interests to declare relevant to this article's content.

References

1. INE, Estimativas Provisórias de População Residente 2011–2020, pp. 1–11 (2023). www.ine.pt
2. Woodhead, E.L., Yochim, B.: Adult development and aging: a foundational geropsychology knowledge competency. Clin. Psychol. Sci. Pract. **29**(1), 16–27 (2022). https://doi.org/10.1037/cps0000048
3. Coelho, A.R.: Seniores 2.0: inclusão digital na sociedade em rede (2019). http://hdl.handle.net/10071/19753
4. Silva, S., Braga, D., Teixeira, A.: AgeCI: HCI and age diversity. In: Lecture Notes in Computer Science (including subseries Lecture Notes in Artificial Intelligence and Lecture Notes in Bioinformatics), vol. 8515 LNCS, no. PART 3, pp. 179–190 (2014).https://doi.org/10.1007/978-3-319-07446-7_18
5. de Lucca, D.M.: A dimensão política da competência informacional: um estudo a partir das necessidades informacionais de idosos. Encontros Bibli. **20**(43) (2015)
6. Kelly, M.E., et al.: The impact of social activities, social networks, social support and social relationships on the cognitive functioning of healthy older adults: a systematic review. Syst. Rev. **6** (2017)
7. Townsend, B.G., Chen, J.T.H., Wuthrich, V.M.: Barriers and facilitators to social participation in older adults: a systematic literature review. Clin. Gerontol. **44**(4), 359–380 (2021). https://doi.org/10.1080/07317115.2020.1863890
8. Tani, M., Cheng, Z., Piracha, M., Wang, B.Z.: Ageing, health, loneliness and wellbeing. Soc. Indic. Res. **160**(2–3), 791–807 (2022). https://doi.org/10.1007/s11205-020-02450-4
9. Locsin, R.C., Soriano, G.P., Juntasopeepun, P., Kunaviktikul, W., Evangelista, L.S.: Social transformation and social isolation of older adults: digital technologies, nursing, healthcare. Collegian **28**(5), 551–558 (2021). https://doi.org/10.1016/j.colegn.2021.01.005
10. Wang, Y., Chen, Z., Zhou, C.: Social engagement and physical frailty in later life: does marital status matter? BMC Geriatr. **21**(1), 1–11 (2021). https://doi.org/10.1186/s12877-021-02194-x
11. Portugueses passam quase 5 horas por dia a ver TV, Marketeer (2020). https://marketeer.sapo.pt/portugueses-passam-quase-5-horas-por-dia-a-ver-tv
12. Silva, T., Caravau, H., Campelo, D.: Information needs about public and social services of Portuguese elderly. In: ICT4AWE 2017 – Proceedings of 3rd International Conference Information Communication Technol. Ageing Well e-Health, no. Ict4awe, pp. 46–57 (2017). https://doi.org/10.5220/0006284900460057
13. Faria, G.: Assistente pessoal proativo para o contexto do ecossistema televisivo, Repositório Inst. da Univ. Aveiro (2021). http://hdl.handle.net/10773/31617
14. Silva, T., Abreu, J., Antunes, M., Almeida, P., Silva, V., Santinha, G.: +TV4E: interactive television as a support to push information about social services to the elderly. Procedia Comput. Sci. **100**, 580–585 (2016). https://doi.org/10.1016/j.procs.2016.09.198
15. OberCom Observatório da Comunicação, Anuário da comunicação — 2020, p. 167 (2021)
16. Abreu, J.T.F.: Design de Serviços e Interfaces num Contexto de Televisão Interactiva (2007). http://hdl.handle.net/10773/1259
17. Ishibashi, G.A., et al.: Effects of cognitive interventions with video games on cognition in healthy elderly people : a systematic review, pp. 484–491 (2023)
18. Russell, D.W.: UCLA Loneliness Scale (Version 3): reliability, validity, and factor structure. J. Pers. Assess. **66**(1), 20–40 (1996). https://api.semanticscholar.org/CorpusID:7847482

19. Ribeiro, O., et al.: Versão Portuguesa da Escala Breve de Redes Sociais de Lubben (LSNS-6) (2012). https://api.semanticscholar.org/CorpusID:143116827
20. Brooke, J.: SUS: a quick and dirty usability scale. Usability Eval. Ind. **189**(194), 531–536 (1996). https://doi.org/10.4236/9781618961020_0002
21. Abreu, J., Camargo, J., Santos, R., Almeida, P., Beça, P., Silva, T.: UX evaluation methodology for iTV: assessing a natural language interaction system. In: Abásolo, M.J., Abreu, J., Almeida, P., Silva, T. (eds.) jAUTI 2020. CCIS, vol. 1433, pp. 149–161. Springer, Cham (2021). https://doi.org/10.1007/978-3-030-81996-5_11

Experience Design Assisted Healing and Therapeutic Design for Promoting Cultural Heritage: A Case of China Traditional Lingnan Water Village

Ziyi Ma and Zhen Liu(✉)

School of Design, South China University of Technology, Guangzhou 510006, People's Republic of China
liuzjames@scut.edu.cn

Abstract. The traditional Lingnan water village is an important representative of Guangfu culture in China, of which the regional cultural background of "villages built near the water" has created rich historical and cultural resources and a unique natural water village style. However, there are few studies that analyze the problems of the Lingnan water villages from the perspective of experience design, and propose practical solutions. Therefore, the aim of this paper is to investigate the current situation and problems in Lingnan water villages in terms of user experience, and to explore the possibility of implementing healing and therapeutic design with the experience design for Lingnan water villages, and to propose a experience design assisted healing and therapeutic design for promoting cultural heritage.

Keywords: Lingnan Water Villages · Healing · Therapeutic Design · Experience Design · Double Diamond Design Model · Tourism · Cultural Heritage

1 Introduction

The traditional Lingnan water village (TLWV) is an important representative of Guangfu culture in China [1], of which the regional cultural background of "villages built near the water" [2] has created rich historical and cultural resources and a unique natural water village style [3]. The most of the villages are located in the Pearl River Delta region [4]. The list of the fifth batch of traditional villages in China showed that there were 84 traditional villages in these region [5]. China's urbanization is rapidly advancing. In comparison to the Jiangnan water villages, the TLWVs did not receive early theoretical research and planning for preservation, resulting in extensive damage to these settlements [6]. Additionally, the tourism industry and economy in these areas have struggled to keep up, necessitating the urgent need for innovative conservation and development strategies [7].

A. Marcus et al. (Eds.): HCII 2024, LNCS 14714, pp. 86–104, 2024.
https://doi.org/10.1007/978-3-031-61356-2_6

1.1 Traditional Settlement Characteristics

Characteristics of the Social Environment. The Pearl River Delta, home to the TLWVs, typically features flat terrain, dense water networks, abundant rainfall, and rich farmland [8]. As such, the land has been divided into multiple parcels by these water networks, where the most of the villages are surrounded by watercourses, forming different riverine landscape features in the villages [9]. The water network provided convenient transportation and trade, leading to a pattern where "rivers" served as the primary internal and external transportation routes, with "boats" serving as the primary mode of travel [10]. By utilizing local water resources, the ancient people developed a capillary water system consisting of canals and drains that connected settlement sewers, rivers, and ponds, creating a unique artificial landscape. Additionally, TLWVs have retained a significant proportion of ancient tree resources. For instance, in the Xingtan area of Foshan, the saying goes, "Where there are many banyan trees, the land will flourish," referring to the extensive range of ancient trees including the large-leaved banyan, the fine-leaved banyan, the cottonwood, the mango, the water-womb, and the egg-flower tree [11]. Furthermore, the traditional architectural style of the TLWV region is primarily Guangfu architecture. Early Guangfu architecture was heavily influenced by the architectural patterns of the Jiangnan region, typified by wok-ear houses, which were primarily constructed using green bricks, stone pillars, and slabs, often featuring bird and flower motifs on their exterior walls [12]. Hence, the unique geographical setting of the TLWV region has fostered rich natural resources and tranquil, distinctive natural landscapes.

Characteristics of Social Culture. The unique geographical location and natural conditions of the TLWV have fostered the development of a strong culture with regional characteristics. The clan system is particularly well-developed in this region, and the spatial relationship of "living in clans" derived from bloodline and clan is particularly evident in TLWV villages [8]. In these villages, different clans govern different geographical areas and establish settlements. Additionally, as the clan was the basic unit of social and economic activities at the grass-roots level in ancient China, the rulers established ancestral halls to manage clan affairs. Therefore, ancestral halls were very common in the TLWVs [13].

The Guangdong Water God culture is also a significant representation of the TLWV cultural system. Due to frequent waterlogging disasters in this region, the people have a widespread belief in the Water God, with four primary deities being particularly prevalent: the Dragon Mother, the Northern Emperor, the Heavenly Concubine, and the Hong Sheng Water God. The Water God culture of this region exhibits several cultural characteristics, including the diversity of Water God beliefs, the extensive range of worshipping areas, the festive nature of sacrificial practices, and the practical purpose of worship [14].

1.2 Current Status of Experience Design

However, despite the natural beauty and cultural treasures of the TLWVs, the space for places with cultural characteristics and social values is now diminishing [7], and there is a lack of individuals who are willing to uphold, promote, and safeguard their folk culture. Specifically, the cultural and ecological heritage in some water villages lacks comprehensive protection, and traditional architectural complexes, material culture, and water resources have been damaged due to inadequate preservation measures. Therefore, more comprehensive planning and protection measures are necessary [15]. Additionally, the rural population is experiencing a "hollowing out" and aging trend, leading to underdeveloped infrastructure and tourism support services [7].

Currently, most of the studies have adopted the "Progressive Renewal Strategy" [1] and "Acupuncture Renewal Strategy" [16] as the main practical strategies to explore the possibilities of tourism development and village revitalization for Lingnan water villages. Studies have categorized the revitalization of the TLWV into three distinct approaches: government-led landscape transformation, which relies on government funding and emphasizes landscape and environmental enhancement, but often lacks follow-up management in the later stages; autonomous tourism development in villages, which capitalizes on the region's natural beauty and geographical location to focus on the development of the tourism economy; and institution-led cultural intervention, which aims to revitalize villages through artistic interventions [1].

Although tourism is often regarded as the largest experience-producing industry [17] due to its unique ability to create added value by engaging and connecting with customers in a personalized and memorable manner [18], and experience design has been increasingly proposed by cases of tourism [19], there are few studies that analyze the problems of the TLWVs from the perspective of experience design, and propose practical solutions. Moreover, few scholars have paid attention to the actual needs of tourists in experiencing excursion activities in TLWV and the need to alleviate psychological pressure, leading to a research gap in this area.

1.3 The Concept of Healing and Therapeutic Design

In the field of design, healing and therapeutic design refers to the use of design as an intervention [20] that positively impacts people's physical and mental well-being, prevents illness, enhances wellness, reduces stress and anxiety, and increases patient satisfaction [21], for which, art therapy, as an effective non-verbal treatment [22] that promotes wellness [23], is an important part of healing and therapeutic design. After 1940, art therapy emerged as an innovative mental health discipline that is widely utilized today [24]. Through art therapy, therapists can help individuals express their emotions and release pent-up feelings, leading to improved therapeutic outcomes [25]. Art therapy has also been found to effectively enhance subjective well-being in depressed and anxious adolescents [26], and to promote attention regulation, body awareness, and emotion regulation [27]. As a more broadly creative therapy, art therapy can encompass various modalities such as painting, drawing, music, dance, poetry, and bibliotherapy [28]. It can serve as a strategy for psychological and emotional experiences [29], fulfilling user needs and enhancing the overall user experience.

Currently, healing and therapeutic design has been applied to healing architectural design [30] and landscape design [31]. By integrating healing tools with traditional architectural design, healthcare environments that are more conducive to promoting psychological well-being and supporting the healing process of care have been created [32]. Additionally, healing and therapeutic design has been combined with travel experiences [33], with studies showing that nature-based, healing spiritual tourism has become the most popular travel option in the post-COVID-19 era. This is because interacting with the environment enhances one's sense of well-being [34], providing green spaces for healing activities and contemplation, which can alleviate experiencer stress and encourage social interaction, ultimately benefiting people's physical, mental, and social health [35].

As an important representative of Lingnan culture and a model of ecological diversity, the TLWV has high healing properties. However, studies have paid more attention to renovate existing villages, rarely thinking from the perspective of experience design, and have not yet explored the possibility of integrating the concepts of healing and therapeutic design into the experience model of TLWVs for promoting cultural heritage.

Therefore, the aim of this paper is to investigate the current situation and problems in TLWVs in terms of user experience, and to explore the possibility of implementing healing and therapeutic design with the experience design for TLWV, and to propose a experience design assisted healing and therapeutic design for promoting cultural heritage.

2 Method

The paper adopts case study, i.e. a case of Xingtan Township of Foshan City, as the research method, by using the Double Diamond Model [36] of design research technique. A double diamond model (see Fig. 1) was used as a framework and a mixed research methodology was used to underpin the research as a whole. The current state of experience design in TLWV was observed in the field, and key issue areas were identified during the Discover stage. Subsequently, in the Definition phase, focus groups and interviews were conducted to synthesize the perspectives of various stakeholders and their specific needs. This information served as a basis for defining the research content, narrowing down the focus, and framing the research questions.

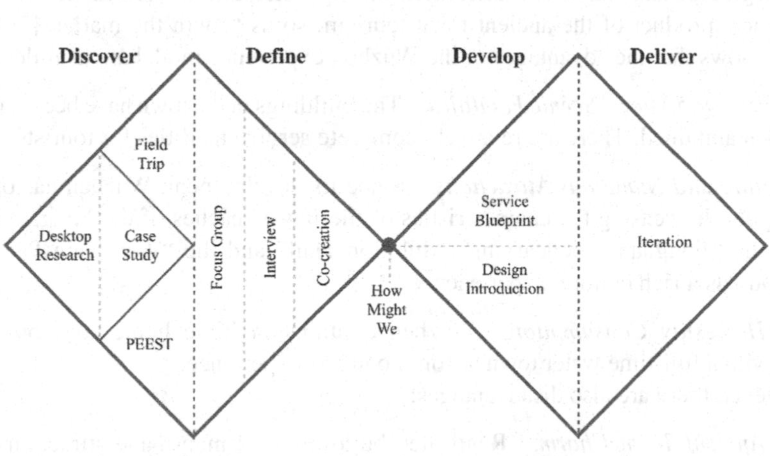

Fig. 1. Double Diamond Model for this study

2.1 Discover

Desktop Research. The TLWV has given birth to many cultural characteristics. The most prominent of these can be divided into the culture of ancestral halls, the culture of water deity worship, and natural culture.

The ancestral hall is the place where the Chinese worship their ancestors. In the water town, different surname families occupy different territories and build ancestral halls, which serve as the spiritual sustenance and the root of the family with the ancestral hall as its core. The culture of water deity worship, the local people go to the water deity temple to sacrifice before each sea voyage, and in addition, it has also spawned folk activities such as dragon boat racing and dragon ship. The natural culture, subtropical monsoon climate plant communities, and the mulberry fish pond are all unique ecological landscapes in the Lingnan water town.

Water (rivers), as the most important element, carries all the culture of the TLWVs. The folk activities involving water include fishing, navigation, domestic water use, and irrigation. At the same time, water has given birth to water town settlements, markets, agriculture, and moats. The most important thing is that water represents a kind of spiritual sustenance, which has spawned folk culture and activities, such as dragon boat racing and the birth of water deities.

Case Study. Wuzhen, located in the Yangtze River Delta region with highly developed water, land, and air transportation, enjoys remarkable location advantages and has preserved a large number of authentic historical and cultural relics. After more than ten years of development, the water town tourism in the lower reaches of the Yangtze River has become one of the characteristic brands of tourism in East China, with Wuzhen as the most representative one [37].

The core model of Wuzhen lies in the formation of a set of systematic solutions that include the scenic company, residents of the ancient town and foreign tourists, and on the basis of forming a win-win situation, the product of the ancient town, which has a high degree of sameness, is transformed into a systematic transformation, forming a brand-new product of the ancient town tourism, so as to win the market [38]. The analysis shows that the advantages of the Wuzhen experience model are as follows:

Comprehensive 5A-level Scenic Facilities. The buildings in the town have been repaired and well-maintained. There are relatively complete service facilities for tourists.

Rich Culture and Numerous Attractions. Since its development, Wuzhen has opened scenic spots showcasing the characteristics of the lower reaches of the Yangtze River, such as the "Jiangnan Woodcarving Exhibition Hall" and the "Wenchang Pavilion," giving tourists a rich cultural experience.

Mature Homestay Consumption. Wuzhen contains multiple homestays, providing tourists with a full-time water town accommodation experience.

However, there are also disadvantages:

Lack of Ancient Town Charm. Renovated buildings and man-made attractions have replaced the original style of the ancient town, lacking original charm.

Few Traditional Cuisine. With serious commercialization, a large number of foreign businesses have settled in the ancient town, and pop restaurants have emerged. There are few local traditional cuisine snacks, and their prices are high.

Poor Cultural Coherence. Scenic spots in areas such as Dongxizha are disorganized and lack storytelling, failing to clarify the overall context of the lower reaches of the Yangtze River.

Less Experience During Peak Season. When the flow of tourists is high, Wuzhen reduces activities and performances, providing tourists with less experience.

Fengjian water town has a TLWV landscape, with abundant water resources, rivers and canals surrounding it, forming an "井" shape with a total length of approximately 28 km. The river is winding and meandering, with clear blue waves, far away from the hustle and bustle of the city, and the ancient village layout of Lingnan is well preserved, making it a representative tourist attraction in the TLWV area [39].

The analysis shows that the advantages of the Fengjian water town experience model are as follows:

Well-Preserved Ancient Buildings. Fengjian water town has well-preserved ancient buildings, including ancient bridges, ancestral halls, dwellings, and religious buildings. There are as many as 19 well-preserved ancestral halls in Fengjian water town.

Rich Resources of Specialty Cuisine. Fengjian water town is known as the "world capital of food," with rich resources of specialty cuisine.

Rich Folk Activities. In recent years, Fengjian water town has begun to hold folk activities such as the Water Town Cultural Festival and dragon boat racing, which are cultural activities with traditional Lingnan characteristics. These activities enrich the cultural resources of the scenic area.

However, there are also disadvantages:

Water Environment Protection Issues. With the development of tourism, water resources have been polluted, and some tourists have reported that the river is muddy and smelly.

Defects in the Spatial Layout of the Scenic Area. The tourist attractions are scattered around community services. The tourist service center is remote and the layout is not convenient for tourists to visit.

Lack of Product System. Tourism products mainly consist of natural and humanistic resources, but the Fengjian water town resources here have not been fully integrated into tourism products, making it difficult to form a solid product system for tourism products.

Through the above case studies, it can be found that it is particularly important to determine a good experiential strategy model, and the focus is to explore the unique folk experience and theme culture of ancient villages [40]. In the context of TLWV, it should be specifically reflected in the experiential model, which should show the charm of ancient water towns and give play to the architectural style; designers should make full use of the local water culture, pay attention to the logic of planning, and create a moving cultural story; designers should also consider the periodic nature of folk activities.

Field Trip. Four main villages were visited in Xingtan Township: Longtan Village, Maning Village, Madong Village, and Changjiao Village. The fieldwork focused mainly on local culture, landscape, and issues (see Fig. 2).

It can be found that the TLWV in Xingtan Town is relatively typical and well-preserved, with a low degree of urbanization. The local area has retained a large number of Qing Dynasty brick structure buildings, including residential houses, ancestral halls, and water temples. However, only a few buildings are open to the public and in use, with few administrators, limited interpretive resources, and room for improvement in scenic area maintenance and service.

In addition, it was observed that there were floating leaves and impurities in the waterways of the TLWV, which are difficult to clean up due to the narrowness of some of the waterway areas.

As a settlement group built near the water, it can be observed that important ancestral halls and water temples are all built facing the waterways, which facilitates the organization of folk activities. In the waterways, one can see submerged dragon boats, which is a locally distinctive scene: during non-folklore events, dragon boats are submerged underwater for protection. The water in which the dragon boats have been soaked represents auspicious meanings, and thus the local area has also developed the custom of washing with dragon boat water.

Fig. 2. Field trip process

PEEST. A policy, economic, environmental, social, and technological (PEEST) analysis was conducted to comprehensively evaluate the current state of tourist experience in Lingnan water villages across the five major dimensions: policy, economic, environmental, social, and technological (see Fig. 3).

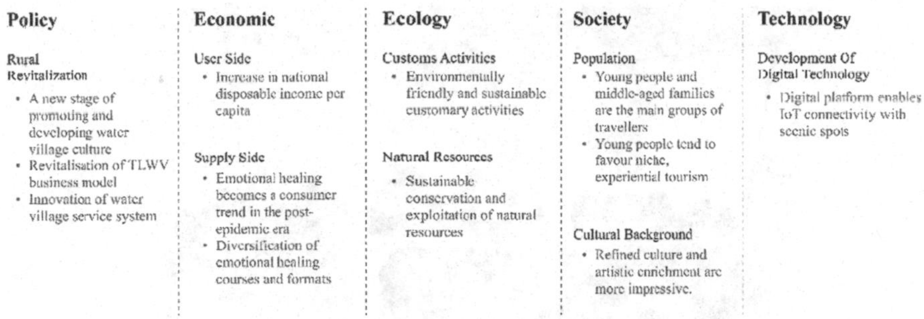

Fig. 3. PEEST analysis

2.2 Define

Focus Group. According to the age segmentation ratio of Chinese tourists in 2022, 37% of them belong to the post-90s generation, who are young people entering society and tend to travel with friends and explore new activities. On the other hand, 34% of the tourists belong to the post-80s generation, who are mostly family-oriented groups, placing more emphasis on parent-child education and tourism leisure. Therefore, it can be determined that the main target group of TLWV is the post-90s generation, followed by the post-80s generation.

The focus group selected different types of post-90s people for a joint discussion (see Fig. 4), including 3 tourists of water towns, 1 student with a background in tourism management, and 1 dragon boat athlete. The discussion lasted for 2 h.

The discussion mainly focused on the following questions aimed at analyzing user needs for TLWV experience and ideas for healing:

1 Please share your preferences when visiting TLWVs.
2 What are your interests in the unique features of TLWVs and why?
3 Do you think there are any areas for improvement in these existing TLWV tourism experiences?
4 Have you participated in any healing activities, and what are your interests in healing?
5 Which new healing method do you think is more suitable for combining with TLWV, and what are your visions and solutions?

Interview. The main target group for the interviews was 80s family travelers, with the aim of understanding their preferences, visions, and needs for water town tourism, as well as their demand for healing activities.

In total, two water town tourists were interviewed. The first was a 40-year-old male who had visited Lingnan and Jiangnan water towns before. The second was a 43-year-old female who had worked as a tour guide and had experience leading groups in water towns. Each interview lasted half an hour, and the questions are shown in Table 1:

Co-creation. Co-creation is a powerful tool that actively involves users in the design process. It empowers potential users by providing them with specific tools to express their personal needs and encouraging them to think outside the box. This approach fosters creativity and generates innovative ideas (see Fig. 5). On April 27th, 2023, an exploration

Fig. 4. Focus group discussion process

Table 1. Interview questions

No	Classification	Question
1	Basic Information	How old are you?
2		What's your job?
3	Tourism Situation	How often do you usually travel?
4		Where do you usually go?
5		What travelling means to you?
6		What TLWVs have you visited? What is the frequency?
7		What do you like to travel in TLWV?
8		Who do you travel with?
9		Are there any problems encountered?
10		What to expect from TLWV tourism?
11	Thoughts on Healing Events	How is the usual stress and how do you relieve it?
12		How to relieve stress by travelling?
13		What aspects of water village travel help you to relieve stress and relax?
14		What healing activity would you like to try?

was conducted in Xingtan Town, located in Foshan City. The final co-creation process was developed at the South China University of Technology (SCUT) University City Campus, spanning a total duration of 7 h. The specific processes to be carried out are as follows:

Field Experience. Six people who were interested in the healing of TLWV were invited to participate in the co-creation, and they were led to TLWV and asked to experience and observe the local area in depth, and record what they saw and thought at any time.

Introduction of Background. The facilitator of the co-creation opened the formal discussion by introducing the background and importance of the project to the participants, as well as guiding them to discuss positively without criticizing each other.

Likes and Dislikes. Stickers and map tools were used. Participants were asked to make subjective judgements about the places and contents of the tour, and to use emoticon stickers to express their emotions to paste them on the map.

Writing Questions. Sticky notes and map tools were used. Participants wrote down the questions during the experience and pasted them to the corresponding locations in the map.

Insight Statements. A question form was used. Write down the challenges of the water village as well as write down the reasons behind multiple challenges.

What Can We Do? (How Might We Approach). The question form was used. Write down how you can help TLWV as well as the main directions to help. Discussed openly at the end of the session to make sure everyone was unified in one direction.

Program Statement. Sticky notes were used. This round can be subdivided into two rounds; in the first round each participant is not constrained to think of five options each. In the second round, participants can use other people's ideas on sticky notes to develop new ideas and share them with others.

Field Experience
Invite 6 young people who are interested in Lingnan water village
Introduction
Introduce the background and importance of the project to the participants
Likes And Dislikes
Stick emoji stickers to express the participants' love for each location
Write Questions
Use sticky notes to write down questions about a location
Insight Statements
Write down the challenges and what the reasons are behind the water village
How Might We ?
Write out how we are going to help water village by serving our users
Program Statement
Participants use the map to talk about the final solution

Fig. 5. Co-creation process

3 Results

3.1 Phase of Discover: Experience Design Issues in the TLWV

Through the discover phase of the study, the following experience design issues facing TLWV can be identified:

Single Scenery and Cultural Content. Primarily, TLWVs generally share similar cultural traits and natural landscapes, leading to a lack of distinctiveness and few unique features that could appeal to tourists. Secondly, the tourism experience often lacks notable highlights, preventing it from effectively capturing the essence of the visit. Additionally, the various attractions within the TLWVs are often scattered, resulting in a fragmented and incomplete experience. The absence of clear signage or directional instructions further compounds this issue, preventing visitors from fully engaging with the environment and deriving a sense of immersion.

Difficulty of Activities to Continuously Attract Tourists. The folklore activities related to water in TLWVs are indeed captivating, including dragon boat experiences and the Water God's Birthday Temple Festival. However, most of these activities are only held during the annual characteristic festivals, making it challenging for users to experience the characteristic culture and folklore when the events are not organized, ultimately reducing their expectations. Therefore, it is crucial to carefully consider how to create continuous experience activities that allow tourists to immerse themselves in the folklore whenever they visit the water town.

Weak Healing Attributes. TLWVs possess ample green vegetation and rivers, which have the potential to provide a certain natural healing effect. However, currently there are no specific healing attributes or supporting facilities, preventing users from fully extracting the emotional healing value during their experience. Therefore, it is essential to consider integrating healing elements and amenities to enhance the overall emotional well-being of visitors.

A Lot of Unused Resources. There are a lot of unused resources in the TLWV, such as dragon boats, ancestral halls, and residential houses, etc., which do not have the opportunity to be used in normal times.

3.2 Phase of Define: The Possibility of Implementing Healing and Therapeutic Design

Through the discover phase of the study, the following experience design issues facing TLWV can be identified:

Journey Map. Based on the study, it can be concluded that the users' existing participation in the process of touring the TLWVs (see Fig. 6).

User Persona. The following user persona for primary (see Fig. 7) and secondary (see Fig. 8) users, respectively, include the user's experience goals, pain points, and influencing factors.

Classification of Needs. By sorting out the experience needs of TLWV users, they can be summarized into the following three categories:

Pressure Relief Needs. Users can relax their tense emotions and nerves in the water village, forgetting the busyness of work or life; users can interact with the natural and humanistic architecture in the water village, immersing themselves in the quiet environment; and obtaining self-relief.

Cultural and Folklore Experience. Allow users to experience the local culture in depth and keep them interested for a longer period of time; travel at a slower pace and remain in a healing experience throughout; participate in the experience with a friend; and show users the story behind the culture in a fun way.

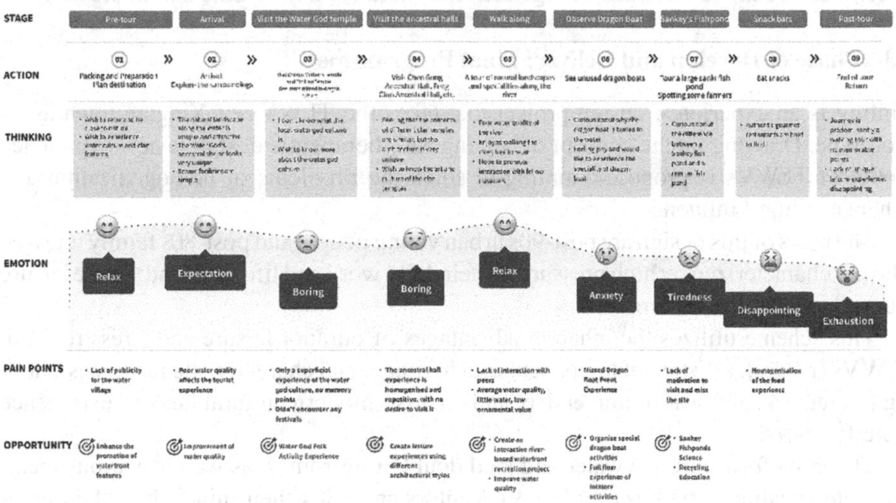

Fig. 6. Journey map

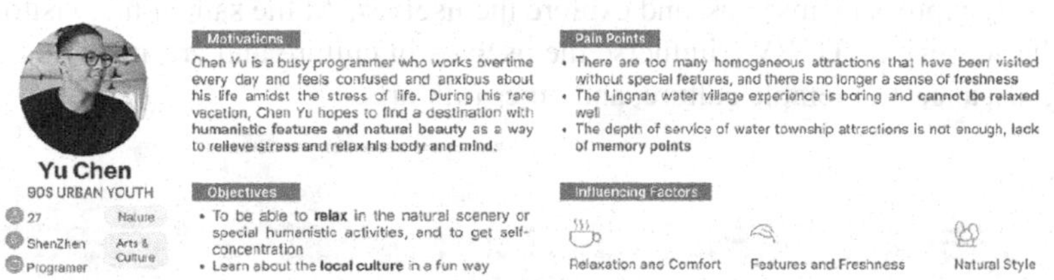

Yu Chen
90S URBAN YOUTH
27
ShenZhen
Programer
Nature
Arts & Culture
Motivations
Chen Yu is a busy programmer who works overtime every day and feels confused and anxious about his life amidst the stress of life. During his rare vacation, Chen Yu hopes to find a destination with humanistic features and natural beauty as a way to relieve stress and relax his body and mind.
Objectives
• To be able to relax in the natural scenery or special humanistic activities, and to get self-concentration
• Learn about the local culture in a fun way
Pain Points
• There are too many homogeneous attractions that have been visited without special features, and there is no longer a sense of freshness
• The Lingnan water village experience is boring and cannot be relaxed well
• The depth of service of water township attractions is not enough, lack of memory points
Influencing Factors
Relaxation and Comfort
Features and Freshness
Natural Style

Fig. 7. User persona for primary user

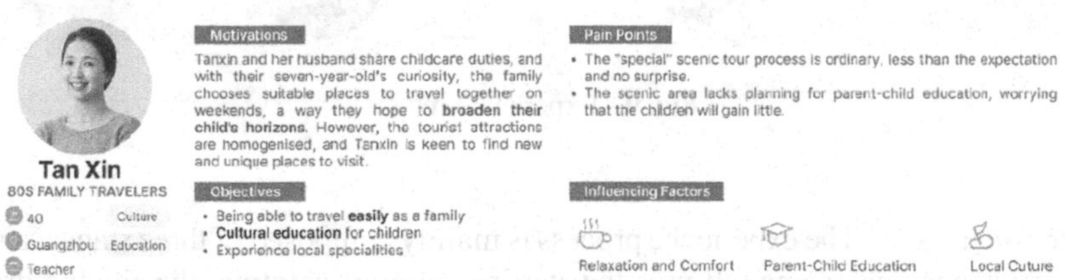

Tan Xin
80S FAMILY TRAVELERS
40
Guangzhou
Teacher
Culture
Education
Motivations
Tanxin and her husband share childcare duties, and with their seven-year-old's curiosity, the family chooses suitable places to travel together on weekends, a way they hope to broaden their child's horizons. However, the tourist attractions are homogenised, and Tanxin is keen to find new and unique places to visit.
Objectives
• Being able to travel easily as a family
• Cultural education for children
• Experience local specialities
Pain Points
• The "special" scenic tour process is ordinary, less than the expectation and no surprise.
• The scenic area lacks planning for parent-child education, worrying that the children will gain little.
Influencing Factors
Relaxation and Comfort
Parent-Child Education
Local Cuture

Fig. 8. User persona for secondary user

Emotional Value Demand. It can preserve users' memories of their visit to the water village; it can make users feel that they have gained something, such as emotional catharsis, or some souvenir items of the experience.

How Might We. Through the How Might We method, the main directions and objectives of the program are presented:

1. How do we make visitors interact and relax in TLWV?
2 How do we make each attraction and building present different characteristics?
3 How do we make the water village activities held for a long time and interesting?

3.3 Phase of Develop and Deliver: Final Programme

Xinling is an experience design project that takes the TLWVs of Xingtan town as its prototype. Drawing on the concept of healing and therapeutic design, a new experience model of TLWVs is proposed, aiming to solve the problems of homogenization and enhance cultural influence.

The users of this design are post-90s urban young people and post-80s family tourists, who are characterized by high pressure in their daily work and life, and tend to take leisure tourism to relax themselves.

This scheme utilizes the inherent advantages of outdoor leisure and stress relief in TLWVs (natural, artistic, intangible cultural heritage, and characteristic resources), hoping to create a safe, warm, immersive, and creative modern cultural healing experience route for users.

The main forms are the water and land double tour routes, as well as various local-integrated healing activities (see Fig. 9). Visitors can relax their minds, heal their emotions, and satisfy the psychological needs of "relieving stress through tourism", effectively helping them improve their self-confidence and self-awareness, better understand themselves, express themselves, and explore themselves. At the same time, visitors can enjoy the scenery of TLWVs, immerse themselves in culture and art, including water, water gods, ancestral temple culture, and other folk arts.

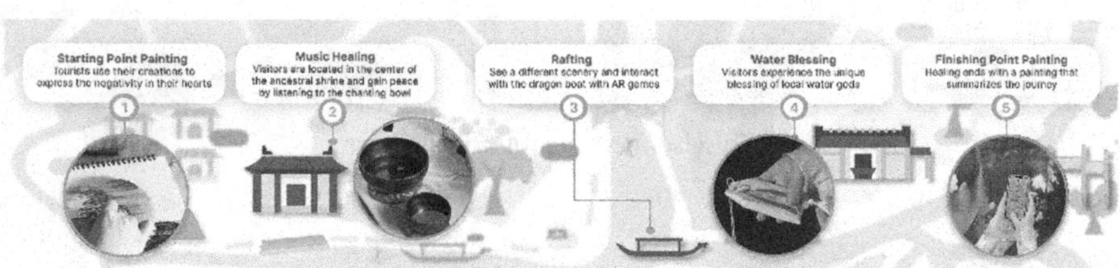

Fig. 9. Experience map

Service Blueprint. The experience process is mainly composed of three stages: awareness, acceptance, and change. It uses the starting point of painting, the sinking dragon boat, music healing, boat riding, the blessing of the water gods, and the ending point of painting as the touchpoints for the experience. The entire process is linked by the "XinLing" boat, and on the river channels of the water town, tourists will board the "XinLing" boat and visit various scenic spots to participate in healing activities and absorb the local cultural atmosphere (see Fig. 10).

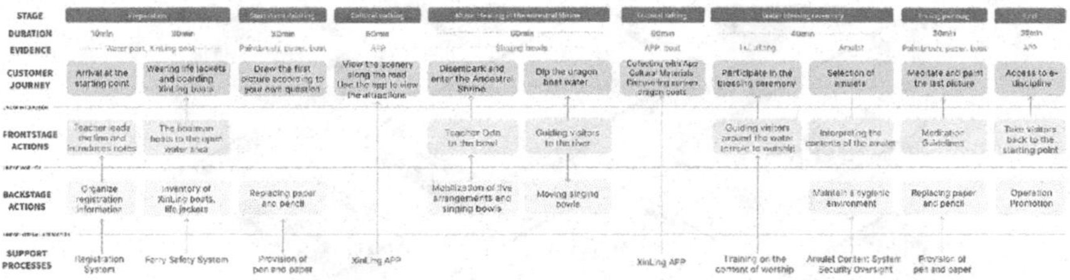

Fig. 10. Service blueprint

"XinLing" Boat. The boat (see Fig. 11) will connect the tourists' water journey, providing an immersive, quiet, and comfortable space for meditation, allowing tourists to focus on their own experience and feelings during the painting process. The hull design can be combined with existing idle dragon boats, and only the internal structure of the dragon boat needs to be replaced. The rest of the dragon boat, including the head and tail, can be removed.

Fig. 11. XinLing Boat renderings

APP. The APP (see Fig. 12) will cooperate with the entire tour to enhance the fun of the experience. It mainly provides users with a cultural camera that allows them to take pictures and record their psychological feelings at any time. Other features include map viewing, healing journeys, shopping mall, etc.

Amulet of the Water God. Visitors choose amulets (see Fig. 13) and soak them in the river water to make the originally invisible water god patterns appear, thus obtaining the water gods that guard them. This product mainly provides spiritual value support for tourists, guiding them to calm down and guide themselves during the prayer process, leaving a memory carrier for the healing journey.

Fig. 12. XinLing APP

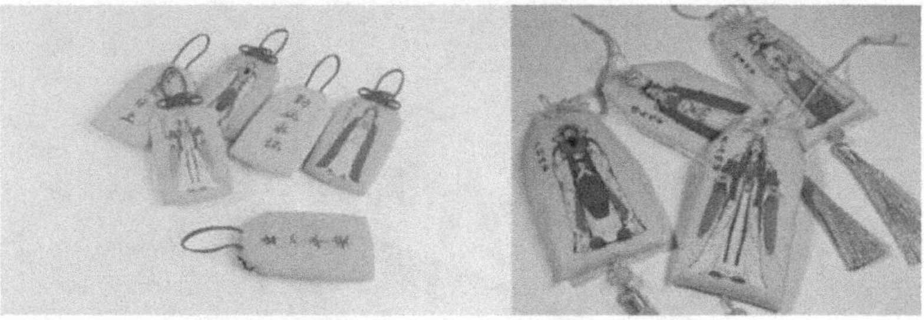

Fig. 13. Amulet design

4 Discussion

In the Discover phase, through field research and literature review, we gained an understanding of the current status and challenges in TLWV experiences, including issues with monotonous scenery and cultural content. This information will assist local tourism authorities in improving the tourism system and foster consensus among scholars on TLWV-related topics. In the Define phase, we employed techniques such as User Journey Mapping, User Profiling, Needs Classification, and How Might We to gain a deeper understanding of the TLWV audience and their healing needs. This phase enabled us to confirm the feasibility of integrating Healing and Therapeutic Design with experience design. In the Develop and Deliver phase, we formally propose an experience model that integrates Healing and Therapeutic Design into experience design. This model not only extends the scope of experience design research but also provides a valuable case study for TLWV.

However, due to limitations such as small sample size, this article still has some limitations. In the future, scholars can further explore different combinations and details of different water towns, as well as further research on diversified healing experience models, including targeting different age groups. More empirical validation can also be conducted to verify the effectiveness of the proposed experiential design model.

5 Conclusion

This paper introduces a novel experience model, designed to support the principles of healing and therapeutic design, which is developed by exploring challenges and issues within TLWVs and analyzing the healing needs of primary user groups. A set of healing experiences tailored for post-90s urban youth and post-80s family travelers in TLWVs is proposed, which includes the creation of design products like the Xinling Boat, Water God Amulet, and Xinling App. The experiential journey centers around the core product, i.e. the Xinling Boat, navigating through waterways that lead key locations of cultural heritage of TLWVs such as clan temples, water god temples, and sunken dragon boats. The incorporation of healing services, including painting therapy, music therapy, and cultural therapy, facilitates the relaxation of user' body and mind. These interventions have been designed to address uncertainties, allowing users to immerse themselves authentically in the cultural richness of water villages during their tours.

This innovative ideas and solutions for the cultural revitalization of TLWVs are anticipated to augment the appeal of tourism in TLWVs by fostering new attractions. Additionally, this paper contributes to the field of healing and therapeutic design and expands the potential for integrating healing and therapeutic design with experience design in promoting cultural heritage.

Acknowledgments. This study was funded by "2022 Constructing Project of Teaching Quality and Teaching Reform Project for Undergraduate Universities in Guangdong Province" Higher Education Teaching Reform Project (project No. 386), 'Innovation and practice of teaching methods for information and interaction design in the context of new liberal arts' (project grant number x2sj-C9233001).

Disclosure of Interests. The authors have no competing interests to declare that are relevant to the content of this article.

References

1. Mei, C., He, C.: Exploration and practice of gradual renewal strategy in lingnan water towns: a case study of Xingtan Town in Shunde. Rural Economy and Technology. **32**, 242–244 (2021)
2. Wei, C., Cheng, Y., Zhong, Z., Xiao, D.: Research on implementation and management evaluation system for protection and utilization of traditional villages: a case study of traditional chinese villages in Lingnan Waterfront. J. South Architect. **1**, 61–72 (2024). https://doi.org/10.33142/jsa.v1i1.10435
3. Wei, C., Miao, K., Huang, D., Xiao, D.: Research on comprehensive evaluation system of traditional village infrastructure: a case study of the pearl river delta. Res. Urban Regional Plann. **9**, 112–126 (2017)

4. Yuan, S., Tang, G., Zhang, H., Gong, Q., Yin, X., Huang, G.: Spatial distribution patterns of traditional villages in Guangdong and their ethnic characteristics. Trop. Geogr. **37**, 318–327 (2017)
5. Zhong G.: The influence of urbanization on the ecological space of lingnan water towns and strategies for restoration: a case study of Xiaozhou Village in Guangzhou. Anhui Architect. **29**, 3–6 (2022). https://doi.org/10.16330/j.cnki.1007-7359.2022.03.001
6. Ye X.: Comparative Study on the spatial morphological characteristics of traditional settlements in Lingnan and Jiangnan water towns, https://kns.cnki.net/kcms2/article/abstract?v=Epsgq4wCkk2kwqlQvwHn0ADwMzi_g8jjwMW8B9XIW0hhRzKwvaff3F84QfvmTnJIsHRxCm7p_u5p-k9V3jY9INJLbhYrKFgZSgv4g7vkENQitmGHjOr9NuCWki32r97d9WEavi_JzaYCLwsa1Iz98g==&uniplatform=NZKPT&language=CHS. (2011)
7. Li Z.: Analysis of conservation and tourism development in Lingnan water towns: a case study of Xiong village in Lingchuan County, Guilin City. House. Sci. **41**, 51–54 (2021). https://doi.org/10.13626/j.cnki.hs.2021.02.011
8. Mei, W.: Research on the spatial morphological characteristics of traditional settlements in Lingnan water towns. ART PANORAMA, pp. 88–89 (2018)
9. Chen Y., Lu Q.: Landscape design of traditional villages in Lingnan water towns based on 'Water Law'. Huazhong Architecture. **36**, 111–114 (2018). https://doi.org/10.13942/j.cnki.hzjz.2018.02.026
10. Xie Y.: Research on the cultural ecological characteristics and conservation strategies of traditional villages in Lingnan Water Towns. https://kns.cnki.net/kcms2/article/abstract?v=Epsgq4wCkk33v0UgijEedY__--TwBlELjCfvDvyGtNR3b-NdNaJi2N3Dv-bZV5G-ZK_kJ0ZdlxK4fxC-d6kv-lwmnV9hhpQ8epje__vqmq6qp6i9eJX6NZlEkQzcOrL-pBhzcV-zHQS1n_fJhQKOUg==&uniplatform=NZKPT&language=CHS. (2021)
11. Liao H.: Heritage cognitive system and conservation strategies of traditional settlement clusters in Lingnan Water Towns. https://kns.cnki.net/kcms2/article/abstract?v=Epsgq4wCkk0oTxbl6IcX2AEZL0XNXgxkKtRVxyPWUlrqG9i281MNito0HAsZwtCuHS_FjobVDdOrQk9rnW3Qs10mJpRXh5muiPqZgAYtLRs3XjDPXGp8AuGkVwgM-O6LpZ8zyBLyxX1dRvaDaHbKcA==&uniplatform=NZKPT&language=CHS. (2022)
12. Fu, J., Xu, J., Xiao, D.: Study on the Adaptability of Traditional Village Morphology and Landscape in Southern Regions to Water Environments. classical Chinese garden. 29, 120–124 (2013)
13. Zhang, F.L., Ayoungman, F.Z., Islam, M.: Institutional capital, ancestral hall, and the reshaping of ancient rule: an empirical analysis of the new energy of chinese heritage elements in rural revitalization. J. Knowl. Econ. (2023). https://doi.org/10.1007/s13132-023-01243-7
14. He M.: Preliminary exploration of water deity beliefs and water deity culture in Lingnan. Guangzhou cultural museum, pp. 346–355 (2012)
15. Wei, C., Zhong, Z., Liao, H.: Analysis of Spatial Formation and Cultural Ecological Characteristics of Ancient Water Towns: A Case Study of Traditional Village Culture. South Architecture/Nanfang Jianzhu. (2021)
16. Chen, X.: 'Acupuncture-style' renovation practice of public spaces in Lingnan water towns: a case study of Xiaozhou village in Guangzhou. Architect. Design Manage. **39**, 61–66 (2022)
17. Dekker, E.B., Teun Den: Agenda for Co-Creation Tourism Experience Research. In: Marketing of Tourism Experiences. Routledge (2010)
18. Fitzsimmons, J.A., Fitzsimmons, M.J.: Service management: Operations, strategy, and information technology. Irwin/McGraw-Hill (2004)
19. Tussyadiah, I.P.: Toward a theoretical foundation for experience design in tourism. J. Travel Res. **53**, 543–564 (2014). https://doi.org/10.1177/0047287513513172
20. Liu, Z., Yang, Z., Liang, M., Liu, Y., Osmani, M., Demian, P.: A conceptual framework for blockchain enhanced information modeling for healing and therapeutic design. Int. J. Environ. Res. Public Health. **19**, 8218 (2022)

21. Schweitzer, M., Gilpin, L., Frampton, S.: Healing spaces: elements of environmental design that make an impact on health. J. Alt. Complement. Med. **10**(supplement 1), S-71-S−83 (2004). https://doi.org/10.1089/acm.2004.10.S-71
22. Kometiani, M.K., Farmer, K.W.: Exploring resilience through case studies of art therapy with sex trafficking survivors and their advocates. Arts Psychother. **67**, 101582 (2020)
23. Daykin, N., Byrne, E., Soteriou, T., O'Connor, S.: Review: the impact of art, design and environment in mental healthcare: a systematic review of the literature. J. Royal Society Promotion of Health. **128**, 85–94 (2008). https://doi.org/10.1177/1466424007087806
24. Hogan, S.: Healing arts: The history of art therapy. Jessica Kingsley Publishers (2001)
25. Levy, B.: Art therapy in a women's correctional facility. Art Psychother. **5**, 157–166 (1978)
26. Kim, S., Kim, G., Ki, J.: Effects of group art therapy combined with breath meditation on the subjective well-being of depressed and anxious adolescents. Arts Psychother. **41**, 519–526 (2014)
27. Newland, P., Bettencourt, B.A.: Effectiveness of mindfulness-based art therapy for symptoms of anxiety, depression, and fatigue: a systematic review and meta-analysis. Complement. Ther. Clin. Pract. **41**, 101246 (2020)
28. Geue, K., Goetze, H., Buttstaedt, M., Kleinert, E., Richter, D., Singer, S.: An overview of art therapy interventions for cancer patients and the results of research. Complement. Ther. Med. **18**, 160–170 (2010)
29. Yang, Z., Liu, Z., Zhang, K., Xiao, C.: Potential Usability Design Strategies Based on Mental Models, Behavioral Model and Art Therapy for User Experience in Post-COVID-19 Era. In: Soares, M.M., Rosenzweig, E., Marcus, A. (eds.) Design, User Experience, and Usability: Design for Diversity, Well-being, and Social Development, pp. 548–561. Springer International Publishing, Cham (2021)
30. Khaled Sayed Asfour: Healing architecture: a spatial experience praxis. Archnet-IJAR: Int. J. Architect. Res. **14**(2), 133–147 (2020). https://doi.org/10.1108/ARCH-03-2019-0055
31. Belčáková, I., Galbavá, P., Majorošová, M.: Healing and therapeutic landscape design–examples and experience of medical facilities. ArchNet-IJAR: Int. J. Architect. Res. **12**, 128 (2018)
32. Mazuch, R., Stephen, R.: Creating healing environments: humanistic architecture and therapeutic design. J. Public Mental Health **4**(4), 48–52 (2005). https://doi.org/10.1108/17465729200500031
33. Han, Z.: Exploring health contributing elements of healing travel: focusing on Gangneung coffee healing camp participants. J. Tourism Sci. **37**, 137–158 (2013)
34. Little, J.: Transformational tourism, nature and wellbeing: new perspectives on fitness and the body*. Sociol. Rural. **52**, 257–271 (2012). https://doi.org/10.1111/j.1467-9523.2012.00566.x
35. Jiang, S.: Therapeutic landscapes and healing gardens: a review of Chinese literature in relation to the studies in western countries. Front. Architect. Res. **3**, 141–153 (2014)
36. Council, D.: Design methods for developing services. Keeping Connected Business Challenge Competition Material, London (2015)
37. Wang, L., Lu, L., Tong, S.: Preliminary exploration of tourism development strategy for ancient towns in the Jiangnan water towns: an empirical analysis of Wuzhen in Zhejiang. Resources Environ. Yangtze River Basin. **12**, 529–534 (2003)
38. Zheng, S., Wang, D.: Analysis of tourism development models in Wuzhen. Areal Res. Develop. **31**, 85–88 (2012)
39. He, Y., Yang, L., Yang, L.: Exploration on the protection and development of ancient town tourism characteristic resources: a case study of Fengjian Water Town in Shunde, Guangdong. Guangdong Sericulture (2022)

40. Deng, M., Zhen, W., Wang, Q.: Research on the tourism development of ancient villages: a discussion based on the ecotourism development model. Agricult. Technol. **28**, 100–103 (2008)

The Experience of Portuguese Visually Impaired with Interactive Television (iTV) Services: A Questionnaire Survey

Rita Oliveira(✉), Luísa Júlio, and Ana Patrícia Oliveira

DigiMedia, Department of Communication and Art, University of Aveiro, Aveiro, Portugal
{apoliveira,luisaamj,ritaoliveira}@ua.pt

Abstract. The evolution of interactive television (iTV) services offers diverse functionalities and resources, revolutionizing audiovisual consumption. Despite advancements in making iTV accessible to visually impaired users in Portugal, significant room for improvement remains. Addressing this, the MEO4ALL research project introduces an iTV solution targeted to users with blindness and low vision and other users with special needs like the elderly. This solution aims to enhance the TV experience of these users through easy and assisted access to menus and functionalities. To identify users' needs and expectations in order to shape the functional and technical requirements of the iTV solution, a questionnaire survey was carried out. This article details the questionnaire's development process, focusing on characterizing the experience of blind and low-vision individuals with Portuguese iTV services and devices. Results suggest that enhancing accessibility in TV content and technology for visually impaired individuals is crucial to improving their television experience. A clearer awareness of features like audio description and contextual help is needed. Improving usability, especially with voice control, can also contribute to a greater experience.

Keywords: Accessibility · Disability · Interactive Television · Visual Impairment · User Experience

1 Introduction

Today's interactive television (iTV) services offer a wide variety of functionalities and resources alongside an extensive range of television channels, providing their users with new experiences of interaction and audiovisual consumption [1]. In Portugal, despite the progress made in recent years in iTV services to make them accessible to visually impaired users (with blindness and low vision), there are still significant opportunities for improvement so that these services can respond more efficiently to the needs of this audience [2]. At the same time, current iTV distribution infrastructures have the technological capacity to improve this type of service, resulting in favorable socio-economic impacts [3]. In Portugal, around 1 million visually impaired citizens [4] cannot fully benefit from the potential of the current television paradigm and have many difficulties in operating and benefiting from interactive features, since these solutions usually involve a strong visual component.

A. Marcus et al. (Eds.): HCII 2024, LNCS 14714, pp. 105–115, 2024.
https://doi.org/10.1007/978-3-031-61356-2_7

It is in this context that the MEO4ALL research project was created, which consists of an iTV solution that allows easy and assisted access to the service's menus, options, and functionalities, improving the television experience for visually impaired users and, in a universal design logic, other users with special needs, such as elderly. The project's development was divided into three phases: conceptualization, implementation, and validation of the iTV solution. In the first phase (conceptualization) the needs and expectations of the target audience were identified through a questionnaire survey to define the functional and technical requirements based on the results obtained. This article presents in detail the questionnaire that was developed to characterize the experience of blind and low-vision people with Portuguese interactive television services, as well as with television content and devices.

In the next section, the Portuguese television panorama about services that consider accessibility for visually impaired people is presented. The method used to create the questionnaire survey is identified and explained in Sect. 3. Finally, in Sect. 4. The results of the questionnaire obtained are presented and discussed and in the last section the conclusions are formulated.

2 ITV Portuguese Panorama

When it comes to television content, accessibility options in Portugal are limited to programs with audio description. Since the 2011 revision of the Television Law [5], a multi-annual plan has been put in place establishing obligations for Portuguese television channels to make their content accessible to people with disabilities, and since 2005, RTP [6] has been trying to ensure this offer, which includes audio description. Originally, this option was based only on the regular broadcast of a program with AD, but this service was transmitted over the airwaves, in analog form, and visually impaired citizens found it difficult to use the service and were forced to own two devices, the television and the radio [7]. Later, in February 2018, RTP's AD service, in collaboration with the three main cable distribution platforms in Portugal, NOS, MEO, and Vodafone, implemented a dual audio system [6]. Before a program with AD starts, RTP provides a text and audio warning (Fig. 1).

When the user realizes that the program contains this feature, must manually change the audio track (by selecting the track with AD), which forces him to navigate the TV service's menus. This solution is not at all accessible, because none of the services include Voice Over (VO), implying additional difficulties for the user. It should also be noted that RTP advertises this service at no cost to the user, but the cable services that support this solution are paid for.

In Portugal, there are also streaming services, such as Netflix, which offer some movies and series with AD [8]. On the other hand, there are TV boxes that allow the installation of services/applications such as Netflix and YouTube. One such box is Apple TV, which integrates VO functionality, benefiting people with visual impairments [9].

Since the end of 2013, the Portuguese commercial IPTV solution MEO provides the Audio Zapping service [10] at no extra cost to the user. This is an accessibility feature designed to allow blind and low-vision users to obtain audio cues for certain actions carried out with the MEO remote control, using a previously recorded voice. With this

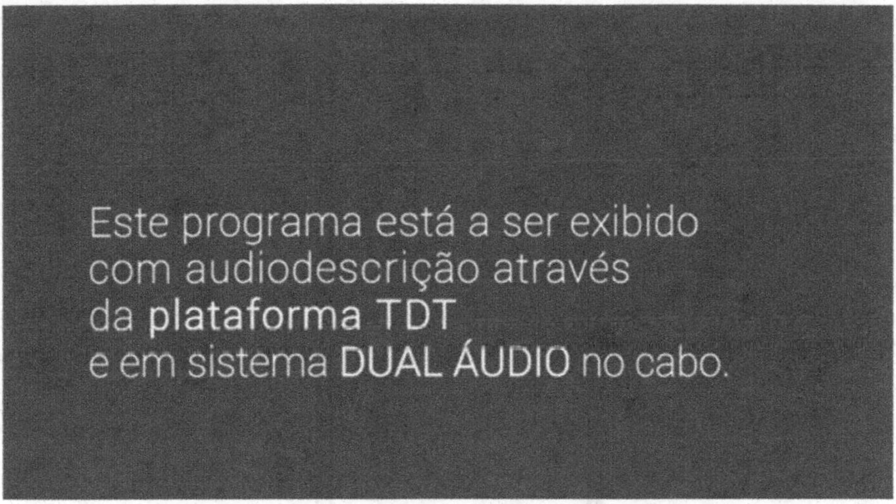

Fig. 1. Warning of a program with audio description on RTP

feature, visually impaired users can use the MEO service more easily, as they are given audible indications of which channel they are on, and which channel they are switching to when zapping. However, the user must install the functionality beforehand and the MEO service does not have VO. The MEO service offers Voice Control (VC), but in a second-screen application named MEO Remote (Fig. 2), and its controls are limited [11].

Considering the existing offers on the TV sets in Portugal, Samsung offers the VO functionality and other features like high-contrast, color inversion, and text magnification, specifically designed for visually impaired users [12]. One of the differentiating features is the existence of specific areas of the interface for the user to hear what each key on the remote control does when it is pressed and the functions that the service provides.

Typically, cable television services in Portugal are complemented by second-screen applications, both to access their range of channels and content outside the home and some service areas directly. VO and VC functionalities are offered by most mobile operating systems. Apple offers its VO "VoiceOver" system and VC functionality from Siri [13] and Google offers the VO "TalkBack" system [14] and VC from Google Assistant. If these options are activated, it is possible to read the screen sequentially and give voice commands. Therefore, second-screen applications for television services can be accessible if they are developed by accessibility standards (this is the only way these features can work fully), which is not seen in most cases.

Fig. 2. Voice Control option in the MEO Remote application

3 Method

Through a questionnaire survey, the needs and experience of blind and low-vision people with Portuguese interactive television services, content, and devices were identified. The data collected made it possible to define the functional and technical requirements of the MEO4All iTV solution.

The strategy for recruiting respondents involved contacting institutions with connections to visual impairment and/or special needs people to ask for help in disseminating the questionnaire among their users and/or members.

At the start of the survey, participants were acquainted with the questionnaire's subject matter and the overarching research project. The questionnaire was organized into distinct sections, each of which will be delineated shortly.

A.Participants' Characteristics. Since the intended audience comprises individuals who are blind or have low vision, a section of this questionnaire had been dedicated to ascertaining the participant's diagnosis of their type of visual impairment.

B.Participants' Interaction with Television Content and Services. The following sections of the questionnaire aimed to understand participants' interaction with television content and services, using diverse methods such as remote control, audiodescription, other tools/functionalities, voice control, and contextual help.

B1. Remote Control. Regarding the use of the remote control as a way of interacting with the television, the aim was to comprehend the extent to which users employ the remote control, identify the keys they deem essential, and ascertain which additional keys they would like to incorporate in the remote control.

B2. Audio Description. In the context of audiodescription, it was important to gauge participants' familiarity with this feature. Therefore, the subsequent subsection provided a definition of audiodescription, enabling participants answer the following questions with enhanced understanding. With this approach, the participants were in a better position to answer questions such as the perceived value of this feature, the use of audiodescription, the activation process, and their ability to identify channels offering audiodescription. Furthermore, it was sought to discern the participants' proficiency in determining the availability of audiodescription on specific channels and the significance they attribute to this information.

B3. Other Tools/Features. To gather insights into alternative modes of interaction, such as services already in place, a dedicated section of the questionnaire had been allocated to explore various tools and functionalities.

B4. Voice Control. For voice control, awareness of this feature was assessed, followed by a definition of voice control as a form of interaction. This methodology made it possible to understand whether participants perceived added value in voice control and actively used it in their interactions. It also sought to understand the specific scenarios in which users used voice control and how their behaviour might vary depending on the spoken command. Finally, participants were asked to indicate which areas/functions they considered voice control to be available for, such as changing channels or viewing automatic recordings.

B5. Contextual Help. This section focused on contextual help interaction, where the participant was again asked if they knew the term, and after the definition was given, an attempt was made to understand the added value of this form of interaction. In addition, information was gathered on when contextual help was most needed and in what situations contextual help had been in use.

4 Results

A few weeks after the questionnaire was sent out, many responses were received (66 answers), with promising results, which allowed the project team to improve the solution that was under development, since the creation process is iterative.

A.Participants' Characteristics. In this study, 66 participants were involved, with different degrees of visual impairment. Out of this, 34 individuals reported experiencing blindness, while 24 participants had been diagnosed with low vision. Additionally, 4 participants were found to have myopia. Notably, after excluding participants with no visual disability (4 participants with myopia), the analysis was conducted on a subset of 62 individuals.

B. Participants' Interaction with Television Content and Services. *B1. Remote Control.* Regarding the use of the remote control as a way of interacting with television content and services, 69,4% (n = 43) of the participants use the remote control, while the other 30,6% (n = 19) do not.

Among the 43 participants who use this type of interaction with the television, the keys considered essential are (Fig. 3): directional keys (up, down, right, left arrows) with a percentage of 83,7% (n = 36); numbers, with 76,7% (n = 33); OK button, with 67,4% (n = 29); menu button, with 62,8% (n = 27); emission control keys (forward, backward, pause/play) with a percentage of 55,8% (n = 24); and Google Assistant button, with 41,9% (n = 18). Additionally, some participants mentioned other remote-control keys they found essential: volume control keys, with a percentage of 6,9% (n = 3); channel change keys, with 2,3% (n = 1); and exit button, also with a percentage of 2,3% (n = 1).

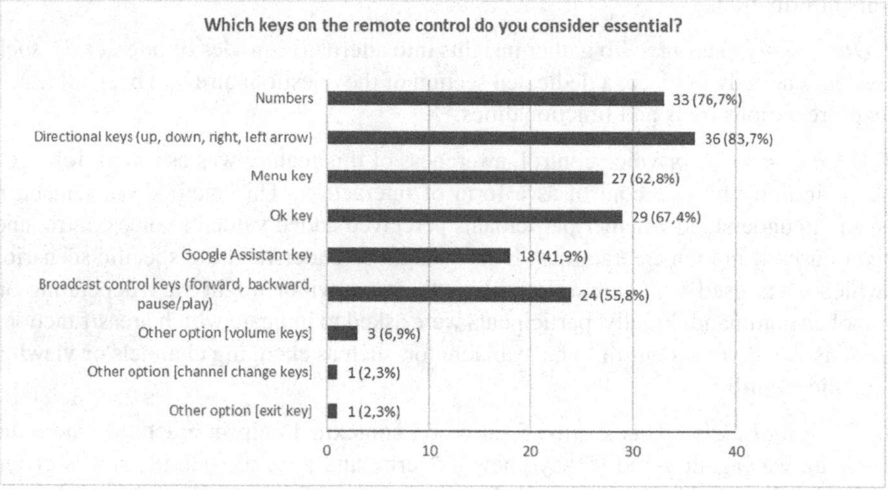

Fig. 3. Which keys on the remote control participants consider essential

Beyond the essential keys, 33 participants indicated other keys they wished the remote control would incorporate. Six participants (18,2%) emphasized the importance of tactile markings on keys for differentiation (like braille keys, for example). Requests were made for features like audio description (9,1%; n = 3) and subtitle reading (6,1%; n = 2) activation keys. Accessibility features such as voice command (12,1%; n = 4), audio feedback (24,2%, n = 8) for menu navigation, and larger and more visible keys were desired (12,1%; n = 4). Overall, participants highlighted the need for remote controls to be more inclusive and user-friendly for individuals with different abilities.

B2. Audio Description. Regarding the audiodescription as way to interact with television content and services, from the 62 participants, 77,4% (n = 48) knew what audiodescription is, and the other 22,6% (n = 14), did not knew.

The participants overwhelmingly recognize the substantial value that audio description brings to individuals with visual impairments. They view it as a critical tool that enriches the television and film viewing experience, offering essential information about scenes, characters, and visual elements that would otherwise be inaccessible to them. Most participants emphasized that audio description enables them to fully comprehend and engage with audiovisual content, enhancing their overall enjoyment and understanding. Furthermore, participants highlighted various benefits of audio description, such as: allowing for a deeper understanding of scenes and contexts; providing access to non-verbal cues and details crucial for understanding plot developments; enabling individuals to independently access and enjoy content that would otherwise be challenging or impossible to comprehend; fostering inclusivity by ensuring that individuals with visual impairments can fully participate in shared cultural experiences, such as watching movies or television shows; enhancing social integration by enabling discussions and shared experiences with peers who may have sight. In summary, participants overwhelmingly agree that audio description is an indispensable tool that greatly enhances the television and film viewing experiences for individuals with visual impairment, ensuring their equal participation and enjoyment in the multimedia landscape.

Among the 62 participants, only 38,7% (n = 24) use audio description to interact with television content and services, while 61,3% (n = 38) do not use this functionality. Considering these responses, only participants who use audio description answered the subsequent questions about this feature. Out of the 24 participants who use audio description, a mere 16,7% (n = 4) are aware of how to activate this functionality. Conversely, the majority, comprising 83,3% (n = 20) expressed a lack of knowledge regarding its activation. Of the 4 participants who knew how to activate audio description, 3 reported to rely on assistance from individuals without disabilities to activate audio description, indicating a limitation in accessibility and independence.

Out of the 24 participants, only 29,2% (n = 7) know which channels offer audio description and were able to identify the Portuguese channels RTP1 and RTP2, however, they also point out that it's not available on all programs of the channels, and the activation process is not straightforward, making it rarely used. It was also suggested that this feature should also be available on the channels' websites and respective mobile TV applications. This information indicates a limited awareness among participants regarding the availability of audio description on television channels, with the majority (70,8%; n = 17) unaware of this fact. The responses also highlight some challenges related to the activation process and suggest improvements for enhancing accessibility to audio description features across different media platforms.

All participants (n = 24) agreed that it is highly important to identify channels and programs which offers audio description when accessed. They provided various reasons supporting this stance, such as: program selection, where participants emphasized that knowing which channels offer audio description helps them decide which programs to watch; accessibility assurance, with the identification of channels with audio description gives individuals confidence that they will have access to fully accessible content; simplified activation, making it easier for individuals to navigate through channels and select those offering audio description; informed viewing decisions, which ensures visually impaired persons can anticipate and select programming that aligns with their accessibility needs and preferences. Overall, participants unanimously agreed on the critical importance of identifying channels and programs offering audiodescription.

B3. Other Tools/Features. Out of the 62 participants, a mere 8,1% (n = 5) have used other tools or features to support their television experience. The overwhelming majority, comprising 91,9% (n = 57), have never utilized such tools or functionalities. When asked to specify which tools or functionalities they have used, participants mentioned a few examples. Two participants mentioned using 'Audio zapping' from MEO, but they indicate that this solution has limitations, because it provides only audio feedback in few actions (e.g.: changing channels). Additionally, other two participants referred the use of voice commands, and one participant indicated the of an unspecified app.

B4. Voice Control. Regarding the voice control as way to interact with television content, from the 62 participants, 67,7% (n = 42) knew what voice control was, and the other 32,3% (n = 20) did not knew.

Voice control is perceived as highly valuable by participants, with various justifications provided. Most participants view it to facilitate interaction with television devices, offering a comprehensive control option without the need for visual cues. Additionally, some participants highlighted its potential to provide inclusivity and independence. However, there are also concerns raised, notably regarding the effectiveness and accessibility of voice control features for individuals with visual impairment. Despite these considerations, the overall sentiment is positive, with voice control seen as a significant enhancement to the television viewing experience, providing faster access to desired content and improving usability for a diverse range of users.

Only a minority of participants, constituting 24,2% (n = 15), use voice control as a means of interaction, with the majority, comprising 75,8% (n = 47), not using this feature.

From the responses detailing the use of voice control, it appears that participants primarily use it for basic functions such as changing channels, turning the television on or off, searching for content, or accessing certain features like radio or music streaming services. Some participants express satisfaction with the performance of voice control, while others note limitations or difficulties, such as the need for articulating commands slowly or experiencing challenges in accessing specific content.

According to the responses provided, there are several areas and functionalities where it would make sense for voice control to be available, enabling direct navigation and activation (Fig. 4): watching automatic recordings, with the ability to specify the series or movie desired for playback, this feature was supported by 80% (n = 12); changing channels by specifying the channel name, which received support from 80% (n = 12); accessing recommended content, with 73,3% (n = 11) expressing interest in this functionality; activating audio description, which received significant support at 93,3% (n = 14), this feature is crucial for users with visual impairment to access TV content; playing user manuals or instructions, if available, was considered valuable by 60% (n = 9), this feature could enhance accessibility by providing spoken guidance for device usage; activating other areas or functionalities, which garnered interest from 73.3% (n = 11), this could include various system preferences or customization options. Three participants specified other areas/functionalities where voice control could be beneficial, such as: all the features and areas of the service should be voice-controlled (n = 2) and the feature of increasing the size of subtitles (n = 1).

B5. Contextual Help. Regarding contextual help, only 6,5% of the participants (n = 4) are familiar with this feature, while the vast majority, 93,5% (n = 58), have no knowledge of this functionality.

When the participants were asked what benefits they identified in the use of contextual help, the majority admitted to not knowing what contextual help is (even after providing an explanation of what the functionality is). The remain participants recognized potential

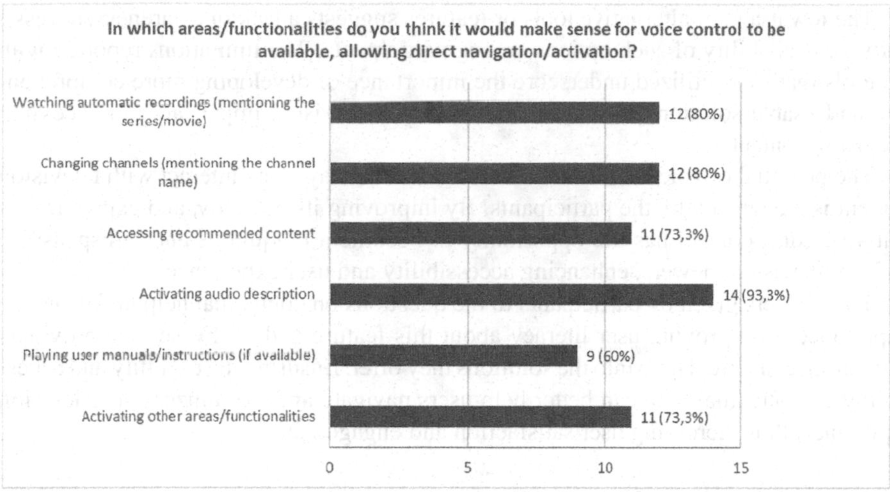

Fig. 4. Areas/Functionalities participants think it would make sense for voice control to be available

utility of contextual help if properly implemented and if information was provided in an accessible format.

The responses regarding the moments when individuals feel the greatest need for contextual help when interacting with TV content/services reveal once more that most participants cannot identify those moments because does not understand what contextual help entails. However, some respondents indicated specific scenarios where they felt contextual help would be valuable, such as when navigating menus, searching for programs, or understanding content in a foreign language without subtitles.

From the 62 participants, only a very small percentage of participants, 3,2% (n = 2), have used contextual help while interacting with TV content/services. The vast majority, comprising 96,8% (n = 60), have not used this feature. From the two participants, one mentioned using contextual help while navigating through the various options available on the television. The other participant stated that contextual help is used when accompanied by others.

4.1 Discussion

Firstly, regarding the use of remote control, there is a need for these devices to be more inclusive and user-friendly for persons with visual impairment. Accessibility features such as tactile markings, activation keys of accessibility functions, and keys with audio feedback can enhance the user experience of remote controls.

While there is widespread recognition of the value of audio description, there are significant barriers to its effective utilization, including limited awareness, accessibility challenges, and a lack of knowledge regarding activation processes. Addressing these barriers is essential to ensure equal access to TV content for viewers with visual impairment.

The low usage of alternative tools or features suggests a lack of awareness, accessibility, or availability of such options among participants. The limitations reported with the tools that were utilized underscore the importance of developing more comprehensive and usable solutions to support individuals with visual impairment in accessing television content.

The potential of voice control to revolutionize the way users interact with television content is recognized by the participants. By improving its usability, and expanding its features, voice control has the opportunity to become a ubiquitous and indispensable tool for television viewers, enhancing accessibility and user experience.

The answers given by participants to the questions on contextual help underline the importance of improving user literacy about this feature and of TV service providers integrating contextual help into the solutions they offer. Ensuring the usability and accessibility of contextual help can better help users navigate and maximize their television experience, thus increasing user satisfaction and engagement.

5 Conclusions and Future Work

The results of the questionnaire survey emphasize the importance of enhancing accessibility and inclusivity in interactive television services, content, and devices for individuals with visual impairment. This includes not only providing essential features like voice over and audio description but also ensuring that remote controls and other interaction methods are designed with accessibility in mind.

There is a need for clearer awareness regarding available accessibility features, such as audiodescription and contextual help. Building initiatives for improving the knowledge of both users and service providers about the existence and benefits of these features is crucial for increasing their adoption and ensuring that individuals with visual impairment can fully use them.

Improving accessibility, usability, and integration of features like voice control could significantly enhance the TV viewing experience for users with visual impairment. This may involve streamlining activation processes, providing clear instructions, and ensuring compatibility with a wide range of devices and services.

Continued efforts are required from both industry stakeholders and service providers to address the identified challenges and ensure equal access to TV content and services for all users. Companies involved in TV technology and content creation should recognize the diverse needs of their audience and work towards developing solutions that cater to these needs effectively. This may involve collaboration with disability advocacy groups and incorporating feedback from individuals with visual impairment into the design process.

The results obtained from the questionnaire will allow the final definition of the technical and functional requirements of the iTV MEO4ALL solution. After this definition, it will be possible to develop and implement the solution and validate it iteratively in terms of user experience, considering three essential aspects: accessibility, usability and interaction design.

Acknowledgements. Acknowledgements. The authors would like to thank the AlticeLabs@UA laboratory that funded the MEO4ALL project and the associations that publicized the survey, namely: ACAPO - Association of the Blind and Visually Impaired of Portugal (the main association and its delegations in Viana do Castelo, Castelo Branco, and Leiria), APCSM (Association of Cerebral Palsy of São Miguel), School of Guide Dogs in Mortágua, ABAADV (Association of Guide Dogs for the Blind), Association of 'Bengala Mágica' (Magic Cane), and APD - Portuguese Association of the Disabled.

References

1. Boehm, K., Esser, R., Klein, F., Mogg, A., Lee, P., Raab, J. : The future of the TV and video landscape by 2030. Deloitte – center for the long view. Issue 8/2018 (2018). https://www2.deloitte.com/content/dam/Deloitte/be/Documents/technology-media-telecommunications/201809%20Future%20of%20Video_DIGITAL_FINAL.pdf
2. Oliveira, R., Prata, A., Miranda, J.C., Ferraz, J., de Abreu, A., Almeida, M.: Accessibility Solutions for Visually Impaired Persons: A Digital Platform Conceptualization. In: Carvalho, L.C., Reis, L., Prata, A., Pereira, R. (eds.) Handbook of Research on Multidisciplinary Approaches to Entrepreneurship, Innovation, and ICTs:, pp. 331–348. IGI Global (2021). https://doi.org/10.4018/978-1-7998-4099-2.ch015
3. da Silva Klehm, V., de Souza Braga, R., de Lucena, V.F.: A survey of digital television interactivity technologies. Sensors. **22**, 6542 (2022). https://doi.org/10.3390/s22176542
4. Instituto Nacional de Estatística: Censos - O que nos dizem os Censos sobre as dificuldades sentidas pelas pessoas com incapacidades - 2021. INE (2022). https://www.ine.pt/xurl/pub/66200373
5. Diário da República: Lei n.º 8/2011, D.R. n.º 71 (Série I). 11 de Abril de 2011. http://www.dre.pt/pdf1s/2011/04/07100/0213902175.pdf
6. Rádio Televisão Portuguesa (RTP): RTP Acessibilidades - Audiodescrição. RTP (2024). http://www.rtp.pt/wportal/acessibilidades/audiodescricao.php.
7. Oliveira, R., de Abreu, J.F., Almeida, A.M.: Promoting Interactive Television (ITV) accessibility: an adapted service for users with visual impairments. Univ. Access Inf. Soc. **16**, 533–544 (2016). https://doi.org/10.1007/s10209-016-0482-z
8. Netflix: Help Center – Audio Descriptions for Netflix Movies and TV Shows. Netflix (2024). https://help.netflix.com/en/node/25079
9. Apple: Manual do Utilizador da aplicação TV – Usar o VoiceOver na aplicação TV. Apple (2024). https://support.apple.com/pt-pt/guide/tvapp/atvbfa4ff6cd/web
10. MEO: Sabe o que é Áudio Zapping?. Blog MEO (2014). https://blog.meo.pt/sabe-o-que-e-audio-zapping-113236
11. MEO: App MEO Remote. MEO (2024). https://www.meo.pt/tv/novidades/melhor-experiencia-tv/meo-remote
12. Samsung: Accessibility - Vision | Samsung Jordan. Samsung (2024). https://www.samsung.com/levant/sustainability/accessibility/vision/
13. Apple: Manual de Utilização do iPhone – Ativar VoiceOver e praticar a sua utilização no iPhone. Apple (2024). https://support.apple.com/pt-pt/guide/iphone/iph3e2e415f/ios
14. Google: TalkBack – Acessibilidade do Android Ajuda. Google (2024). https://support.google.com/accessibility/android/topic/3529932?hl=pt&ref_topic=907884

Challenges and Gaps in Promoting Inclusive Spaces: A Study Based on Interviews

Francisca Rocha Lourenço(✉), Rita Oliveira, and Oksana Tymoshchuk

University of Aveiro, Campus Universitário de Santiago, 3810-193 Aveiro, Portugal
franciscalourenco@ua.pt

Abstract. This study focuses on promoting inclusive spaces specifically designed to support People with Disabilities (PwD). These spaces play a crucial role in providing services and digital resources that enable these people to increase their autonomy, independence, accessibility, communication, and quality of life.

The overall impact of these spaces depends largely on proper dissemination. It is therefore of the highest importance to design and implement effective promotion strategies to ensure that PwD are aware of the existence of these spaces and have the necessary information to access them.

In this qualitative study 16 interviews with representatives of different disability-inclusive spaces in the Community of Portuguese Language Countries, namely Angola, Brazil, and Portugal are analyzed. The main objective was to identifying and understanding the gaps and challenges in promoting inclusive spaces.

The study's findings reveal that participants recognize the importance of implementing communication strategies, but various obstacles often limit their implementation. These challenges include lack of strategic planning, limited time and financial resources, operational capacity constraints, reluctance to join communication channels, and lack of communication skills.

Recognizing these challenges and gaps enables the implementation of significant improvements in the promotion of inclusive spaces and empowers teams in these and other types of spaces and communities. This will make it possible to adapt communication strategies informally, optimizing their dissemination process and effectively promoting inclusion.

Keywords: Disability · Inclusive Spaces · Inclusion · Disability · Dissemination · Accessibility · Communication

1 Introduction

According to the World Health Organization, approximately 1.3 billion people – around 16% of the world's population - have some significant disability [1]. This number is rising substantially, making it a priority issue [2].

People with Disabilities (PwD) and their caregivers often face significant social challenges such as stigma, exclusion, lack of opportunities and difficulty accessing resources

A. Marcus et al. (Eds.): HCII 2024, LNCS 14714, pp. 116–129, 2024.
https://doi.org/10.1007/978-3-031-61356-2_8

and support. In addition, PwD may encounter obstacles due to physical or digital accessibility, a lack of accessible information and resources, and a general unawareness about their needs [3–5].

Inclusive spaces can foster social and digital inclusion, and accessibility – core values in contemporary society [6] – and support PwD to live in their community in a meaningful way, making it easier for them to overcome many challenges [4].

An inclusive space is a human environment that provides conditions for everyone's inclusion in various areas of society, by eliminating any barriers and considering the diversity of people [7]. They are designed to welcome and ensure accessibility for people of all backgrounds, abilities, and identities, recognizing and valuing the differences of each member of the community, promoting equal participation and a sense of belonging, respect, and dignity for all [7, 8].

In the context of disability, these spaces can be defined as accessible and welcoming places where PwD, regardless of their abilities or characteristics, can be understood, respected, supported, and feel integrated into the community. Besides removing physical or digital barriers, these spaces constitute large support networks that recognize the needs of PwD and their families and caregivers, providing personalized support and resources and services that facilitate care and develop PwD' abilities and autonomy. These spaces ultimately promote integration and participation in society, community involvement and a sense of belonging for PwD [9, 10] – essential factors for their well-being and quality of life [4].

The characteristics of these spaces can facilitate overcoming the challenges and problems faced by PwD, providing an environment of contact with diverse resources for inclusion, where there are equal opportunities and where these people feel integrated, valued, and included, free from stigma and discrimination [4, 9]. By creating support networks, promoting autonomy, the exchange of knowledge and full participation in society, these spaces contribute to building a more inclusive society. In this way, they play a key role not only in promoting inclusion, but consequently in improving the autonomy, accessibility, independence and quality of life of PwD [10], allowing them to interact with other people, take part in daily activities, explore new forms of learning and leisure, access various sources of information, establish contacts, exchange information and expand relationships and horizons in the same way as the non-disabled population [13].

The effectiveness of these spaces in promoting inclusion depends largely on adequate dissemination. It is therefore essential to promote these spaces effectively, so that PwD are aware of them and can take advantage of their benefits [10].

In this sense, this study analyzed how some inclusive spaces in the Community of Portuguese Language Countries promote their work (Sect. 2. Methodology), identifying some gaps and challenges in terms of dissemination (Sect. 3. Results). This analysis will provide a deeper understanding of the promotion and dissemination methods used by the spaces studied, serving as a starting point for developing improved, adapted, and planned strategies, considering the gaps and challenges identified (Sect. 4. Discussion).

2 Methodology

2.1 Research Design

This study adopted a qualitative and exploratory approach to understand the dissemination strategies used by several inclusive spaces in the area of disability for their promotion, thus making it possible to identify the gaps and challenges that these spaces face in this process.

For this purpose, 16 semi-structured interviews were conducted with representatives from various inclusive spaces. These interviews provided in-depth insights into the participants' perspectives, experiences, and understanding about this topic.

2.2 Participants

The participants were selected by purposive sampling, based on specific criteria, to ensure a diverse and comprehensive representation, namely: i) to include spaces that promote inclusion; ii) to include spaces from different geographical areas of the Community of Portuguese Language Countries; and iii) to include spaces from different sectors (education, health, and technology).

In this way, 16 participants were interviewed, corresponding to the representatives of each space included in the study. This sample represents the variety of inclusive spaces located in Portugal (13), Brazil (2) and Angola (1). The participants were representatives from the following spaces: Disability Support Associations (5), Digital Inclusion Resource Centers (2), ICT Resource Center (2), Social Inclusion Support Center (1), Cooperative for the Education and Rehabilitation of People with Disabilities (1), Medical and Rehabilitation Center (1), Technology and Innovation Center (1), Telecommunications Company (1) Assistive Technology and Occupational Performance Laboratory (1), and Support Product Developer (1).

2.3 Instruments

The researchers developed a semi-structured script to conduct the interviews with the representatives of each venue. This script included 17 open-ended questions, which made it possible to obtain more detailed answers about the characterization of the space, the characterization of the team, the target audience and the communication strategies adopted.

This instrument underwent a pilot test, the results of which required refinements and improvements to improve its reliability and validity.

The researcher himself conducted the interviews, ensuring consistency in data collection.

2.4 Procedures

The interviews took an average of around an hour each, whit four conducted face-to-face and the rest twelve online.

Each participant was informed about the purpose of the study, ensuring informed consent. The participants duly signed, permitting the interview recording for analysis and data collection.

2.5 Data Collection and Analysis

Data was collected by audio recording all the interviews, the content of which was then transcribed into textual format, where data analysis began. These transcripts were imported into NVivo data analysis software, where all the data was managed and coded.

The data was coded based on the following categories: i) promotion/communication goals of each space; ii) perceived difficulties in promoting the spaces; and iii) communication strategies and media used by each spaces.

This process revealed recurring response patterns, providing the researchers valuable insights into the promotion practices of the inclusive spaces studied.

3 Results

3.1 Goals of Inclusive Spaces

Early in the interviews, participants were asked to explain the objectives of the space they were representing. The main strategic goals of the inclusive spaces were: support and intervention for PwDs (75% of spaces have this goal), training (50%), evaluating and prescribing support products (44%), research and development (25%), innovation (19%), promoting collaboration through partnerships and collaborations (19%), defending and promoting the rights of PwD (19%), and supporting studies (13%).

Therefore, the most common goal among inclusive spaces is supporting and intervening in PwD, with 75% of respondents reporting that they do this in their represented spaces.

3.2 Goals of Promoting Inclusive Spaces

Specific goals related to promoting or disseminating these spaces included making the space known was identified as the predominant goal, with nine spaces (out of 16) reporting having this goal (56%), followed by reaching out to PwD, their families or carers (38%). Less predominantly, there are also spaces that want to make connections (31%) with other spaces, organizations, or companies, such as nursing homes and hospitals, for example. In addition, other promotion goals include: disseminating good practices and success stories (19%), raising financial support (13%), raising awareness (13%) and selling training courses (6%) (Fig. 1).

3.3 Communication Strategies Used to Promote Inclusive Spaces

Regarding the communication strategies to promote inclusive spaces, six of the 16 spaces interviewed (38%) did not mention any specific strategy for this purpose or claimed not to have any defined strategy for this promotion (Fig. 2).

However, of the remaining spaces that do use promotion strategies, most of them revealed that their most used strategies are: sharing testimonies and real stories (4 out of 16 spaces, or 25% of the spaces interviewed), presenting concrete examples of people showing how the space has changed their lives; promoting the space and its activities and

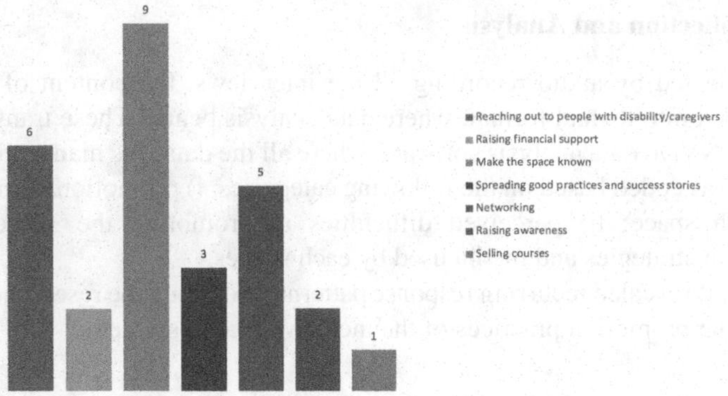

Fig. 1. Goals of dissemination for each participating space.

services in institutions such as schools and universities (25%); and promotion through partners or external entities (25%) (Fig. 2).

In addition, three participants revealed that they use strategies related to social media (19%), and three participants explained that they use inclusive communication as a strategy (19%), opting for communication that is accessible to all. Finally, only 1 participant mentioned each of the following strategies: dissemination in companies or institutions (6%), humanization (6%), innovation (6%) and sending an e-mail newsletter (6%) (Fig. 2).

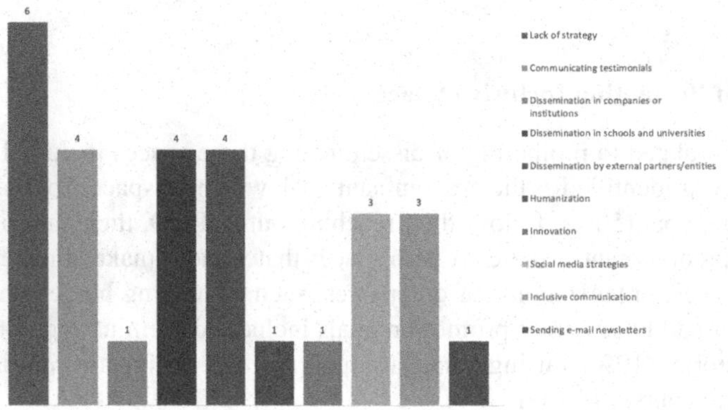

Fig. 2. Main strategies used to promote the participating inclusive spaces.

3.4 Media Used to Promote Inclusive Spaces

The participants showed that they use various media to promote their spaces. The most common is their website, used by 15 of the 16 spaces interviewed (94%), followed by social media (Facebook (81%), Instagram (44%), LinkedIn (12.5%), Pinterest (6%), Youtube (6%) and WhatsApp (6%)), used by 13 of the 16 spaces interviewed (81%) (Fig. 3).

In addition, many participants said that they often used "word of mouth" (informal communication) to let people know about the space (44%), as well as presentations, meetings and/or debates between schools, companies, and institutions (44%) (Fig. 3).

After this, it was also observed that presenting work at conferences and congresses (38%), using the press (38%), and posting flyers and posters (38%) still have some significance among the spaces interviewed, as do email marketing (31%), hosting events in the community (31%) and using promotional or explanatory videos (31%) (Fig. 3). Finally, forums (13%), outdoors (6%) and phone communication (6%) were also used (Fig. 3).

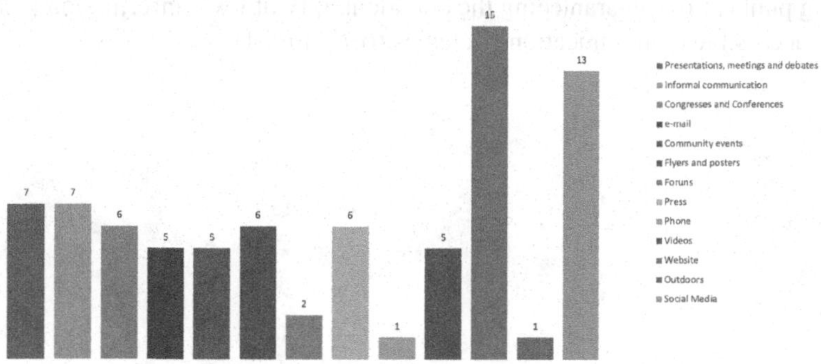

Fig. 3. Media used to promote the participating inclusive spaces.

3.5 Challenges Faced in Promoting Inclusive Spaces

To understand what difficulties participants face in communicating and promoting inclusive spaces, they were asked to identify and address the biggest difficulties and challenges they identify in this sense.

The most significant difficulty documented in disseminating these spaces is the lack of communication strategies, representing the biggest challenge in this regard, with 4 participants (25%) assuming that they don't adopt any kind of strategy (Fig. 4).

Previously, six spaces had already realized that they did not adopt any strategy. However, only one of these six spaces is shared in this awareness of the lack of strategies. This means that of the participants who now identify the lack of strategies as a challenge in this sense, only one is in common with those who said they didn't use communication strategies. In other words, 83% (5) of the spaces that consider the lack of strategies do not see it as a problem or challenge in promoting inclusive spaces. In addition, the total number of spaces that do not actually have strategies defined for their promotion is nine spaces (56%).

Other participants did not directly state that they did not adopt communication strategies. Still, they did say that they did not adopt any communication channels (13%), that they did not have enough time to devote to promoting and disseminating the spaces in question (13%), and that they did not have enough financial resources to invest in disseminating them (6%) (Fig. 4). In addition to this, the participants mentioned that the staff who make up the spaces interviewed lack skills and/or training in the area of communication and disseminating information (6%), as well as the lack of employees which compromises disseminating activities (6%) (Fig. 4). Also identified as a challenge was the low adherence/difficulties that some PwD still experience in using technology and social media (13%).

In addition to these gaps, challenges were identified related to the operational capacity of the spaces, where participants revealed that they were unable to reconcile the responsibilities inherent in the daily work of the teams involved with the task of disseminating their services (6%) (Fig. 4). In addition, other challenges faced by the inclusive spaces interviewed are: lack of external cooperation and collaboration (6%); difficulty in creating publications guaranteeing the confidentiality of PwD information (6%); and not using accessible communication strategies (6%) (Fig. 4).

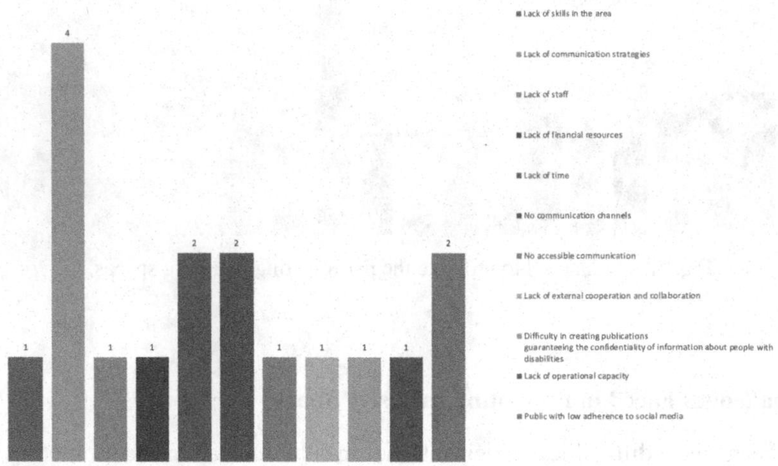

Fig. 4. Difficulties and limitations identified by the participants in promoting the spaces.

3.6 Type of Content/Media with Most Impact on the Audience

Participants were asked to indicate the most influential media or content type for the target audience at the final stage of the interviews. 44% of the respondents (7 of the 16 interviewees) said that sharing testimonies or real stories from real people is the most impactful strategy for the public. On the other hand, 18% of respondents say that social media is a tool that impacts on the public. A further 18% of respondents refer specifically to the substantial impact that sharing videos on social media has on the target audience. In addition, they refer, in the same proportion, to direct contact with people and/or recommendations (18%). Other components identified by the participants as having an impact on the public were: inclusion and training programs (13%), visual and multimedia content (6%), sharing the work they do daily (6%), and the technological component (6%) (Fig. 5).

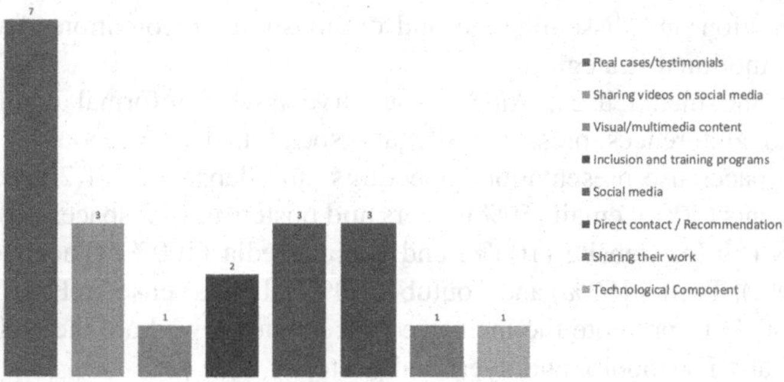

Fig. 5. Type of content/media that participants consider to have the greatest impact on the audience.

3.7 Communication Strategies: Comparing Countries

A comparative analysis between countries shows that the predominant goal of the spaces in Brazil (2 out of 2 spaces (100%)) and Portugal (7 out of 13 spaces (54%)) is to make the space known. The only goal of the only space interviewed in Angola is to raise awareness (100% of the Angolan spaces interviewed).

Regarding the communication strategies used, the space that uses the most disseminating strategies is in Portugal. On the other hand, 5 other spaces in Portugal do not apply any communication strategy to their spaces, as well as the participating space in Angola, which doesn't mention using any type of communication strategy.

Thus, the communication strategies used by the 13 spaces in Portugal are: disseminating in schools and universities (used by 4 out of 13 participating spaces, that is, 31%); communicating testimonies (23% (3 out of 13 spaces)); disseminating through external partners/entities (15% (2 out of 3 spaces)); using accessibility resources such as subtitles, braille, audio description, etc. (15%); social media strategies (15%); disseminating to companies/institutions (8% (1 in 13 spaces)); sending a newsletter by email (8%); humanization (8%); innovation (8%), concluding that the strategy most used by Portuguese participants is disseminating to schools and universities (31%). The fact that the strategy most used by Portuguese spaces is disseminating information in schools and universities suggests that there is recognition in Portugal of the importance of involving educational institutions in this process [11].

In Brazil, the communication strategies used by the spaces interviewed are: disseminating through external partners (100% (2 out of 2 spaces)); social media strategies (50% (1 out of 2 spaces)); communicating testimonials (50%); and using accessibility resources (50%). The most used strategy is disseminating through partners outside the spaces interviewed (100%), which suggests a strategic approach of collaboration with other institutions/organizations and may indicate the lack of resources or time constraints these spaces face. Through these partnerships, these types of limitations can be overcome, taking advantage of the resources and influence of organizations to achieve their promotion goals more effectively [12].

In Brazil, in contrast to Portugal and Angola, all the participants said they used disseminating strategies to promote their spaces, which suggests an awareness of the need for promotion and dissemination and demonstrates recognition of the need to implement promotional strategies.

Regarding the media used, Angola uses five media: informal communication, congresses and conferences, press, website, and social media (Facebook).

Brazilian spaces use presentations, meetings, and debates (1 of 2 spaces (50%)), community events (50%), email (50%), flyers and posters (2 of 2 spaces (100%)), press (50%), videos (50%), website (100%) and social media (100%) (Facebook (100%), Instagram (50%), Twitter (50%) and Youtube (50%)). In this sense, in Brazil, the media most used (100%) to promote the inclusive spaces interviewed are the website, social media (essentially Facebook), and flyers and posters.

Portuguese spaces also essentially use the website (92% (12 out of 13 spaces)) and social media (77% (10 out of 13 spaces)) (Facebook (77%, Instagram 46%, LinkedIn (15%), Pinterest (8%) and WhatsApp (8%)), but also other media such as presentations, meetings and debates (46% (6 out of 13 spaces)), informal communication (46% (6 out of 13 spaces)), congresses and conferences (38% (5 out of 13 spaces)), email (31% (4 out of 13 spaces)), community events (31%), flyers and posters (31%), press (31%), videos (31%), forums (15% (2 out of 13 spaces)) and outdoors (8% (1 out of 13 spaces)).

The use of media in Brazil, with an emphasis on presentations, meetings, debates, and flyers, reflects a more tangible and physical strategy. The emphasis on websites and social media in Portugal suggests a more digital approach. Regarding the challenges encountered in promoting inclusive spaces, the Angolan spaces point to the lack of external cooperation and collaboration as the main and only difficulty they encounter in this context.

The challenges in promoting Brazilian spaces are essentially related to the lack of financial resources (1 of 2 spaces (50%)), lack of time (50%), the difficulty in creating publications guaranteeing the confidentiality of PwD information (50%), and the space's lack of adherence to specific communication channels (50%).

Concerning Portugal, the challenges that Portuguese inclusive spaces have faced in the context of their promotion are: lack of communication strategies (31% (4 out of 13 spaces)); lack of staff (15% (2 out of 13 spaces)); lack of time (15% (2 out of 13 spaces)); non-existence/lack of the space's adherence to communication channels (15%); lack of skills in communication (8% (1 out of 13 spaces)); lack of accessible communication (8%); lack of operational capacity (8%); low adherence of the disabled public to social media (8%); lack of financial resources (8%).

In Portugal and Brazil, the challenges identified in terms of dissemination are expected, except for the difficulty in creating publications guaranteeing the confidentiality of PwD information, which only happens in Brazil, and the lack of staff, lack of skills in the area of communication, lack of accessible communication, lack of operational capacity, low adherence of the disabled public to social media, and lack of communication strategies as a barrier in terms of promotion, which only happens in Portugal.

It is important to note that challenges can be intrinsically interconnected, creating a scenario in which one challenge can trigger or aggravate another. In addition, differences in economic and social development levels between countries can impact on the availability of resources [14] and the ability to implement effective strategies [15].

4 Discussion

Analysis of the results relating to the goals of the inclusive spaces interviewed, in which the predominant goal of support and intervention for PwD, mentioned by 12 of the 16 spaces interviewed (75%) of the participants, highlights the emphasis of these spaces on providing support for PwD and improving their quality of life.

The significant presence of goals related to research and development (25%) demonstrates a commitment to seeking innovations that can benefit the disabled community. In addition, the evaluation and prescription of support products (44%) and training (50%) indicate the importance of training and making resources available to meet the individual needs of PwD. The promotion goals of collaboration and defence of the rights of PwD (19%) highlight awareness of the importance of involving other entities in this type of space and the need to defend the rights of PwD actively.

In addition, the diversity of strategic goals identified in the spaces studied reflects the intrinsic complexity of the needs of PwD.

It should be noted that a significant proportion of the participants (75%) identified supporting and intervening with PwD as their main strategic goal. However, when analyzing the specific goals of promoting inclusive spaces, only 38% of the spaces may indicate their focus is on directly reaching PwD, their caregivers and/or family members. This discrepancy suggests that, although there is a commitment to providing support and intervention, as well as assessing and prescribing support products (44%) and other goals aimed at PwD and their caregivers/family members, the emphasis on promotion directed at this target audience may not be as widely adopted as might be expected. To promote inclusion effectively, it is essential to align these goals, ensuring that the promotion of spaces also caters directly to the public seeking this support.

On the other hand, 56% of the spaces interviewed aimed to make their spaces better known by promoting them. However, considering the fundamental importance of increasing the visibility of spaces to promote inclusion [10], this percentage is relatively low. Making spaces better known not only helps to promote inclusion and overcome the challenges faced by PwD, but also serves as a foundation for achieving other goals, such as raising awareness, establishing partnerships, and even raising financial support [10].

Analyzing the results regarding the media and communication strategies used to promote inclusive spaces, the quantity (13 types) and diversity of media types that are used by various spaces is evident, concluding that all spaces use at least one of these media. Kreps [16] states that to promote issues related to health and well-being, the use of multiple channels and media should be considered, so that the target audience is exposed to important messages in several different ways [16]. However, the significant percentage of participants who use no defined communication strategy to promote their space (38%) raises the question of the effectiveness of using these media without planning or strategy. This is particularly noticeable in the use of social media, mentioned by 81% of the participating spaces, while only 19% of the same spaces report using communication and publication strategies on social media. This discrepancy highlights the lack of strategic planning to meet the proposed goals, compromising the effectiveness of their communication.

According to Kreps [16], it is extremely important to determine which communication channels are most effective in reaching the target audience, as well as to develop strategic messages adapted to each chosen channel [16]. This communication process requires great planning, strategy, and skill levels to raise awareness and achieve the desired results [17–20].

In this context, to maximize the impact of the chosen media, it is essential to plan, develop and implement clear strategies geared towards the intended goals, ensuring that each channel effectively promotes inclusive spaces, conveying the intended message.

In addition, communication efforts must also be strategically designed to be persuasive, informing, involving, and motivating the target audience, and leading to a change in attitude or the adoption of certain actions [16, 21]. In this context, 25% of interviewees share testimonies and real cases, which allow the target audience to learn about real stories of overcoming and specific examples of people who benefit from a particular inclusive space. According to Atkin & Salmon [22], specific examples of real individuals seek to create emotional involvement and a personal and tangible connection, proving to be a persuasive strategy that can be replicated for other spaces. In addition, 19% of spaces that use inclusive communication strategies demonstrate a commitment to accessibility [22]. It is important to make communication accessible to everyone [23], especially regarding inclusion.

Regarding the difficulties and challenges the participants faced the context of promoting their spaces, most of the spaces identified the lack of communication strategies as their main challenge. However, of the six spaces that had already stated that they didn't adopt any strategy, only one is in common with those that identified the lack of strategies as a challenge. In other words, 83% (5) of the spaces that assume a lack of strategies do not face it as a problem or challenge in their promotion. In addition, the total number of spaces that do not define any strategies for their promotion is nine spaces (56%), which further emphasizes the need to plan their communication and invest in promotion strategies for these spaces to avoid compromising the overall effectiveness of their promotion.

This lack of planning and strategies may indicate a perception that disseminating is not considered a priority compared to other activities and may be related to the other challenges that participants identified, namely the lack of time available to dedicate to promoting and disseminating inclusive spaces, the lack of financial resources, the lack of skills and/or training in the area of communication, the lack of operational capacity, and the lack of employees. Other participants may not consider it pertinent to invest in disseminating strategies, as they believe that the target audience still has difficulties or does not adhere to social media/technology.

On the other hand, the challenge of reluctance to join communication channels or lack of communication channels may be related to a lack of technological knowledge or understanding of the potential of modern communication channels. In addition, the lack of time to devote to promoting spaces may be due to prioritizing customer service and other related tasks, leaving little time for this task, also resulting in a lack of operational capacity, where participants explain not being able to reconcile daily work responsibilities with the task of promoting spaces. In addition, the lack of workers specialized in communication can also affect the effectiveness of space promotion. Wijaya [24] highlights the role of planning and defining communication strategies in overcoming communication barriers and achieving the goals set. According to this author, planning is essential for developing successful communication strategies, starting with identifying and analyzing the needs of the target audience, followed by defining communication goals; designing the message; choosing appropriate media and communication channels; developing specific strategies considering each communication goal and chosen media/channel; and estimating the impact of the whole process [10, 24]. This planning allows for developing strategies aligned with the needs of the target audience and the organizational goals [24].

Regarding the media, participants considered to have the most impact on the public, sharing of testimonies and real stories stands out (44%). It is positive to note that participants know this can be a very effective strategy for promoting awareness [25]. However, only 25% of the sample adopted it. This suggests a disconnect between perception and implementation, possibly influenced by the challenges already identified (time constraints, lack of staff, skills in the area, financial resources, and the operational capacity of spaces). In addition, the reference to social media also highlights the relevance of these channels, as they are an effective tool for conveying messages and engaging the public [21, 26].

Communication is an impactful tool for generating awareness, promoting understanding and inspiring action [27]. However, the spaces studied face multifaceted challenges that compromise the effectiveness of their disseminating. It is, therefore, essential to take concrete steps to overcome the challenges identified, ensuring that PwD, family members and caregivers have access to information and resources from these spaces effectively.

5 Conclusions

This study shows that some inclusive spaces have been investing in promoting themselves. It is encouraging to note that online dissemination, through websites and social media, is becoming a common practice among these spaces, reflecting the recognition of digital presence's importance in this context. However, there are still gaps to be filled. Participants recognize the importance of implementing certain strategies, but their implementation is limited due to a lack of strategic planning and other challenges they encounter, such as lack of strategic planning, lack of time and financial resources, lack of operational capacity, reluctance to join communication channels, and communication skills.

This lack of strategic planning and strategy implementation is a critical barrier that can limit the reach of disseminating messages and restrict people's access to information about these inclusive spaces.

However, by recognizing and addressing these gaps, this study contributes to the awareness of this problem, offering the opportunity to bridge these gaps. The in-depth understanding of the challenges and gaps faced by the inclusive spaces studied not only highlights the critical points in the promotion of these spaces, allowing for the implementation of significant improvements in this regard, but also alerts the managers and workers of these types of spaces to adapt the communication strategies implemented in an informed way, optimizing the effectiveness of their communication.

The main limitation of this study is related to the geographical concentration of the sample in Portugal. There was an uneven distribution of participants, with significant representation in Portugal, while Brazil and Angola had limited representation, which may affect the generalizability of the results. It is important to consider this limitation in future research, seeking a more equitable sample for a more comprehensive analysis.

In addition, future work could focus on understanding how effectively the disseminating strategies implemented reach the target audience and what repercussions not using them has. To fill the gap in the literature, it would also be useful to develop practical guidelines for implementing effective communication strategies in the context of inclusive spaces.

Acknowledgements. This work is financially supported by national funds through FCT – Foundation for Science and Technology, I.P., under the project UIDB/05460/2020.

References

1. World Health Organization. Disability. https://www.who.int/news-room/fact-sheets/detail/disability-and-health. Accessed 3 Dec 2023
2. World Health Organization: Global report on health equity for persons with disabilities, Geneva (2022)
3. Sri Ramakrishna Hospital: What are the Challenges Faced by the People with Disabilities? https://www.sriramakrishnahospital.com/blog/orthopaedics/what-are-the-challenges-faced-by-the-people-with-disabilities/. Accessed 20 Jan 2024
4. Hung, L., et al.: Creating dementia-friendly communities for social inclusion: a scoping review. Gerontol. Geriatr. Med. **7**, 1–13 (2021). https://doi.org/10.1177/23337214211013596
5. World Health Organization: World Report on Disability. Geneva (2011)
6. Isăilă, N.: Social inclusion in the context of informational society. Procedia Soc. Behav. Sci. **46**, 1006–1009 (2012). https://doi.org/10.1016/j.sbspro.2012.05.239
7. Palatna, D.: Inclusive environment: Developing integrated definition. **Вісник Київського національного університету імені Тараса Шевченка. Серія «Соціальна робота»**(5), 20–23 (2019)
8. Zhou, S.: Understanding 'Inclusiveness' in Public Space: Learning from Existing Approaches. Vancouver (2019)
9. Gray Group International. Disability Inclusion: Building an Accessible and Empathetic World. https://www.graygroupintl.com/blog/disability-inclusion. Accessed 16 Jan 2024
10. Rocha Lourenço, F., Oliveira, R., Tymoshchuk, O.: Best-practices for developing effective communication campaigns to promote assistive technology resource centres. In: ICERI Proceedings, pp. 3999–4008 (2023). https://doi.org/10.21125/iceri.2023.1003
11. Milot, É., Ruest-Paquette, A., Fortin, G., Letscher, S., Dogba, M.: Active involvement of people with disabilities in education: a literature review. Développement Humain, Handicap et Changement Social **24**(1), 95–107 (2018). https://doi.org/10.7202/1086207ar
12. Livestorm. What is Partnership Marketing and How it Can Help With Lead Generation? https://livestorm.co/blog/partnership-marketing. Accessed 18 Dec 2023
13. Godinho, F.: Internet para Necessidades Especiais. GUIA/UTAD, Vila Real (1999)
14. IEEE Connecting the Unconnected. Impact of the digital divide: economic, social, and educational consequences. https://ctu.ieee.org/impact-of-the-digital-divide-economic-social-and-educational-consequences/. Accessed 16 Jan 2024
15. Argenti, P.A., Howell, R.A., Beck, K.: The strategic communication imperative. MIT Sloan Manag. Rev. **46**(3), 83–89 (2005)

16. Kreps, G.: Addressing resistance to adopting relevant health promotion recommendations with strategic health communication. Inf. Serv. Use **43**(2), 131–142 (2023). https://doi.org/10.3233/ISU-230187
17. Kreps, G.: Disseminating relevant health information to underserved audiences: implications of the digital divide pilot projects. J. Med. Libr. Assoc. **93**(4), S68–S73 (2005)
18. Kreps, G.: Enhancing access to relevant health information. In: Carveth, R., Kretchmer, S.B., Schuler, D., (eds.) Shaping the Network Society: Patterns for Participation, Action, and Change. CPSR, Palo Alto, CA, pp. 149–152 (2002)
19. Kreps, G.: Public access to relevant cancer information: results from the health information national trends survey and implications for breast cancer education in Malaysia. In: Hashim, Z. (ed.) Proceedings of the Malaysian National Breast Cancer Education Summit. Universiti Putra Malaysia Press, Kuala Lumpor (2007)
20. Kreps, G., Viswanath, K., Harris, L.: Advancing communication as a science: research opportunities from the federal sector. J. Appl. Commun. Res. **30**(4), 369–381 (2002)
21. Melo, A., Ruão, T., Balonas, S., Alves, M., Ferreira, M.: Guia de comunicação em saúde: Boas práticas (2023). https://doi.org/10.21814/1822.78904
22. Atkin, C., Salmon, C.: Persuasive strategies in health campaigns. In: Dillard, J.P., Shen, L. (eds.) The SAGE Hand-Book of Persuasion: Developments in Theory and Practice, 2nd edn., pp. 278–295. SAGE Publications, Thousand Oaks (2013)
23. Flores, A., Meunier, J., Peacock, G.: "Include Me": implementing inclusive and accessible communication in public health. Assistive Technol. Outcomes Benefits **16**(2), 104–110 (2022)
24. Wijaya, I.: PERENCANAAN DAN STRATEGI KOMUNIKASI DALAM KEGIATAN PEMBANGUNAN **17** (2015). https://doi.org/10.21093/LJ.V17I1.428
25. Rice, R.E., Atkin, C.: Public Communication Campaigns. 4th edn. SAGE Publications, Inc., 55 City Road, London (2013). https://doi.org/10.4135/9781544308449
26. Tench, R., Gordon, G.: Developing effective health communication campaign. UMinho Editora/CECS eBooks, Leeds, United Kingdom. https://doi.org/10.21814/uminho.ed.46.4
27. Thomas, R.: Health Communication. Springer, US, Boston (2006). https://doi.org/10.1007/b136859

Big Movements or Small Motions: Controlling Digital Avatars with Single-Camera Motion Capture

Mingyang Su[1(✉)], Binlin Feng[2], Junfan Zhao[1], Haoqian Yu[1], Keyi Zeng[1], and Xiu Li[1]

[1] Tsinghua Shenzhen International Graduate School, Shenzhen, China
sumy22@mails.tsinghua.edu.cn

[2] Shenzhen University, Shenzhen, China

Abstract. Digital human avatars provide users with more natural interactions in virtual reality, games, and specific scenarios and enhance user immersion. This study explores the ways of controlling a digital human avatar and the effects of different movement amplitudes on the user experience, using a monocular motion capture technology, Mediapipe, for whole-body and hand joint information capture and digital human control. The study tested the interaction with different movement magnitudes (small, medium, and large) by designing two game tasks - simple walking and complex gesture manipulation. The results show that small-range actions are easy to control and improve ease of use in simple tasks. In contrast, medium-range actions provide a higher immersion and engagement experience in complex tasks. These findings provide new insights into designing user-friendly digital avatar interactions that can help improve user satisfaction and the quality of virtual experiences. We expect these insights to guide the development of digital incarnation technology.

Keywords: Digital Human · Avatar · Motion Capture · Video Game · User Study

1 Introduction

Digital human avatars play an increasingly important role in today's virtual worlds. Digital human avatars provide users with more natural interactions in virtual reality, games, and specific scenarios and enhance their immersion [25]. These avatars act as a bridge between the user and the virtual world and can interact with the digital world on behalf of the user, making the virtual world more prosperous and fascinating.

The key to a better digital human avatar experience for users is better controlling these avatars. Currently, research on digital avatars focuses on the optimization of modal interaction devices, such as keyboards, joysticks, and wear, able motion capture devices, to achieve more accurate control of digital avatars

A. Marcus et al. (Eds.): HCII 2024, LNCS 14714, pp. 130–148, 2024.
https://doi.org/10.1007/978-3-031-61356-2_9

Fig. 1. Walking task of park visitors (left) and interaction with King of Fighters action (right)

and better simulate the user's behavior [26,27]. However, with the continuous development of motion recognition technology, monocular motion capture technology provides new possibilities for users to control digital human avatars, which is unique in that no additional equipment is required, and the user is not constrained by the hardware medium for a more accessible control experience. However, this requires the user to operate the avatar with realistic full-body movements. This control method also brings more physiological burdens for the user to produce effects and even lead to fatigue. Therefore, an in-depth study is needed to investigate the range of movements suitable for monocular motion capture when the user controls the avatar.

Our study investigates the effects of different movement ranges on the user's experience of controlling the avatar under monocular kinematic capture. Using the monocular motion capture technology Mediapipe, we have successfully achieved accurate recognition of the user's whole body and hand joint information to capture whole body movements. In order to gain insights into the user's preference for the magnitude of movement in a monocular kinaesthetic environment, we further designed two game tasks, ranging from simple to complex, in order to encapsulate as much as possible the user's needs when controlling a digital avatar with monocular kinaesthetic.

To be clear, we defined small-range movements as those that included stepping and natural finger movements. In contrast, medium-range movements covered those that required gesture control and walking in place. On the other hand, large-range movements include movements that require more effort from the user to achieve displacement and a wide range of shoulder joint movements. This categorization helps to understand the user's preferences for different movement ranges more precisely.

We chose the most common walking task in games as the simple task, as shown in Fig. 1 left. We designed a beautiful park scene in the Unity engine, allowing the player to take on the role of a park visitor, stroll through it, and enjoy the different views. In our comparison experiments for the simple walking task, we used slight in-place padding, in-place stepping, and real walking as different movement interactions.

In the complex task, the player will take on the role of Kyo Kusanagi, one of the most iconic characters from the KOF games, as shown in Fig. 1 right. We employ Python combined with OpenCV and Mediapipe components to recognize the whole body and hand joint information and write the corresponding search and matching logic to capture the sequence of actions performed by the player. The player can release the character's skills by performing the corresponding gestures. To meet the needs of our comparative experiments, we designed different gesture magnitudes for three different ranges of movement interactions.

To evaluate our research content, we chose the NASA-TLX questionnaire to measure the player's task load. We combined it with the USE questionnaire to evaluate the player's experience with different ranges of gestures. We invited players to participate in the experiment. Through quantitative analyses, we found that in simple tasks, small-range actions are not only easy to control but also show high performance in ease of use, providing users with a natural and relaxing way of interacting, which can improve the overall quality of user experience. In contrast, medium-range actions are more advantageous in complex tasks. While these actions require more effort and body movement from the user, they provide a higher level of immersion and a more engaging experience.

The study provides new insights into how to control the interaction of digital human avatars, which can help improve user satisfaction and the quality of the virtual experience. We expect the findings of this study to provide inspiration and guidance for future development and innovation in digital avatar technology.

2 Related Work

2.1 Avatar

Virtual characters have been widely utilized in digital environments and electronic games. They are often seen as a tangible representation of personal identity [1].

The evolution of digital avatars has progressed from basic imagery to highly realistic 3D models. A digital avatar is a computer model that accurately represents the physical characteristics and features of a human [2]. It is a visual, adjustable, and controllable virtual existence [3]. The development of digital avatars has involved transitioning from basic modeling to utilizing OpenSim for precise simulation of human actions. Modern game engines such as Unity3D, Unreal Engine, and CryEngine have made it possible to create lifelike digital avatars. The goal of these technologies is to enable digital avatars to exhibit natural behavior during interactions with products and users [4].

Previous research conducted in the fields of virtual reality, electronic games, social media, and metaverses has shown that digital avatars, serving as a link between users and virtual worlds, can impact users' immersion and sense of identification through image differences and design mechanisms.

Max V. Birk et al. [5] analyzed data from 126 participants playing a customized endless runner game and found that similarity identification, embodiment identification, and wishful identification with virtual character agents can enhance autonomy, immersion, effort investment, enjoyment, and positive impact, thereby strengthening players' intrinsic motivation.

MARTIN et al. [6] Exposure Task for Social Anxiety] had participants solve math problems at a virtual store checkout, while facing observations and negative evaluations from simulated audience members in the virtual world. It was discovered that participants who customized their virtual avatars experienced a higher degree of identification, and this sense of identification significantly influenced expected fear and actual fear levels, particularly among participants with higher social anxiety.

The research by Laura et al. [7] demonstrates that similar virtual avatars can reduce social anxiety compared to different virtual images.

Furthermore, incorporating digital avatars into product design can greatly enhance product performance [8]. To achieve this goal, accurately reproducing human movements, appearance, and speech is crucial, as these features directly impact user satisfaction during interactions with digital avatars [23,24].

Hua Wang [9] developed a virtual fitting system based on the metaverse community. This system integrates parametric virtual human modeling and multi-scene, multi-action try-on functionalities. The system enables the construction of personalized virtual human models and serves as a bridge between the metaverse clothing community and the real world, showcasing dynamic fitting effects in various category scenes within the metaverse clothing community platform, thereby enhancing users' immersive experiences in a more realistic and personalized manner.

2.2 Control Technology for Digital Human Avatars

Traditionally, the control of digital avatars has relied mainly on devices such as keyboards, mice, gamepads, and touchscreens.

Currently, there is a wide variety of input devices, each with its unique characteristics and application scenarios. Numerous studies have shown that different control methods can provide users with different experiences in terms of operation precision, immersion, and other aspects for the same task. In the research field of digital avatar control technology, studies can be divided into research on different control devices and research on different control designs within the same device.

For example, Federica Pallavicini et al. [10] compared the experiences of 30 young people playing racing games using VR and desktop computers and found that the sense of immersion and flow were more significant when using VR devices. On the other hand, Masaki Oshita et al. [11] compared the performance of gamepads and touchscreens in action selection tasks in computer games and found that touchscreens outperformed or performed equally well as gamepads in certain aspects.

Furthermore, our investigation has also found that even with the same control device, different mapping methods can affect the user's immersive experience. Matthias et al. [12] pointed out in their study on virtual gamepads for smartphones that different mapping methods can affect the user's attention, operation precision, immersion, and speed, even when controlling digital avatars using smartphones.

In today's rapidly developing interactive technology, control methods for virtual avatars have also entered a new stage. Modern technologies such as virtual reality (VR), Kinect, and motion capture suits have become important tools for controlling virtual avatars. For example, Asako Soga et al. [13] developed a novel VR system that allows real-time control of dancers' movements in virtual space through input from VR devices, greatly enhancing the expressive power of body movements. On the other hand, Masaki Oshita [14] introduced a motion-capture-based third-person view VR control framework, which enables users to directly control the full-body movements of avatars in virtual environments using motion capture devices. Additionally, adopting a third-person perspective allows users to intuitively understand their own movements in the virtual environment and their interactions with other characters or objects, effectively addressing the challenges of physical interaction and virtual environment navigation.

Georges Gagneré et al. [15] explored the generation and performance of virtual characters in traditional 3D world scenes, particularly in the context of virtual "avatars" and new performance processes in theater. Through case studies, they demonstrated how digital avatars can be combined with live performers for artistic performances. These advanced control technologies provide broad creative and design possibilities for digital human virtual avatars, but as the design space expands, the impact of different mapping methods on user experience becomes a topic that urgently needs further research.

In the context of rapid advancements in computer technology and deep neural network models, computer vision has also significantly improved in terms of recognition accuracy and stability. Take Mediapipe, for example, it is a mature visual model for motion capture that can capture full-body movements and perform joint skeleton positioning using a regular camera without the need for specialized motion capture equipment. This model has demonstrated high stability and recognition accuracy in various application scenarios. For instance, Huaizhong Zhu et al. [16] used Mediapipe to recognize 21 key points of hand gestures and developed a system for recognizing English letter gestures. Additionally, Khuat Duy Bach et al. [17] proposed a sign language gesture recognition method that combines the Mediapipe hand tracking framework with a recurrent neural network (RNN). By generating training data from input videos using deep learning models and multi-hand tracking techniques, this model achieves high accuracy in recognizing common Vietnamese word gestures based on hand landmark features extracted from each frame.

The above research indicates that Mediapipe has the potential to provide control for digital human virtual avatars through whole-body skeleton positioning. However, the focus of this paper is on how to choose appropriate whole-body motion mapping schemes based on different difficulties and tasks, and to study the impact of these schemes on the usability and efficiency of control methods.

3 Concept

In the current research, many interactive games and applications gradually adopt gesture and body movement-based recognition techniques [18–20]. Such technologies usually rely on specialized recognition systems that are costly and not portable. However, with the development of motion capture technology, monocular camera-based motion capture offers new possibilities for controlling digital characters. Its distinctive feature is that users do not need additional equipment, which frees them from hardware dependence and allows them to enjoy a more accessible control experience without increasing their burden.

In this study, we designed both simple and complex tasks. For the simple task, we built a delicate park scene in the Unity engine, where the player can control the movement, position, and rotation of the digital characters in the scene by simulating the walking movement to achieve free roaming and landscape viewing in the park.

We chose the classic fighting game King of Fighters as the experimental object for the complex task. The player can control the character "Kyo Kusanagi" by waving his arm and performing a specific skill, "Orochi Nagi."

We developed a search and matching algorithm that combines Python, OpenCV, and Mediapipe tools to recognize the player's current movement sequence, including whole body and hand joint information. Through socket technology, we transmit the recognition results from the Python motion detection system to Unity, enabling the implementation of virtual character walking control for simple tasks. Since no source code is provided for King of Fighters, we use Win32API to simulate keyboard input to control the game character and perform the corresponding skills indirectly. This method of simulating keyboard input, where the simulated keyboard signals are passed through the operating system to the game program, introduces an additional processing layer and some latency. However, our tests show that the latency is still within acceptable limits.

4 Pilot Study

4.1 Task

In the experiments of this study, participants were assigned two tasks: a simple task and a complex task.

Simple Task (The walking task of park visitors). For simple tasks, we have created a virtual scenic environment for participants. This virtual park features lush plants, babbling brooks, and colorful flowers. Participants take on the role of strollers, tasked with maneuvering their characters through the three-dimensional environment along winding paths to visit three featured scenic spots in the park, as shown in Fig. 2. Each of these spots has its own unique characteristics: the first is a dense forest, the second is the central fountain, and the third is a bridge spanning the stream. Participants simply need to guide their characters to each of these three locations in sequence, "checking in" at each one to complete the task.

In the complex task, participants' avatars, specifically "Kyo Kusanagi," were placed in the battle scenes of the game "King of Fighters", as shown in Fig. 3. Participants' characters were positioned on the left side of the screen, while the robot opponent appeared on the right side. The actions of the robot opponent

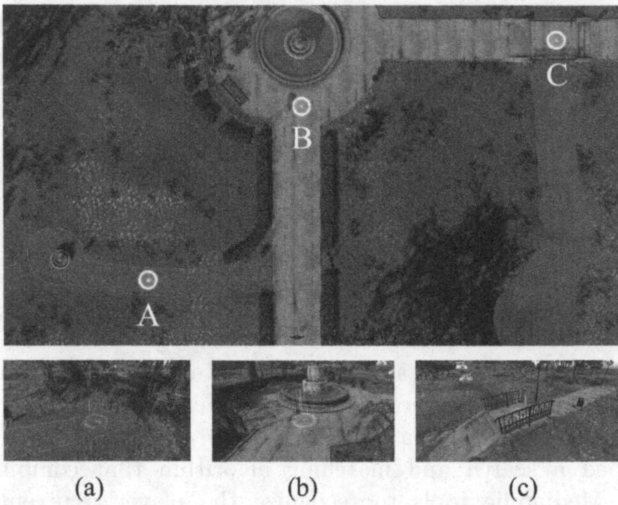

Fig. 2. Three punch points and their locations: the dense forest (a), the central fountain (b) and the bridge spanning the stream (c)

were limited to basic attack and defense moves, with a low difficulty level that posed no significant threat to the participants. This design was intended to allow participants to experience the game process fully. In the game, participants needed to use their left hand to control their character's movement, while their right hand was responsible for executing specific actions to unleash skills. Their task was to avoid the robot's attacks as much as possible and ultimately defeat its opponent. **Complex Task** (Fighting task in King of Fighters).

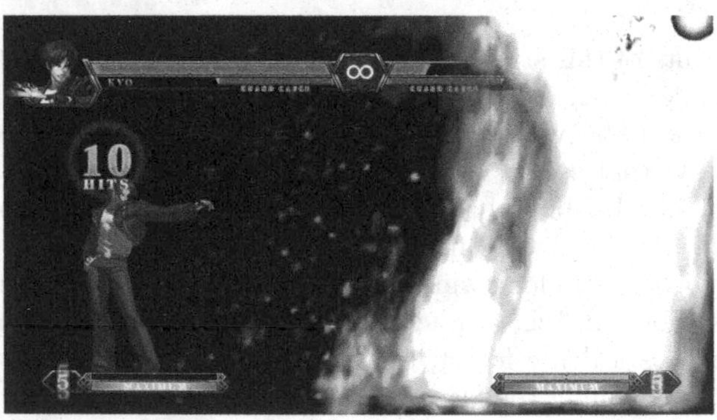

Fig. 3. The Kyo Kusanagi's Super Desperation Move

4.2 Conditions and Metrics

Various Motion Scales of Two Tasks. This study defines small-scale motion as involving small movements of the distal limbs, such as light footsteps and finger gestures. Medium-scale motion refers to activities that involve arm control and walking in place. Large-scale motion requires the user to exert more physical effort and perform larger displacements involving extensive shoulder joint movements.

In the simple task segment, participants were required to control the virtual character in the game by simulating different scales of walking motions. Small-scale motion required participants to perform slight walking and small swinging motions of the arms, with the main active joints being the ankles and wrists. Medium-scale motion required participants to walk in place, involving more significant movements of the knee and elbow joints. The large-scale motion required participants to perform more significant amplitude movements and achieve actual displacement in space, involving greater angles of movement in the lower-scale joints and significant movements of the shoulder and hip joints.

In the complex task segment, participants were required to perform different scales of motion to simulate the release of Kyo Kusanagi's skill "Orochi Nagi." Participants needed to rotate their wrists counterclockwise in small-scale motion to draw a small circle—medium-scale motion required rotating the elbow joint to perform a similar action. In large-scale motion, participants had to rotate the wrist, elbow, and entire arm continuously to draw a larger circle, thus completing the skill's release.

Metrics. This study employed subjective evaluation methods to investigate the impact of different motion scales on player interaction experience in simple and complex tasks, including the USE (Usefulness, Ease of Use, Ease of Learning, and Satisfaction) questionnaire [21] and the NASA-TLX questionnaire [22].

The USE questionnaire aims to comprehensively assess four core dimensions of usability: usefulness, ease of use, ease of learning, and satisfaction. The questionnaire consists of 30 evaluation items, validated for effectiveness and reliability in previous studies [1]. Evaluation is conducted using a seven-point rating scale based on Likert scales, ranging from "strongly disagree" to "strongly agree," to quantitatively measure the degree of agreement with each evaluation item. Higher scores reflect better performance in the corresponding dimension.

The NASA-TLX questionnaire provides a quantitative score of overall workload through the weighted average scores of six subscales: mental demand, physical demand, temporal demand, performance, effort, and frustration. The NASA-TLX is primarily used to assess the cognitive and emotional burden imposed by tasks. Each evaluation dimension uses a seven-point scale, with 21 gradations formed by increments of high, medium, and low ratings. It is worth noting that in the evaluation of performance, a score of 0 represents "perfect performance," while a score of 100 indicates "poor performance," which is contrary to the usual intuition.

4.3 Participants and Apparatus

This study recruited 12 participants from the affiliated units of the school, including six men and six women. The average age of these participants was 21.8 years old, with a standard deviation of 1.55. Importantly, before the experiment began, all participants had no experience with the game "King of Fighters" or any other motion-sensing games.

The experiment used a Lenovo ThinkBook 14 laptop as the program running platform. The device was equipped with a Windows 10 operating system and a 2-megapixel front-facing camera to capture the participants' movements. The input devices included a membrane keyboard with an essential travel of 1.3 mm and an external HPS300 wired mouse; both kept at factory settings. The experimental space was a $2 \times 4 \times 2$ cubic meter area with a standard computer desk. The laptop was placed on an adjustable stand. It calibrated the participants' activity range within the experimental area using colored transparent tape to ensure the camera could capture their whole body. For complex tasks, the King of Fighters 13 version on the Steam platform was selected, while for simple tasks, a self-made park-visiting game based on Unity 2021.3.11f1c1 editor was used.

To collect the participants' subjective feedback, the NASA-TLX and USE questionnaires were used and filled out on another computer via electronic spreadsheets. After completing the questionnaires, the results were analyzed in-depth through interviews to explore the reasons behind them.

4.4 Procedure

In the initial phase of this study, participants were thoroughly introduced to the overall design of the experiment. They had to sign an informed consent form to confirm their understanding and agreement with the experimental content. Subsequently, we collected and organized basic information from the participants. Based on this, we elaborated on the specific procedures and tasks of the two experiments. We addressed any questions raised by the participants to ensure their clear understanding of the specific standards and considerations for task completion. Participants were then guided into the experimental environment and instructed to stand within a designated area marked with colored tape. To ensure the accuracy of the experiment, we adjusted the height of the computer stand according to each participant's height to ensure that the laptop's camera could fully capture their entire body.

The experiment began with simple tasks. Prior to the execution of each task, participants were given 5 min to learn and understand the task. We assisted participants in mastering the experimental rules and becoming familiar with the environment by reading the control rules and on-site demonstrations. Once the participants were ready, we initiated the motion capture system implemented through the Mediapipe framework using the Python programming language. We started the park viewing program after confirming that the video system could fully capture the participants' full-body movements. We established a socket connection to the Python-side socket server. In this phase, we conducted ten repetitions of experiments for the small, medium, and significant action dimensions, respectively, and provided participants with 30 s of rest time after each experiment.

Following the completion of each experiment for each action dimension, participants were given 1 min of rest time. Subsequently, participants filled out the NASA-TLX questionnaire on another computer to assess their mental workload during the task execution. Participants also completed the User Satisfaction Evaluation (USE) questionnaire to evaluate their user experience.

After completing the experiments for the simple tasks, we conducted brief semi-structured interviews with the participants to obtain qualitative feedback about their experiences. Subsequently, participants were allowed a 5-min break before commencing the experiments for complex tasks, the procedure of which was similar to that of the simple task experiments.

5 Results

5.1 Simple Task: Walking

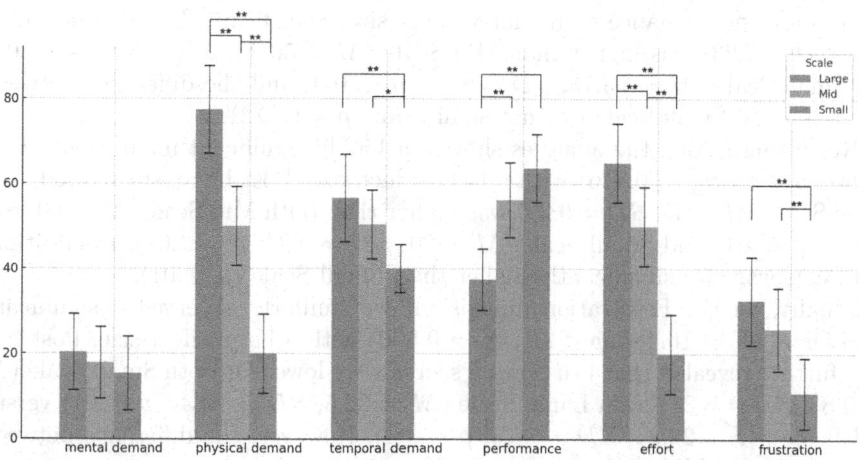

Fig. 4. In the Simple Task, subjects rated the NASA-TLX questionnaire, the Mean (SD) of Mental Demand, Physical Demand, Temporal Demand, Performance, Effort, and Frustration rated in the NASA-TLX questionnaire under six different companionship. Higher scores indicate a higher burden on the corresponding dimension. In particular, in Performance, a score of 0 means "perfect", while a score of 100 means "failure". The error bars denote standard deviation, $*$ and $**$ significant differences at $p < 0.05$, and $p < 0.01$ levels respectively.

NASA-TLX. As shown in Fig. 4, we first analyzed the effect of different Scales on users in terms of Mental Demand; Scale had no significant effect on it, showing consistency ($F = 1.003$, $p = 0.378$, $\eta_p^2 = 0.057$).

We first analyzed the effect of different Scales on users in the Physical Demands dimension. On the Physical Demand dimension, we observed a significant main effect by questionnaire ($F = 106.512$, $p < .01$, $\eta_p^2 = 0.866$) with a large effect size. Post hoc tests indicated that participants had significantly lower Physical Demand in the Mid Scale ($M = 50$, $SD = 9.29$, $p < .01$) and Small Scale ($M = 20$, $SD = 9.29$, $p < .01$) conditions compared to the Large Scale ($M = 77.5$, $SD = 10.34$). In addition, Physical Demand was also significantly higher for Mid Scale than Small Scale ($p < .01$).

Next, we analyzed the effect of different Scales on users regarding Temporal Demand. Analyses on the Temporal Demand dimension revealed a significant main effect ($F = 12.535$, $p < .01$, $\eta_p^2 = 0.432$), indicating a medium effect size. Post hoc tests revealed that on Temporal Demand, Small Scale ($M = 40$, $SD = 5.64$) was significantly lower than Large Scale ($M = 56.67$, $SD = 10.30$, $p < .01$) vs. Mid Scale ($M = 50.42$, $SD = 8.11$, $p < .5$). However, the difference between Large Scale and Mid Scale was not significant ($p = 0.167$).

We also observed a significant main effect on the Performance dimension ($F = 33.868$, $p < .01$, $\eta_p^2 = 0.672$), suggesting that the difference in Scale significantly affected user performance with a large effect size. Specifically, Large Scale ($M = 37.5$, $SD = 7.23$) was higher than Mid Scale ($M = 56.25$, $SD = 8.82$, $p < .01$) and Small Scale ($M = 63.75$, $SD = 8.01$, $p < .01$), and the difference between Mid Scale and Small Scale was not significant ($p = 0.072$).

Regarding Effort, the analyses showed a highly significant main effect ($F = 72.947$, $p < .01$, $\eta_p^2 = 0.816$) with a large effect size. Post hoc tests showed that Large Scale ($M = 65$, $SD = 9.29$) was higher than both Mid Scale ($M = 50$, $SD = 9.29$, $p < .01$) and Small Scale ($M = 20$, $SD = 9.29$, $p =< .01$). In addition, Mid Scale was also significantly higher than Small Scale ($p < .01$).

Finally, on the Frustration dimension, we similarly observed a significant main effect ($F = 16.485$, $p < .01$, $\eta_p^2 = 0.500$) with a large effect size. Post hoc tests further revealed that Frustration scores were lower for both Small Scale ($M = 10.83$, $SD = 8.21$) than Large Scale ($M = 32.5$, $SD = 10.34$, $p < .01$) versus Mid Scale ($M = 25.83$, $SD = 9.73$, $p < .01$). However, the difference between Large Scale and Mid Scale was not significant.

There were significant differences in Frustration scores between Small Scale ($M = 10.83$, $SD = 8.21$, $p = .0010$) and between Mid Scale ($M = 25.83$, $SD = 9.73$) and Small Scale ($p = .0013$), indicating that in the Small Scale condition ($p = 0.211$).

USE. As shown in Fig. 5, we found that the Scale showed consistency and no difference in Usefulness ($F = 1.739$, $p = 0.191$, $\eta_p^2 = 0.095$) and Ease of Learning ($F = 0.402$, $p = 0.672$, $\eta_p^2 = 0.024$).

For Ease of Use, on the other hand, we observed a significant main effect ($F = 4.004$, $p < .05$, $\eta_p^2 = 0.195$) with a small effect size. Post hoc tests showed that

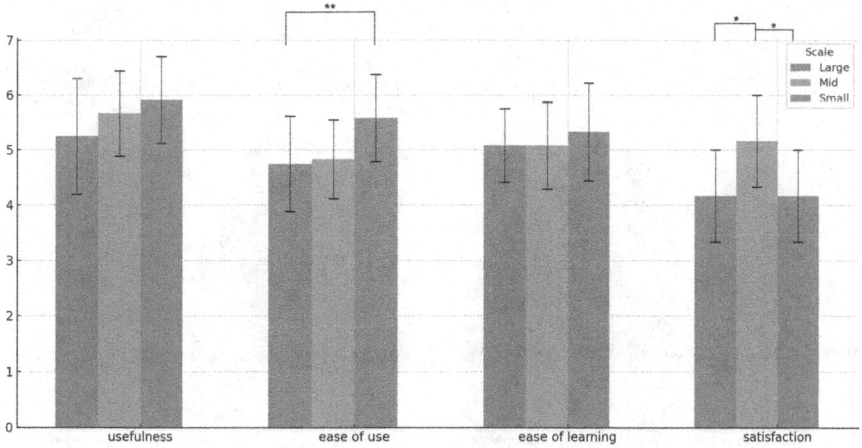

Fig. 5. In the Simple Task, subjects rated the USE questionnaire, the Mean (SD) of Usefulness, Ease of use, Ease of learning, and Satisfaction rated in the NASA-TLX questionnaire under six different companionship. Higher scores show greater recognition of the corresponding dimensions by the subjects. The error bars denote standard deviation, $*$ and $**$ significant differences at $p < 0.05$, and $p < 0.01$ levels respectively.

Large Scale ($M = 4.75$, $SD = 0.87$) scores were lower than Small Scale ($M = 5.58$, $SD = 0.79$, $p < .05$). While the differences between Large Scale and Mid Scale ($M = 4.83$, $SD = 0.72$, $p = 0.90$) and Mid Scale and Small Scale ($p = 0.068$) were not significant.

Finally, we analyzed the effect of different Scales on user satisfaction and observed a significant main effect on satisfaction ($F = 5.739$, $p < .01$, $\eta_p^2 = 0.258$), indicating a medium effect size. Post hoc tests showed that Mid Scale ($M = 5.17$, $SD = 0.83$) was rated higher than Small Scale ($M = 4.17$, $SD = 0.83$, $p < .05$) and Large Scale ($M = 4.17$, $SD = 0.83$, $p < .05$). And there was no significant difference between Large Scale and Small Scale ($p = .90$).

5.2 Complex Missions: Combat

NASA-TLX. As shown in Fig. 6, in analyzing the Complex Task data, we first examined the effect of different Scales on the user's Mental Demand. scale had a non-significant effect ($F = 1.913$, $p = 0.164$, $\eta_p^2 = 0.104$), showing consistency.

Next, we analyzed the impact of Physical Demand. On this dimension, we observed a significant main effect ($F = 66.848$, $p < .01$, $\eta_p^2 = 0.802$) with a large effect size. Post hoc tests showed that Physical Demand was significantly higher in the Large Scale ($M = 88.33$, $SD = 6.51$) than in the Mid Scale ($M = 72.50$, $SD = 8.39$, $p < .01$) and Small Scale ($M = 52.92$, $SD = 7.53$, $p < .01$), and the Mid Scale was also significantly higher than between Small Scale ($p < .01$).

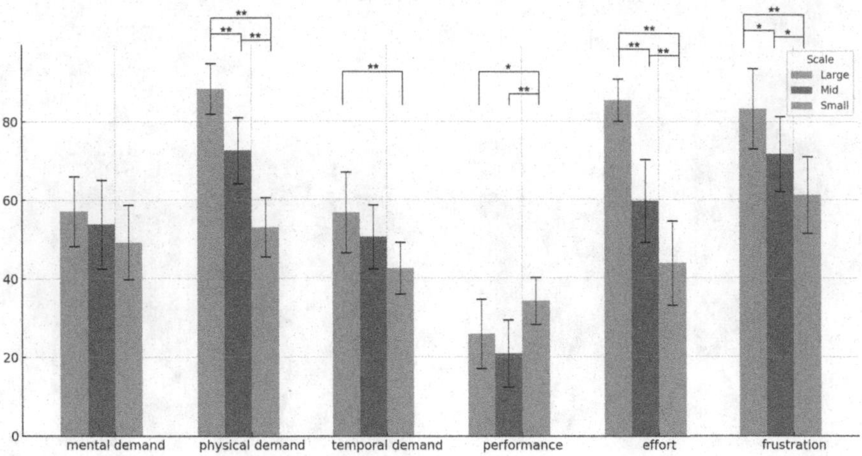

Fig. 6. In the Complex Task, subjects rated the NASA-TLX questionnaire, the Mean (SD) of Mental Demand, Physical Demand, Temporal Demand, Performance, Effort, and Frustration rated in the NASA-TLX questionnaire under six different companionship. Higher scores indicate a higher burden on the corresponding dimension. In particular, in Performance, a score of 0 means "perfect", while a score of 100 means "failure". The error bars denote standard deviation, $*$ and $**$ significant differences at $p < 0.05$, and $p < 0.01$ levels respectively.

Regarding Temporal Demand, analyses revealed a significant main effect ($F = 8.441$, $p < .01$, $\eta_p^2 = 0.338$) with a medium effect size. Our further post-hoc tests revealed that Temporal Demand was significantly higher for Large Scale ($M = 56.67$, $SD = 10.30$) than Small Scale ($M = 42.50$, $SD = 6.57$, $p < .01$), whereas for Large versus Mid Scale ($M = 50.42$, $SD = 8.11$, $p = 0.182$), the difference between Mid and Small Scale was not significant ($p = 0.071$).

On the Performance dimension, we similarly observed a significant main effect ($F = 8.872, p < .01, \eta_p^2 = 0.350$) with a medium effect size. Post hoc tests showed that Performance was lower for Small Scale ($M = 34.17$, $SD = 5.97$) than for Large Scale ($M = 25.83$, $SD = 8.75$, $p < .05$) and Mid Scale ($M = 20.83$, $SD = 8.48$, $p < .01$), whereas Large and Mid Scale ($M = 20.83$, $SD = 8.48$, $p = 0.276$) were not significant. Again, it is emphasized that lower Performance in the NASA-TLX questionnaire represents more success.

The scale had a significant main effect on Effort ($F = 62.516$, $p < .01$, $\eta_p^2 = 0.791$) with a large effect size. Our further post hoc test analyses found that Effort was significantly higher for Large Scale ($M = 85.42$, $SD = 5.42$) than Mid Scale ($M = 59.58$, $SD = 10.54$, $p < .01$) and Small Scale ($M = 43.75$, $SD = 10.69$, $p < .01$), and that Mid Scale's Effort was also significantly higher than Small Scale ($p < .01$).

Finally, we found that different Scales showed significant differences in Frustration ($F = 14.919$, $p < .01$, $\eta_p^2 = 0.475$). Post hoc tests showed that Large Scale ($M = 83.33$, $SD = 10.30$) was higher than Mid Scale ($M = 71.67$,

$SD = 9.61$, $p < .05$), Mid Scale was higher than Small Scale ($M = 61.25$, $SD = 9.80$, $p < .05$), corresponding to Large Scale being significantly higher than Small Scale ($p < .01$).

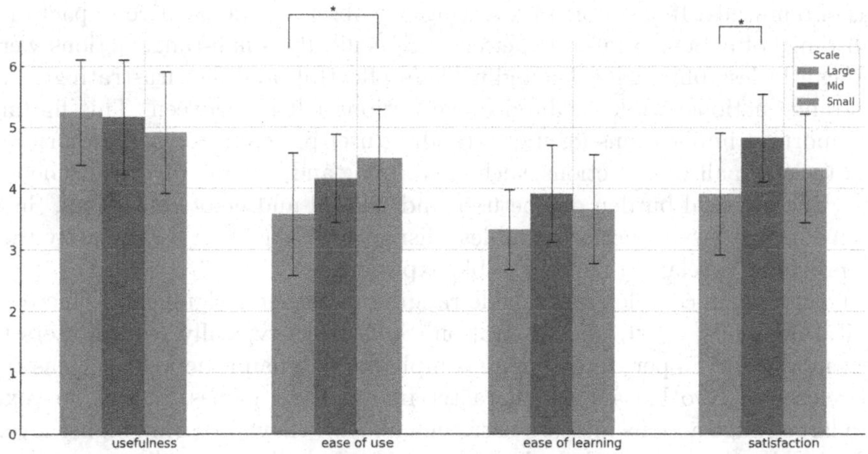

Fig. 7. In the Complex Task, subjects rated the USE questionnaire, the Mean (SD) of Usefulness, Ease of use, Ease of learning, and Satisfaction rated in the NASA-TLX questionnaire under six different companionship. Higher scores show greater recognition of the corresponding dimensions by the subjects. The error bars denote standard deviation, $*$ and $**$ significant differences at $p < 0.05$, and $p < 0.01$ levels respectively.

USE. As shown in Fig. 7, the effect of Scale on both the Usefulness and Ease of Learning dimensions was not significant, showing consistency, respectively, for Usefulness ($F = 0.413$, $p = 0.665$, $\eta_p^2 = 0.024$) and Ease of Learning ($F = 1.675$, $p = 0.203$, $\eta_p^2 = 0.092$).

For Ease of Use, we observed a significant main effect ($F = 3.615$, $p < .05$, $\eta_p^2 = 0.180$) with a small effect size. Post hoc tests showed higher ratings with Small Scale ($M = 4.50$, $SD = 0.80$) than Large Scale ($M = 3.58$, $SD = 1.00$, $p < .05$). Whereas the differences between Large Scale and Mid Scale ($M = 4.17$, $SD = 0.72$, $p = 0.224$) and Mid Scale and Small Scale ($p = 0.597$) were not significant.

Finally, the Scale showed significance for Satisfaction ($F = 3.304$, $p < .05$, $\eta_p^2 = 0.167$). Further post-hoc test analyses yielded that Large Scale ($M = 3.92$, $SD = 1.00$) was rated lower than Mid Scale ($M = 4.83$, $SD = 0.72$, $p < .05$), whereas the difference between Large Scale and Small Scale ($M = 4.33$, $SD = 0.89$, $p = 0.483$) and Mid Scale and Small Scale ($p = 0.353$) were not significant.

6 Discussion

6.1 User Experience and Magnitude of Motion

The relationship between user experience and action magnitude became a key focus of our study. In a simple task setting, we observed the positive impact of a small range of actions on user experience. Specifically, small-range actions were significantly less physically demanding, less effortful, and less frustrating than large-range actions, while medium-range actions fell in between. This finding has important implications for understanding user preferences when performing easier tasks. Small-range actions, such as stepping and natural finger movements, reduce the physical burden on the user and mental and emotional stress. Such movements are easy to perform and less disruptive to the user's daily activities, thus providing a relaxing and enjoyable experience.

In contrast, in complex tasks, wide-ranging movements significantly increase physical demands, effort, and frustration. Such tasks typically require users to invest more effort in performing more complex and dynamic actions, such as the skill release of Kyo Kusanagi's character in the KOF games. In this context, while large-range actions increase user engagement, they also bring higher levels of physical burden and psychological frustration. In addition, medium-range and small-range actions performed better in user experience in complex tasks, probably because they reduced the user's physical and psychological burden while keeping the interaction rich and challenging.

6.2 Performance and Efficiency

In the simple task scenarios, our findings suggest that a large range of actions performs lower than the medium and small range of actions. This result may reflect that in more relaxed and natural environments, users are more likely to control and perform small- and medium-range actions, making them feel more relaxed. For example, small padding or stepping in simple tasks drastically reduces their physical demands and completes the corresponding task at a smaller cost. As a result, they performed better in terms of efficiency and accuracy of execution. However, the difference in performance between medium and small ranges of motion was insignificant, which may mean that in simple tasks, medium ranges of motion provide an equally efficient and natural experience.

Small range movements performed lower than medium- and large-range movements in complex tasks. This phenomenon reveals that larger range movements may be more appropriate in more complex and precision-demanding tasks. For example, in Kyo Kusanagi role-playing, the user must perform a series of specific gestures and movements to release a skill. These actions often require a large range and precise control, so large- and medium-range actions may be more efficient in such complex tasks.

6.3 Ease of Use and Satisfaction

Regarding ease of use, our study found that small-range and medium-range movements performed better in simple tasks. This result emphasizes that in tasks that do not require highly complex and precise movements, users prefer to use a small range of movements that are easy to control and perform. These actions are not only more natural and consistent with everyday habits. However, they are also more intuitive and simpler to use, thus providing a better ease-of-use experience for the user. For example, in walking in the park, the character can easily achieve small-range actions such as padding or slight stepping and are more in line with the user's daily behavioral patterns.

However, in the complex task, ease of use did not differ significantly between different action ranges. This may be because complex tasks inherently require a higher degree of concentration and skill, and users need to invest in a similar learning and adaptation process, whether for small, medium, or large range of movements. In this case, ease of use depends more on the user's proficiency and personal preference for the particular type of movement than on the magnitude of the movement itself.

Regarding satisfaction, our findings suggest that mid-range actions received the highest ratings regarding user satisfaction in simple tasks. This may be because mid-range movements provide a comfortable and natural experience while giving the user a degree of involvement and control. Users may feel that such movements are neither overly effortful nor overly passive, thus enjoying a relaxing gaming experience while remaining moderately engaged.

In complex tasks, satisfaction was higher for medium and large-range actions than for small-range actions. This may reflect that a larger range of movements can bring a stronger sense of immersion and achievement when performing game tasks with more complex skills and movements. For example, in the role of Kyo Kusanagi, executing a complex series of large-range gestures and movements may make players feel more excited and engaged, thus increasing overall satisfaction with the game.

6.4 Findings

This study delves into the specific effects of different movement ranges on user experience. The results show that in austere task environments, small-range actions excel in reducing body burden, lowering effort, and alleviating frustration while demonstrating advantages in ease of use. In contrast, medium- to large-range actions prevail in performance, user satisfaction, and ease of use in complex tasks. These findings provide important insights into the design of virtual reality games and applications, especially critical when considering how to balance task challenges with user comfort appropriately.

For future virtual reality interaction design, we suggest deeper consideration of the characteristics of the task itself and the target user group it is intended to serve. When designing virtual reality applications intended to provide a relaxed and enjoyable experience, it is more appropriate to choose a small range of movements that provide a low-stress and natural interaction. For applications that require a high degree of user involvement and skill, medium to large range of movements may be more appropriate as they enhance the user's involvement and immersion. By taking these factors into account, we can better create virtual reality experiences that meet the needs and expectations of our users.

7 Conclusion

This study aims to investigate the impact of controlling digital human avatars at various scales on the user experience. To this end, we chose monocular motion capture to implement the control of digital human avatars. We developed digital human control tasks based on Unity and Python environments for different scenarios.

By inviting participants to conduct experimental studies, we found that in simple tasks, the small range of movements is not only easy to control but also shows high performance in terms of ease of use, providing users with a natural and easy way of interaction, which can improve the overall quality of user experience. In contrast, medium-range actions are more advantageous in complex tasks. While these actions require more effort and physical movement on the user's part, they provide a higher level of immersion and a more engaging experience.

This critical finding provides new perspectives on designing more user-friendly interactions with digital avatars, emphasizing the need to consider the task's complexity and the user's needs and preferences when designing virtual reality interactions. It also helps to improve user satisfaction and the overall quality of the virtual experience. We expect the findings of this study to provide inspiration and guidance for the future development and innovation of digital incarnation technology.

References

1. Ducheneaut, N., Wen, M., Yee, N., Wadley, G.: Body and mind: a study of avatar personalization in three virtual worlds. In: Proceedings of the SIGCHI Conference on Human Factors in Computing Systems, pp. 1151–1160 (2009). https://doi.org/10.1145/1518701.1518877
2. Chihara, T., Fukuchi, N., Seo, A.: Optimal product design method with digital human modeling for physical workload reduction: a case study illustrating its application to handrail position design. Jpn. J. Ergon. **53**, 25–35 (2017)
3. Zhong, S.: Digital human-a new research field combined information and life science. Sci. Technol. Rev. **23**, 9–12 (2005)
4. Reed, M., Faraway, J., Chaffin, D., Martin, B.: The HUMOSIM ergonomics framework: a new approach to digital human simulation for ergonomic analysis. SAE Technical Paper (2006)
5. Birk, M., Atkins, C., Bowey, J., Mandryk, R.: Fostering intrinsic motivation through avatar identification in digital games. In: Proceedings of the 2016 CHI Conference on Human Factors in Computing Systems, pp. 2982–2995 (2016)

6. Dechant, M., Birk, M., Shiban, Y., Schnell, K., Mandryk, R.: How avatar customization affects fear in a game-based digital exposure task for social anxiety. Proc. ACM Hum.-Comput. Interact. **5**, 1–27 (2021)
7. Aymerich-Franch, L., Kizilcec, R., Bailenson, J.: The relationship between virtual self similarity and social anxiety. Front. Hum. Neurosci. **8**, 944 (2014)
8. Scataglini, S., Danckaers, F., Huysmans, T., Sijbers, J., Andreoni, G.: Design smart clothing using digital human models. DHM Posturography, 683–698 (2019)
9. Wang, H., Liu, X., Jiang, M., Zhou, C.: Garment metaverse: parametric digital human and dynamic scene try-on. In: Proceedings of the 2023 2nd Asia Conference on Algorithms, Computing and Machine Learning, pp. 60–65 (2023)
10. Pallavicini, F., Pepe, A.: Comparing player experience in video games played in virtual reality or on desktop displays: immersion, flow, and positive emotions. In: Extended Abstracts of the Annual Symposium on Computer-Human Interaction in Play Companion Extended Abstracts, pp. 195–210 (2019)
11. Oshita, M., Ishikawa, H.: Gamepad vs. touchscreen: a comparison of action selection interfaces in computer games. In: Proceedings of the Workshop at SIGGRAPH Asia, pp. 27–31 (2012)
12. Baldauf, M., Fröhlich, P., Adegeye, F., Suette, S.: Investigating on-screen gamepad designs for smartphone-controlled video games. ACM Trans. Multimedia Comput. Commun. Appl. (TOMM) **12**, 1–21 (2015)
13. Soga, A., Matsushita, T.: Movement creation by choreographers with a partially self-controllable human body in VR. In: Proceedings of the 29th ACM Symposium on Virtual Reality Software and Technology, pp. 1–2 (2023)
14. Oshita, M.: Motion-capture-based avatar control framework in third-person view virtual environments. In: Proceedings of the 2006 ACM SIGCHI International Conference on Advances in Computer Entertainment Technology, pp. 2–es (2006)
15. Gagneré, G., Lavender, A., Plessiet, C., White, T.: Challenges of movement quality using motion capture in theatre. In: Proceedings of the 5th International Conference on Movement and Computing, pp. 1–6 (2018)
16. Zhu, H., Deng, C., Zhu, Y.: MediaPipe based gesture recognition system for English letters. In: Proceedings of the 2022 11th International Conference on Networks, Communication and Computing, pp. 24–30 (2022)
17. Duy Khuat, B., Thai Phung, D., Thi Thu Pham, H., Ngoc Bui, A., Tung Ngo, S.: Vietnamese sign language detection using Mediapipe. In: 2021 10th International Conference on Software and Computer Applications, pp. 162–165 (2021)
18. Dalsgaard, T., Knibbe, J., Bergström, J.: Modeling pointing for 3D target selection in VR. In: Proceedings of the 27th ACM Symposium on Virtual Reality Software and Technology, pp. 1–10 (2021)
19. Gusmao Lafayette, T., et al.: The virtual Kinect. In: Symposium on Virtual and Augmented Reality, pp. 111–119 (2021)
20. Jiang, F., Zhang, S., Wu, S., Gao, Y., Zhao, D.: Multi-layered gesture recognition with Kinect. J. Mach. Learn. Res. **16**, 227–254 (2015)
21. Gao, M., Kortum, P., Oswald, F.: Psychometric evaluation of the use (usefulness, satisfaction, and ease of use) questionnaire for reliability and validity. Proc. Hum. Fact. Ergon. Soc. Ann. Meet. **62**, 1414–1418 (2018)
22. Hart, S.: NASA-task load index (NASA-TLX); 20 years later. Proc. Hum. Fact. Ergon. Soc. Ann. Meet. **50**, 904–908 (2006)
23. Jia, J., Chung, N., Hwang, J.: Assessing the hotel service robot interaction on tourists' behaviour: the role of anthropomorphism. Ind. Manag. Data Syst. **121**, 1457–1478 (2021)

24. Lu, L., Zhang, P., Zhang, T.: Leveraging "human-likeness" of robotic service at restaurants. Int. J. Hospitality Manag. **94**, 102823 (2021)
25. Sung, E., Han, D., Bae, S., Kwon, O.: What drives technology-enhanced storytelling immersion? The role of digital humans (2022). https://www.sciencedirect.com/science/article/pii/S0747563222000681
26. Tung, Y., et al.: User-defined game input for smart glasses in public space. In: Proceedings of the 33rd Annual ACM Conference on Human Factors in Computing Systems, pp. 3327–3336 (2015). https://doi.org/10.1145/2702123.2702214
27. Abramson, J., et al.: Evaluating Multimodal Interactive Agents (2022)

Functional Effectiveness and User Experience Assessment of Knee Joint Protective Gear Fixation Methods During Physical Activity

Jiayi Tan[1], Xiaoyan Zhu[1], Xiudi Wang[4], Ao Jiang[2,3](✉), Chao Gong[1](✉), Xuechun Jing[1], Moru Fang[1], and Yueyi Wang[1]

[1] Beijing Institute of Technology, Beijing, China
gongc_0@126.com
[2] Nanjing University of Aeronautics and Astronautics, Nanjing, China
ao.jiang23@imperial.ac.uk
[3] Imperial College London, London, UK
[4] Anhui University, Hefei, Anhui, China

Abstract. With the increasing awareness of people's protection during physical activities, the sports sector is gradually moving towards a more diverse and health-oriented development. This trend has propelled the growth of the market for joint protective gear and innovation in gear design. Currently, existing designs for knee joint protection focus on improving the functionality of protective devices but neglect considerations for the user's wearing method and the real experience during actual use. Therefore, this study is based on four common fixation methods for knee joint protective gear (X-shaped patellar strap, double-layer double-sided fixed-open knee protector, double-layer bottom-fixed open knee protector, single-layer magic tape fixed-open knee protector). We measured aspects such as sports restraint, stability, and ease of operation over a certain period, considering the amount of physical activity, knee protector displacement distance, and wearing time. We conducted practical tests with 54 user samples. Through the analysis of objective quantitative data and the combination with subjective qualitative data from users, we believe that the wearing method of the single-layer magic tape fixed-open knee protector provides better sports restraint and stability, and users have a better wearing experience. There is a certain structural-functional relationship between the objective structure of this knee joint protector and human motion data and wearing experience. Furthermore, the initial impression that the product's appearance leaves on users significantly affects their wearing experience. Based on this, the protective gear in this study can provide effective support and protection for the knee joint, offering users a safer and more comfortable sports experience. In addition, the research findings provide design references for the optimization of various wearable/protective devices for joints.

Keywords: Knee Joint Protective Gear · Fastening Methods · Human Movement · Experience Assessment

A. Marcus et al. (Eds.): HCII 2024, LNCS 14714, pp. 149–164, 2024.
https://doi.org/10.1007/978-3-031-61356-2_10

1 Introduction

Knee joint protective products are expected to gain more popularity and dominate the main market for sports protective gear. In sports, the knee joint is a commonly injured area, and with the widespread adoption of the concept of universal sports, people are paying increasing attention to the protection against sports injuries. There is a growing awareness and interest in products related to sports protective gear. Currently, knee protector products with therapeutic and protective functions are widely diverse, primarily falling into several categories: (i) detachable knee braces (used for knee osteoarthritis, providing pain relief and improving functionality), (ii) preventive knee braces (used to protect healthy knee joints from injuries during physical activities), (iii) patellar knee braces (used for anterior knee pain), and (iv) functional knee braces (used to provide stability to unstable knee joints during ligament injuries, such as anterior cruciate ligament tears or ACL reconstruction). Various protective gear options currently offer users a range of joint protection, but there is a need for further optimization in performance and user experience to meet the evolving demands for better protective gear in the future.

So far, research on protective gear products has focused on improving their protective performance and other functionalities. McNair et al. (1996) tested 20 subjects with an average age of 28, recording knee joint angle and force data using a Kin-Com dynamometer during various movements [1]. They analyzed the differences between active and passive limb data and explored the impact of knee joint sleeves on proprioception during normal knee joint dynamic tracking tasks, demonstrating that changes in proprioception caused by knee joint braces may be a major factor in improving knee joint function. Subsequently, Johann et al. (2009) clinically investigated the therapeutic effects of knee joint braces on conditions such as knee joint arthritis and ligament defects from medical and biomechanical perspectives [2]. They proved the effectiveness of braces, knee sleeves, and detachable knee braces in treating knee joint osteoarthritis, standardizing clinical practices for their use. In recent years, Nallavan et al. (2020) explored the role of preventive knee braces made from novel negative Poisson's ratio materials in sports and proposed possible production and improvement strategies [3]. This indicates that the user base for knee joint protective gear is extensive, the functions are diverse, and it is closely related to user health and comfort, making in-depth research on knee joint protective gear design essential. There has been relatively less research focused on the wearable experience of existing related products.

Furthermore, some of the existing research on the wearing experience of knee protectors primarily addresses comfort during wear, with very few cases focusing on the research related to motion restrictions during the wearing experience. Examples include: The American Academy of Orthopedic Surgeons and the American Academy of Pediatrics (1997) explicitly stated in their position statement that there is a lack of evidence for the effectiveness of preventive knee products in reducing the incidence or severity of joint ligament injuries [4]. Additionally, there is evidence suggesting that these products may slow down athletes and inhibit their performance. Shao Yangyang et al. (2022) conducted tests on 15 male health subjects with an average age of around 25 who were passionate about running [5]. They used the Vicon 3D optical motion capture system and AMTI biomechanical force platform to test the range of motion of the subjects' knees, ankles, and hip joints in the sagittal, coronal, and horizontal planes. The focus was on observing the range of motion of the knee joint to assess the fixation effect of knee protectors on the knee joint. The study concluded that wearing knee protectors significantly restricted the flexion and extension range of motion of the knee joint, as well as the range of internal and external rotation, subsequently affecting the motion of the other two joints. The study also found that open-type knee protectors might have adverse effects on the ankle joint and reduce the flexion and extension range of motion of the hip joint. Wearing sleeve-type knee protectors provided some protection to the ankle joint but limited the movement of the hip joint. This type of research lacks subjective user evaluations in the experiments and has not yet compared the same functional attributes of similar products. To advance and improve the development of protective gear, it is essential to comprehensively consider different aspects of gear performance, such as motion stability and wearability, along with corresponding user feedback for optimization and design improvements to meet market demands.

Thus, the assessment dimensions of knee joint protective products, such as motion stability, fixation methods, and wearability, should be considered in the optimization and design of protective gear, taking into account users' subjective experiences. In the future, users' expectations for the user experience of knee protector products will not only focus on good functionality but will also extend to other aspects, such as motion restrictions and wearability. Simultaneously, wearable devices derived from medical, military, disaster relief, and entertainment industries will demand more comprehensive and high-quality designs for knee joint protective gear. Therefore, this study will extract main forms and wearing methods from various knee protector products available in the market, create research samples, design controlled experiments, and compare the wearing effects of different wearing methods. Through a combination of subjective user feedback and measured data, qualitative and quantitative analyses will be conducted. The study aims to identify a sample with significant overall superiority in wearing method and evaluate the functional strengths and weaknesses of different types of knee protectors in terms of motion restraint, stability, and ease of operation. This research will serve as a reference for the optimization design direction of knee protector products and related wearable devices.

2 Method

2.1 Selection of Experimental Test Samples

This experiment selected 56 individuals as user samples for practical use testing, evenly divided into 4 groups with 7 men and 7 women in each group. The male age group was 18–35 years, with an average age of approximately 22.35 years; height ranged from 165.00 to 185.00 cm, with an average height of 173.21 cm; weight ranged from 60.00 to 80.50 kg, with an average weight of 73.31 kg. The female age group was 18–30 years, with an average age of approximately 20.34 years; height ranged from 160.00 to 178.50 cm, with an average height of 164.54 cm; weight ranged from 45.00 to 62.00 kg, with an average weight of 56.55 kg. All test sample users were clearly informed of the experimental process, possessed normal physical capabilities, and were determined to be able to wear the test product samples used in this experiment through preliminary testing.

2.2 Analysis of Existing Wearing Methods Characteristics

There is a wide variety of wearable products for joints, widely used in fields such as protection, correction, and medical rehabilitation. Due to different functional requirements, they adopt different wearing methods. To gain a deeper understanding of the characteristics of these methods, this study selected commonly used magic tape fixation methods in the market and conducted a preliminary investigation and analysis of four different wearing methods, as detailed in Table 1.

2.3 Sample Material and Production Method

1. Materials: In this experiment, we used 200 g and 90 g polypropylene spunbond nonwoven fabric, hook and loop fasteners (nylon), cotton thread, etc., as the materials for producing the test samples. Polypropylene spunbond nonwoven fabric is lightweight, breathable, easy to obtain, and easy to process. Through preliminary experiments, it was determined that the selected specifications of the two nonwoven fabrics, under the equivalent impulse conditions to the typical force applied during regular user movements in this study, did not experience issues such as breakage or tearing. They exhibited minor plastic deformation, allowing us to largely eliminate the influence of the material's inherent elasticity on the results of this study. The choice of hook and loop fasteners as a fixation method will facilitate repeated testing and usage of the samples, thereby expediting the experimental process based on the favorable testing experience for users participating in the experiment.
2. Production Method: Referring to existing products on the market and considering the wearing methods of this type of product, we extracted elements and redesigned the samples. The test samples were handcrafted by cutting the 90 g polypropylene spunbond nonwoven fabric into redesigned wearable pieces to be stitched. The samples were hand-sewn using cotton thread, ensuring that the seam width remained at 8 mm ($\pm$2 mm). Each sample had a similar wearable size and structure. The fixation strap portion used a single layer of 200 g polypropylene spunbond nonwoven fabric folded to increase strength, with a hook and loop fastener fixed at the end. The plan view of the sample is shown in Table 1. The sample connection parts adopted four common wearing methods, as detailed in Fig. 1.

2.4 Experimental Conditions

The testing time for this experiment is flexible, allowing users to choose independently. Sample users must ensure normal physical capabilities, wear clothing that does not affect sample wear, and maintain the integrity of the test during the chosen testing period. Each test session is controlled within a time frame of 4–10 min. The testing location is fixed, utilizing a spacious indoor area (20 °C to27 °C) divided into areas for stationary and slow walking movements. The area designated for slow walking is marked with straight lines to ensure users walk in a straight line. Other potential interference factors, such as noise, accessories, and the emotional state of users, will not impact the results of this experiment and are not considered.

Table 1. Preliminary Research Analysis on Selected Wearing Methods for the Experiment and Plan View of Sample Production

Specimen	Wear Style	Model Production
1	X-shaped Patellar Strap	It forms an X shape, with two fixing straps—one securing below the patella on the patellar tendon, and the other securing above the knee
2	Double-Layer Double-Sided Lixed-Open Knee Support	The inner side of the knee support has a preliminary fixation with magic traps are affixed on both sides to the rear at suitable positions using magic traps are affixed on both sides to the rear at suitable positions using magic tape, depending on the desired tightness
3	Double-Layer Bottom Fixed-Open Knee Support	The inner side of the knee support has a preliminary fixation with magic tape for the supporting functional part. Then, the bottom strap is wrapped to the front and secured on the knee according to the user's comfort and tightness preference
4	Single-Layer Magic Tape Fixed-Open Knee Support	Pull the wide straps on both sides of the knee support from the back of the leg to the front, adjust the position by stretching the length of the knee support, and secure it in place with magic tape

2.5 Experiment Procedure

In this experiment, the models corresponding to the four different wearing methods were divided into four experimental groups. Each group was associated with a specific test model, and each participant wore one model for a series of tests, including wearing speed, stability, and flexibility during movement. The detailed experimental methods for each test are as follows:

1. Wearing Speed Test: Provide the corresponding test model to the participant and demonstrate the correct wearing method in detail, ensuring that each participant understands and is familiar with the model's wearing process. Participants perform three wear operations on the model, and the time taken for each operation is accurately recorded using a stopwatch. To eliminate extreme values caused by operational errors, the median value of each participant's performance is taken as the final data. Participants rate their experience of wearing on a scale (negative ratings as negative numbers, positive ratings as positive numbers, with a maximum score of ten). Conduct follow-up interviews with participants whose objective data and subjective ratings show significant differences, record their user experiences in writing, and gather detailed feedback.

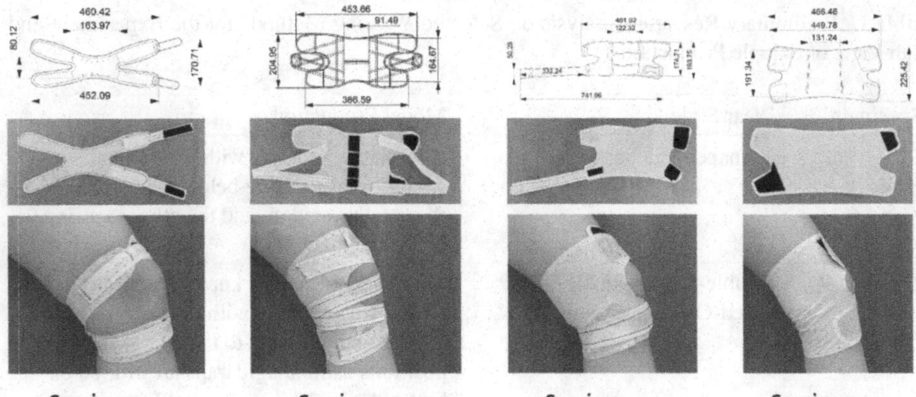

Fig. 1. Model production of four specimens. Specimen 1 represents X-shaped Patellar Strap, Specimen 2 represents Double-Layer Double-Sided Lixed-Open Knee Support, Specimen 3 represents Double-Layer Bottom Fixed-Open Knee Support, Specimen 4 represents Single-Layer Magic Tape Fixed-Open Knee Support.

2. Stability Test: Provide the corresponding test model to the participant and ask them to wear it correctly. Mark the lowest point on the model's lower edge using (paint) after the participant completes the correct wearing. Instruct participants to perform three sets of 60 high leg lifts, with the interval time between each set determined scientifically to ensure consistency. Measure the distance between the edge of the model worn by the participant and the marked position before the test using a tape measure. To eliminate extreme values caused by operational errors, the median value of each measurement result is taken as the final data. Participants rate the firmness of the wear on a scale. Conduct follow-up interviews with participants whose objective data and subjective ratings show significant differences, record their user experiences in writing, and gather detailed feedback.
3. Flexibility During Movement Test: Provide the corresponding test model to the participant, ensuring that each tester completes the wearing process. Conduct three sets of motion tests, including 1 min of deep squats, 1 min of high leg lifts, and 1 min of slow walking, with intervals between each movement determined scientifically to ensure consistency. Record the number of deep squats, high leg lifts, and the distance walked in each of the three tests. To eliminate extreme values caused by operational errors, the median value of each measurement result is taken as the final data. Participants rate the flexibility during movement. Conduct follow-up interviews with participants whose objective data and subjective ratings show significant differences, record their user experiences in writing, and gather detailed feedback.

2.6 Data Collection Standards

The core objective of this experiment is to determine the user experience in terms of wearing speed, stability, and flexibility during movement for four different wearing methods. Based on the data obtained from the aforementioned experimental methods, the data are categorized into three types: objective quantitative data (measurement data), subjective quantitative data (subjective ratings), and textual description information. Further summarization and analysis are conducted as follows:

1. Objective Quantitative Data: Calculate the average of the measured data for each group of participants to obtain data representing the functional effect of each wearing method, ranking the effectiveness of different wearing methods.
2. Subjective Quantitative Data: Calculate the average of the objective quantitative data for each group of participants according to different test items. Use this data as an objective standard for assessing the usability of each type of wearing method. Create scatter plots with the x-axis representing each participant and the y-axis representing subjective quantitative data. Input data for each participant separately. Analyze the distribution of user satisfaction and differences between satisfaction and the objective functional effectiveness of each wearing method. Identify participants with significant differences in subjective and objective data for follow-up interviews. Record detailed feedback to understand the reasons for differentiated experiences.
3. Textual Description Information: Summarize and analyze the textual description information. Distinguish whether the reasons for the textual feedback are individual subjective factors or objective interference factors. Determine if textual feedback had an impact on the experimental results.

3 Experimental Results

3.1 Comparison of Average Values for Each Wearing Method

Utilizing the Statistical Package for the Social Sciences (SPSS) software's bar chart statistical model, the raw data obtained from the experiment was subjected to summary statistics. The statistical results are as follows:

From Fig. 2, it can be clearly observed that the average wearing time for each experimental group is ranked as follows: Single-Layer Velcro Fixed-Open Knee Guard < X-shaped Patellar Strap < Double-Layer Bottom Fixed-Open Knee Guard < Double-Layer Double-Sided Fixed-Open Knee Guard. Therefore, objectively, the difficulty of wearing operations from easy to difficult is as follows: Velcro Fixed-Open Knee Guard, X-shaped Patellar Strap, Double-Layer Bottom Fixed-Open Knee Guard, Double-Layer Double-Sided Fixed-Open Knee Guard. Among them, Velcro Fixed-Open Knee Guard and X-shaped Patellar Strap are relatively close, both ranging from 5 s to 10 s. The Double-Layer Bottom Fixed-Open Knee Guard and Double-Layer Double-Sided Fixed-Open Knee Guard are also close, both ranging from 10 s to 15 s.

At the same time, it is observed that the subjective evaluation by users is ranked from high to low as follows: X-shaped Patellar Strap, Velcro Fixed-Open Knee Guard, Double-Layer Bottom Fixed-Open Knee Guard, Double-Layer Double-Sided Fixed-Open Knee Guard. Among them, the evaluation of Velcro Fixed-Open Knee Guard and X-shaped Patellar Strap is very close.

As shown in Fig. 3, the average displacement during movement for each experimental group is ranked as follows: Single-layer magic tape fixed perforated knee pad < Double-layer bottom-fixed perforated knee pad < X-shaped patellar strap < Double-layer double-sided fixed perforated knee pad. Therefore, the objective stability of wearing, from stable to prone to loosening, is as follows: magic tape fixed perforated knee

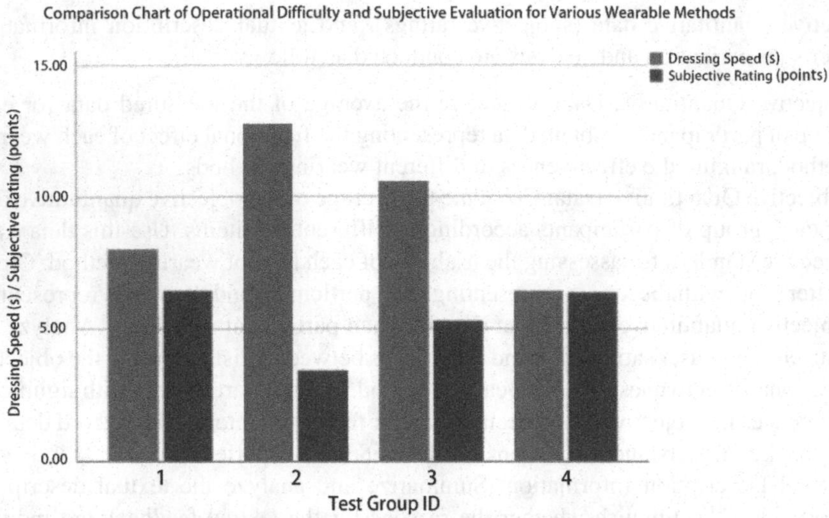

Fig. 2. Comparison of Operational Difficulty and Subjective Evaluation for Various Wearable Methods. X axis labels the ID of test group. Blue bar represents Dressing Speed(s). Green bar represents Subjective Rating (points).

pad, double-layer bottom-fixed perforated knee pad, X-shaped patellar strap, double-layer double-sided fixed perforated knee pad. Among them, the magic tape fixed perforated knee pad and the double-layer bottom-fixed perforated knee pad are relatively close, with an average displacement of less than 1 cm. The X-shaped patellar strap and the double-layer double-sided fixed perforated knee pad are relatively close, with an average displacement between 1 cm and 2 cm.

At the same time, the subjective evaluation by users is ranked from high to low as follows: magic tape fixed perforated knee pad, double-layer bottom-fixed perforated knee pad, double-layer double-sided fixed perforated knee pad, X-shaped patellar strap. Among them, the user's subjective evaluation of the magic tape fixed perforated knee pad is significantly higher than the other groups.

As shown in Fig. 4, the data for 1-min squats and 1-min slow walks are not significantly affected by the independent variable (i.e., different wearing methods) in this experiment. Therefore, subsequent analysis will no longer refer to the results of these two experiments, and further confirmation of the reasons will be sought in the user follow-up.

For the 1-min high-leg lifting exercise, the average number of high-leg lifts for each experimental group is ranked as follows: X-shaped patellar strap < Double-layer double-sided fixed perforated knee pad < Double-layer bottom-fixed perforated knee pad < Single-layer magic tape fixed perforated knee pad. Therefore, the objective impact of each wearing method on the movement state is as follows, from small to large: magic tape fixed perforated knee pad, double-layer bottom-fixed perforated knee pad, double-layer double-sided fixed perforated knee pad, X-shaped patellar strap. Among them, the double-layer double-sided fixed perforated knee pad and the double-layer bottom-fixed

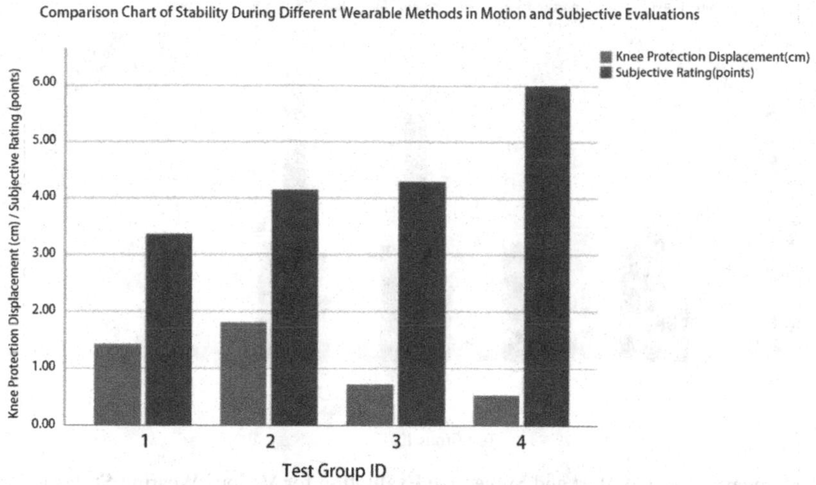

Fig. 3. Comparison of Stability During Different Wearable Methods in Motion and Subjective Evaluations. X axis labels the ID of test group. Blue bar represents Knee Protection Displacement (cm). Green bar represents Subjective Rating (points). (Color figure online)

perforated knee pad are relatively close, while the X-shaped patellar strap significantly lags behind in hindering user movement.

At the same time, the subjective evaluation by users is ranked from high to low as follows: magic tape fixed perforated knee pad, double-layer double-sided fixed perforated knee pad, double-layer bottom-fixed perforated knee pad, X-shaped patellar strap. Among them, the user's subjective evaluation of the magic tape fixed perforated knee pad is significantly higher than the other groups; X-shaped patellar strap receives relatively negative feedback regarding the degree of movement restriction.

3.2 The Distribution of Subjects Regarding the Ease of Wearing and Subjective Evaluation

Using the multivariate regression analysis method with SPSS as the tool, the experimental data was processed and analyzed. Each sample score of the experimental data was plotted on a scatter plot, with objective data on the x-axis and subjective evaluations on the y-axis. Based on the distribution, an approximate curve was fitted, as shown in the following Figs. 5, 6.

As shown in Figs. 5 and 6, the scatter distribution of the X-shaped patella strap is mainly concentrated in the region of faster dressing speed and higher ratings. There are instances of slow dressing but good ratings and instances of fast speed but not high ratings. The scatter distribution of the double-layer bilateral fixed-open knee support is mainly centered around slower dressing speed and moderate ratings, with one instance of very slow dressing speed but moderate ratings. The scatter distribution of the double-layer bottom-fixed open knee support is mainly in the region of moderate speed but high scores, with one instance of moderate speed but very high scores. The scatter distribution of the magic tape fixed-open knee support is mainly in the region of fast dressing speed

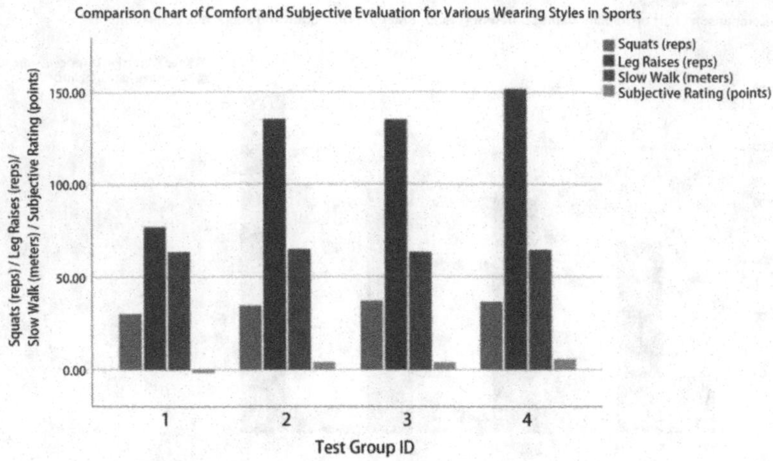

Fig. 4. Comparison of Comfort and Subjective Evaluation for Various Wearing Styles in Sports. X axis labels the ID of test group. Blue bar represents Squats (reps). Green bar represents Leg Raises (reps). Red bar represents Slow Walk (meters). Brown bar represents Subjective Rating (points). (Color figure online)

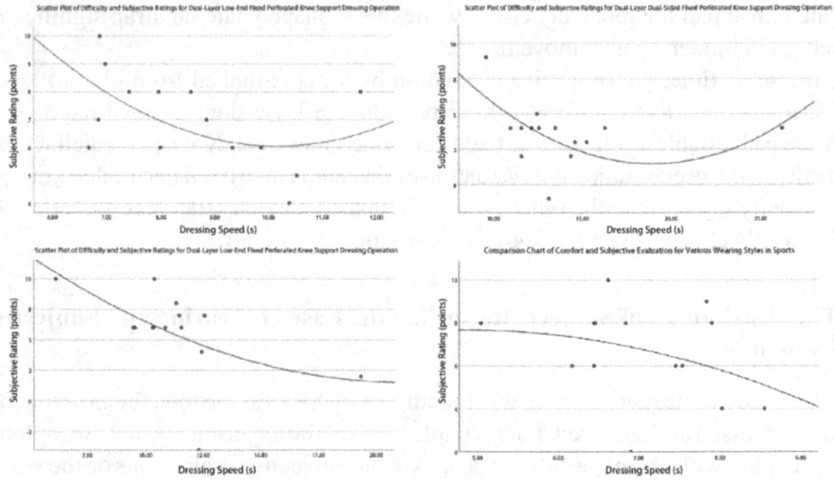

Fig. 5. Scatter Plot of Difficulty and Subjective Ratings for Dual-Layer Low-End Fixed Perforated Knee Support Dressing operation of four Specimens. X axis labels Dressing Speed(s). Y axis labels Subjective Rating (points). Using the multivariate regression analysis method with SPSS as the tool, the experimental data was processed. Based on the distribution, an approximate curve was fitted. The plot in the top left corner is Specimen 1, the plot in the top right corner is Specimen 2, the plot in the bottom left corner is Specimen 3, the plot in the bottom right corner is Specimen 4.

and high ratings, with one instance of moderate speed but high ratings, two instances of slow speed but high ratings, and one instance of slow speed with very low ratings.

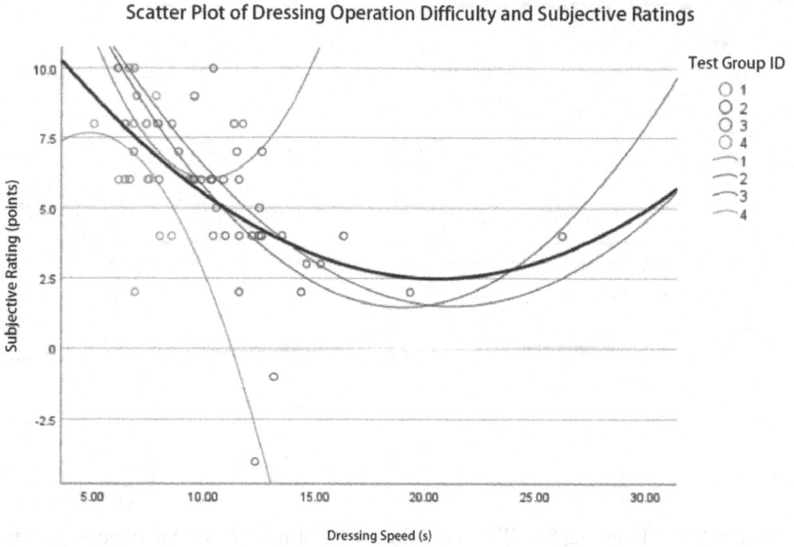

Fig. 6. Integration of the four Scatter Plots in Fig. 5. Blue data points and line represents Specimen 1. Green data points and line represents Specimen 2. Red data points and line represents Specimen 3. Brown data points and line represents Specimen 4. (Color figure online)

Overall, user subjective ratings tend to decrease with the increase in dressing time and decrease in dressing speed.

3.3 Distribution of Subjects in Terms of Dressing Firmness and Subjective Evaluation

Using the multivariate regression analysis method with SPSS as the tool, the experimental data was processed and analyzed. Each sample score of the experimental data was plotted on a scatter plot, with objective data on the x-axis and subjective evaluations on the y-axis. Based on their distribution, an approximate curve was fitted, as shown in the following Figs. 7, 8.

As shown in Figs. 7 and 8, the scatter plot distribution for the X-shaped patellar strap is mainly concentrated in the moderate displacement distance with relatively favorable evaluations. There is an instance where the displacement distance is moderate but the evaluation is extremely low. The scatter plot for the double-layer double-sided fixed-opening knee brace is primarily centered around a longer displacement distance with moderate evaluations, and no abnormal experimental results were observed. The scatter plot for the double-layer bottom-fixed opening knee brace is mainly distributed in the moderate displacement distance with moderate ratings. There is one instance where the displacement distance is moderate but the rating is extremely low, and another instance where the displacement distance is relatively large but the rating is still positive. The scatter plot for the magic tape fixed-opening knee brace is mainly distributed in the short displacement distance with higher evaluations. There are three instances with short displacement distances but lower evaluations.

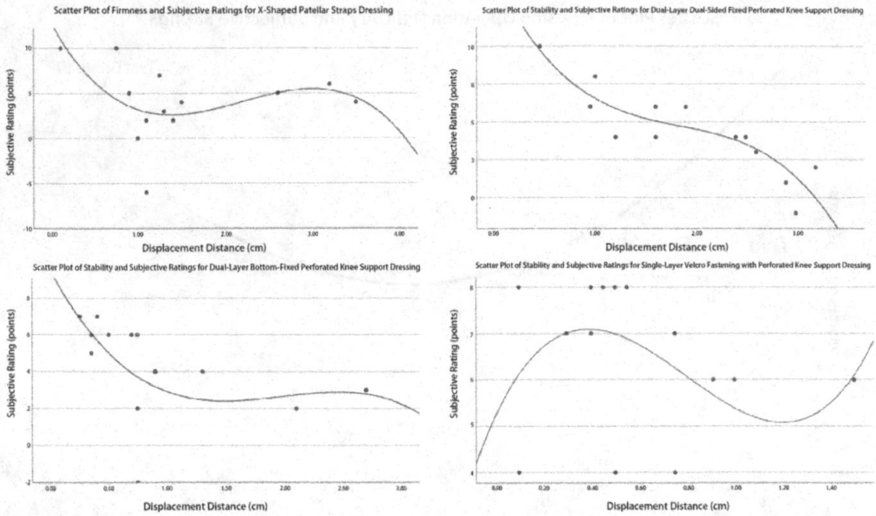

Fig. 7. Scatter Plot of Dressing Stability and Subjective Ratings of four Specimens. X axis labels Displacement Distance (cm). Y axis labels Subjective Rating (points). Using the multivariate regression analysis method with SPSS as the tool, the experimental data was processed. Based on the distribution, an approximate curve was fitted. The plot in the top left corner is Specimen 1, the plot in the top right corner is Specimen 2, the plot in the bottom left corner is Specimen 3, the plot in the bottom right corner is Specimen 4.

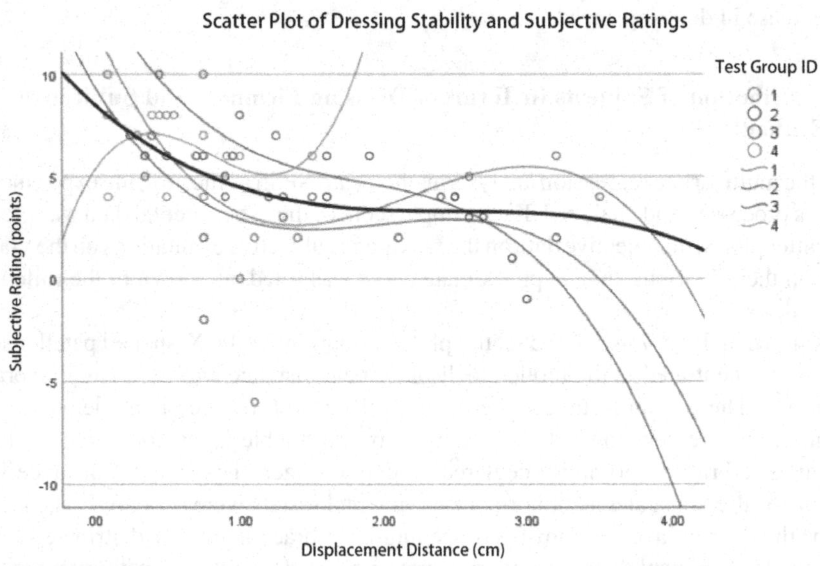

Fig. 8. Integration of the four Scatter Plots in Fig. 7. Blue data points and line represents Specimen 1. Green data points and line represents Specimen 2. Red data points and line represents Specimen 3. Brown data points and line represents Specimen 4. (Color figure online)

3.4 The Distribution of Post-wearing Comfort During Movement and Subjective Evaluations of the Participants

Through multivariate regression analysis using SPSS as the tool, the experimental data was processed and analyzed. Each sample score of the experimental data was plotted on a scatter plot, with objective data on the x-axis and subjective evaluations on the y-axis. Based on their distribution, an approximate curve was fitted, as shown in the following Figs. 9, 10.

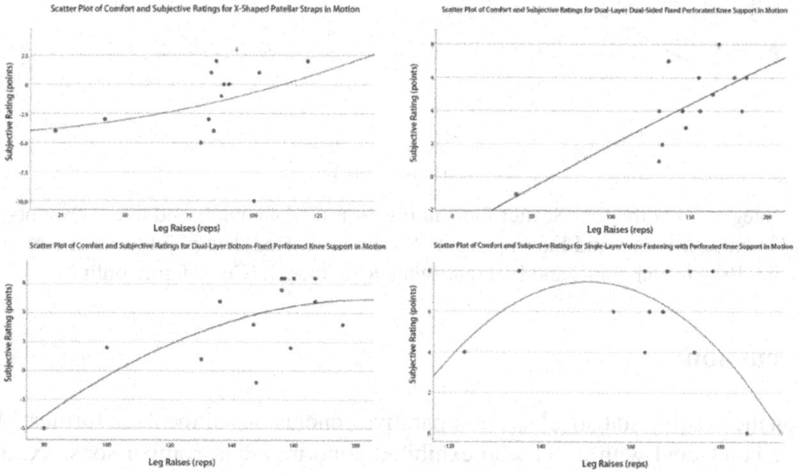

Fig. 9. Scatter Plot of Exercise Comfort and Subjective Ratings of four Specimens. X axis labels Leg Raises (reps). Y axis labels Subjective Rating (points). Using the multivariate regression analysis method with SPSS as the tool, the experimental data was processed. Based on the distribution, an approximate curve was fitted. The plot in the top left corner is Specimen 1, the plot in the top right corner is Specimen 2, the plot in the bottom left corner is Specimen 3, the plot in the bottom right corner is Specimen 4.

As shown in Figs. 9 and 10, the scatter distribution of the X-shaped patellar strap is mainly concentrated in the area of a lower number of leg lifts and lower evaluations, with one case showing a moderate number of leg lifts but extremely low ratings. The scatter distribution of the double-layer double-sided fixed-open knee support is mainly concentrated in the area of a higher number of leg lifts and higher evaluations, with no abnormal experimental results. The scatter distribution of the double-layer bottom-fixed open knee support is mainly in the area of a higher number of leg lifts and higher evaluations, with one case having a higher number of leg lifts but lower ratings. The scatter distribution of the magic tape fixed-open knee support is concentrated in the area of a higher number of leg lifts and higher evaluations, with one case having an extremely high number of leg lifts but very low ratings, and two cases having higher leg lift data but moderate ratings.

Overall, user subjective ratings tend to increase with a higher number of leg lifts and a decrease in hindrance to movement.

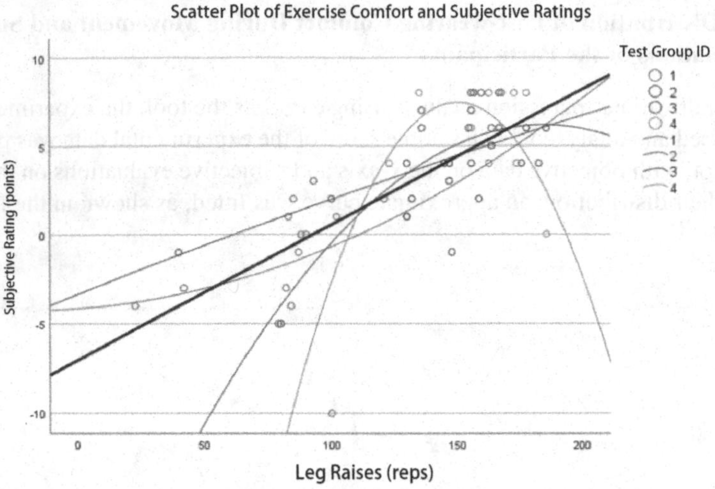

Fig. 10. Integration of the four Scatter Plots in Fig. 9. Blue data points and line represents Specimen 1. Green data points and line represents Specimen 2. Red data points and line represents Specimen 3. Brown data points and line represents Specimen 4. (Color figure online)

4 Discussion

Based on the existing statistical and comparative conclusions of the data, further follow-ups were conducted with users who exhibited abnormal data comparisons, extracting keywords from their responses. These keywords helped eliminate additional factors such as subjective preferences, past experiences, and physical conditions during the experiment that might affect user feedback. The following conclusions were drawn in response to the initial research questions:

1. According to the aforementioned experimental results, the experimenter subjectively believes that the objective impact of wearing methods on the ease of wearing primarily depends on the number of layers (i.e., the number of straps) required by each wearing method. This provides a reference for knee protector products that emphasize visual design (Man, Yue & Tian, 2022) [6]. The factors influencing user subjective evaluations mainly depend on the range of motion and the number of steps involved. For product design and optimization of user experience, this conclusion is of significant importance. Applying these research findings can aid in designing safer, more comfortable, and more practical sports protective gear, better meeting the needs of users.
2. Different fixation methods have varying effects on the stability of knee protectors, primarily depending on their fixation level at the lower end of the knee protector (lower leg area). This is corroborated by user feedback, demonstrating that the skin stretchability in different areas of the legs during lower limb movement is not uniform. Significant stretching is mainly concentrated in the outer side of the thigh and knee area (Wang, Wang, Zhang & Wu, 2013) [7–9]. This insight plays a crucial guiding role in the design and improvement of protective gear. It helps designers focus specifically

on the fixation level at the lower part of the knee when considering fixation methods, ensuring stability during the use of knee protectors [10, 11].

3. The sample production process in this experiment involved subjective extraction and imitation of the forms of existing knee protector products. The manual stitching method used in the production process involved stitching multiple pieces together to form a surface, which differs from the stitching method used in actual products that involves stitching the edges of wrapping fabrics. Although this difference is not directly related to the measured variables in this experiment, users might potentially provide biased evaluations of the usability of the samples used in this study due to their visual perception and expectations of knee protector products (Sonderegger, A., & Sauer, J., 2010) [8, 12–15]. This could potentially have a positive or negative impact on the subjective evaluation results of users.

5 Conclusion

The single-layer magic tape fixed open-knee protector exhibits the most advantages in both user perception and objective data. Although the double-layer double-sided fixed open-knee protector provides average feedback in objective data, users subjectively rate it highly. The X-shaped patellar band has advantages only in the ease of wear, while other aspects, including objective data and user perceptions, are relatively poor. This suggests that a single convenient wearing method may not effectively achieve the protective function of knee protection. The double-layer bottom-fixed open-knee protector has objective stability advantages, but apart from being perceived as convenient to wear, it receives poor subjective evaluations in other aspects [16–18].

The impact of different fixation methods on the stability of knee protection mainly depends on their fixation level at the lower end of the knee protector (lower leg area). In this experiment, samples with better feedback results in terms of motion stability exhibit the characteristic of lower limb segment fixation, which is more stable compared to the overall sample fixation.

References

1. McNair, P.J., Stanley, S.N., Strauss, G.R.: Knee bracing: effects on proprioception. Arch. Phys. Med. Rehabil. **77**, 287–289 (1996)
2. Beaudreuil, J., Bendaya, S., Faucher, M., et al.: Clinical practice guidelines for rest orthosis, knee sleeves, and unloading knee braces in knee osteoarthritis. Joint Bone Spine **76**, 629–636 (2009)
3. Nallavan, G.: Impact of recent developments in fabrication of Auxetic materials on safety and protection in sport. AIP Conf. Proc. **2271**, 030006 (2020)
4. American Academy of Orthopaedic Surgeons: Position Statement: The Use of Knee Braces. American Academy of Orthopaedic Surgeons, Rosemont, IL (1997)
5. Yangyang, S., Junxia, Z., Meijiao, J., et al.: Kinematic characteristics of lower limb joints in young men wearing knee protectors on the dominant and non-dominant sides during running. Chin. J. Tissue Eng. Res. **26**(06), 832–837 (2022)
6. Man, K., Yue, F., Tian, W.: A design method of knee pad based on user data. In: Soares, M.M., Rosenzweig, E., Marcus, A. (eds.) HCII 2022. LNCS, vol. 13323, pp. 187–199. Springer, Cham (2022). https://doi.org/10.1007/978-3-031-05906-3_14

7. Wang, Y., Wang, J., Zhang, Y., Wu, T.: A study on skin stretching under running motion state. J. Text. Res. **34**(8), 115–120 (2013)
8. Sonderegger, A., Sauer, J.: The influence of design aesthetics in usability testing: effects on user performance and perceived usability. Appl. Ergon. **41**(3), 403–410 (2010)
9. Jiang, A., Foing, B.H., Schlacht, I.L., Yao, X., Cheung, V., Rhodes, P.A.: Colour schemes to reduce stress response in the hygiene area of a space station: a Delphi study. Appl. Ergon. **98**, 103573 (2022)
10. Jiang, A., et al.: The effect of colour environments on visual tracking and visual strain during short-term simulation of three gravity states. Appl. Ergon. **110**, 103994 (2023)
11. Yu, K., Jiang, A., Wang, J., Zeng, X., Yao, X., Chen, Y.: Construction of crew visual behaviour mechanism in ship centralized control cabin. In: Stanton, N. (ed.) AHFE 2021. LNNS, vol. 270, pp. 503–510, Springer, Cham (2021)
12. Jiang, A., et al.: Space habitat astronautics: multicolour lighting psychology in a 7-day simulated habitat. Space Sci. Technol. (2022)
13. Jiang, A., et al.: Short-term virtual reality simulation of the effects of space station colour and microgravity and lunar gravity on cognitive task performance and emotion. Build. Environ. **227**, 109789 (2023)
14. Jiang, A., Yao, X., Westland, S., Hemingray, C., Foing, B., Lin, J.: The effect of correlated colour temperature on physiological, emotional and subjective satisfaction in the hygiene area of a space station. Int. J. Environ. Res. Public Health **19**(15), 9090 (2022)
15. Jiang, A.O.: Effects of colour environment on spaceflight cognitive abilities during short-term simulations of three gravity states. Doctoral dissertation, University of Leeds (2022)
16. Jiang, A., Zhu, Y., Yao, X., Foing, B.H., Westland, S., Hemingray, C.: The effect of three body positions on colour preference: an exploration of microgravity and lunar gravity simulations. Acta Astronaut. **204**, 1–10 (2023)
17. Huang, Z., Wang, S., Jiang, A., Hemingray, C., Westland, S.: Gender preference differences in color temperature associated with LED light sources in the autopilot cabin. In: Krömker, H. (ed.) HCII 2022. LNCS, vol. 13335, pp. 151–166. Springer, Cham (2022)
18. Jiang, A., Yao, X., Hemingray, C., Westland, S.: Young people's colour preference and the arousal level of small apartments. Color. Res. Appl. **47**(3), 783–795 (2022)

Gamified Participatory Design Empowers Blind People's Emotional Experience - Take "Sound·Sound" as an Example

Hanchao Yu(✉), Hao He, and Qi Tan

Central Academy of Fine Arts, No. 8 Huajiadi South Street, Chaoyang District, Beijing, China
347942711@qq.com

Abstract. In the era of global competition, technology has fundamentally lowered the entry threshold for competition. Greater engagement is the real competitive advantage, and gamification design provides us with ways to enhance engagement. Today, gamification interaction methods have gradually penetrated and spread from specific groups of people to the field of ordinary workers. For blind users, the product's humanistic care and satisfaction of emotional needs play a positive role in their confidence and self-esteem. Leverage gamification to help and transform blind people's life participation and experiences. It makes complex behaviors simple and sustainable. This study used a questionnaire survey to explore the relationship between blind somatosensory games and the mental health of blind people.

Keywords: physical and mental health of blind people · participatory design · self-esteem · self-confidence

1 Introduction

Gaming is almost as old as human civilization. Even the most novel form of video games is 40 years old, creating a massive global industry worth $70 billion annually. The game has received a warm welcome regardless of people's race, age and gender [1]. Gamification is not a goal, but a capability. The key to "product gamification" is not games, but stimulating people's inner motivation. Through the new science of thinking and behavior, we can change our personal thinking patterns and turn mundane and trivial things into interesting things that we actively want to accomplish. The essence of gamification thinking is to influence user behavior by designing the emotions generated at each stage of interaction between users and products. This is not entertainment, but a fusion of humanity and design. Make products interesting and fun, enhance their appeal to users, explore user needs beyond core needs, strengthen users' emotional experience and the added value of the product, gamify the product, and complete the transformation from a tool to a toy. Of course, this is all achieved without compromising an experience that meets the core needs of users. Gamification is a complete system that requires the clever and organic combination of multiple mechanisms, rather than the separate

A. Marcus et al. (Eds.): HCII 2024, LNCS 14714, pp. 165–174, 2024.
https://doi.org/10.1007/978-3-031-61356-2_11

application of a certain mechanism. This system includes challenges, opportunities, competition, cooperation, feedback, resource acquisition, rewards, transactions, rounds, victory and defeat, etc., forming a complete gamification system. Play (especially in the form of sport), as an element of our evolutionary heritage and to some extent as the first element of culture, can be described as a "mode of cognition", a way of permeating all human behavior. The intelligence of domain expertise [2].

2 Problem Focus

2.1 Current Situation of Blind People

Blind people have strong resistance to special designs. Mr. Ma Linshun, a blind man, mentioned in the article "Special Products Make Me Inferior" that some special products on the market designed for blind people are very complex and impractical. At present, the research on sensory fitness games for blind people is still in its infancy, and relevant research mainly focuses on game design, user experience and technology application [3]. In recent years, with the continuous improvement of health awareness, fitness exercises have attracted more and more attention and attention from countries around the world. However, for blind people, participating in fitness activities faces many challenges due to the lack of visual ability. In response to this problem, fitness games for the blind came into being. Blind fitness games input information through the senses such as sound, touch, smell, etc. to help blind friends exercise, strengthen their physical fitness, and improve their mental health. As one of the most important cognitive methods for blind people, meeting and ensuring effective tactile cognitive learning for blind people is essential in society [4] (Fig. 1).

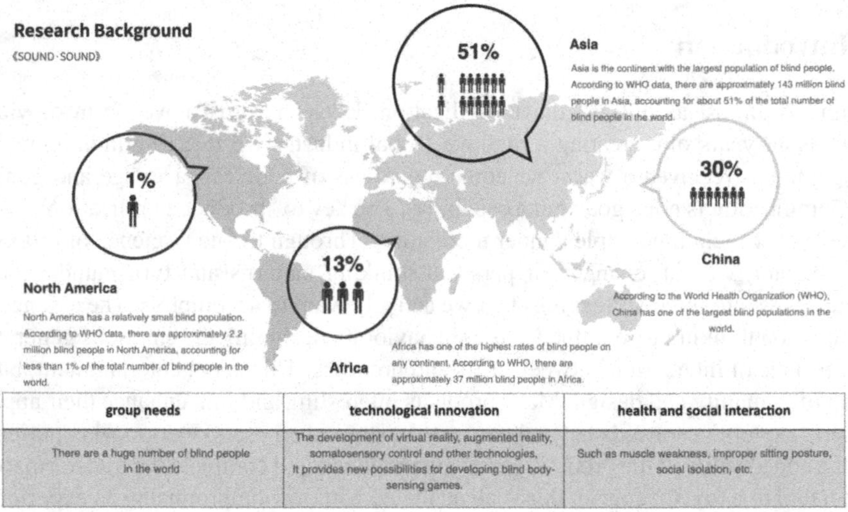

Fig. 1. Research Background

Blind people face many challenges in daily life, one of which is the lack of visual information to enjoy games, entertainment and physical exercise opportunities [5]. Traditional game entertainment methods are often vision-oriented and difficult to meet the needs of blind users. Therefore, developing blind body-sensing games can provide blind users with a new way of entertainment and exercise to meet their needs. Blind people also face many physical and mental health challenges, such as muscle weakness, poor sitting posture, and social isolation. By developing blind somatosensory games, we can provide blind users with a beneficial way of physical exercise, promote muscle activity and body coordination, and promote communication and social interaction between blind users and ordinary sighted people through social interaction in the game, improving their quality of life and well-being. At the same time, blind somatosensory games also have certain social significance. With the development and progress of society, more and more people are paying attention to the lives and needs of blind people. In recent years, research on tactile sensors has made tremendous progress. In addition, the collaboration of medical skills and modern technology is increasingly required to develop assistive devices for the visually impaired [6]. By developing blind somatosensory games, we can provide blind people with a new way of entertainment and at the same time promote society's understanding and attention to the blind group.

2.2 Analysis of Mental Health Status of Blind People

Loneliness: Little is known about whether and to what extent loneliness affects the lives of blind people. Vision is a key sensory modality for interpersonal and social communication. Blind people have fewer opportunities to learn and socialize, and many suffer from severe autism, which exacerbates feelings of isolation [7].

Inferiority complex: This mainly comes from the heart of blind people. They do not agree with their own changes and think that they are worse than others in all aspects of study and life. This also comes from the social environment's inaccurate understanding and evaluation of visually impaired people. Extreme phenomena may also occur, resulting in a sense of inferiority [8].

Depressed mood: Research suggests that blind people may be more susceptible to depression than the general population. Depressed mood has been linked not only to stress in daily life but also to stress caused by visual impairment, suggesting that disability can have a negative impact on mental health in addition to the inconveniences it brings [9].

2.3 Analysis of Spatial Perception Characteristics of Blind People

Blind people use hearing to perceive and understand spatial information in their environment. They rely on characteristics such as direction, distance and echoes of sound to determine the location and spatial layout of objects. This is the auditory spatial perception characteristic of blind people. For example, a blind person can quickly judge the size and shape of a room by hearing changes in the direction of sound. Blind people perceive spatial information such as the shape, texture, and size of objects through touch [10, 11].

Blind people use tactile feedback from their hands and body to understand spatial relationships by touching, groping, and feeling the edges, surface features, and geometry of objects. This is the tactile spatial perception characteristic of blind people. For example, learn about different destinations by touching the texture of the ground, feeling the smoothness of the walls, and touching the contours of objects. Blind people perceive space through their own movement and body sensations. They rely on walking, running or exploring the environment to perceive the spatial relationships around them through the body's sense of balance, gravity and motion feedback. For example, you can judge the height and slope of a mountain by feeling the slope of the ground, the height difference of stairs, and the speed of body movement. This is the characteristic of motion perception in blind people. Blind people develop spatial memory and navigation strategies to understand and manipulate their environment. They use everyday experiences and environmental features to remember and recognize different spatial locations and paths. By memorizing landmarks, a sense of direction, and spatial relationships, blind people can navigate and orient themselves in unfamiliar environments [12].

3 Concept Explanation

3.1 Gamified Participatory Design

Gamification is not a goal, but a method. "Sound·Sound" uses this method to change people's mentality, thereby improving the emotional cognition of blind people. Gamification design is to design through gamification thinking to enhance users' participation in products and tap into users' potential needs and motivations. Gamification design is more than just designing games. The core is "gamification thinking", which makes the original business more interesting, thereby improving user stickiness and experience satisfaction [13]. Combining product goals and features, deeply understand target users and user behavior logic, and create scenes that people are willing to immerse themselves in. Through quantitative and qualitative user research, determine and draw user portraits, output user experience maps, and gain insight into and explore users' potential underlying needs [14].

Participatory design means that user participation reaches a deeper level and users can participate more actively in the design process. Saunders defines participatory design as a new attitude towards design that requires new ways of thinking and working. Additionally, Sanders introduced the concept of something that people can co-design. This way, people will have the opportunity to get better ideas and scale their ideas more efficiently [15]. Currently, participatory design is defined as a set of theoretical and practical methods that emphasize that the user's role should be fully involved in the entire design process. Basically, users are the people involved in the design. Participatory design is increasingly mentioned and used as a first step in user-centered design [16].

3.2 The Emotional Value that Gamified Participatory Design Brings to the Blind Group

The essence of gamification thinking is to influence user behavior by designing the emotions generated at each stage of interaction between users and products. This is not entertainment, but a fusion of humanity and design. "Sound·Sound" is designed in this way, to gamify the product and complete the transformation from tool to toy. It enhances the user's emotional experience and the added value of the product, turning mundane and trivial things into interesting things that they actively want to accomplish.

4 Creative Exploration

4.1 "Sound·Sound" Design Concept

"Sound·Sound" somatosensory fitness game is a two-person somatosensory fitness game for blind people. Using the most commonly used guide stick for blind people, different vibration points are set on the handle to help blind people complete fitness movements, exercise, strengthen their physical fitness, and improve their mental health through input from the ears, body and other senses and sounds [17]. And through changes in touch vibration points, more difficult movements can be completed. You can realize that blind people are more sensitive to touch and hearing and respond faster to sounds than ordinary people. This innate advantage improves the self-confidence of blind people [18]. Establish communication and present yourself positively in two-player games.

4.2 "Sound·Sound" Work Display

Game goal: The main goal of "Sound·Sound" is to use the auditory and somatosensory movements of blind players to complete a series of physical challenges with another player to improve physical fitness. The game is designed to provide blind users with a fitness experience to participate in with visually impaired friends or family members through a combination of hearing and body movements, promoting physical and mental health and interaction.

Game interface: Played on a somatosensory device, using somatosensory controllers, motion sensors, etc., players can interact with the game through sound guidance and vibration feedback.

Fitness challenges: Design a variety of fitness challenges, aerobic exercise, flexibility training, etc. These challenges will be combined with music and sound effects to allow players to perceive through hearing and make corresponding somatosensory actions.

Cooperation mode: mainly two people compete to complete the fitness challenge through two people's competition. Blind players can interact and collaborate with other players through auditory and tactile guidance.

Customizable: Offers customizable options including challenge difficulty, music selection and fitness goals. Players can adjust game settings according to their needs and health for the best experience.

Action recognition: Use somatosensory technology, accelerometers, gyroscopes, etc. to capture the player's body movements and recognize them in real time, converting them into in-game operating instructions.

Fitness guidance: Provide professional fitness guidance and suggestions, including warm-up, stretching, etc., to help players perform fitness exercises correctly to ensure safety and effectiveness.

Action recognition process: Obtain three-axis acceleration through a three-axis accelerometer -> Store the data in a circular queue -> Dynamic time warping algorithm calculates the similarity between the obtained sequence and the template academic qualification -> Deduced the action type based on the similarity.

Game flow control: The host randomly generates an action sequence -> the host sends the action sequence to the slave -> the state machine controls the conversion of the action sequence -> compares the completion time difference between the host and slave action sequences -> calculates the winner.

Technical difficulties: motion path detection, scoring rule formulation, data filtering (Kalman filter), state machine, instruction synchronization, miniaturization, etc.

"Sound·sound" is an innovative blind two-person fitness somatosensory game that allows players to enjoy fitness, improve physical health through the combination of hearing and somatosensory movements, [19] gain fun and a sense of accomplishment in two-person sports (Fig. 2).

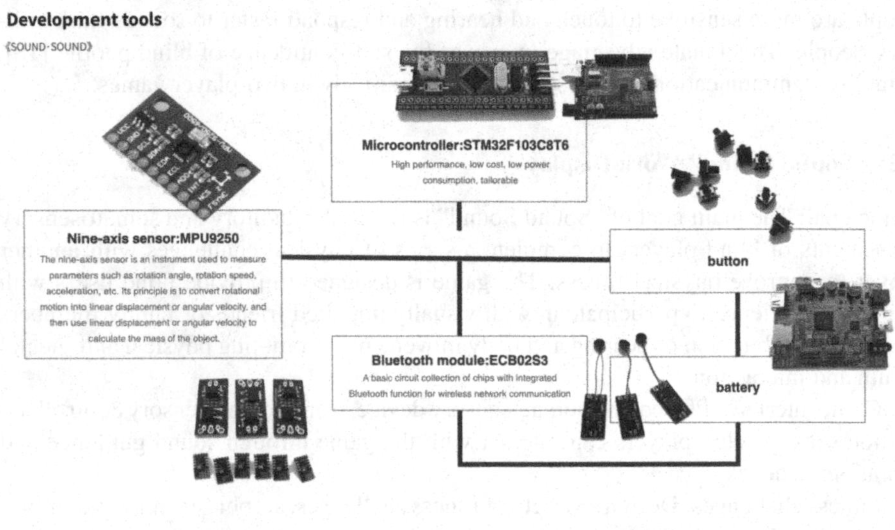

Fig. 2. Development tools

Aiming at the problems of blind people and achieving emotional and creative breakthroughs, this two-person body-sensing fitness game based on guide sticks, compared to the existing smart wearable entertainment devices for blind people on the market, "sound · sound" uses the Arduino series of microcontrollers as the microcontroller. Completed by gyro sensor and vibration motor module and audio module. Cost reduced to one third. "Sound · Sound" can realize: monitoring changes in people's posture and movement, and using vibration modules to transmit information to blind people. It is also equipped with an MP3 portable sound module and reflective signs to relieve the pressure of blind people traveling at night. Different from traditional somatosensory games, "Sound · Sound" adds a small special configuration of double speed. The voice tutorial broadcast settings are mainly at the elementary level and do not involve too many professional vocabulary, vague vocabulary, and abstract vocabulary. The blind cane is the most dependent and accustomed tool for blind people. The handle of "sound·sound" can be connected to the guide cane through rotation. The handle not only senses the blind person's movement direction through vibration, but is also a mobile speaker. The positions of the X-axis and Y-axis are connected through the USB serial port and transmitted to the motherboard in real time to complete motion monitoring. The game tasks fully reflect the somatosensory characteristics and spatial perception abilities of blind people. Among them, some task designs require blind people to accurately judge distance, direction, height, etc. This can not only improve the blind people's perception, but also increase the challenge and interest of the game. The application of gamified participatory research methods brings positive emotional value to the blind group.

4.3 Thoughts on the Design of "Sound·Sound"

Game tasks should be able to fully reflect the somatosensory characteristics and spatial perception abilities of blind people. For example, some tasks that require blind people to accurately judge distance, direction, height, etc. can be enriched. This will not only improve the perception of blind people, but also increase the challenge and interest of the game.

This study mainly uses questionnaire survey and experimental research methods. Although the sample has certain representativeness and credibility, the results may have certain flaws. The development of body-sensing fitness games for the blind is still in its infancy, and the quantity and quality of relevant research need to be further improved and improved. Therefore, future research can further increase the sample size and research time, strengthen the research and promotion of sensory fitness games for the blind, and further explore the relationship between sensory fitness games for the blind and the mental health of the blind. Provide guidance for the development of fitness games for the blind. Provide more scientific support and guarantee (Fig. 3).

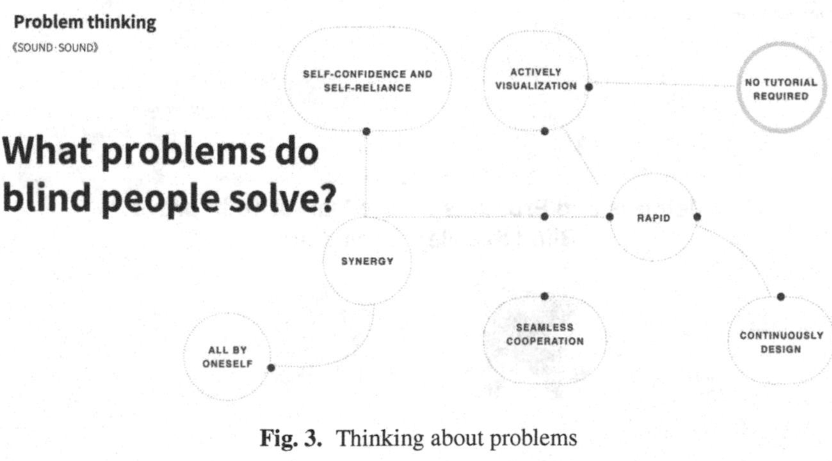

Fig. 3. Thinking about problems

4.4 Use Charts and Other Forms to Demonstrate the Future Emotional Value Trends that Gamified Participatory Design Will Bring to the Blind Group

See Fig. 4.

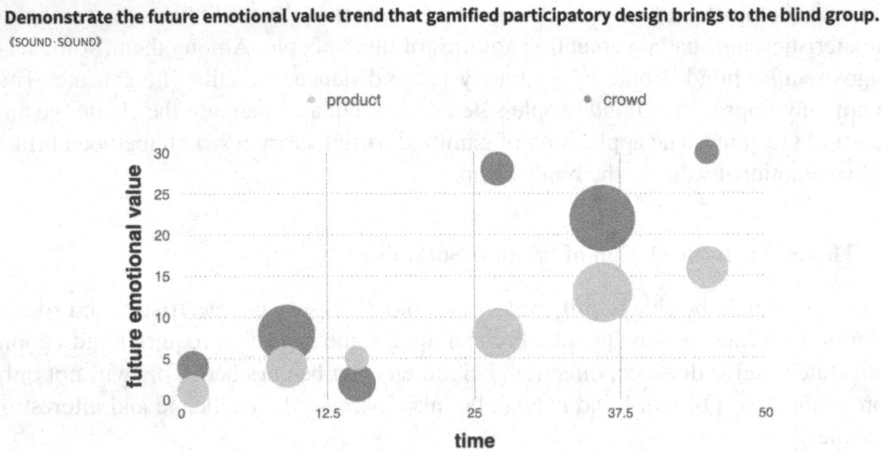

Fig. 4. Development Trend

5 Conclusion

Propose Future Research Suggestions on Emotion Recognition Training for Blind People

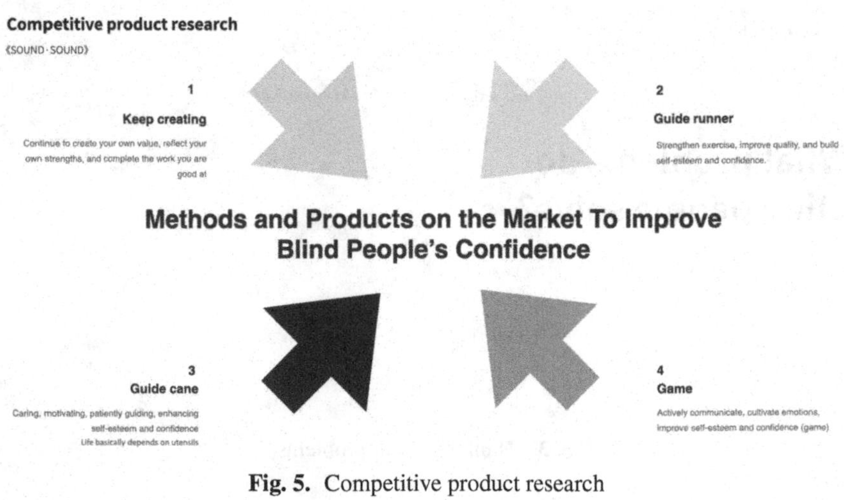

Fig. 5. Competitive product research

Improvement of emotion recognition technology: Focus on the development of more intelligent and accurate emotion recognition technology, including the use of biometric technology, voice recognition technology and facial expression recognition technology to help blind people better understand and identify the emotions of others (Fig. 5).

Design of emotional feedback system: Develop an emotional feedback system suitable for blind people to help blind people better perceive their own emotional changes and adjust their emotional state in a timely manner through sound, touch or other forms of feedback mechanisms.

Development of emotion recognition auxiliary tools: Design and develop emotion recognition auxiliary tools for blind people, including emotion maps, emotion labeling systems, etc., to help blind people better understand and identify various emotions and learn to respond appropriately.

Optimize emotion cognition training methods: further explore and improve the methods and strategies of emotion cognition training for blind people, combine cognitive psychology and education theory, and design a more effective and systematic emotion cognition training program [20].

Research on the relationship between emotional cognition and quality of life: In-depth study of the relationship between the emotional cognition level of blind people and their quality of life, exploring the impact of emotional cognition training on the mental health and life satisfaction of blind people, and providing theoretical support and practicality for improving the quality of life of blind people guide.

Offers customizable options including challenge difficulty, music selection and fitness goals. Players can adjust game settings according to their needs and health for the best experience.

References

1. Ziyu "Reading Essays": What exactly does gamification bring to business? (2021)
2. Scott Kretchmar, R.: Human evolution, movement, and intelligence: why playing games counts as smart. Quest **70**(1), 1–11 (2018). https://doi.org/10.1080/00336297.2017.1359636
3. Nan, J., He A, W.: Directional thinking and design of intelligent interactive products for blind people. Mech. Electr. Prod. Dev. Innov. **31**(3) (2018)
4. Zhang, X., Tian, J., Gao, T., Zhang, D., Zhou, H.: Tactile cognition and art product design for the blind based on emotional interaction. In: Stephanidis, C., Antona, M., Ntoa, S., Salvendy, G. (eds.) HCII 2022. CCIS, vol. 1654, pp. 233–238. Springer, Cham (2022). https://doi.org/10.1007/978-3-031-19679-9_29
5. Brady, E., Morris, M.R., Zhong, Y., White, S., Bigham, J.P.: Visual challenges in the everyday lives of blind people. In: Proceedings of the SIGCHI Conference on Human Factors in Computing Systems (CHI 2013), pp. 2117–2126. Association for Computing Machinery, New York (2013). https://doi.org/10.1145/2470654.2481291
6. Siddhartha, B., Chavan, A.P., Uma, B.V.: An electronic smart jacket for the navigation of visually impaired society. Mater. Today Proc. **5**(4), 10665–10669 (2018)
7. Brunes, A., Hansen, M.B., Heir, T.: Loneliness among adults with visual impairment: prevalence, associated factors, and relationship to life satisfaction. Health Qual. Life Outcomes **17**, 24 (2019). https://doi.org/10.1186/s12955-019-1096-y
8. Demmin, D.L., Silverstein, S.M.: Visual impairment and mental health: unmet needs and treatment options. Clin. Ophthalmol. **14**, 4229–4251 (2020). https://doi.org/10.2147/OPTH.S258783

9. Kim, A.M., Park, J.-H.: Mental health and depressive mood in people with visual impairments. J. Vis. Impair. Blindness **117**(4), 314–325 (2023). https://doi.org/10.1177/0145482X231193970
10. Cotzin, Dallenbach: Facial vision: the role of pitch and loudness in the location of obstacles by the blind. Am. J. Psychol. (1950)
11. Rosenblum, L.D., Gordon, M.S., Jarquin, L.: Echolocating distance by moving and stationary listeners. Biol. Psychol. 12(31), 81–206 (2000)
12. Arthur, P., Passimi, R.: Wayfinding: People, Signs, and Architecture. Mcgraw-Hill, USA (1992)
13. Zhao A, X.: The enlightenment of video games on vocational education and teaching in blind schools China's education informatization (2017)
14. Wu A, J.: Embodied practice in somatosensory games - taking the game "ring fit adventure" as an example "new media research"
15. Sanders, E.B.-N.: From user-centered to participatory design approaches. In: Design and Social Science (2002)
16. He J, H.: Design, user experience and usability of future museums Gamified participatory museum experiences (2019)
17. Chen, X.: The process of construction of spatial representation in the unfamiliar environment in the blind: the role of strategies and its effect. https://doi.org/10.3724/SP.J.1041.2016.00637
18. Chen, C.: A study of ergonomic design for the blind: the perspective of human-sense characteristics
19. Hull, J.M.: Touching the rock: an experience of blindness
20. Salimi, S., Sadeghi, A.: A comparison of emotion regulation strategies of blind students with sighted students (2016). https://doi.org/10.18869/nrip.irj.14.2.127

Human-Centered Design for Social Impact

Perceived Value of UX in Organizations: A Systematic Literature Review

Louis Amant[1(✉)], Luka Rukonić[1,2], and Suzanne Kieffer[1]

[1] Université Catholique de Louvain, Institute for Language and Communication, Louvain-la-Neuve, Belgium
{louis.amant,luka.rukonic,suzanne.kieffer}@uclouvain.be

[2] AISIN Europe, Connected and Sharing Solutions, Braine l'Alleud, Belgium

Abstract. This systematic literature review (SLR) examines what factors affect the perceived value of user experience (UX) in organizations. Integrating UX activities into organizational processes and software development is a widely addressed topic in the literature. However, although the social perception of the UX integration process is key for its successful execution, we do not have a concise understanding of this concept. To bridge this gap, we conducted an SLR answering two research questions: 1) What factors influence the perceived value of UX in organizations? and 2) What are the existing tools to measure or evaluate the perceived value of UX? Database search retrieved 49 publications, and we analyzed the content of 14 papers published between 2012 and 2023. The results are divided into six themes, each describing the positive and negative impacts on the perceived value of UX: understanding UX, UX resources, UX culture, perceived UX value, UX management, and UX work organization. Also, we found that the concept of the perceived value of UX is not yet developed in the HCI literature, and no tools have been developed to measure it. Therefore, further research on defining this concept is needed to understand better how social perception of UX affects its integration.

Keywords: User experience · UX perceived value · UX maturity · UX culture · Systematic literature review

1 Introduction

The perception of organizational agile software development (ASD) practices by employees has been studied extensively, mainly due to a lack of empirical studies that could illustrate the quantitative benefits of agile practices [19]. For instance, team members' perception of agile team productivity relates to the mature use of iteration planning and development agile practices [14]. Implementing the continuous delivery practice benefits customers and clients, from improved product quality and productivity to smoother collaboration and communication between them [21]. Therefore, the perception of organizational practices might influence

A. Marcus et al. (Eds.): HCII 2024, LNCS 14714, pp. 177–194, 2024.
https://doi.org/10.1007/978-3-031-61356-2_12

organizational outcomes, commitment to organizational goals, and project success. This paper focuses on the non-user experience (UX) staff (e.g., software developers, managers, project leads) perceptions of UX practices and the consequences their perceptions might produce. Specifically, we looked into literature on what barriers, misunderstandings, collaboration, and communication issues happen and what solutions, strategies, and frameworks exist to integrate UX and ASD practices in organizations from the social perspective.

A survey of User-Centered Design (UCD) practitioners in the industry [43] showed that they believe UCD practices improve product usefulness and usability. However, they lacked measures and evaluation criteria to show UCD's effectiveness and often relied on internal measures, such as customer satisfaction or enhanced ease of use. Later work on the return on investment of UX (UX ROI) [4] is divided into three types: social, internal, and external. Although UX work is expensive, indicators such as competitive advantage, increased user satisfaction, reduction of development costs, reuse of design principles, or innovations brought forward by UX research represent useful justifications for the investment in UX activities [4]. Nevertheless, direct revenues from UX work are difficult to calculate and precise methods to do so do not exist.

Issues impeding high UX maturity include blocking factors leading to strategic planning issues include the lack of management support and resistance among engineers and/or management to usability [36] and the lack of sensitivity and responsivity among developers toward the work of usability practitioners [44]. Cost-justifying usability can help overcome these issues [4,31]. However, struggles remain when integrating UCD or UX into formal software development models because various social aspects influence the context in which the integration happens [2,10,38].

UX capability/maturity models (UXCMMs) offer structured solutions for step-by-step integrations of UX practices into organizations. UX maturity refers to how consistently an organization implements UX processes to achieve UX goals [37]. UXCMMs enable assessing software engineering organizations' UX capabilities and maturity. Based on these assessments, such models recommend moving toward a higher UX maturity level, i.e., optimizing UX processes and their ROI [9,10,37]. See [27] for a systematic literature review (SLR) about UXCMMs.

To the best of our knowledge, neither the implementation of the UCD approach nor the integration of UX practices in organizations has been studied from the social perception perspective. Concretely, integrating UX and UCD practices into software development processes affects how developers, designers, and managers execute their work tasks and might change their perception of contributions toward achieving business goals. Understanding how stakeholders perceive UX practices can provide insights into the organizational culture, collaboration dynamics, and the overall effectiveness of UX integration. Although some papers draw attention to the social aspects of stakeholders' perception of UCD or UX [3,22], little is known about the social ROI of UCD or UX.

To identify and synthesize the relevant published research on the social ROI of UX, we conducted an SLR. Specifically, we aim to answer the following research questions:

- **RQ1:** What factors influence the perceived value of UX in organizations for UX and non-UX-trained staff?
- **RQ2:** What are the existing measures and tools to evaluate the perceived value of UX?

The contribution of this paper is to define a baseline or to identify avenues for future research regarding the increase of social ROI of UX while integrating UX. The increase in social ROI and UX perceived value would, we believe, significantly facilitate and improve the integration of UX into software development models, as well as help organizations in their quest to increase UX maturity.

2 Background and Related Work

2.1 User Experience

The concept of UX emerged from closely related disciplines such as usability engineering, UCD, and human-centered design (HCD) [15,17]. These approaches share a common thread in placing the user in the center of the development process and designing systems based on user needs, guided by user research data.

The International Organization for Standardization [20] defines UX as "a person's perceptions and responses that result from the use or anticipated use of a product, system or service". Thus, UX is context-dependent and subjective, allowing designers to only design for desired experiences without guaranteeing that the target users will live them. The definition deliberately excludes any dimension associated with the practice of design. The definition articulates UX in terms of the dynamic interaction between the user and a system across various temporal dimensions. We fully endorse this definition and assert that design shapes UX. In this context, UX is intricately connected to the essence of the system, and the design of the system can exert a notable influence, either positively or negatively, on the overall UX.

Hence, we rely on specific processes and practices to design for UX, using the process reference model (PRM) [23] as our primary reference. The PRM delineates four UX processes: analysis, design, formative evaluation, and summative evaluation. Additionally, it incorporates a suite of supporting UX methods designed to address these processes, ensuring the achievement of expected outcomes.

2.2 UX Integration

In the ever-intensifying landscape of competition, organizations often rely on products' UX as a pivotal differentiator, influencing product quality and, consequently, business success [16,40]. However, organizations opting to integrate UX activities into their established ASD processes, like Scrum, Extreme Programming, Kanban, or Crystal, must accommodate time and resources to conduct them to achieve UX integration [23]. Due to their shared characteristics, including constant collaboration, iterative approaches, swift testing, adaptability, and stakeholder involvement, UX and ASD are frequently combined [41]. Despite their theoretical compatibility, organizations often encounter challenges in this integration venture [11,22,39]. To overcome these difficulties, several integration strategies have been used in industry and documented in the literature. A literature review [3] addressed this issue by creating a framework listing different integration mechanisms in five main categories: practices integration, process integration, technology integration, people integration, and social integration. In a comprehensive literature review [6], the authors adopted the classification established by [3], shedding light on the constituent principles of UX and ASD integration. Their research underscores a growing interest within the research community in the social dimension of UX ASD integration. UX maturity assessment implies using UXCMMs to evaluate both UX capabilities and maturity within software engineering organizations. Each UXCMM describes an incremental path from lower to higher maturity levels, where competencies and capabilities increase at each level. Various maturity indicators identified in the literature include the timing of UX involvement, UX expertise and resources, the use of appropriate techniques and deliverables, UX-aware leadership and culture, the integration of UX processes with other corporate processes, resource availability, and user involvement [9,10].

As UXCMMs assume an incremental improvement of the aforementioned maturity indicators, UX maturity is inherently linked to the level of UX integration in an organization and the mindset of individuals in it. Reaching higher levels of UX maturity requires individuals to have a strong awareness of the UX ROI, develop a user-first mindset, and contribute toward building positive perceptions and attitudes about UX activities. Thus, enhancing the perceived value of UX (social ROI) is posited to correlate directly with a positive impact on UX maturity. This correlation, in turn, fosters a more robust organizational UX culture, facilitating the transition from intermediate to advanced stages of maturity. Existing literature identifies these transitional phases as intricate milestones to effectively integrating UX principles [46].

2.3 UX Return on Investment

Given that UX is grounded in UCD [28], metrics to assess the ROI of UCD also apply to UX. Examples of metrics include increased sales and revenues, reduced development time and costs, or reduced technical support and training needs [45]. The ROI is broken down into internal, external, and social. Internal ROI refers to the improvement of the system development lifecycle resulting from better UCD practices and, therefore, can be attributed to the UCD staff (i.e., UX designer, UX researcher, UX lead, UX strategist, UX analyst, UX evaluator, UX manager, field study specialist, or interaction designer [8]). External ROI refers to the improvement of the system and thus affects users and customers.

Social ROI refers to the organizational benefits stemming from improving the attitudes, beliefs, and perceptions of non-UCD staff toward UCD, UCD staff, and users. The authors specify that the credibility of UCD practitioners may depend as much on perceptions of ROI as on actual ROI metrics. Social ROI is characterized by buy-in from management, the belief that UCD is beneficial, and a supportive network that will allow UCD processes to reach their highest possible capability.

2.4 UX Culture

Combining previously mentioned theoretical concepts, building organizational UX culture is a key strategic goal to achieve good UX integration. Previous studies [9,13] found that, building an organizational UX culture takes years. Evangelizing UX practice to stakeholders and teaching UX skills to colleagues showed a fruitful enhancer toward UX-oriented cultures organizations. The flow of competence from individual UX staff to other stakeholders can be achieved through sharing UX knowledge and raising awareness of the successful contributions of UX staff to product development. Additionally, organizing workshops to teach UX concepts, educating management on the importance of user testing and UX design, and building an internal stakeholder supporter base all contribute toward building a stronger UX culture [9]. Moreover, building UX capacity through hiring UX staff, dedicating budget to UX, and investing in materials and infrastructure results in a more UX-oriented culture where the organization understands the value of UX and is ready to integrate UX practices into its software development processes [30]. We drew on these concepts to build our search queries and define the hypotheses for this SLR. Finally, building a UX culture requires a holistic approach to UX practices, making them part of the organization's strategic goals and including all participating stakeholders in the UX work rather than just a small team of UX practitioners [18].

3 Methodology

We followed Kitchenham's methodology [25] to conduct the SLR. This methodology covers three phases (Fig. 1): planning, conducting, and reporting. The planning phase is covered in this paper's introduction and background sections, laying out the reasons for conducting this SLR and formulating the research questions. The conducting phase is explained in this section, while the reporting phase is covered in Sect. 4.

3.1 Conducting the Literature Review

Search Process. We consider UX to form part of human-computer interaction (HCI), a research discipline building on top of (1) behavioral sciences such as psychology, anthropology, sociology, ergonomy and cognitive sciences; (2) design such as graphic design, information design and interaction design; (3) computer

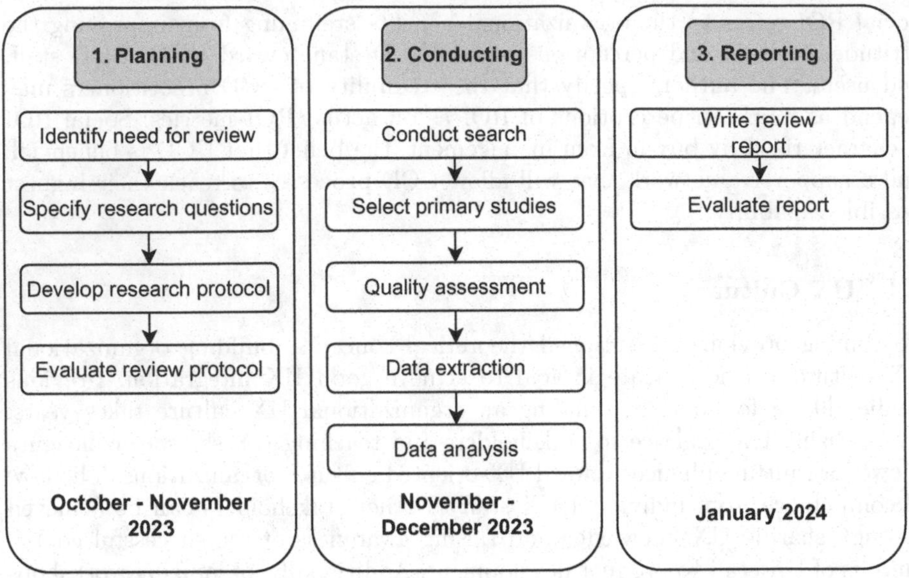

Fig. 1. SLR Process by [25]

science such as computer graphics and computer vision. To avoid retrieving duplicates, we looked for results in Scopus and ACM Digital Library (ACM DL), which index publications in HCI from other relevant databases like IEEE and ScienceDirect. We referred to the works of key authors [4,6] to determine our query keywords. However, queries involving keywords "perceived value" and "social ROI", being less common in HCI literature, yielded no results, and despite testing various queries with synonyms, none proved fruitful. Therefore, we expanded our query to include concepts such as UX maturity, UX awareness, and UX culture. Although guidelines for conducting an SLR recommend consulting various sources, such as digital libraries, journals, grey literature, magazines, conferences, research registers, and internet sources, we focused only on databases that index peer-reviewed academic literature to examine the scientific understanding of the issue. Accordingly, we designed this query for Scopus:

TITLE-ABS-KEY ("ux maturity" OR "ux culture" OR "ux transformation" OR "ux integration" OR "ux awareness").

We modified the query to fit ACM DL's search engine design and extracted the articles from both databases on November 8, 2023.

Study Selection and Eligibility Criteria. First, as our study specifically focuses on UX, we only considered papers explicitly mentioning UX, excluding those discussing solely usability engineering, UCD, or HCD. Second, we established the inclusion and exclusion criteria while identifying concepts and keywords for the query. The iterative task of refining the query to achieve the desired outcome is a crucial means of delineating what is considered outside the scope of the study. This process aids in defining eligibility criteria (Table 1) for guiding the subsequent screening. Using Microsoft Excel, we screened the content of the retrieved articles in two steps:

1. title, keywords, and abstract screening;
2. full-text screening.

Table 1. Inclusion and exclusion criteria

Criteria	Inclusion	Exclusion
1) Language	English or French	other
2) Peer-reviewed	yes	no
3) Document type	conference paper or article	conference proceedings preface, workshops, posters, magazine articles, tutorials, and non-primary studies (systematic mapping and systematic, narrative, and semi-SLRs)
4) Content criteria	discussing perceived value of UX within an organization	not discussing the perceived value of UX within an organization
5) Content criteria	focusing on the perceived value of UX processes for different stakeholder type	focusing (only) on product perception for users
6) Content criteria	focusing on system development by adopting UX processes and practices	Focusing on system development without considering the adoption of UX processes and practices

The third author acted as a final decision-maker when the two first authors disagreed on including or excluding a paper. We recorded all disagreements and their reasons throughout both screening steps. We defined two types of eligibility criteria: metacriteria and content criteria. The first three are metacriteria and are applied using database filters, except for language in ACM DL. The remaining three are content criteria and helped us select primary studies during the screening process. To identify and remove duplicates, we applied Excel's *conditional formatting* to the authors' information and the article title, and then applied *highlight cells*, followed by *duplicate values* feature. This allowed us to double-check the presence of any duplicates within our results. Two duplicates occurred in our results. These co-occurrences are due to the presence of each of these papers in the two databases queried. We only retrieved papers from selected databases to limit duplicates, avoiding overlaps in what each indexed, as explained in Sect. 3.1. We excluded one paper from the analysis as the full text was inaccessible.

Quality Assessment. The first and third authors conducted the quality assessment (QA) similarly to another SLR [24] for assessing the eligibility of the retrieved papers. Their QA methodology relies on *QualSyst*, a tool developed by [26]. This is a standardized checklist for evaluating primary research from different fields. The tool proposes an adapted version for qualitative and quantitative research and a concrete guide in appendices on applying the QA checklist. As the retrieved papers contain mainly qualitative results, we decided to use the *Checklist for assessing the quality of qualitative studies* presented in Table 2 of [26] without criteria 10 due to its irrelevancy in HCI. Each checklist criteria was rated according to fulfillment level (2 = yes, 1 = partial, 0 = no) defined in *QualSyst.* Criteria not applicable to a specific study design were labeled 'n/a' and not considered when calculating the final score. The overall score was calculated by dividing the total points earned by the study on the checklist by the maximum possible points. For example, if there is one 'n/a', the maximum possible score is 16 points (9 criteria x 2 points = 18 points). To maintain a high-quality standard, we excluded papers scoring less than 75% from this study according to the QA scoring procedure outlined by [42]. Therefore, we excluded five papers at this stage.

Table 2. Average QA scores (2 reviewers) per paper (column 1) across nine criteria from [26]. Ref. stands for reference, Max. for the maximum score possible, n.a. for non-applicable.

Ref.	1	2	3	4	5	6	7	8	9	Total	Max.	%
[1]	1	2	2	2	2	1.5	2	2	2	16.5	18	91.60
[2]	2	2	2	2	2	2	2	2	2	18	18	100.00
[3]	2	2	2	2	2	2	1.5	2	2	17.5	18	94.40
[8]	2	2	2	2	2	1	2	0	2	15	18	83.30
[9]	2	2	2	2	2	2	2	2	2	18	18	100.00
[18]	2	2	2	2	2	2	2	2	2	18	18	100.00
[22]	2	2	2	2	2	2	2	2	2	18	18	100.00
[29]	1.5	2	2	2	2	2	2	2	2	17.5	18	94.40
[30]	2	1.5	2	2	n.a	n.a	n.a	2	2	11.5	12	95.80
[32]	2	2	2	2	2	2	2	2	2	18	18	100.00
[33]	2	2	2	2	2	2	2	2	2	18	18	100.00
[34]	2	2	2	2	1.5	2	2	2	2	17.5	18	94.40
[35]	2	2	2	2	2	2	2	2	2	18	18	100.00
[46]	2	2	2	2	2	2	2	2	2	18	18	100.00

Data Extraction. We extracted the following data for each study: title, keywords, abstract, study type (i.e., theoretical, empirical, model construction), methodological choices (i.e., interview, survey, observation), research questions or study objectives, and main research findings.

Deviation from the SLR Protocol. We decided to manually include two papers that were not found by the query we ran on databases:

- Study [3] was authored by productive authors within the realm of the perceived value of UX and the social capital associated with UX. It was not indexed by the databases we searched in.
- Study [18] was found while selecting keywords for our query. We could not incorporate keywords from this paper into our search query for Scopus and maintain a reasonable number of papers for screening. Neither the title, the abstract, nor the keywords of this article match our query because the authors use the keyword "organizational culture" instead of "UX culture".

Data Analysis. The two first authors analyzed the data using the thematic analysis (TA) method from [5]. We chose TA because this methodology is known for its application flexibility regarding sample size, research questions, and meaning generation approach. This flexibility should comply with the iterative SLR process. To a greater degree, we believe this methodological choice is suitable to deliver both outcomes of this SLR, i.e., identification of factors influencing the perceived value of UX and identification of its measurement tools. Using TA allowed us to create themes and discuss key aspects of the perceived value of UX using inductive open coding established from the first full-text reading of the included primary studies. This process is, therefore, a bottom-up process.

We generated an initial set of codes during the second screening step according to the TA methodology [5], i.e., "Familiarizing yourself with your data" and "Generating initial codes". After data extraction, we coded the papers by thoroughly reading the full text and searching for data relevant to our research questions. For example, ideas, results, or data related to the perceived value of UX were extracted into an Excel sheet and assigned one or multiple codes. While coding, we discussed codes by sharing codebooks and analyzed potential similarities and differences, thus continuously adapting the codes according to phases 3, 4, and 5 of the TA methodology, respectively "Searching for themes", "Reviewing themes", and "Defining and naming themes". We present phase 6 of the TA, i.e., "Producing the report", in Sect. 4. Figure 2 presents the PRISMA flow diagram tracking the complete selection process of primary studies.

4 Results

Table 3 lists the 14 studies included in this SLR that passed the screening based on our eligibility criteria and QA. The articles were published between 2012 and 2023. The data analysis resulted in 25 codes. We consolidated 24 of them into 6 themes answering RQ1 and used the remaining one to answer RQ2 (Sect. 4).

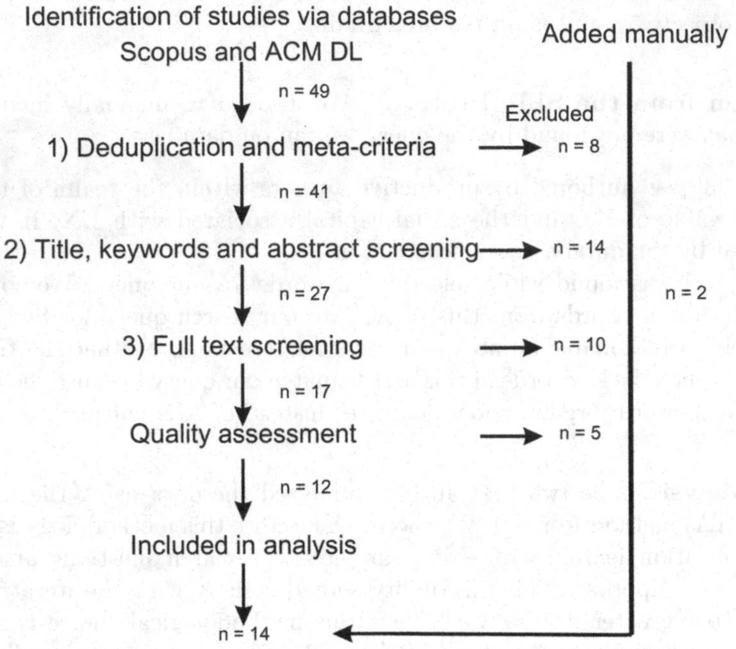

Fig. 2. PRISMA flow diagram/paper selection process

Table 3. Included papers. "CS" stands for Case Study.

Ref.	Year	Study type	Approach type
[1]	2020	Empirical	Mixed
[2]	2023	Empirical/double CS	Qualitative
[3]	2012	Theoretical + framework construction	Mixed
[8]	2018	Empirical/CS	Qualitative
[9]	2023	Empirical/ multiple CS	Qualitative
[18]	2013	Empirical/CS	Qualitative
[22]	2019	Empirical/CS	Qualitative
[29]	2017	Empirical	Qualitative
[30]	2019	Theoretical + model construction	Qualitative
[32]	2023	Empirical/CS	Qualitative
[33]	2023	Empirical/CS	Qualitative
[34]	2015	Empirical/CS	Qualitative
[35]	2023	Empirical	Mixed
[46]	2020	Empirical	Mixed

4.1 RQ1: What Factors Influence the Perceived Value of UX in Organizations for UX and Non-UX Trained Staff?

Theme 1: Understanding UX Terminology, Concepts, and Metrics. Stakeholders' understanding of UX processes, UCD, and related concepts is essential for building a positive perceived value of UX. Knowing what UX practitioners do and how they can collaborate with other team members, such as developers, plays a vital role in valuing UX work [18]. Interestingly, developers can find it easy to connect with the wireframes provided by UX consultants and yet consider UX as a "black box" [8]. This aligns with other studies that also reported stakeholders considering UX as a "black box" appearing before development [32,33]. Furthermore, in low-UX maturity organizations, UX professionals must invest significant effort in educating both clients and colleagues about UX to get the necessary buy-in [2,9,18,30]. Finally, the complexity and wide range of UX responsibilities makes it hard for organizations to understand and agree on the UX outcomes [8,22].

We identified several strategies for improving the understanding of UX practices in organizations. For instance, ensuring that stakeholders have at least a theoretical understanding of UX positively affects the perceived value of UX. Poor understanding of UX results in considering it resource-intensive and might make UX work deprioritized [32] and UX practitioners isolated and misunderstood [29]. Additionally, knowledge transfer from UX practitioners to non-UX staff (i.e., developers, clients, management) helps improve organization-wide UX integration and understanding, leading to more willingness to do UX work and better team collaboration throughout projects [3,30,33]. Finally, organizing regular UX trainings [9,32,35] for developers and educating clients on UX [9] seem to produce good results for generating positive perception of UX.

Theme 2: UX Resources. Numerous studies link the lack of UX resources to a deficiency in organizational UX strategy [9,33,34]. This lack of UX resources stems from negative perceptions of UX, further constraining available resources for UX activities [32], compelling UX staff to juggle multiple projects with tight deadlines [2], and posing challenges in scoping UX work for practitioners [29]. In addition, it manifests in UX activities occurring late in the development process [9], leading to bottlenecks and delayed outcomes [2].

Hiring UX staff is often the initial step toward advancing UX maturity. Typically, organizations increase the resources allocated to UX [34,35] after achieving a successful buy-in by hiring UX staff, investing in UX infrastructure, and/or allocating time for conducting UX work [30]. However, hiring UX staff is often the most expensive investment in UX [30]. To expedite the integration of UX, it is crucial to involve management with a strong grasp of the significance of including users in the design process [29]. Nevertheless, integrating newly hired team members into existing structures can lead to tensions [3]. To address this challenge, [30] suggests prioritizing hiring UX staff with broad knowledge and skills capable of contributing to the development of organizational UX capacity.

For instance, developers with an interest or background in UX can significantly enhance awareness of its importance.

Theme 3: Organizational UX Culture. Developing a UX culture is essential to create favorable conditions for UX integration. UX culture or mindset stems from realizing that addressing user needs makes way for better products and gaining competitive advantage [9]. However, that does not always lead to immediate product redesigns [30].

There are multiple interventions that can help organizations build a UX culture. For example, active participation in UX activities results in higher awareness of the day-to-day responsibilities of UX practitioners [9,18,30]. Similarly, observation of UX activities may help non-UX staff grasp the essence of UX, minimizing resistance to the new methods of working necessary for UX integration. Also, engaging in discussion about UX and producing educational materials for how UX could benefit product development helps to accept UX as a strategic asset [22]. Further, evangelizing UX wider than direct management, such as to marketing departments, is key for making UX institutionalized [9]. Other interventions include organizing company events where employees can attend field studies [30], creating dedicated UX teams [29], broadly sharing UX knowledge and results [30], and starting marketing campaigns to promote the experience with products organizations develop [22].

Theme 4: Perceived UX Value. The value of UX is perceived as low in organizations that fail to acknowledge the importance of hiring UX professionals with formal UX practices and instead consider UX work as "soft skills" that everyone possesses [32,35]. Giving UX practitioners a defined and stable job position with career prospects is a strong signal of UX strategy [35]. In addition, the fun experienced by UX practitioners while conducting UX activities also influences the perceived value of UX [32], which aligns with prior work [7]. Further, stakeholders' perceived value of UX can be either influenced by the external ROI (economic benefits) or by the internal ROI (process optimization), which is also in line with prior work [45].

One strategy to demonstrate the impact of external ROI on perceived UX value is to select a product that serves as a flagship for UX in the product line, ensuring a positive association between UX and its system-wide impact [18]. Another strategy lies in involving stakeholders in UX activities and colocating them in shared offices with UX practitioners can enhance internal ROI [32], aligning their mindsets, limiting the black box effect, and demystifying UX work for non-UX staff. Stakeholders' involvement strategy induces UX transversality across stakeholder groups, making them actors of UX integration [2]. Customers' high perception of UX value motivates, even enforces, organizational UX buy-in [22]. Finally, organizations that institutionalized UX exhibit higher perceived UX value [29]. For example, organizations recognizing the value of UX and allocating more UX resources increase UX maturity [46]. These findings underscore a direct connection between the value of UX and the themes explored in this

SLR. Such insights should inspire UX practitioners to extend their efforts beyond simply raising awareness of UX among their colleagues.

Theme 5: UX Management. Attitudes and behaviors of both UX and non-UX managers toward UX practices significantly impact UX integration in organizations. Non-UX managers' perceived UX ROI greatly impacts UX practices in corporate environments. Projects receive financial support accelerating positive outcomes when non-UX managers acknowledge UX ROI [9], whereas non-UX managers' negative perceptions of UX lead to individuals' resistance to UX [32]. To address such resistance, organizations could create a UX guild that brings together UX representatives to ensure UX consistency across the organization and builds a common ground for structuring UX practices and management [22]. Such guild and UX representatives can embody the UX leadership to limit the feeling of "noise" and allow stakeholders to understand UX processes. This avoids the feeling of having "three captains on one ship" [9], which can be detrimental to perceived UX value as a serious, structured practice. It is crucial for executive managers to support UX practices, as their perceived value of UX shapes how employees approach UX. In case of high perceived UX value, UX managers can make decisions and document the decision-making process [2]. If there is no designated UX manager, employees who are well-liked and trusted can be identified to act as UX "flag holders" who spread a good perceived UX value [32]. UX flag holders know the organization's inner workings and unwritten rules and can facilitate UX integration.

Theme 6: UX Work Organization. One key finding lies in the value delivery from UX to development processes. As explained by [34], breaking down UX tasks and linking them to agile sprint goals can enhance the transparency of value deliveries to the development process. Consequently, understanding these processes can greatly improve the perceived value of UX and foster behaviors and attitudes conducive to adherence to the practice. When UX is integrated into an organization, UX processes have to fit in with pre-existing processes and the teams in place who operate these processes. For example, [9] suggest understanding organizational processes better by mapping the role of each of its stakeholders to identify the key supportive figures to become UX champions. Strategically, organizations can also opt for a pilot project to raise awareness of these processes and make existing teams understand the new UX-related practices by demonstrating them as easy and accessible [22]. This strategy diminishes the discovery effect and accompanies employees in their discovery to encourage the development of an attitude and behaviors inclined to embrace UX. In fact, a good understanding and visibility of the benefits of UX practices increases their perceived value, leading to greater acceptance and integration by employees. This awareness can also be raised by demonstrating the benefits of certain UX methods for information management, such as mock-up or storyboarding, which are simple, accessible, and impactful [22].

Finally, the second key finding touches on the lack of perceived value in UX, which often leads to a lack of prioritization in various aspects of the project. In fact, prioritization is a mechanism that manifests itself in the timing of processes, the prioritization of requirements (user and functional), the allocation of budget adapted to the research objectives (access to users, building prototypes for user testing, acquiring materials required to implement UX methods, etc.) and in the recruitment of human resources adapted to the research needs and to the performance of UX activities in the best possible circumstances (validity of results, workload, etc.). Indeed, UX in a low perceived value context is often disadvantaged. As reported in an observational study [2], it is not uncommon to witness a temporarily halted development cycle. However, for this to occur, it is essential for the project manager to have a perceived value of UX that enables them to make choices regarding prioritization. To conclude, power dynamics and challenging communication between developers and UX practitioners are often cited as barriers to the integration of UX and the cohesion of teams toward successfully integrating both approaches to unleash their full potential. In this regard, [3] suggests utilizing meetings to announce and publicly emphasize instances where collaboration between the two teams has led to the success of system development. This strategy aims to diminish counterproductive behaviors toward UX practitioners by raising the perceived value brought by their contribution.

4.2 RQ2: Measures and Tools to Evaluate Perceived Value of UX

We found only one study dealing with tools for measuring the perceived value of UX [1]. The author asked information technology practitioners to rate how much their organization values UX on a 7-point scale, where a higher rating meant a higher perceived value of UX. However, this was based on only one question in the survey, and it was not further described in the paper. All other studies in this SLR were qualitative and descriptive of the organizational UX strategy and employees' attitudes toward UX practices.

5 Conclusion

Perception of UX value is a complex construct determined by several factors. In low UX-maturity organizations, individual employees shed light on the importance of UX and start advocating for user-centered practices. Organizational buy-in happens after successful project contributions become clear to a wider scope of stakeholders, which primarily means convincing the management of its positive contributions. Often, UX work is perceived as a black box whose processes and practices are not understood by the organization and thus often underestimated in the time, staff, and budget required. The perception usually changes thanks to UX champions who promote UX and advocate for its strategic integration into organizational processes (i.e., evangelization). Nevertheless, both UX training and including non-UX staff in UX activities are key activities helping increase the positive perceived value of UX in organizations.

The key finding from this SLR is that understanding UX and its practices is the initial step toward enhancing perceived UX value and UX integration, which aligns with [2,9,22]. The six themes uncovered in this SLR provide a strong foundation for future work. This future work endeavors to construct a framework for assessing individuals' perceived UX value based on the six related influencing factors and their associated codes. The perceived UX value, being a continuum, will likely entail the utilization of a declarative scale questionnaire.

Finally, we raise two hypotheses regarding the struggles impeding UX integration: the successful integration of UX is correlated with the perceived value of UX (H1), and the high perceived value of UX in organizations generates social ROI (H2).

Acknowledgments. This research was funded by the Service Public de Wallonie, project UX-DI (grant number 8637) and AISIN Europe. We thank the anonymous reviewers for their comments on improving this paper.

Disclosure of Interests. All authors declared that they have no conflict of interest relevant to the content of this article. Luka Rukonić is an employee of AISIN Europe.

References

1. Alhadreti, O.: Exploring UX maturity in software development environments in Saudi Arabia. Int. J. Adv. Comput. Sci. Appl. **11**(12) (2020). https://doi.org/10.14569/IJACSA.2020.0111221
2. Azevedo, D., Rukonić, L., Kieffer, S.: The gap between UX literacy and UX practices in agile-UX settings: a case study. In: Abdelnour Nocera, J., Kristín Lárusdóttir, M., Petrie, H., Piccinno, A., Winckler, M. (eds.) Human-Computer Interaction – INTERACT 2023: 19th IFIP TC13 International Conference, York, UK, August 28 – September 1, 2023, Proceedings, Part II, pp. 436–457. Springer Nature Switzerland, Cham (2023). https://doi.org/10.1007/978-3-031-42283-6_24
3. Barksdale, J.T., McCrickard, D.S.: Software product innovation in agile usability teams: an analytical framework of social capital, network governance, and usability knowledge management. Int. J. Agile Extreme Softw. Develop. **1**(1), 52–77 (2012). https://doi.org/10.1504/IJAESD.2012.048302
4. Bias, R.G., Mayhew, D.J.: Cost-justifying usability: an update for an Internet age, vol. Elsevier, Second (2005)
5. Braun, V., Clarke, V.: Using thematic analysis in psychology. Qual. Res. Psychol. **3**(2), 77–101 (2006). https://doi.org/10.1191/1478088706qp063oa
6. Brhel, M., Meth, H., Maedche, A., Werder, K.: Exploring principles of user-centered agile software development: a literature review. Inf. Softw. Technol. **61**, 163–181 (2015). https://doi.org/10.1016/j.infsof.2015.01.004
7. Browne, J., Green, L.: The future of work is no work: A call to action for designers in the abolition of work. In: Extended Abstracts of the 2022 CHI Conference on Human Factors in Computing Systems. CHI EA '22, Association for Computing Machinery, New York, NY, USA (2022). https://doi.org/10.1145/3491101.3516385, https://doi.org/10.1145/3491101.3516385

8. Bruun, A., Larusdottir, M.K., Nielsen, L., Nielsen, P.A., Persson, J.S.: The role of UX professionals in agile development: a case study from industry. In: Proceedings of the 10th Nordic Conference on Human-Computer Interaction, pp. 352–363. NordiCHI '18, Association for Computing Machinery, New York, NY, USA (2018). https://doi.org/10.1145/3240167.3240213
9. Buis, E., Ashby, S., Kouwenberg, K.: Increasing the UX maturity level of clients: a study of best practices in an agile environment. Inf. Softw. Technol. **154**, 107086 (2023). https://doi.org/10.1016/j.infsof.2022.107086
10. Chapman, L., Plewes, S.: A UX maturity model: effective introduction of UX into organizations. LNCS (including subseries Lecture Notes in Artificial Intelligence and Lecture Notes in Bioinformatics) **8520 LNCS**(PART 4), 12–22 (2014). https://doi.org/10.1007/978-3-319-07638-6_2
11. Choma, J., Guerra, E.M., Alvaro, A., Pereira, R., Zaina, L.: Influences of UX factors in the agile UX context of software startups. Inf. Softw. Technol. **152**, 107041 (2022)
12. De Bruin, T., Rosemann, M., Freeze, R., Kaulkarni, U.: Understanding the main phases of developing a maturity assessment model. In: Australasian Conference on Information Systems (ACIS), pp. 8–19. Australasian Chapter of the Association for Information Systems (2005)
13. Gray, C.M., Toombs, A.L., Gross, S.: Flow of competence in UX design practice. In: Proceedings of the 33rd Annual ACM Conference on Human Factors in Computing Systems, pp. 3285–3294. CHI '15, Association for Computing Machinery, New York, NY, USA (2015). https://doi.org/10.1145/2702123.2702579
14. Gren, L.: The links between agile practices, interpersonal conflict, and perceived productivity. In: Proceedings of the 21st International Conference on Evaluation and Assessment in Software Engineering, pp. 292–297. EASE '17, Association for Computing Machinery, New York, NY, USA (2017). https://doi.org/10.1145/3084226.3084269
15. Hassan, H.M., Galal-Edeen, G.H.: From usability to user experience. In: 2017 International Conference on Intelligent Informatics and Biomedical Sciences (ICIIBMS), pp. 216–222. IEEE (2017). https://doi.org/10.1109/ICIIBMS.2017.8279761
16. Hassenzahl, M.: User experience (ux) towards an experiential perspective on product quality. In: Proceedings of the 20th Conference on l'Interaction Homme-Machine, pp. 11–15 (2008). https://doi.org/10.1145/1512714.1512717
17. Hassenzahl, M., Tractinsky, N.: User experience-a research agenda. Behav. Inform. Technol. **25**(2), 91–97 (2006)
18. Heikkinen, M., Määttä, H.: Design driven product innovation in enhancing user experience oriented organisational culture in b-to-b organisations. In: 2013 IEEE Tsinghua International Design Management Symposium, pp. 127–135. IEEE (2013)
19. Holgeid, K.K., Jørgensen, M.: Benefits management and agile practices in software projects: how perceived benefits are impacted. In: 2020 IEEE 22nd Conference on Business Informatics (CBI), vol. 2, pp. 48–56. IEEE (2020)
20. ISO: Ergonomics of human-system interaction part 210: Human-centred design for interactive systems. Standard ISO 9241-210:2019, International Organization for Standardization, Geneva, CH (2019). https://www.iso.org/standard/77520.html
21. Itkonen, J., Udd, R., Lassenius, C., Lehtonen, T.: Perceived benefits of adopting continuous delivery practices. In: Proceedings of the 10th ACM/IEEE International Symposium on empirical software engineering and measurement, pp. 1–6 (2016)
22. Kashfi, P., Feldt, R., Nilsson, A.: Integrating UX principles and practices into software development organizations: a case study of influencing events. J. Syst. Softw. **154**, 37–58 (2019)

23. Kieffer, S., Rukonić, L., Kervyn de Meerendré, V., Vanderdonckt, J.: A process reference model for UX. In: Cláudio, A.P., et al. (eds.) Computer Vision, Imaging and Computer Graphics Theory and Applications: 14th International Joint Conference, VISIGRAPP 2019, Prague, Czech Republic, February 25–27, 2019, Revised Selected Papers, pp. 128–152. Springer International Publishing, Cham (2020). https://doi.org/10.1007/978-3-030-41590-7_6
24. Kim, Y.M., Rhiu, I., Yun, M.H.: A systematic review of a virtual reality system from the perspective of user experience. Int. J. Human-Comput. Interact. **36**(10), 893–910 (2020)
25. Kitchenham, B.: Guidelines for performing systematic literature reviews in software engineering. Tech. rep, EBSE Technical Report (2007)
26. Kmet, L.M., Cook, L.S., Lee, R.C.: Standard quality assessment criteria for evaluating primary research papers from a variety of fields. Tech. rep, Alberta Heritage Foundation for Medical Research (2004)
27. Lacerda, T.C., von Wangenheim, C.G.: Systematic literature review of usability capability/maturity models. Comput. Standards Interfaces **55**, 95–105 (2018). https://doi.org/10.1016/j.csi.2017.06.001
28. Law, E.L.C., Roto, V., Hassenzahl, M., Vermeeren, A.P.O.S., Kort, J.: Understanding, scoping and defining user experience: a survey approach. CHI 2009 **23**(1), 23–32 (2009). https://doi.org/10.1145/1518701.1518813
29. MacDonald, C.M.: "It Takes a Village": On UX Librarianship and Building UX Capacity in Libraries. J. Libr. Adm. **57**(2), 194–214 (2017). https://doi.org/10.1080/01930826.2016.1232942
30. MacDonald, C.M.: User experience (UX) capacity-building: A conceptual model and research agenda. In: Proceedings of the 2019 on Designing Interactive Systems Conference, pp. 187–200. DIS '19, Association for Computing Machinery, New York, NY, USA (2019). https://doi.org/10.1145/3322276.3322346
31. Nielsen, J., Berger, J., Gilutz, S., Whitenton, K.: Return on investment (ROI) for usability (2013)
32. Nielsen, S., Ordoñez, R., Skov, M.B., Jochum, E.: Strategies for strengthening UX competencies and cultivating corporate UX in a large organisation developing robots. Behav. Inform. Technol. 1–29 (2023). https://doi.org/10.1080/0144929X.2023.2227284
33. Nielsen, S., Skov, M.B., Bruun, A.: User experience in large-scale robot development: a case study of mechanical and software teams. In: Abdelnour Nocera, J., Kristín Lárusdóttir, M., Petrie, H., Piccinno, A., Winckler, M. (eds.) Human-Computer Interaction – INTERACT 2023: 19th IFIP TC13 International Conference, York, UK, August 28 – September 1, 2023, Proceedings, Part II, pp. 40–61. Springer Nature Switzerland, Cham (2023). https://doi.org/10.1007/978-3-031-42283-6_3
34. Øvad, T., Larsen, L.B.: The prevalence of UX design in agile development processes in industry. In: 2015 Agile Conference, pp. 40–49. IEEE (2015). https://doi.org/10.1109/Agile.2015.13
35. Phesto P. Namayala, T.S.K., Mselle, L.J.: The factors affecting user experience maturity in free and open source software community: an empirical study. Int. J. Human-Comput. Interact. 1–17 (2023). https://doi.org/10.1080/10447318.2023.2262270
36. Rosenbaum, S., Rohn, J.A., Humburg, J.: A toolkit for strategic usability: results from workshops, panels, and surveys. In: Proceedings of the SIGCHI Conference on

Human Factors in Computing Systems, pp. 337–344. CHI '00, Association for Computing Machinery, New York, NY, USA (2000). https://doi.org/10.1145/332040.332454
37. Rukonić, L., Kervyn de Meerendré, V., Kieffer, S.: Measuring UX capability and maturity in organizations. In: Marcus, A., Wang, W. (eds.) Design, User Experience, and Usability. Practice and Case Studies: 8th International Conference, DUXU 2019, Held as Part of the 21st HCI International Conference, HCII 2019, Orlando, FL, USA, July 26–31, 2019, Proceedings, Part IV, pp. 346–365. Springer International Publishing, Cham (2019). https://doi.org/10.1007/978-3-030-23535-2_26
38. Salah, D., Paige, R., Cairns, P.: A practitioner perspective on integrating agile and user centred design. In: Proceedings of the 28th International BCS Human Computer Interaction Conference on HCI 2014 - Sand, Sea and Sky - Holiday HCI, pp. 100–109. BCS-HCI '14, BCS, Swindon, GBR (2014). https://doi.org/10.14236/ewic/hci2014.11
39. Salah, D., Petrie, H., Paige, R.F.: Towards a framework for integrating user centered design and agile software development processes. Proc. Irish CHI 2009 (2009)
40. Sauro, J., Johnson, K., Meenan, C.: From snake-oil to science: measuring UX maturity. In: Proceedings of the 2017 CHI Conference Extended Abstracts on Human Factors in Computing Systems, pp. 1084–1091. CHI EA '17, Association for Computing Machinery, New York, NY, USA (2017). https://doi.org/10.1145/3027063.3053350
41. Schön, E.M., Thomaschewski, J., Escalona, M.J.: Agile requirements engineering: A systematic literature review. Comput. stand. Interfaces **49**, 79–91 (2017). https://doi.org/10.1016/j.csi.2016.08.011
42. Van Cutsem, J., Marcora, S., De Pauw, K., Bailey, S., Meeusen, R., Roelands, B.: The effects of mental fatigue on physical performance: a systematic review. Sports Med. **47**(8), 1569–1588 (2017). https://doi.org/10.1007/s40279-016-0672-0
43. Vredenburg, K., Mao, J.Y., Smith, P.W., Carey, T.: A survey of user-centered design practice. In: Proceedings of the SIGCHI Conference on Human Factors in Computing Systems, pp. 471–478. CHI '02, Association for Computing Machinery, New York, NY, USA (2002). https://doi.org/10.1145/503376.503460
44. Wilson, C.E.: Please listen to me! or, how can usability practitioners be more persuasive? Interactions **14**(2) (2007)
45. Wilson, C.E., Rosenbaum, S.: Categories of return on investment and their practical implications. In: Cost-justifying usability, pp. 215–263. Elsevier (2005)
46. Young, S.W., Chao, Z., Chandler, A.: User experience methods and maturity in academic libraries. Inform. Technol. Libr. textbf39(1) (2020). https://doi.org/10.6017/ital.v39i1.11787

Thinking Interactions and Their Social Impact Through Human-Centred Design

Carolina Bozzi[1](✉), Marco Neves[1], and Claudia Mont'Alvão[2]

[1] CIAUD, Research Centre for Architecture, Urbanism and Design, Lisbon School of Architecture, Universidade de Lisboa, Lisbon, Portugal
{carolinabozzi,mneves}@fa.ulisboa.pt

[2] LEUI, PUC-Rio, Rio de Janeiro, Brazil
cmontalvao@puc rio.br

Abstract. Design has contributed significantly to the development of digital projects that are more intuitive and user-friendly. However, there has been a more significant focus on experience and behaviour lately. From this perspective, where the focal point of the design process is no longer the object, but the behaviour and experience, there is a demand for investing in different pathways for the field. The scope expands beyond the immediate interaction of users with artefacts to include the influence of design within more complex social, physical, economic, and technological systems, and research strategies must go beyond laboratory tests. HCD is often used generically to cover a range of distinct research topics. HCD is not only about optimising the technical capabilities of machines but recognising and respecting the organisations or other forms of human social organization. The term is used interchangeably with user-centred design, and one could say, there is no general understanding of the term. In this paper, through the review of relevant literature, we will conceptualize, discuss, and compare Human-centred design (HCD) to user-centred design to create interactions that focus on the whole journey, not only on the 'user moment' to include social impacts in the pre- and post-user phases that are often overlooked in UCD. We conclude that this perspective of HCD as a paradigm shift takes the term 'human-centred' to mean more than simply considering the user in technology development. The HCD principles go beyond ergonomic, psychological, sociological, and anthropological studies of what fits the human body and mind. HCD is a search for what can support human dignity in its social, political, economic, and cultural life.

Keywords: human-centred design · interaction design · user-centred design · social impact

1 Introduction

Design has played a pivotal role in evolving more intuitive and user-friendly digital projects. Design mediates the relationship between people and their activities to interact with the environment [1]. However, how this mediation occurs has been changing to increasingly focus on the experience and behaviour resulting from this interaction as the design practice becomes more complex [2].

A. Marcus et al. (Eds.): HCII 2024, LNCS 14714, pp. 195–204, 2024.
https://doi.org/10.1007/978-3-031-61356-2_13

The focal point of the design process is no longer on the object, thus demanding different pathways for the field. The scope expands beyond the immediate interaction of users with artefacts to include the influence of design within more complex social, physical, economic, and technological systems, and research strategies must go beyond tests performed in ergonomics laboratories to environments where research-relevant behaviour can be observed [2]. The paradigm shift from technology-centred to human-centred [3], from object to experience, underscored the need to design interactive systems that go further; those that are also socially responsible take a more holistic approach.

To this end, successful interaction design projects focus on people, not machines [4]. The author argues that we are moving from designing interfaces between people and machines to designing 'interspaces' inhabited by "multiple people, workstations, servers, and other devices" in a complex web of interactions [4, p. 39]. Redirecting the attention to the human body in space and the environment where activities are performed becomes more pronounced [5].

In this paper, through the review of relevant literature, we will conceptualize, discuss, and compare Human-centred design (HCD) to user-centred design to create interactions that focus on the whole journey, not only on the 'user moment' to include social impacts in the pre-and post-user phases that are often overlooked in UCD.

2 Theoretical Background: Defining Human-Centred Design

Human-centred design (HCD) is often used generically to cover a range of distinct research topics, such as interaction design and intelligent systems, human-computer interaction, and others, without any commitment to an encompassing conceptual framework [5].

This perspective of HCD as a paradigm shift perceives 'human-centred' as surpassing mere consideration of users in technology development. Instead, it places our understanding of people, their concerns, and their activities at the forefront of the design of new technologies [5].

Buchanan [6] discusses the significance of HCD and compares it to user-centred design (UCD) in the sense that HCD is not limited to the usability of a system or product but to the user moment. An example of Buchanan's [6] critique of HCD is in Maguire [7], where he mainly considers the importance of usability in a design project.

The principles that guide HCD are not exhausted when we finish the ergonomic, psychological, sociological, and anthropological studies of what fits the human body and mind. HCD is a search for what can support human dignity in its social, political, economic, and cultural life [6]. The question of what problems are being solved is paramount. Systems that seek only to respond to a very narrow technical or economic agenda or a set of theoretical technical points do not belong under HCD.

2.1 HCD and UCD

The motto 'know the user' endorsed the user-centred approach, it historically focused on human users as information processing mechanisms. The human being was seen as a set of factors that should be considered in the design process, but the notion of the user as an active actor in the process was missing [8].

Bannon [8] argues that human-computer interaction (HCI) has moved from evaluating interfaces through systems design to creating a general sense of our world and needs reconstruction. The area of concern is much broader than the match between people and technology to improve productivity, and it covers a much more challenging territory that includes people's goals and activities, their values, and the tools and environments that help shape their daily lives. It can also be seen more radically as a shift from a psychological to a sociological perspective on human work and activity, emphasising field observation methods rather than laboratory studies [8].

For some, combining this plethora of approaches under the old HCI banner is too limiting, and even the field of interaction design is not broad enough. As a result, the terms 'human-centred computing' and 'human-centred design' have been touted as possible replacements for HCI (Bannon, 2011).

Although we consider the terms 'user-centred' and 'human-centred' to be distinct, some authors use them interchangeably [9]. For example, Friess [10], does not clearly distinguish between UCD and HCD. The study carried out by Zoltowski et al. [11] revealed significant misunderstandings about what HCD means.

Kling and Star [12] explain that the word 'human' represents a person, not a task or a set of cognitive processes. Humans are not divisible into parts, such as tasks. So, a design that optimises a task's performance but does not consider ergonomics, activities, feelings, and the socio-cultural context does not effectively consider the human. The term human encompasses and goes beyond individuals and their cognition to include the activity and interactions of people with various groups, organisations, and segments of larger communities [12].

HCD is not about optimising machines' technical capabilities but about recognising and respecting the organisations or other forms of human social organisation in which they are embedded. HCD considers the various ways stakeholders and organisations are connected with social relationships and information flows [12].

Kling and Star [12] point out that to be human-centred, such systems must consider the following:

- An analysis that encompasses the complexity of the social organisation and the state of the art of the technique. The analysis cannot be based on a vague idea of what a generic individual would like, sitting at a keyboard in social isolation or in a stereotypical situation that effectively ignores the varieties of concrete social locations. One quickly trivialises the concept of a human-centred system by homogenising people and places into 'all humans' and 'everywhere'.
- Human-centredness is not a unique or timeless attribute of a system at a particular point in time. Rather, it is a process considering how evaluation criteria are generated and applied and for whose benefit, including stakeholder participation.
- The architecture of systems and products that incorporates livability, usability, and sustainability issues.

Systems that seek only to respond to a very narrow technical or economic agenda, or a set of theoretical technical points do not belong under the human-centred approach. What fundamentally separates HCD from other approaches is its specific focus on the user experience (UX) [13]. HCD starts by observing people's behaviour and designing services according to their needs. We serve other people by strengthening their individual dignity and supporting collective social values, all within the pluralism of the human experience [14]. To be focused on the user experience, we must include the whole journey, the expectations of the use, and the impression and impacts after an interaction, as UX is defined as a person's perceptions and responses that result from the use and/or anticipated use of a product, system or service." [15].

Giacomin [16] believes that the heart of any design activity is the identification of the meaning that the product, system, or service should offer people. Furthermore, for him, the HCD definition is a pragmatic and applied approach to identifying what Holt and Cameron [17] call 'ideological opportunities' and realising what they call 'cultural design'. HCD is thus distinct from many traditional design practices because the natural focus of questions, perceptions, and activities lies with the people for whom the product, system, or service is intended rather than in the designer's creative process or within the material and technological substrates of the artifact. In its most basic form, HCD leads to products, systems, and services that are physically, perceptually, cognitively, and emotionally intuitive.

Giacomin [16] proposes an HCD pyramid in which the classical rhetorical questions of the antiquity of *Quis* (who), *Quid* (what), *Quando* (when), *Quem ad Modum* (how), and *Cur* (why) have been associated with current design semantics to structure the increasing layers of complexity. This new interpretation of HCD stems from a hierarchy based on scientific facts about human physical, perceptual, cognitive, and emotional characteristics, followed by progressively more complex, interactive, and sociological considerations. At its apex, the model contains the metaphysical meaning that individuals form that originates from their contact with design. In the view that the model summarises, metaphysical meaning, whether pre-existing or yet to be created through contact, is vital to social acceptance, commercial success, brand identity, and business strategy. Designs whose features answer questions and curiosities that are higher up the pyramid would be expected to offer a broader range of possibilities to people and to embed themselves more deeply into minds and everyday life.

Giacomin's [16] model of HCD aligns with Pullin's [18] definitions and examples, which acknowledge the importance of resolving issues while prioritizing a mindset that is receptive to new ideas, critical of established limits, and mindful of the impact of actions and societal structures. The model outlines a series of concerns and inquiries that commence with the human body's tangible, sensory, intellectual, and interactive abilities and culminate with the eventual implications that the outcome, system, or offer will have on an individual's psychological, sociological, and communal environment.

IDEO [19] defines HCD as a process and a set of techniques for creating solutions for the world. These solutions include products, services, environments, organisations, and modes of interaction. This process is human-centred because it starts with the people we are designing for [19].

This definition of HCD is consistent with Zhang and Dong's [20] review of various HCD approaches. All have humans as central characters in the process, involve users throughout the design process, and seek to understand them holistically.

Krippendorff [3] identifies three characteristics shared by HCD methods:

- Employ divergent and convergent thinking.
- Use processes concerned with how stakeholders attribute meaning using the proposed design.
- Include prototypes and other ways for stakeholders to test their design ideas.

Note that the above definitions describe the HCD as distinct from the design of something user-friendly, or user centred. Instead, HCD involves and values stakeholders throughout the design process rather than checking the ease of use at the end [11]. A critical part of design thinking and HCD is understanding the affected people involved [11] as well as their environment. HCD is, in our view, a more comprehensive approach than UCD. It includes the 'user moment' and goes beyond, considering the post-use and social impacts. HCD also involves stakeholders throughout the process.

HCD Models. Among the HCD models are those explicitly referred to as 'human-centred' and various human-centred models but not strictly labelled as such. Considering these different models helps to illuminate what it means to be human-centred and the variation between HCD approaches.

As mentioned previously, user-centred design focuses on the product's end user, in contrast, the HCD considers all stakeholders more broadly than the stereotypical user [3].

Zoltowski et al. [11] bring us a comprehensive review of some of these approaches, some examples are described below:

- Empathic design: empirical research techniques that provide designers access to how users experience their material surroundings and the people who are part of it to include themselves as key characters in their everyday lives [21]. Although the design team generates solutions, the aim is always to keep in mind, who you are designing for.
- Participatory design: stemmed from work that began in the early 1970s in Norway [22] and is defined by Kensing and Blomberg [23, p. 181] as "...a commitment to worker participation in the design and an effort to rebalance the power relations between users and technical experts and between workers and managers".
- Contextual design: focuses on understanding how the individual works or the context in which the product is used [24]. It involves exploring individuals and their environments through ethnographic research and then building working models that capture this information. Individual perspectives are consolidated to reveal common patterns and structures and complete a working practice redesign.
- Inclusive design: is a design philosophy and methodology that aims to enable as many people as possible to use the designed product. It is a derivative of user-centred design [25, 26].

Adding to the above, Norman [27] recently used the term 'humanity-centred design', whose definition is aligned with our concept of human-centred design. He explains that designers must expand the HCD scope to all living things: land quality, water, and air, the loss of species, and climate changes.

The author defines what he considers are the four HCD principles that must be considered when designing human-centred projects. According to Norman [27], despite

Table 1. Transforming human-centred principles into humanity-centred according to Norman [27].

HCD Principles	Transforming human-centred into Humanity-centred
1. Solve the core, root issues, not just the problem as presented (which is often the symptom, not the cause).	1. Solve the core, root issues, not just the problem as presented (which is often the symptom, not the cause).
2. Focus on the people.	2. Focus on the entire ecosystem of people, all living things, and the physical environment.
3. Take a systems point of view, realizing that most complications result from the interdependencies of the multiple parts.	3. Take a long-term, systems point of view, realizing that most complications result from the interdependencies of the multiple parts and that many of the most damaging impacts on society and the ecosystem reveal themselves only years or even decades later.
4. Continually test and refine the proposed designs to ensure they truly meet the concerns of the people for whom they are intended.	4. Continually test and refine the proposed designs to ensure they truly meet the concerns of the people for whom they are intended.
	5. Design with the community and, as much as possible, support designs by the community. Professional designers should serve as enablers, facilitators, and resources, aiding community members to meet their concerns.

the importance of these principles, they ignore the problems of sustainability, inequity, and bias and do not consider the long-term impact (our view of HCD includes the latter). To become humanity-centred, HCD must take on an additional principle (principle 5) and widen the range of issues being addressed by principles 2, 3, and 4 (Table 1) [27].

2.2 Design Thinking as a HCD Approach

Design thinking has long been associated with human-centred approaches. Kimbell [28] defines and discusses design thinking through a critical literature review. She presented some opposing views on the subject and what it was like when it emerged. She criticises designers' simplistic approach to design thinking as something to solve complex social issues as if they were in their domain, yet not always working closely with other experts.

The author mentions three fundamental texts that address the conceptualisation of design thinking: 'The Reflective Practitioner' by Donald Schön [29], 'How Designers Think' by Bryan Lawson [30], and 'Design Thinking' by Peter Rowe [31]. Schön [29] used the term reflection-in-action, while Lawson [30] and Rowe [31] used the term design thinking; in both cases, they referred to a way of seeing and understanding the world while working to bring about a desired change. Each of the authors set out to analyse the design process and identify the characteristics of designers.

Much of the work on design thinking has attempted to generalise how designers work and think, implying that this differs from what non-designers do [32, 33]. Cross [33–35] sees designers' way of problem-solving as solution oriented as they deal with ill-defined problems, and the author situates this within a larger argument about design as a coherent discipline of study distinct from the sciences and humanities.

Buchanan's [32] article *Wicked Problems in Design Thinking* moved design theory from its legacy in craft and industrial production to more generalised design thinking.

Brown and Katz [36] emphasise design thinking as a human-centred activity and describe the three spaces of the design thinking process: inspiration, ideation, and implementation [37]. Supporting this approach is the idea of empathy; designers are perceived as being able to understand and interpret end-users' perspectives and the problems they face, which, according to Brown and Katz [36], is perhaps the most crucial distinction between academic thinking and design thinking. Design thinking aims to translate observations into insights and insights into products and services that will improve lives. For the authors, a successful design outcome exists at the intersection of three concerns: what is desirable from the users' perspective, what is technically feasible, and what is commercially viable for the organisation.

Also, according to Brown and Katz [36], as an approach, design thinking harnesses the capabilities we all have but which are neglected by more conventional problem-solving practices. Design thinking relies on our ability to be intuitive, recognise patterns, construct emotionally meaningful and functional ideas, and express ourselves in means other than words or symbols [37].

For Bauer and Eagen [38], analytical thinking is part of, not the opposite of, design thinking. While analytical thinking provides the epistemic basis of capital, they believe that design thinking represents the epistemology of creative work.

According to Brown and Wyatt [37], this type of activity is no longer focused on product design and has become an activity to design consumer experiences. Contrasting with what Hassenzahl [39] argues, according to him, it is not possible to design an experience, only to design for it. Designers can create possibilities but not certainties. By stating that a group of recommendations will always produce certain emotions, one risks going beyond what can be fulfilled.

The discourse on design thinking reveals a nuanced landscape, with different perspectives and definitions and it is far from reaching a common ground. Kimbell's [28] critical examination sheds light on the complexities of design thinking, cautioning against oversimplified approaches in addressing intricate social issues. However, in its essence, design thinking can be a transformative process, emphasizing reflection-in-action and a holistic understanding of the world.

3 Conclusion

We conclude that this perspective of HCD as a paradigm shift takes the term 'human-centred' to mean more than simply considering the user in technology development. Instead, it places our understanding of people, their concerns, and their activities at the forefront of the design of new technologies (Bannon, 2011).

Rather, HCD should also comprehend the impacts of products and systems on our environment, anticipating damages to our society. This involves, for instance, designing products' end-cycle, using materials that are easy to replace, reuse, or recycle, or optimizing processes to make them greener.

Including stakeholders also means elucidating consumers about supply chains and educating them about the impacts that actions that seem harmful might have on the environment.

In the evolution of HCD, there has been a development from a focus on physical ergonomics, usability, the context of use, and user goals to a focus on emotions and user experiences. The design innovation methods consider human needs beyond usability and emotions and investigate deeper needs and aspirations instead. Bijl-brouwer and Dorst [40] use the term 'aspiration' to focus on immediate needs and include long-term hopes, desires, and ambitions.

Bijl-brouwer and Dorst [40] state that compared to the more traditional HCD, these methods are not meant to address needs but include a more strategic exploration of what could provide significant value to stakeholders. So that one has the framework creation method presented to them.

Furthermore, human-centred strategic innovation requires a holistic approach. We then need to ask ourselves who should be at the centre of the strategic application of HCD. It is no longer just about users but about customers, service providers, citizens, and other stakeholders, including people who make decisions regarding strategy, business models and organisational transformation.

Acknowledgments. This work is financed by national funds through FCT - Fundação para a Ciência e a Tecnologia, I.P., under the Strategic Project with the references UIDB/04008/2020 and UIDP/04008/2020.

References

1. Kaptelinin, V., Nardi, B.: Acting with technology: activity theory and interaction design. First Monday (2007). https://doi.org/10.5210/fm.v12i4.1772
2. Davis, M.: Why do we need doctoral study in design? Int. J. Des. (2008)
3. Krippendorff, K.: The Semantic Turn. Taylor and Francis, Boca Raton (2006)
4. Winograd, T.: From computing machinery to interaction design. In: Denning, P., Metcalfe, R. (eds.) The Design of Interaction, pp. 149–161. Springer, New York (1997)
5. Bannon, L.: Reimagining HCI: toward a more human-centered perspective. Interactions **18**(4), 50–57 (2011). https://doi.org/10.1145/1978822.1978833
6. Buchanan, R.: Human dignity and human rights: thoughts on the principles of human-centered design. Des. Issues **17**(3), 35–39 (2001). https://doi.org/10.1162/074793601750357178
7. Maguire, M.: Methods to support human-centred design. Int. J. Hum. Comput. Stud. **55**(4), 587–634 (2001). https://doi.org/10.1006/ijhc.2001.0503
8. Bannon, L.J.: From human factors to human actors: the role of psychology and human-computer interaction studies in systems design. In: Greenbaum, J., Kyng, M. (eds.) Design at Work: Cooperative Design of Computer Systems, pp. 25–44. Lawrence Erlbaum Associates, Hillsdale (1991)

9. Oviatt, S.: Human-centered design meets cognitive load theory. In: Proceedings of the 14th Annual ACM International Conference on Multimedia - MULTIMEDIA 2006, pp. 871–880 (2006). https://doi.org/10.1145/1180639.1180831
10. Friess, E.: The sword of data: does human-centered design fulfill its rhetorical responsibility? Des. Issues **26**(3), 40–51 (2010). https://doi.org/10.1162/DESI_a_00028
11. Zoltowski, C.B., Oakes, W.C., Cardella, M.E.: Students' ways of experiencing human-centered design. J. Eng. Educ. **101**(1), 28–59 (2012)
12. Kling, R., Star, S.L.: Human centered systems in the perspective of organizational and social informatics. ACM SIGCAS Comput. Soc. (1998). https://doi.org/10.1145/277351.277356
13. Barlow, M., Lévy-Bencheton, C.: Human-centered design. In: Smart Cities, Smart Future: Showcasing Tomorrow. Wileys, New Jersey (2019)
14. Buchanan, R.: Human-centered design: changing perspectives on design education in the east and west. Des. Issues **20**(1), 30–39 (2004). https://doi.org/10.1162/074793604772933748
15. International Standard Organization: ISO 9241-210:11 ergonomics of human-system interaction - Part 11: usability: definitions and concepts. International Standard Organization, Genebra (2010)
16. Giacomin, J.: What is human centred design? Des. J. **17**(4), 606–623 (2014). https://doi.org/10.2752/175630614X14056185480186
17. Holt, D., Cameron, D.: Cultural Strategy: Using Innovative Ideology to Build Breakthrough Brands. Oxford University Press, Oxford (2010)
18. Pullin, G.: Design Meets Disability. MIT Press, Cambridge (2009)
19. IDEO: Human centered design toolkit. IDEO, Palo Alto (2011)
20. Zhang, T., Dong, H.: Human-centred design: an emergent conceptual model (2009)
21. Koskinen, I., Mattelmäki, T., Battarbee, I.K.: Empathic Design. IT Press, Helsinki (2003)
22. Sanoff, H.: Special issue on participatory design. Des. Stud. **28**(3), 213–215 (2007). https://doi.org/10.1016/j.destud.2007.02.001
23. Kensing, F., Blomberg, J.: Participatory design: issues and concerns. Comput. Support. Coop. Work (1998). https://doi.org/10.1023/A:1008689307411
24. Beyer, H., Holtzblatt, K.: Contextual design: defining customer-centered systems (1998)
25. Clarkson, J., Coleman, R., Keates, S., Lebbon, C.: Inclusive Design: Design for the Whole Population. Springer, London (2003). https://doi.org/10.1007/978-1-4471-0001-0
26. Keates, S., Clarkson, J.: Countering Design Exclusion: An Introduction to Inclusive Design. Springer, London (2003). https://doi.org/10.1007/978-1-4471-0013-3
27. Norman, D.: Design for a Better World: Meaningful, Sustainable, Humanity Centered. MIT Press, Cambridge (2023)
28. Kimbell, L.: Rethinking design thinking: Part I. Des. Cult. **3**(3), 285–306 (2011). https://doi.org/10.2752/175470811x13071166525216
29. Schön, D.A.: The Reflective Practitioner: How Professionals Think in Action. Basic Books, New York (1983)
30. Lawson, B.: How Designers Think, 3rd edn. Architectural Press, London (1997)
31. Rowe, P.: Design Thinking. MIT Press, Cambridge (1987)
32. Buchanan, R.: Wicked problems in design thinking. Des. Issues (1992). https://doi.org/10.2307/1511637
33. Cross, N.: Designerly ways of knowing. Des. Stud. (1982). https://doi.org/10.1016/0142-694X(82)90040-0
34. Cross, N.: Designerly ways of knowing: design discipline versus design science. Des. Issues (2001). https://doi.org/10.1162/074793601750357196
35. Cross, N.: Design Thinking: Understanding How Designers Think and Work. Berg, Oxford (2011)
36. Brown, T., Katz, B.: Change by Design. Harper Collins, New York (2009)

37. Brown, T., Wyatt, J.: Design thinking for social innovation. Stanford Soc. Innov. Rev. Winter, 30–35 (2010). https://doi.org/10.1108/10878571011042050
38. Bauer, R., Eagen, W.: Design thinking: epistemic plurality in management and organization. Aesthesis Int. J. Art Aesthet. Manag. Organ. Life (2008)
39. Hassenzahl, M.: Emotions can be quite ephemeral; we cannot design them. Interactions **11**(5), 46 (2004). https://doi.org/10.1145/1015530.1015551
40. Van Der Bijl-brouwer, M., Dorst, K.: Advancing the strategic impact of human-centred design. Des. Stud. **53**, 1–22 (2017). https://doi.org/10.1016/j.destud.2017.06.003

Redesigns in Enterprise Resource Planning Modules Using User-Centered Design Methods: A Systematic Literature Review

Fátima Cruzalegui(✉), Rony Cueva, and Freddy Paz

Pontificia Universidad Católica del Perú, San Miguel, Lima 15088, Peru
{fatima.cruzalegui,cueva.r}@pucp.edu.pe, fpaz@pucp.pe

Abstract. Nowadays, usability is a fairly important attribute within all types of systems. However, there is a type of system in which the lack of this stands out. These types of systems are ERP systems. Taking this into account, this article focuses on carrying out a systematic review of the literature regarding the redesign of the graphical interfaces of ERP systems, treating and identifying different methods, especially User-Centered Design methods. In this way, the review seeks to focus on this type of methods, their definitions and uses, how they are used to solve the different usability problems found and identified in graphical interfaces in ERP systems and what are the impacts of some strategies or commonly used methods. In the same way, an analysis of the results obtained through this review will be sought, so that useful information can be collected to be focused on the redesign of ERP system interfaces. This article also details the studies found, the respective search strings, selection criteria, search engines or databases and a conceptual framework oriented to the topic.

Keywords: Human-Computer Interaction · User Experience · Usability · ERP · Inspection Methods · Software products

1 Introduction

Usability is a relevant quality aspect that must be considered in developing products, systems, and services to achieve artifacts that are easy to use, understandable, and attractive [28]. If a software product fails to be usable and generates a lousy interaction experience, people will look for a better alternative that meets their expectations in the current highly competitive market. This statement also applies to Enterprise Resource Planning systems, known by their acronym ERP, which are software products developed to support the core business processes of various types of corporations.

The problem with ERP systems is that since they have been built to support business models of a different nature, their architecture and design are complex

A. Marcus et al. (Eds.): HCII 2024, LNCS 14714, pp. 205–222, 2024.
https://doi.org/10.1007/978-3-031-61356-2_14

[26]. It is for this reason that its graphical interaction interfaces are overloaded with many elements in a way that makes it possible to manage any information required by the company that will implement this system. Nevertheless, the fact that graphical interfaces have multiple elements to support all types of business scenarios makes them challenging to use. Many of the design elements are not used by users since some fields are irrelevant to store or manage. Likewise, the mechanisms of use are complex, generating unnecessary delays and difficulties for a company's employees to get used to using the system [31]. It is due to the complexity of the interfaces of ERP systems that adaptations are made to make them more usable and attractive.

To carry out redesigns and adaptations of the graphical interfaces of software products, User-Centered Design (UCD) methods are usually used, which consider end-users' opinions to obtain an interface that adjusts to their needs and expectations. Likewise, UCD methods guarantee the achievement of a product that is perceived positively and whose interaction is satisfactory. In this study, through a systematic review of the literature, we explore case studies that report redesigns of graphical user interfaces of ERP system modules through the use of UCD methods. The purpose is to identify why these redesigns are carried out, the problems ERP system graphical interfaces generate, and the most used methods to solve usability issues. This study can be used as a guide for industry and academia in redesigning interfaces.

Although the importance of usability for ERP systems for acceptance and project success has been highlighted, the individualization of enterprise systems is commonly bound to the use of favourites and the like. Because of that and the increasing possibilities and demands towards mobile operation, the group of ERP systems may add responsive designs and web-based approaches in their portfolio and they may support newer forms of interaction, that do not only rely on predefined forms [6]. In this way, this study also seeks to determine certain shortcomings in the graphical interfaces of ERP systems so that they can be taken into account when designing or redesigning them.

2 Conceptual Framework

In this section, the definitions and concepts that were required for the development of this study are presented. This research aimed to conduct a Systematic Literature Review (SLR) of all case studies in which the User-Centered Design (UCD) framework or related methods were employed to solve design problems in graphical interfaces of Enterprise Resource Planning (ERP) systems.

2.1 Enterprise Resource Planning Systems

In today's economy, organizations require software products that can support their business processes and facilitate the communication of the different organizational units as well as the exchange and access to data throughout the process.

In this way, Enterprise Resource Planning (ERP) systems emerge as an alternative solution that can help companies manage and optimize their processes and improve efficiency, visibility, and decision-making across all functions [32].

An ERP system can be described as a business information system designed to integrate and optimize business processes and transactions within a corporation [21]. Likewise, ERP systems are currently involved in all aspects of an organization, as they provide a highly integrated solution to find necessary information from the system [30].

ERP systems are highly configurable and can be adapted to different business scenarios. The concept of ERP can be approached from different perspectives [12]. ERP systems are considered software products that map all processes and data of an enterprise into a comprehensive integrative structure. In addition, ERP systems can be seen as the critical element of a technological infrastructure that delivers a solution to a business. For this reason, they are complex, broad systems that work with different business applications to manage and integrate business functions.

An example of this type of system is SAP, which is a leading ERP system in the business software application market. This system is developed by SAP SE, a company founded in 1972, that has a rich history of innovation and growth as a true industrial leader. Additionally, SAP is ranked as the number one independent ERP software provider in the world. Likewise, SAP integrates all the main functions of the company's business, including finance, sales, customer relationship management, inventory, and operations [30].

2.2 User-Centered Design Framework

Nowadays, companies aim to offer technological products and services that are easy to use, understandable, and attractive to their users and customers [27]. This fact occurs because companies are aware of making a difference in a highly competitive market where many options are available for the same purpose. Likewise, it has been demonstrated that products that are not understandable or generate a negative perception in people have quickly stopped being used and have been forced to leave the market, causing significant financial losses for companies. For this reason, specialists have proposed some procedures and work guides that consist of continuous participation of the end users to ensure interaction designs and graphical interfaces that meet expectations and, simultaneously, are usable. User-centered design emerges as an approach that ensures, through multiple phases and methods, a high degree of usability of software products and a satisfactory interaction experience.

User-Centered Design is defined as an iterative design process framework that incorporates user-based validations during each development phase, in constant interaction with the end-users [19]. This work guide describes a set of design phases, focused on understanding the people who will use the final product. This framework is explicitly based on understanding users, tasks, and environments, addressing the entire user experience. In addition, it involves users throughout the design life cycle. The general phases of the Centered Design framework are

[10,18]: (1) Understanding and specifying the context of use, (2) Specifying the user requirements, (3) Producing design solutions, and (4) Evaluating the design.

Understanding and Specifying the Context of Use. When a product, system, or service is developed, it is used within a certain context. For this reason, it is important to understand this context, which involves a population of users with certain characteristics, objectives, and performance of certain tasks. Additionally, the software product will be used within an environment with technical, physical, and social conditions that will affect its use.

Specifying the User Requirements. Obtaining and analyzing design requirements is crucial to the graphical user interface design process. Even the success of a design proposal depends mainly on how well this phase is carried out. To develop appropriate interaction interfaces, it is necessary to establish requirements associated with users' needs and expectations.

Producing Design Solutions. Design solutions emerge in different ways, from copying logic and developing previous designs to new, creative, and innovative designs. Whatever the source, design ideas must go through an iterative process. Mockups and system simulations are necessary to support this iterative design cycle. These simulations or prototypes can be easily carried out in the early stages of the system development cycle for evaluation by specialists. Changes can be made quickly in response to user feedback.

Evaluating the Design. Designs should be evaluated throughout development, initially using low fidelity and followed by more sophisticated prototypes. This activity is essential in the product life cycle as it helps confirm the extent to which user and organizational objectives have been met and provides more information to refine the design.

3 A Systematic Literature Review

In this chapter, we are carrying out our research through a systematic literature review, which is defined by Kitchenham and Charters as "a form of secondary study that uses a well-defined methodology to identify, analyze and interpret all available evidence related to a specific research question in a way that is unbiased and (to a degree) repeatable" [11].

In order to that, the present work was performed following the methodology described by Kitchenham and Charters [11]. In that way, the steps of this methodology are presented in the subsequent sections, as well as the three questions formulated to guide the review.

3.1 Research Questions

The purpose of this work was to analyze and determine the techniques and methods that have been used as an attempt to make the design or redesign of graphical user interfaces of an ERP using User-Centered Design framework. Moreover, this review shows the usability issues and impacts related to methods and strategies used to solve them. In that way, we formulated the following research questions:

RQ1: *What usability problems do studies report about graphical user interfaces of ERP systems and how do these problems affect the interaction experience and the achievement of user goals?*

RQ2: *What methods or strategies are reported to solve usability problems present in the graphical user interfaces of ERP systems and how have they been executed?*

RQ3: *What are the impacts generated by the application of methods and strategies to solve usability problems in graphical interfaces of ERP systems and how have they influenced the interaction experience and the achievement of user goals?*

To structure the research questions and conduct the process for this systematic review, we have delimited the general concepts defined by PICOC. These fundamental components include Population, Intervention, Comparison, Output, and Context. However, it is pertinent to highlight that the "Comparison" criterion has been excluded from our considerations, as the primary objective of this research is not the comparative analysis of interventions (Table 1).

Table 1. Definition of PICOC criteria for the systematic review

Criterion	Description
Population	Graphical User Interfaces
Intervention	Usability practices
Comparison	It does not apply
Output	Problems, methods, impacts and redesign
Context	ERP Systems

3.2 Source Selection

For the systematic review to be carried out, the following search engines and databases have been chosen, which have been selected for their relevance in the area of Computer Science and their significant content on topics such as Software Engineering and usability:

- Scopus (www.scopus.com)
- IEEE Xplore (ieeexplore.ieee.org)
- ACM Digital Library (dl.acm.org)

3.3 Search Strategy

Table 2. Delimited terms for the search string

General concepts	Terms
GC1 - Graphical User Interfaces	graphical user interface, GUI, interaction interface, user interface, UI, graphical interface, software interface
GC2 - Usability practices	usability, UX, user experience, user centered design, HCI, UCD, user centered, user-centred
GC3 - Problems	problem, challenge, issue, barrier, obstacle, conflict, difficulty, trouble
GC4 - Methods	approach, procedure, study case, method, process, technique, analysis, evaluate, evaluation, assess, analyzing, methodology
GC5 - Impact	impact, influence, change, effect
GC6 - Redesign	design, redesign
GC7 - ERP Systems	ERP, enterprise resource planning

Delimitation of Search Terms. To construct the search string, the four used concepts of PICOC were taken into account [29], so that keywords were defined in relation to each criterion, as well as their synonyms and related words (Table 2).

Delimitation of Search String. Once we establish the search terms and the keywords or synonyms, the following search string is obtained:

("graphical user interface" **OR** "GUI" **OR** "interaction interface" **OR** "user interface" **OR** "UI" **OR** "graphical interface" **OR** "software interface") **AND** ("usability" **OR** "UX" **OR** "user experience" **OR** "user centered design" **OR** "HCI" **OR** "UCD" OR "user centered" **OR** "user-centred") **AND** (("problem" **OR** "challenge" **OR** "issue" **OR** "barrier" **OR** "obstacle" **OR** "conflict" **OR** "difficulty" **OR** "trouble") **OR** ("approach" **OR** "procedure" **OR** "study case" **OR** "method" **OR** "process" **OR** "technique" **OR** "analysis" **OR** "evaluate" **OR** "evaluation" **OR** "assess" **OR** "analyzing" **OR** "methodology") **OR** ("impact" **OR** "influence" **OR** "change" **OR** "effect") **OR** ("design" **OR** "redesign")) **AND** ("ERP" **OR** "enterprise resource planning")

Finally, it is pertinent to comment that the search strings were adapted according to the syntax of each search engine and database.

3.4 Inclusion and Exclusion Criteria

To filter the articles obtained through the search process carried out, certain criteria were defined in favor of the selection of the documents used. The defined criteria are inclusion and exclusion criteria, which helped to obtain the most relevant literature to resolve the research questions.

Hereunder are the inclusion criteria considered for the selection of the documents:

1. The study provides information about the problems, challenges, obstacles and difficulties related to usability and user experience in ERP systems.
2. The study details any evaluation, methodologies, protocols or procedures used in the design of interfaces, usability or graphical interfaces of ERP systems.
3. The study reports on the impacts and effects about different User-Centered Design, usability or user experience practices on an ERP system.
4. The study describes a use case in which a design or redesign is applied to some interface of an ERP system.
5. The study indicates the use of software tools for the design or redesign of an ERP system.

Likewise, the exclusion criteria considered are presented:

1. The study is written in a language different than English.
2. The study refers to the redesign or design in interfaces other than that of an ERP system.
3. The study is not related to usability issues, user experiences, graphic interfaces or user-centered design.
4. The study describes only the titles of the published articles.
5. The study focuses on the design of algorithms for the generation of usable interfaces.

3.5 Data Extraction

The search strings have been executed on October 6th 2023, according to the engines mentioned above. The search gave us 124 study results. Of these, 13 were duplicate articles and 27 were selected using the inclusion and exclusion criteria described previously in this document.

Table 3 shows the number of articles classified by search engine and according to the number of results, duplicates, and selected studies and Table 4 shows the details about the selected studies.

Table 3. Summary of search results

Database name	Search Results	Duplicated studies	Relevant studies
Scopus	66	0	23
IEEE Xplore	25	8	1
ACM Digital Library	11	5	3
Total	**102**	**13**	**27**

Table 4. Summary of search results

ID	Paper title	Author(s)	Database	Year
P01 [32]	Qualitative techniques for evaluating enterprise resource planning (ERP) user interfaces	Brenda Scholtz, Charmain Cilliers, André Calitz	ACM	2010
P02 [37]	User Interface Redesign of Dental Clinic ERP System using Design Thinking: A Case Study	Amalia Suzianti, Galang Arrafah	ACM	2019
P03 [1]	Engineering adaptive user interfaces for enterprise applications	Pierre Akiki	ACM	2013
P04 [31]	Usability Evaluation of ERP Systems: A Comparison between SAP S/4 Hana & Oracle Cloud	Karim Osama Saad Soliman	IEEE	2021
P05 [22]	Towards a Methodology to Evaluate User Experience with Personalized Questionnaires for the Developments of Custom Systems	Jenny Morales, Germán Rojas, Gamadiel Cerda	Scopus	2022
P06 [4]	Improving ERP Usability Through User-System Collaboration	Tamara Babaian, Wendy Lucas, Heikki Topi	Scopus	2006
P07 [3]	Collaborating to improve ERP usability	Tamara Babaian, Wendy Lucas, Heikki Topi	Scopus	2004
P08 [7]	Working beyond technical aspects: An approach for driving the usability inspection adding the perspective of user experience	Joelma Choma, Lucianza Zaina, Tiago Da Silva	Scopus	2016
P09 [34]	User Interaction Satisfaction with Simulation Games Used in Learning about ERP Systems	Sung Shim	Scopus	2022
P10 [9]	A novel usability matrix for ERP systems using heuristic approach	Chaudhry Faisal, Sohail Tariq, Tooba Ahtram, Muhammad Shabbir, Sameet Sarwer, Ali Selamat	Scopus	2012
P11 [24]	An adaptive system architecture for devising adaptive user interfaces for mobile ERP apps	Khalil Omar, Jorge Gomez	Scopus	2018
P12 [14]	Commonalities and contrasts: An investigation of ERP usability in a comparative user study	Christian Lambeck, Corinna Fohrholz, Christian Leyh, Inese Supulniece, Romy Muller	Scopus	2014

continued

Table 4. continued

ID	Paper title	Author(s)	Database	Year
P13 [33]	Evaluation and Redesign of SAP Portal for University Students	Yukta Sharma, Anirban Chowdhury	Scopus	2021
P14 [15]	Mastering ERP interface complexity a scalable user interface concept for ERP systems	Christian Lambeck, Rainer Groh	Scopus	2013
P15 [5]	ERP prototype with built-in task and process support	Tamara Babaian, Jennifer Xu, Wendy Lucas	Scopus	2018
P16 [2]	A Systematic Review of User-Centered Design Framework Applied to the Redesign of Purchase Order Modules	Alexis Avelino, Rony Cueva, Freddy Paz	Scopus	2022
P17 [35]	Evaluation criteria for assessing the usability of ERP systems	Akash Singh, Janet Wesson	Scopus	2009
P18 [38]	Complexity in enterprise applications vs. simplicity in user experience	Matthias Uflacker, Daniela Busse	Scopus	2007
P19 [36]	The design of adaptive interfaces for enterprise resource planning systems	Akash Singh, Janet Wesson	Scopus	2011
P20 [30]	A Usability Study of an Enterprise Resource Planning System: A Case Study on SAP Business One	Ronaldo Polancos	Scopus	2019
P21 [20]	Quality improvement of ERP system GUI using expert method: A case study	Marek Milosz, Małgorzata Plechawska-Wójcik, Magdalena Borys, Maciej Laskowski	Scopus	2013
P22 [16]	(Re-)Evaluating user interface aspects in ERP systems - An empirical user study	Christian Lambeck, Romy Muller, Corinna Fohrholz, Christian Leyh	Scopus	2014
P23 [8]	Usability evaluation of in-housed developed ERP system	Chaudhry Faisal, Muhammad Shakeel, Zahid Javed	Scopus	2011
P24 [17]	Implementing design principles for collaborative ERP systems	Wendy Lucas, Tamara Babaian	Scopus	2012
P25 [23]	Using activity descriptions to generate user interfaces for ERP software	Timothy O'Hear, Yassin Boudjenane	Scopus	2009
P26 [25]	Heuristic evaluation checklist for mobile ERP user interfaces	Omar Khalil, Barbara Rapp, Jorge Gomez	Scopus	2016
P27 [13]	Metric based efficiency analysis of educational ERP system usability-using fuzzy model	Anil Kumar, Reza Tadayoni, Lene Sorensen	Scopus	2016

4 Analysis of the Results

4.1 Usability Problems in ERP Systems Interfaces

Results Report. To answer the first review question (*What usability problems do studies report about graphical user interfaces of ERP systems and how do these problems affect the interaction experience and the achievement of user goals?*) a total of 21 studies were identified. From these studies, numerous usability problems were identified in relation to the question posed. However, of these, about 5 that stand out are repetitive and mentioned in most studies.

Analysis of Results. Based on the results obtained, it is observed that the greatest number of usability problems reported by studies about the graphical user interfaces of ERP systems are those mentioned hereunder, with their respective descriptions and impacts that they generate in the experience of interaction and achievement of user goals.

- **Difficulty locating required functionalities or information** (P01, P02, P03, P12, P13, P14, P15, P17, P18, P20, P21, P22). Although ERP systems are systems rich in functionalities, the complexity of their location induces confusion, frustration, failures and other negative emotional responses in the user, which lead to the appearance of errors (P02, P17, P21), especially by novice users (P15). Furthermore, the studies highlight that both the search and the organization and navigation of information is complex and tedious, generating a bad experience for the user (P01, P03, P12, P14, P15, P17, P18, P20, P22). Likewise, they mention overload information, a delay in accessing it due to its complexity and the lack of help to find the correct information (P01, P13). Furthermore, in relation to the functionalities, they indicate the lack of some of these in certain screens, since they cannot identify them, which results in dissatisfaction of the user as they cannot complete their goals (P01, P17, P19).
- **System complexity** (P01, P03, P12, P14, P15, P16, P17, P18, P19, P20, P22, P27). This difficulty lies in the "unfriendly" nature of the interface, which results in a system with poor usability and a frustrating experience at the time of use (P16, P20, P27). Furthermore, it is indicated that, in relation to this problem, effect problems arise such as system output limitations (P12, P14), complications in terminologies (P01, P15, P17, P22) and even moral damage to the employee and their productivity. (P16, P18, P19).
- **Inadequate support in the execution of transactions** (P04, P12, P14, P15, P17, P22, P27). This usability problem details that there is no consistent relationship between the transactions and the characteristics of their function, which is why it is not possible to identify or access to correct functionalities and nor to have help regarding the execution of the transactions carried out, depending on the goal to accomplish (P04, P12, P14, P15, P17, P22). Furthermore, a guide on the use of transactions is not provided, nor is it

clear what is the next step to be executed to achieve the fulfillment of a task, which means that the user is not clear about the use or role of transactions and not understand the business process (P04, P17).

- **Complex visual composition** (P01, P02, P03, P16, P17, P18, P19, P22). Most ERPs have a fairly complex user interface. This includes complex screen display (P17, P22), difficult to understand menu compositions (P01), abundance and complexity of tab usage (P19), and complex integration of processes and data (P01, P02, P03). Altogether, the aforementioned makes it impossible for the user to achieve their goals when carrying out their work, negatively affecting both the usability of the system and themselves (P16, P18).
- **Unintuitive system with little capacity for rapid learning** (P01, P03, P13, P17, P18, P19, P20, P21, P22, P27). The graphical user interface of ERP systems is not intuitive in nature and has difficulties in learning and training its use (P01, P17, P18, P20, P22, P27), being notoriously challenging to learn how to use. Furthermore, some studies indicate that the time required to learn about the details of the screens and functions of ERP systems is excessive (P01, P03, P13, P17, P20), since these systems are not designed to provide teaching support. This causes system users to only focus on completing practical exercises, without being able to understand how their work contributes to business objectives (P19, P21).

4.2 User-Centered Design Methods for Redesigning ERP System Interfaces

Results Report. To answer the second review question (*What methods or strategies are reported to solve usability problems present in the graphical user interfaces of ERP systems and how have they been executed?*), a total of 25 studies were identified. From these studies, numerous reported UCD methods or strategies that were identified to solve usability problems in relation to the question posed. However, of these, about 6 that stand out are repetitive and mentioned in most studies.

Analysis of Results. Based on the results obtained, it is observed that the largest number of methods or strategies are reported to solve usability problems present in graphical interfaces are those mentioned hereunder, with their respective descriptions and the ways in which they have been executed.

- **Case studies** (P01, P10, P15). This strategy consists of being able to generate an answer to the questions of "Why", "What" and "How", so that it is possible to understand situations in non-numerical ways, opting for an analysis instead of a statistical generalization. The strengths that this strategy offers us include the establishment of deep knowledge and rapport with the subject of study. It should be noted that, despite the different benefits provided by the use of case studies, these are an approach that can hardly be used alone, so most of the time they are combined with some other techniques to act as sources of evidence, corroborating the information. This includes interviews, observations, documented evidence and questionnaires. Case studies are usually carried out by researchers with a small group of people or participants in depth, who are studied in order to identify and describe the problems or difficulties with the use of some tool or system and then proceed with solution ideas (P01).

- **Questionnaires** (P02, P04, P05, P08, P09, P10, P12, P13, P15, P16, P20). Questionnaires are methods used to carry out usability or user experience evaluations, relating them to a specific context and considering users and clients, in addition to emphasizing the particularities of a personalized design (P05). There is a wide variety of questionnaires, including some of the aforementioned: SUS (System Usability Scale) questionnaires (P04, P05, P08, P15, P20), PSSUQ (Post-Study System Usability Questionnaire) (P02), SUMI questionnaires (Software Usability Measurement Inventory) (P05), QUIS (Questionnaire for User Interface Satisfaction) questionnaires (P05, P08, P09), UEQ (User Experience Questionnaire) questionnaires (P05, P16), USE (Usefulness, Satisfaction and Ease of Use) questionnaires (P05), etc. In this way, the application of this method occurs through the measurement provided by users in relation to their satisfaction and experience with a product and the information that can be extracted from the questionnaire applied to them (P05).
- **Interviews** (P01, P05, P10, P20, P23). Interviews are a research strategy that can be used to evaluate the user interfaces of a software application. These can help find valuable information such as the description of the problem that a system solves, requirements documentation and other documents that describe the context of the system (P23). In addition, they allow us to know the key actors within the context. Likewise, the application and execution of this strategy occurs in a similar way to questionnaires, since both are methods of consultation with users in which there must be an interaction with them to obtain the necessary information (P01, P05, P20).
- **Usability and user experience tests** (P01, P02, P05, P17, P23). These are a set of tests that make use of participants representing a target population in order to evaluate the degree to which the presented product meets specific usability criteria (P01). Usually these types of tests are given to evaluate "real world" products, after they have been launched into production (P01). Usability tests provide the evaluator or expert with results to identify how the interfaces help the user in completing tasks, including techniques such as: coaching method, joint discovery learning, performance measurement, question protocol, remote testing, retrospective testing, monitoring method, teaching method and the think-aloud protocol (P23).
- **Heuristic evaluations** (P08, P10, P15, P16, P17, P22, P26). These types of evaluations are an informal method of usability analysis where evaluators examine the user interface and judge its compliance with known usability principles, such as Nielsen's 10 heuristics (P08, P15 P17, P26). After raters have associated the usability problems with the respective heuristic violations,

they can score the problems according to their level of severity (P08, P17). Some of the benefits of this evaluation include its low level of cost, its use early in the development process, the low need for advanced planning, its effective conduct without the need for professional evaluators, and its ease of learning (P17, P26).

- **User-Centered Design** (P06, P16, P18, P20). User-Centered Design is a framework that involves the participation of users in the design process (P06, P20). In this way, users can present intense participation in each stage of development as partners (P16). Overall, the evaluation of satisfaction, experience, and objective characteristics confirm the usefulness of this User-Centered Design framework (P16). It is also valid to mention that user intervention is not only important when deciding which methods to apply, but it is essential to consult with the user how these methods should be applied, achieving an optimal balance between the solution for users and the correct understanding of software use (P16, P18).

4.3 Impacts Generated by the Application of Methods to Solve Usability Problems in ERP Systems Interfaces

Results Report. To answer the third review question (*What are the impacts generated by the application of methods and strategies to solve usability problems in graphical interfaces of ERP systems and how have they influenced the interaction experience and the achievement of user goals?*) a total of 17 studies were identified. From these studies, certain impacts of some methods and strategies that have attempted to solve usability problems are identified. However, of the total, a number of 3 methods or strategies stand out with their respective impacts, some being mentioned in other studies.

Analysis of Results. Based on the results obtained, it is observed that the greatest number of methods and strategies are those mentioned hereunder, with their respective descriptions and impacts to solve usability problems in graphical interfaces of some ERP systems, as well as their influences on the experience of interaction and the achievement of user goals.

- **Heuristic evaluation** (P15, P16, P17, P26, P27). This method allows you to evaluate the user interface and judge compliance with known usability principles. Its use provides a significant impact since usability can be measured at an earlier stage of process development, advance planning is not required, evaluations can be carried out effectively without the use of professional evaluators and it is simple to understand and easy to use (P17, P26). Furthermore, it allowed analysis and the possibility of verification of task completion and a task-based accessibility assessment in the cases in which it was applied (P26, P27). On the other hand, through its use, the fulfillment of the user's goals and quick navigation is identified (P15). Some of the benefits of heuristic evaluations include: Low-cost means to measuring usability, usability can measured earlier in the development process, no advanced planning is required, evaluations can be conducted effectively without using professional evaluators and the method of conducting a heuristic evaluation is easy to learn (P02).

- **Prototyping** (P02, P03, P06, P07, P13, P15, P19, P20, P25). It is a technique or practice through which a prototype is created that reproduces the interaction of sequences in real time based on previously generated usage log data (P15). This approach results as a more flexible and low-cost alternative (P15). In this way, a previous design of an interface is created interactively, which can be tested and evaluated (P02). This practice has had a lot of influence in different case studies, which is why it has been used as an alternative to display a design or redesign proposal (P06, P07, P13, P15, P19, P20, P25). Furthermore, the use of the method allows us to simulate the complete flow of a system, improving the user experience and personalizing their needs (P02). Likewise, through its use, the reduction of system use time, access to data and processes, improvement of usability (P06, P07, P15), compliance with user objectives and tasks (P15) is verified, as well as the simple and fast navigation and familiarization with icons (P20, P25). Some of the impacts or benefits found due to prototyping are: Develop a clickable design and design something that visually mimic function flow form an original system (P02).
- **Questionnaires** (P02, P12, P13, P22, P23). This method allows usability evaluation to be carried out quickly, cost-effectively and easily for data collection (P23). In addition, it makes it possible to identify satisfaction with usability, task completion time and text readability. However, it presents certain negative impacts such as the risk of reliability due to limitations in relation to resources such as the time and reluctance of participants to participate or the number of them, giving less appropriate results (P12, P13, P23).

5 Conclusions and Future Works

The systematic review that has been carried out has identified that the graphical user interfaces of ERP systems report several usability problems. Studies establish that the interfaces are hard to use because they support multiple business scenarios, and many graphical elements are only occasionally used or required. This situation generates delays in the use of the system, long periods of learning time, and user dissatisfaction. Some of the forms are overloaded with information and elements, and the expressions used in the design are generic and not adapted to the local cultural environment or the company. Due to this situation, the team in charge of the company's information technology area must make modifications and adapt the design according to the needs and requirements of the units. In the identified studies, case studies are reported in which redesigns are carried out using User-Centered Design methods to improve the usability of these software products.

The systematic review shows numerous efforts to improve the design of the graphical interfaces that are by default in ERP systems. Design and development teams use user-centered methods to redesign and improve the graphical interfaces. One of the most used approaches is the questionnaire due to its simplicity, speed, and practicality of application. Even the questionnaires have been applied asynchronously, not necessarily in a testing scenario but as a survey through digital media to the workers of those companies that have implemented the ERP system. Another of the methods most preferred by academics, according to the systematic review carried out and the case studies reported is heuristic evaluation. This inspection method provides the opportunity to identify design problems by verifying compliance with specific guidelines or general usability rules. The preference for this approach is that specialists can execute it without requiring the participation of real users. However, in the execution of this method, it can be observed that they are not necessarily directed by specialists in the area of Human-Computer Interaction (HCI) as established by the original definition. Likewise, there are slight differences in how the inspection is carried out. However, the benefits obtained as a result have been highlighted in all the articles that show the application of User-Centered Design methods to improve the usability of ERP systems, regardless of the method used. The benefits of improving the user experience of systems outweigh the efforts and costs associated with method implementation and redesign.

Regarding the impacts generated by carrying out redesigns and usability evaluations through UCD methods, it is possible to mention that the improvements reported are significant. Through the methods, it is possible to identify critical design problems that substantially affect the interaction experience, and after being identified, it is possible to solve them from a perspective based on the end user. Some methods require greater resources to be executed, but it will depend on the specific conditions of the business scenario to apply one or another method that best suits the IT team. Suppose the company needs more resources to conduct a usability test in a controlled environment; quick and simple methods, such as inquiry methods, can easily collect direct information from users. Likewise, it will always be better to carry out evaluations and use UCD methods to improve graphical interfaces than to implement ERP systems as they come by default.

As future works, case studies can be carried out where different methods are applied to verify how each method contributes to identifying usability problems and improving the interaction experience. Likewise, it is possible to compare different ERP systems to determine which is the most usable in terms of usability. Finally, a methodology could be proposed that involves the most relevant methods to adapt the graphical interfaces of ERP systems to specific business environments.

Acknowledgement. This study is highly supported by the *Section of Informatics Engineering* of the *Pontifical Catholic University of Peru* (PUCP) - Peru, and the "HCI, Design, User Experience, Accessibility & Innovation Technologies" Research Group (HCI-DUXAIT). HCI-DUXAIT is a research group of PUCP.

References

1. Akiki, P.A.: Engineering adaptive user interfaces for enterprise applications. In: Proceedings of the 5th ACM SIGCHI Symposium on Engineering Interactive Computing Systems, EICS 2013, pp. 151–154. Association for Computing Machinery, New York, NY, USA (2013). https://doi.org/10.1145/2494603.2480333
2. Avelino, A., Cueva, R., Paz, F.: A systematic review of user-centered design framework applied to the redesign of purchase order modules. In: Soares, M.M., Rosenzweig, E., Marcus, A. (eds.) Design, User Experience, and Usability: Design Thinking and Practice in Contemporary and Emerging Technologies, pp. 106–123. Springer, Cham (2022). https://doi.org/10.1007/978-3-031-05906-3_9
3. Babaian, T., Lucas, W., Topi, H.: Collaborating to improve ERP usability. In: Sixth International Conference on Enterprise Information Systems, pp. 164–168 (2004). https://doi.org/10.5220/0002655101640168
4. Babaian, T., Lucas, W., Topi, H.: Improving ERP usability through user-system collaboration. Int. J. Enterp. Inf. Syst. **2**(3), 10–23 (2006). https://doi.org/10.4018/jeis.2006070102
5. Babaian, T., Xu, J., Lucas, W.: ERP prototype with built-in task and process support. Eur. J. Inf. Syst. (2017). https://doi.org/10.1057/s41303-017-0060-3
6. Bender, B., Bertheau, C., Gronau, N.: Future ERP systems: a research agenda. In: Proceedings of the 23rd International Conference on Enterprise Information Systems (ICEIS 2021), pp. 776–783. Science and Technology Publications (2021). https://doi.org/10.5220/0010477307760783
7. Choma, J., Zaina, L.A., da Silva, T.S.: Working beyond technical aspects: an approach for driving the usability inspection adding the perspective of user experience. In: Proceedings of the 34th ACM International Conference on the Design of Communication, SIGDOC 2016. Association for Computing Machinery, New York, NY, USA (2016). https://doi.org/10.1145/2987592.2987607
8. Faisal, C.M.N., Shakeel Faridi, M., Javed, Z.: Usability evaluation of in-housed developed ERP system. In: SPIE - The International Society for Optical Engineering (2011). https://doi.org/10.1117/12.913212
9. Faisal, C.M.N., Tariq, S., Ahtram, T., Abbasi, M.S., Sarwer, S., Selamat, A.: A novel usability matrix for ERP systems using heuristic approach. In: 2012 International Conference on Management of e-Commerce and e-Government, pp. 291–296 (2012). https://doi.org/10.1109/ICMeCG.2012.34
10. ISO: Ergonomics of human-system interaction - Part 210: Human-centred design for interactive systems (ISO/IEC 9241-210:2019). Standard, International Organization for Standardization, Geneva, CH (2019)
11. Kitchenham, B., Charters, S.: Guidelines for performing systematic literature reviews in software engineering. Technical report. EBSE 2007-001, Keele University and Durham University (2007)
12. Klaus, H., Rosemann, M., Gable, G.G.: What is ERP? Inf. Syst. Front. **2**(2), 141–162 (2000). https://doi.org/10.1023/A:1026543906354
13. Kumar, A., Tadayoni, R., Sorensen, L.T.: Metric based efficiency analysis of educational ERP system usability-using fuzzy model. In: 2015 Third International Conference on Image Information Processing (ICIIP), pp. 382–386 (2015). https://doi.org/10.1109/ICIIP.2015.7414801
14. Lambeck, C., Fohrholz, C., Leyh, C., Šūpulniece, I., Müller, R.: Commonalities and contrasts: an investigation of ERP usability in a comparative user study. In: Twenty Second European Conference on Information Systems (2014)

15. Lambeck, C., Groh, R.: Mastering ERP interface complexity - a scalable user interface concept for ERP systems. In: 15th International Conference on Enterprise Information Systems (ICEIS-2013), pp. 170–178 (2013). https://doi.org/10.5220/0004566601700178
16. Lambeck, C., Müller, R., Fohrholz, C., Leyh, C.: (Re-)evaluating user interface aspects in ERP systems – an empirical user study. In: 2014 47th Hawaii International Conference on System Sciences, pp. 396–405 (2014). https://doi.org/10.1109/HICSS.2014.57
17. Lucas, W., Babaian, T.: Implementing design principles for collaborative ERP systems. In: Peffers, K., Rothenberger, M., Kuechler, B. (eds.) DESRIST 2012. LNCS, vol. 7286, pp. 88–107. Springer, Heidelberg (2012). https://doi.org/10.1007/978-3-642-29863-9_8
18. Maguire, M.: Methods to support human-centred design. Int. J. Hum Comput Stud. **55**(4), 587–634 (2001). https://doi.org/10.1006/ijhc.2001.0503
19. Mao, J.Y., Vredenburg, K., Smith, P.W., Carey, T.: The state of user-centered design practice. Commun. ACM **48**(3), 105–109 (2005). https://doi.org/10.1145/1047671.1047677
20. Milosz, M., Plechawska-Wojcik, M., Borys, M., Laskowski, M.: Quality improvement of ERP system GUI using expert method: a case study. In: 2013 6th International Conference on Human System Interactions (HSI), pp. 145–152 (2013). https://doi.org/10.1109/HSI.2013.6577815
21. Moon, Y.B.: Enterprise resource planning (ERP): a review of the literature. Int. J. Manag. Enterprise Dev. **4**(3), 235–264 (2007). https://doi.org/10.1504/IJMED.2007.012679
22. Morales, J., Rojas, G., Cerda, G.: Towards a methodology to evaluate user experience with personalized questionnaires for the developments of custom systems. In: Kurosu, M., et al. (eds.) HCI International 2022 - Late Breaking Papers. Design, User Experience and Interaction, pp. 267–281. Springer, Cham (2022). https://doi.org/10.1007/978-3-031-17615-9_19
23. O'Hear, T., Boudjenane, Y.: Using activity descriptions to generate user interfaces for ERP software. In: Jacko, J.A. (ed.) HCI 2009. LNCS, vol. 5613, pp. 577–586. Springer, Heidelberg (2009). https://doi.org/10.1007/978-3-642-02583-9_63
24. Omar, K., Gómez, J.M.: An adaptive system architecture for devising adaptive user interfaces for mobile ERP apps. In: 2017 2nd International Conference on the Applications of Information Technology in Developing Renewable Energy Processes & Systems (IT-DREPS), pp. 1–6 (2017). https://doi.org/10.1109/IT-DREPS.2017.8277812
25. Omar, K., Rapp, B., Gómez, J.M.: Heuristic evaluation checklist for mobile ERP user interfaces. In: 2016 7th International Conference on Information and Communication Systems (ICICS), pp. 180–185 (2016). https://doi.org/10.1109/IACS.2016.7476107
26. Omieno, K.K.: Evaluating the usability maturity of enterprise resource planning systems. In: Metrics and Models for Evaluating the Quality and Effectiveness of ERP Software, pp. 171–199 (2020). https://doi.org/10.4018/978-1-5225-7678-5.ch008
27. Paz, F., Lecaros, A., Falconi, F., Tapia, A., Aguirre, J., Moquillaza, A.: A process to support heuristic evaluation and tree testing from a UX integrated perspective. In: Latifi, S. (ed.) ITNG 2023 20th International Conference on Information Technology-New Generations, pp. 369–377. Springer, Cham (2023). https://doi.org/10.1007/978-3-031-28332-1_42

28. Paz, F., Paz, F.A.: A comparison between usability evaluation methods: a case study in the e-commerce domain. In: 8th International Conference on Human Interaction and Emerging Technologies (IHIET 2022), pp. 436–444 (2022). https://doi.org/10.54941/ahfe1002762
29. Petticrew, M., Roberts, H.: Systematic reviews in the social sciences: a practical guide. Wiley-Blackwell (2006). https://doi.org/10.1002/9780470754887
30. Polancos, R.V.: A usability study of an enterprise resource planning system: a case study on SAP business one. In: Bagnara, S., Tartaglia, R., Albolino, S., Alexander, T., Fujita, Y. (eds.) IEA 2018. AISC, vol. 824, pp. 1203–1223. Springer, Cham (2019). https://doi.org/10.1007/978-3-319-96071-5_121
31. Prasetyo, Y.T., Soliman, K.O.S.: Usability evaluation of ERP systems: a comparison between SAP S/4 HANA & Oracle cloud. In: 2021 IEEE 8th International Conference on Industrial Engineering and Applications (ICIEA), pp. 120–125 (2021). https://doi.org/10.1109/ICIEA52957.2021.9436697
32. Scholtz, B., Cilliers, C., Calitz, A.: Qualitative techniques for evaluating enterprise resource planning (ERP) user interfaces. In: Proceedings of the 2010 Annual Research Conference of the South African Institute of Computer Scientists and Information Technologists, SAICSIT 2010, pp. 284–293. Association for Computing Machinery, New York, NY, USA (2010). https://doi.org/10.1145/1899503.1899535
33. Sharma, Y., Chowdhury, A.: Evaluation and redesign of SAP portal for university students. In: Chakrabarti, A., Poovaiah, R., Bokil, P., Kant, V. (eds.) ICoRD 2021. SIST, vol. 221, pp. 413–422. Springer, Singapore (2021). https://doi.org/10.1007/978-981-16-0041-8_35
34. Shim, S.J.: User interaction satisfaction with simulation games used in learning about ERP systems. In: 2022 8th International Conference of the Immersive Learning Research Network (iLRN), pp. 1–5 (2022). https://doi.org/10.23919/iLRN55037.2022.9815920
35. Singh, A., Wesson, J.: Evaluation criteria for assessing the usability of ERP systems. In: Proceedings of the 2009 Annual Research Conference of the South African Institute of Computer Scientists and Information Technologists, SAICSIT 2009, pp. 87–95. Association for Computing Machinery, New York, NY, USA (2009). https://doi.org/10.1145/1632149.1632162
36. Singh, A., Wesson, J.: The design of adaptive interfaces for enterprise resource planning systems. In: 13th International Conference on Enterprise Information Systems (ICEIS-2011), pp. 281–286 (2011). https://doi.org/10.5220/0003486302810286
37. Suzianti, A., Arrafah, G.: User interface redesign of dental clinic ERP system using design thinking: a case study. In: Proceedings of the 5th International Conference on Industrial and Business Engineering, ICIBE 2019, pp. 193–197. Association for Computing Machinery, New York, NY, USA (2019). https://doi.org/10.1145/3364335.3364369
38. Uflacker, M., Busse, D.: Complexity in enterprise applications vs. simplicity in user experience. In: Jacko, J.A. (ed.) HCI 2007. LNCS, vol. 4553, pp. 778–787. Springer, Heidelberg (2007). https://doi.org/10.1007/978-3-540-73111-5_87

A Case Study Analyzing an Interdisciplinary Effort to Guide the Development and Design of a Human-Centered, Digitally Facilitated System of Care to Support Diabetes Self-management Education and Support (DSMES) in Rural Parts of Texas

Michael R. Gibson(✉)

The University of North Texas, Denton, TX 76201, USA
Michael.gibson@unt.edu

Abstract. One of the primary reasons for the higher incidences of diabetes and prediabetes in rural counties in Texas is that the people who live in them tend not to have easy access to what are known as "*Diabetes Self-Management Education and Support*," or *DSMES* programs. (A rural county in Texas has a population that numbers less than 20,000 people.) More specifically, in 153 out of 254 counties (60.3%), they have little or no access to these programs because they either do not exist in those locations as physically available initiatives, or, if they are available but are only accessible online, they require levels of broadband internet connectivity and types of computational resources that many people living in these areas do not have. Additionally, in many cases, the structure and delivery of the content that constitutes the (mostly) web-facilitated programs that rural Texans living with diabetes do have access to has not been designed or written in ways that account for the lower quality and lower levels of education prevalent among this population (compared to those who have been educated in the state's more urbanized areas). Web-facilitated, diabetes-related content that is written and presented in a manner that makes it difficult to understand for this group of users can contribute to a phenomenon known as "diabetes distress," which occurs when someone feels frustrated, defeated, or overwhelmed by having to live with diabetes, or having to care for someone who is.

This problem is further exacerbated by the fact that the organizational structure, user interface design, and linguistic style and tone of many of the extant web-facilitated DSMES programs available to people living with diabetes in rural Texas do not appear to have not been informed by one or more types of user research. Specifically, regarding its potential to affect the development and design of these programs, no methodic study of some number of these people appeared to have been operated to determine their needs and wants, or what was causing them one or more types of difficulty, as they attempted to manage their treatment of diabetes. Additionally, these programs do not appear to have undergone much of the kinds of iteratively guided, heuristically informed cycles of prototypical development that allows for various versions of their system components, features, and

A. Marcus et al. (Eds.): HCII 2024, LNCS 14714, pp. 223–236, 2024.
https://doi.org/10.1007/978-3-031-61356-2_15

functionalities to be operated and critically assessed by either their potential users or their stakeholders.

In this context, potential users are not only those living with diabetes in rural Texas, but those who are involved in caring for them, or who are affected in some way by their need for day-to-day treatment, or some combination of these. Stakeholders are comprised of the endocrinologists and other physicians who help those living with diabetes in rural Texas plan and manage their care, along with those who administrate the healthcare systems of which many of these healthcare providers are a part. Other stakeholders include those who facilitate the operation of the insurance companies and (in some cases) government-run programs that help pay for diabetes treatments and care regimens, and those who fulfill roles in some rural areas of Texas as "diabetic educators" to help especially those newly diagnosed learn to effectively understand and manage the day-to-day responsibilities that living with diabetes entails.

The combined effects of rural Texans living with diabetes not having easy access to physically available or well-designed, web-facilitated, DSMES programs was a key factor that triggered the initiation of the applied design research endeavor that is described in this paper. Another was the lack of hospital-based or other dedicated, high-operational-level healthcare facilities necessary to support the ministration and treatment needs of many of these people, especially if they live in one of the 77 Texas counties that does not have a hospital, or if they are among the almost one in three rural Texans who does not have health insurance.

In January of 2023, this set of circumstances began to fuel a series of conversations between a noted endocrinologist with over 20 years of experience treating people with diabetes, or who were or are prediabetic, in rural and urban areas of Texas, and the author of this paper. The endocrinologist was and is Dr. Wasim Haque, M.D., F.A.C.E. who was and is a is Board Certified in Endocrinology and is a fellow of the American College of Endocrinology, a member of the American Diabetes Association, and the Denton County (Texas, U.S.A.) Medical Society. His primary areas of interest are insulin resistance, hyperlipidemia, thyroid disorders, osteoporosis, and diabetes mellitus. The author of this paper is a Full Professor of Visual Communication Design embedded in the Department of Design at The University of North Texas, a tier one research university located in the Dallas/Fort Worth, Texas metropolitan area of the U.S.

Speculation by Dr. Haque and two of his colleagues about how a DSMES that would be specifically tailored to meet the needs of rural Texans living with diabetes had led them to develop a crude-but-operational, online-facilitated DSMES to address these in October and November of 2022. This was used as a "starting point" from which a much more comprehensive digitally facilitated system of care could evolve. What follows describes the research that informed the design decision-making processes that affected the initial-to-mid-level development and design of the uniquely tailored DSMES system that came to be known as "*EndoMD: an Initative to Empower Rural Texans Living with Diabetes*," or, more simply, "*EndoMD*."

Keywords: diabetes · human-centered · healthcare · health literacy · user experience design · rural Texas · Diabetes Self-Management Education and Support · DSMES · co-design

1 Introduction: Framing and Defining a Widespread Dilemma

DSMES (Diabetes Self-Management, Education, and Support) programs can be crucial to helping people living with diabetes plan and facilitate "…the comprehensive blend of clinical, educational, psychosocial, and behavioral aspects of care needed for [effective] diabetes self-management." (see Footnote [13]) Living with diabetes demands that those who have it plan and manage a treatment and *daily care regimen* to limit the levels of sugar that enters their bloodstreams. According to research published by the *American Centers for Disease Control and Prevention* in late 2023, people living with diabetes who *consistently* make effective use of the kinds of personal care management information provided by a DSMES program are three times more likely to avoid diabetes-related health problems than those who do not (see Footnote [8]).

The lack of easy access to DSMES programs in rural areas of Texas is associated with two other significant factors that inhibit the ability those who live there to engage in the daily care and treatment regimens necessary to effectively manage the disease. The first of these is that they have difficulty accessing credible, medically well-vetted information about preventing diabetes, much less managing it, due to a combination of a lack of well-functioning hospital and health clinic infrastructures (see Footnote [13]) coupled with less-than-robust internet connectivity. (For people who rely mostly or solely on their smartphones to access the internet in rural areas—in Texas and across the U.S.—accessing so-called 'telemedicine-based services' to facilitate various aspects of healthcare delivery, "… inhibits the ability of many … to obtain health care services via telemedicine." (see Footnote [9])) The second of these is the sheer amount of misinformation that is currently—as of this writing in late January of 2024—circulating online about diabetes care and treatment. According to a recent study carried out by the *International Diabetes Foundation,* "…one in five Google searches for terms related to diabetes reveal[ed] inaccurate information about the condition and how to manage its complications." (see Footnote [10]) Interviews with 61 people living with diabetes, or caring for them, in rural areas of Texas, 37—67.2%—revealed that they'd encountered what they believed to be false or misleading information online related to diabetes within 30 days of being interviewed.[1] 30 of these 37 —81%—revealed that they had also encountered this type mis- and dis-information on at least two social media platforms within 30 days of being interviewed. *Facebook* and *X* (formerly *Twitter)* were the platforms that were most commonly mentioned, as they were cited by 32 of these 37—86%. For people living with diabetes, acting on inaccurate information that, for example, suggests that one can be 'weaned off of insulin' as they 'reverse' or 'cure' their diabetes can literally be life-threatening (see Footnote [15]).

Adding to the array of challenges that rural Texans living with diabetes must confront are three other factors. The first is that they tend *not* to have easy access to doctors, or well-stocked grocery stores, pharmacies, clinics, or hospitals (see Footnote [14]). (This set of circumstances exists because Texas has more people living in rural areas than any other state in the U.S., and it is the size of France and Switzerland combined. This means that many rural Texans must transport themselves dozens of miles or more to reach these

[1] These were conducted by the author, one of his professorial colleagues, and team of five of their graduate students between March and June of 2023.

kinds of places, a feat that is logistically difficult for many of them (see Footnote [6]).) The second factor is that roughly one in six—more than five million, or 18%—of Texans lack health insurance, which makes gaining and then sustaining a regimen of care that is supervised by a doctor or other licensed healthcare provider virtually impossible for them to obtain (see Footnote [12]). This also makes it difficult for many rural Texans living with diabetes to afford the relatively high cost of many of the medications that are now commonly prescribed to help them manage the day-to-day demands of this disease. The third factor is that many rural Texans have only limited access to the kinds of public health-related materials and resources that have been prepared for general use by state, federal, and private sector information providers. Not having ready access to this kind of information, and—if they do—not having it written and presented in ways that make it easy to understand and act upon is dangerous for significant portions of this population.[2] Not being able to gain key understandings about how diabetes can and will affect their physiologies if it is not treated effectively carries grave health risks, as it is a disease that grows progressively worse if it cannot be controlled.

This combination of problems was brought to the attention of the author of this piece—a professor in the user experience and interaction design programs at *The University of North Texas*—in November of 2022. They were initially described by an endocrinologist with over 20 years of experience treating people living with diabetes in Texas' north central region (particularly in and around the Dallas/Fort Worth metropolitan region, as well as the rural areas that surround it). The initial conversations between this user experience and interaction design professor and this endocrinologist led them to begin work during the early spring of 2023 on an applied design research project that they believed would yield results that could help at least some rural Texans living with diabetes. This endeavor has since come to be known as *"EndoMD: an Initative to Empower Rural Texans Living with Diabetes,"* or, more simply, *"EndoMD."*

A group of 15 graduate and undergraduate students enrolled in the university's interaction and user experience design programs were then afforded opportunities to contribute to the development of this project as part of their classroom learning experiences beginning in early March of 2023. Shortly thereafter, *EndoMD* received its initial round of funding in April of that year, which allowed four and eventually five of these students began contributing to its development and design as paid members of a *co-design team* that has also included significant input from 38 potential users. All but six of them have Type 1 or Type 2 diabetes, and 19 of them also help care for others in their families and communities that live with diabetes. Four of them are diabetes educators.[3] As of this writing in late January of 2024, various members of the *EndoMD* co-design team

[2] Gursul, D. "NIHR Evidence: Health Information: are you getting your message across?" *National Institute for Health and Care Research,* June (2022). https://evidence.nihr.ac.uk/collection/health-information-are-you-getting-your-message-across/ (Accessed January 20, 2024).

[3] Diabetes care and education specialists are an essential part of any diabetes health care team. They provide evidence-based diabetes self-management education and support (DSMES) services and help people live well with diabetes. They also can play an important role in helping people prevent type 2 diabetes. Excerpted from "Diabetes Care and Education Specialists," *Centers for Disease Control and Prevention,* 19 April 2023. https://www.cdc.gov/diabetes/professional-info/diabetes-care-education-specialists.html (Accessed January 31, 2024).

have met more than 25 times to use and learn from each other's stores of knowledge and understandings, as the group of potential users has worked with the group of students, the user experience and interaction professor and one of his colleagues, and the endocrinologist. These "exchanges" informed critical discussions of and about how and why particular kinds of information should be organized, made accessible and understandable, and be supported by various kinds of content (i.e., still- and motion-based imagery, informational diagrams, charts, and maps, and various types of language) across the structure of this DSMES. They also guided 11 rounds of qualitative usability testing (of wireframes, paper prototypes, and, since early in July of 2023, seven iterations of functional, digitally operationalized prototypes) that sought to identify problems in its design, uncover opportunities to improve it, and learn more about the preferences and behaviors of rural Texans living with diabetes. (see Footnote [11]) *EndoMD* received its second round of funding in November of 2023, which has allowed the co-design team to 1) expand the scope of the content that will be developed and tested for possible inclusion in this DSMES, and 2) refine its overall organization and the aesthetic design and writing that will constitute its subject matter.

An overarching goal that was articulated early on during this process was to ensure that whatever would be designed and implemented, as features and as functionalities, would meet the psychological and physiological needs and wants of rural Texans living with diabetes. This case study chronicles and analyzes the co-creative, design decision-making processes that guided the iterative, heuristically informed evolution of a high-fidelity prototype of the *EndoMD* DSMES. As this 'working version' incorporated its essential structure, features, and functionalities, it could be and was broadly and deeply tested by this assortment of 38 potential users; a synopsis of what these tests revealed and suggested will also be shared in this piece.

2 A Synoptic Exploration of Key Healthcare-Related Communication Challenges Faced by Rural Texans Living with Diabetes

Over a five-week period at the outset of the *EndoMD* project, an initial round of interviews with 61 people living with or caring for those with diabetes in rural Texas (55 of these people were over the age of 50) was conducted by the author, one of his professorial colleagues, and five members of the student team. The 38 "potential users" that eventually participated in the activities of the co-design team that guided the development and design of the *EndoMD* project emerged from this initial round of interviews. During this span of time, the author, his professorial colleague, and five members of the student team also conducted three in-depth interviews (IDIs) with two nurse practitioners and the endocrinologist who is an essential partner in this endeavor. These interviews were intended to surface information and guide the construction of understandings about how those living in rural Texas with diabetes located, perceived, and acted upon various types of information about diabetes treatment and management.

One of the key revelations gleaned from these initial interviews informed a key tenet of the user experience design approach to this project. Specifically, these exchanges of information revealed that slightly over half of the group of 61—34, or 55.7%—read most comfortably at what is known in the U.S. as "the seventh-grade reading level." This meant that they could determine the central theme of a given text, identify details that relate to it, identify how and why particular points of view presented within a given discourse are similar or different, recognize relationships between narrative elements, and draw key inferences from what they have read (see Footnote [2]).

43—roughly 70%—of these potential users spoke about how they were often frustrated during their attempts to read various examples of diabetes care and treatment information because they encountered prose and design structure that impeded their ability to interpret meaning. Of particular note (among 28—45.9%—of the group of 61) were complaints offered about "relatively recent attempts" to obtain information about a specific aspect of living with diabetes, such as understanding the effects of a given medication, from web-based, diabetes education resources.[4] These complaints were articulated in two ways: interviewees expressed frustration about how often medical terminology was not explained in language they could understand, and about how difficult it often was to locate what they felt was "crucial," or "key," information, much less understandable explanations of these. These revelations came to inform key typographic, language structure, and language usage decisions as the development and design of the *EndoMD* DSMES evolved.

The need to write and design material that satisfied what the team came to refer to as "the seventh-grade standard" was repeatedly stressed by many potential users during the early and more advanced stages of *EndoMD's* content creation. Each particular portion of the content that would constitute each of *EndoMD's* categorical sections evolved into what came to be known as "articles." These would then be designed to conform to a set of physically specific, screen-based parameters that ensured a consistent presentation of typographic and image-based elements across the system. These screen-based parameters also came to guide the configuration and operation of what would become *EndoMD's* user interface.

Understandings that were formed during these initial interviews also revealed that the operation of *EndoMD* as an online-facilitated DSMES would have to work effectively on devices ranging in size from smartphones to desktop computer arrays, with an emphasis on smartphones. The need to ensure the efficacious operation of *EndoMD's* interface and the delivery of its content via smartphone was made clear when 40 of our group of 61—65.5%—indicated that either 1) they did not have or made little use of a desktop computer, or 2) their need to spend large amounts of time driving across rural terrain necessitated an overt reliance on a smartphone to, as six interviewees expressed, "communicate with the world outside of my [car or truck]." Additionally, 24 of the 61—39.3%—indicated that, since they were often in situations where internet connectivity was "less than ideal," driving to a place where this improved enough to "at least access [their] smartphone" was a necessity. This was indicated to be especially true if a given interviewee felt he, she, or they needed to interact with a healthcare or pharmaceutical provider, or needed to gain access to important healthcare information.

[4] These included but were not limited to websites operated by *The American Diabetes Association, The Texas Diabetes Council, The Texas Department of Health and Human Services,* and *The National Diabetes Education Program, The Texas A&M "Healthy Texas" Education Program, and the Rural Health Education Hub.*

3 Utilizing Focused Interactions with Potential *EndoMD* Users to Gain Insights that Could Enhance the Design and Functionality of Content Intended for Their Use

The understandings and insights that were gleaned during the interviews described in Sect. 2 of this piece led the author, his professorial colleague, and the student team to facilitate six, "open card sorting exercises" that involved interacting with the endocrinologist and six smaller groups of rural Texans living with diabetes. These interactions occurred both during and after the members of each of these groups engaged in between two to four usability tests of either two to four extant, online-facilitated DSMES systems, or two to four usability tests of diabetes education websites, or some combination of both. These tests were facilitated within each group by either the author or a member of the student team. Each test challenged a single user or a pair of them to fulfill a realistic task using only the resources available within a given DSMES system or a diabetes education website, such as gaining understandable, useful, and usable information about gestational diabetes. As each test progressed, members of the student team observed the behavior of each user or pair of users as they attempted to fulfill their task, and then engaged them in a conversation intended to elicit critical commentary from them about the relative efficacy of their experience.

Each of these smaller groups numbered between four and nine, and in total involved participation from 38 potential *EndoMD* users (out of the original 61). An open card sorting exercise entails asking those participating in it to critically converse with each other as they arrange a given set of topics into categorized groupings that make sense to them. These exercises can call for participants to write one- to four-word descriptions of the topics at hand on actual, so-called "index cards" or "sticky notes," and then arrange them in groupings which themselves must be labeled with a single card or note. Once this arrangement of single cards or notes into groups has been completed, these groups can, as the participants deem necessary, further arrange them into larger groups or sub-groups. In the realms of user experience and interaction design, open card sorting exercises are often used to design or assess the information architecture[5] of a given website or other type of interactive product (Fig. 1).

The purpose of these open card sorting exercises was threefold:

1. first, they provided a method for allowing their participants to evaluate the categorical arrangement and presentation of the contents of a "diabetes education" website that had been created by the endocrinologist and two of his assistants;
2. second, they provided a method for allowing their participants to evaluate categorical arrangement and presentation of the contents of the extant, web-based diabetes education resources that were described in Sect. 2 of this piece;

[5] "Information architecture (IA) focuses on organizing, structuring, and labeling content in an effective and sustainable way. The goal is to help users find information and complete tasks. To do this, you need to understand how the pieces fit together to create the larger picture, how items relate to each other within the system." Excerpted from "Information Architecture Basics," *Usability.gov,* July (2012): https://www.usability.gov/what-and-why/information-architecture.html (Accessed January 21, 2024).

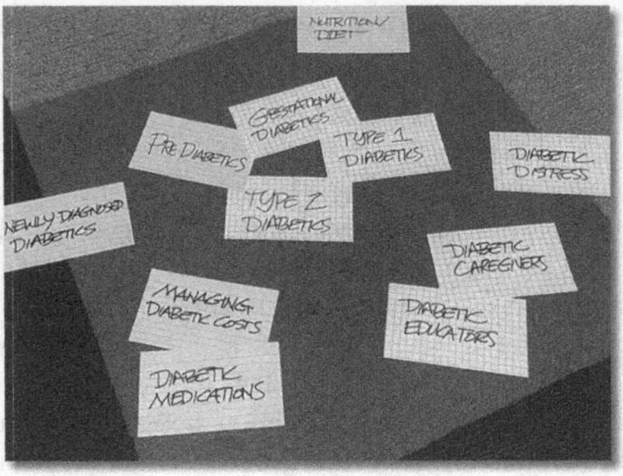

Fig. 1. An example of an early grouping of potential diabetes-related topics that occurred during one of the open card-sorting exercises that were facilitated by the author, the student team, and a group of seven potential users, all of whom were Texans living with diabetes in rural areas.

3. third, the act of engaging in the critical conversations necessary to guide the collective endeavor that constitutes a card sort provided a means for those involved to articulate a set of goals that *EndoMD* would have to satisfy to function as an effective, online-facilitated DSMES (Fig. 2).

These card sorting exercises satisfied the first purpose described above by helping the participants determine that while the "diabetes education" website that had been created by the endocrinologist and two of his assistants contained a wealth of medically credible and pertinent content, this material was arranged within a structure that contained 48 individual web pages. During the card-sort fueled conversations, this was determined among all six groups to be problematic, since the sheer size of all of this content, in terms of data storage and handling capacity, would make it quite difficult for many rural Texans with low-capacity internet access (at best) to access, especially on their smartphones. Comments also emerged from three of the six groups that sought to remind all of the participants that, since "for many rural Texans, their only computer is their smartphone," diabetes-based content disseminated online should be "created… or designed and written… so that it will work well on a smartphone." Further comments emerged from these same three groups that emphasized the importance of making crucial information easy to find "no matter where you are in the system," and that emphasized the importance of providing "easy-to-digest-and-understand" definitions for key terms "wherever they occur in the system."

In the realm of user experience and interaction design, ensuring that online-facilitated content will effectively meet a given user's needs and wants whether he, she, or they is using a smartphone or a desktop computer is referred to as a *responsive approach.* This was communicated by the author or the members of the student team within each of the three groups wherein these types of comments were made. It was also determined during these card-sorting-inspired conversations that the arrangement of the contents into this large number of pages made understanding the overall organizational structure of this more difficult, especially for potential users who had only recently been diagnosed.

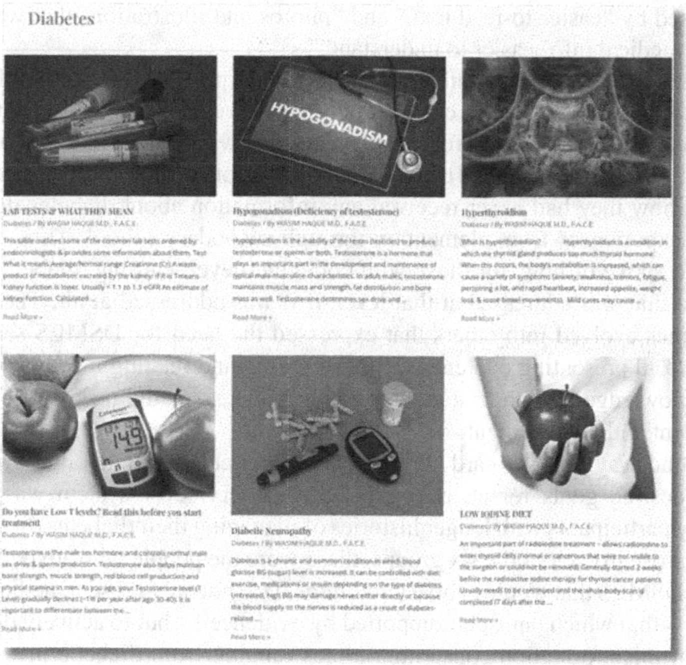

Fig. 2. An example of one of the 48 webpages that were arranged onto the diabetes education website that had been created by the endocrinologist and two of his assistants. This site was assessed during the card sorting sessions to be "chock full of great written information," but was derided for being difficult for users to navigate, especially if those users were operating this on a smartphone.

Additionally, a key insight was articulated as these conversations progressed in two of the groups, which was originally posed as a question. It was, "Why can't all of the various pages and sub-sections of this website be organized so that they're grouped according to information that would be most pertinent to a particular type of user, such as someone dealing with gestational diabetes, or someone who is a caregiver?".

As each group engaged in card sorting activities to evaluate the categorical arrangement and presentation of the contents of three to five extant, web-based diabetes education resources (among these were those operated by *The Rural Health Education Hub, The Texas Diabetes Council,* and *The National Diabetes Education Program),* a consistent criticism of the writing that appears in most of these was voiced. Participants from all six groups offered that, in too many instances, potential users were being challenged to read overlong paragraphs that were laced with difficult-to-understand, medical terminology. Comments emerged from four groups that opined that understanding prose written in this way would be especially difficult for users who do not read or speak English well. Given that over 35% of Texas residents over the age of five speak a non-English language at home, (see Footnote [3]) suggestions emerged from these groups regarding the need to ensure that the contents "whatever the *EndoMD* team would create" would be well-supported by "easier-to-read text," and "photos and illustrations that would make the 'trickier medical info' easier to understand."

The card sorting exercises satisfied their third purpose in three ways. First, they allowed participants to engage in conversations that revealed, especially for those who had been managing their diabetes for several years, how varied their individual, diabetes-based educational experiences had been. In four of the groups, the majority of participants spoke about how they had never received any information about diabetes during their educational experiences from elementary through secondary school. These same participants also spoke of how, for those with collegiate-level learning, diabetes was also not a subject that was addressed at that level, if it was addressed at all. These conversational themes evolved into others that expressed the need for DSMES services and systems to avoid presenting content as if those seeing and reading it somehow *already* possessed knowledge and understandings about diabetes, or the need for it to require daily treatment and management.

The second way that the card sorting exercises yielded insights that evolved into viable and desired goals for an effective DSMES service or system was zealously expressed by participants with longer histories of managing their diabetes. In the conversations that arose in each of the six groups, these were the people who advocated for the need for the DSMES that would evolve into *EndoMD* to not only present medically sound information—that which "must be supported by evidence"—but to actively debunk various types of misinformation concerning topics ranging from diabetic medications to specific types of dietary recommendations.

The third way these exercises yielded insights that could guide future design decision-making was to allow participants, including the endocrinologist and 28 out of 38 participants across all six groups—77.7%—to express their opinions regarding the need for rural Texans living with diabetes to gain and sustain support from family members and other members of their communities. This was articulated as being extremely important as a means to alleviate the psychological phenomenon known as *diabetic distress,* which often affects those living with the disease due to the day-to-day challenges inherent in treating and managing it. The need for *EndoMD* to help rural Texans living with diabetes connect with others who are also having to confront this challenge, especially when they are newly diagnosed, was a theme that was fervently communicated across all six groups.

4 Examining How the Insights Gleaned During Our Focused Interactions with Potential Users Yielded Five Key Principles that Guided the Development of the *EndoMD* DSMES

The focused interactions described in the previous section evolved over a period of slightly more than five months. A series of approximately 20 critical conversations took place over this span of time about what was being learned from the potential users that participated in these rounds of usability testing and card sorts. These conversations transpired between members of the student team, the author and his professorial colleague, the endocrinologist, and, on six occasions, with some of the potential users themselves.

These yielded an ideological and practical platform comprised of five essential principles that would guide the future development of each stage of the *EndoMD* DSMES. These were, and remain as of this writing:

- The need to **educate** rural Texans living with diabetes in ways that make essential information comprehensible and actionable to them so as to enhance their quality of life
- The need for the information presented across the framework of the *EndoMD* DSMES to be communicated **clearly and concisely** so as to help rural Texans living with diabetes more effectively communicate with their caregivers and family members
- The need to ensure that the needs and wants of all rural Texans living with diabetes, regardless of their class status, ethnicity, religious beliefs, or physical or mental abilities, could be **encompassed** within the scope of the *EndoMD* DSMES' functionalities
- The need for individual rural Texans to **build and sustain trust** regarding the credibility of the information-cum-knowledge that the *EndoMD* DSMES makes available across its store of contents
- The need for the *EndoMD* DSMES to operate the scope of its functionalities in ways that facilitate **empathetically guided approaches to care** for rural Texans living with diabetes

These five essential principles can all be closely correlated with what has come to be known across the realm of user experience design as *service design*. In particular, they align well with what software creator, CEO, and service design consultant Marc Stickdorn refers to as the five core principles of *service design thinking*.[6] All of these are intended to guide decision-making in ways that critically account for all of the different types of experiences that a given user might have before, during, and after his, her, or their engagement with a specific service, or an array of them, that a given business—or, in this case, the *EndoMD* DSMES—is striving to provide. Stickdorn refers to this as *sequencing*. His other core principles call upon designers and their collaborators to design their services around their users' needs and wants, and then to ensure that these are being effectively met by asking them questions; this satisfies the definition for the principle of being *user-centered*. Stickdorn's core principle of *co-creativity* has already been discussed at length in this piece: essential stakeholders and users were and will continue to be involved in the ongoing evolution of this project. His principle of *evidencing* has guided and will continue to guide how the *EndoMD* DSMES makes use of visual aids and tools to enhance their communications with each other, stakeholders, and potential users. Finally, the continued development of the *EndoMD* DSMES will require that all those involved in its evolution and maintenance think critically about each aspect of its functionalities, and all of the perspectives within which these are perceived.

[6] Stickdorn, M. & Schneider, J. *This is Service Design Thinking*. New York, NY, USA: John Wiley & Sons, Inc., 2012.

5 Preparing for What's on the Horizon and that's Approaching Quickly

As of this writing in early 2024, the project that began as a conversation about how an extant diabetes education website could be improved by incorporating some minor alterations to its structure has evolved considerably. The *EndoMD* project has been iteratively and heuristically developed to the point where it is has yielded a robustly functional and testable, mid-fidelity, limited access prototype. The design processes that have guided its evolution thus far will soon become more broadly informed as its current iteration is upgraded to a version that will allow it to function as a fully online-facilitated Diabetes Self-Management Education and Support (DSMES) system. As this upgraded version is made accessible via a web domain of its own, the relatively small but highly engaged group of potential users from rural areas of north central Texas that has been involved in its co-creation for over seven months will expand significantly. In early January of 2024, the author and his endocrinologist collaborator began to alert a loosely connected amalgam of endocrinologists affiliated with the *Texas Diabetes Council* and several groups of diabetes educators and healthcare professionals working across rural Texas about their intent to make the online-facilitated version of *EndoMD* more broadly available. It is their intent to make the contents of this version fully web-accessible by the end of April 2024, which will enable members of these groups to interact with and assess the first 30 topically organized content modules *EndoMD* will contain. In turn, these people will be encouraged to share these resources with the rural Texans living with diabetes who are, in one way or another, either under their care or who rely on them for credible advice and counsel regarding their management of the disease.

This expansion of the groups of *EndoMD's* potential users and stakeholders will coincide with the author's and the endocrinologist's plans to secure more external funding, via either government-, private sector-, or philanthropically funded grants and awards. Together, both of these efforts will enable them and the future members of the *EndoMD* student team to continue the iteratively structured and heuristically guided development of this project as a DSMES system tailored to meet the needs of rural north Texans living with diabetes. The need for this project to continue to evolve so it can contribute to the health and well-being of this ever-expanding user group is acute. Rural Texas is home to roughly 3.2 million people—more than live in 18 other American states—and approximately 12% of them are living with diabetes, and this number is projected to increase by at least 4% by 2030.[7]

[7] Author Unknown. "Why Diabetes is a Concern for Rural Communities," *RHIhub,* 23 September 2020. https://www.ruralhealthinfo.org/toolkits/diabetes/1/rural-concerns (Accessed November 20, 2023).

References

1. "Diabetes Care and Education Specialists," Centers for Disease Control and Prevention, 19 April 2023. https://www.cdc.gov/diabetes/professional-info/diabetes-care-education-specialists.html. Accessed 31 Jan 2024
2. Seventh Grade English Language Arts Common Core State Standards. Education.com, 15 July 2023. https://www.education.com/common-core/seventh-grade/ela/. Accessed 25 Jan 2024
3. Top 10 Languages of Texas, Acutrans, 2 June 2023. https://acutrans.com/top-10-languages-of-texas/. Accessed 28 Jan 2024
4. Twenty-five Things to Know About Texas Rural Hospitals. Torchnet, 21 February 2017. https://capitol.texas.gov/tlodocs/85R/handouts/C2102017030910301/be43111d-e0d4-4de3-bc7d-935d111daced.PDF. Accessed 28 Jan 2024
5. What Is Diabetes Distress and Burnout? DiABETES UK, 19 March 2022. https://www.diabetes.org.uk/guide-to-diabetes/emotions/diabetes-burnout#:~:text=Diabetes%20distress%20is%20when%20a,they%20aren't%20going%20away. Accessed 25 Jan 2024
6. Carver, J.L.: Why health care is still hard to access in rural towns near Texas' bigger cities. The Texas Tribune 16 March 2023. https://www.texastribune.org/2023/03/16/texas-health-care-deserts/n. Accessed 13 Jan 2024
7. Centers for Disease Control and Prevention. "Prediabetes: Your Chance to Prevent Type 2 Diabetes," Centers for Disease Control and Prevention, 30 December 2022. https://www.cdc.gov/diabetes/basics/prediabetes.html. Accessed 28 Jan 2024
8. Centers for Disease Control and Prevention. "US Diabetes Surveillance System," Centers for Disease Control and Prevention, 9 October 2023. https://gis.cdc.gov/grasp/diabetes/diabetesatlas-surveillance.html. Accessed 25 Nov 2023
9. Curtis, M.E., Clingan, S.E., Guo, H., Zhu, Y., Mooney, L.J., Hser, Y.: Disparities in digital access among American rural and urban households and implications for telemedicine-based services. J. Rural Health **38**(3), 512–518 (2021). https://onlinelibrary.wiley.com/doi/10.1111/jrh.12614. Accessed 22 Jan 2024
10. Evans, J., et al.: "One in five search results for diabetes reveal misinformation, International Diabetes Federation warns," Diabetes Voice, 6 July 2022. https://diabetesvoice.org/en/news/one-in-five-search-results-for-diabetes-reveal-misinformation-international-diabetes-federation-warns/. Accessed 22 Jan 2024
11. Moran, K.: Usability Testing 101. Nielsen Norman Group, 1 December 2019. https://www.nngroup.com/articles/usability-testing-101/. Accessed 30 Jan 2024
12. Nuila, R.: "Medican't." Texas Monthly, September, 122–123 (2023)
13. Rural Health Information Hub: "Why Diabetes is a Concern for Rural Communities," RHIhub, 23 September 2020. https://www.ruralhealthinfo.org/toolkits/diabetes/1/rural-concerns. Accessed 20 Nov 2023. Wiley & Sons, Inc., 2012
14. United States Department of Agriculture (USDA): Rural-Urban Continuum Codes. Economic Research Service, 15 September 2023. https://www.ers.usda.gov/data-products/rural-urbancontinuum-codes.aspx. Accessed 28 Nov 2023

15. Wagner, B.: Fact check: Facebook ad falsely claims CBD gummies can 'reverse diabetes, USA Today, 11 February 2022. https://www.usatoday.com/story/news/factcheck/2022/02/11/fact-check-facebook-ad-falsely-claims-cbd-gummies-reverse-diabetes/6696378001/. Accessed 31 Jan 2024
16. Wang, Z., Tang, S., Sutton-Jones, K.: Texas rural vs. nonrural school district student growth trajectories on a high-stakes science exam: a multilevel approach. Soc. Sci. **8**(6), 166 (2019). https://doi.org/10.3390/socsci8060166. Accessed 25 Jan 2024

Acceptance of Students and Teachers Regarding a Virtual Reality Tool for Teaching the History of Architecture and Urbanism

Emerson Gomes[1,3](✉), Francisco Rebelo[1,2], and Naylor Vilas Boas[3]

[1] CIAUD, Research Centre for Architecture, Urbanism and Design, Lisbon School of Architecture, University of Lisbon, Lisbon, Portugal
b.emersongomes@gmail.com

[2] ITI/LARSys, University of Lisbon, Lisbon, Portugal

[3] PROURB, Postgraduate Program in Urbanism, Faculty of Architecture and Urbanism, Federal University of Rio de Janeiro, Rio de Janeiro, Brazil

Abstract. With the advancement and increasing accessibility of immersive technologies and metaverses, virtual reality (VR) emerges as a promising educational tool. This study aims to assess student acceptance of VR usage in history of architecture and urbanism classes. The methodology includes the display of a two-minute video that simulates an interactive class, where students, guided by the professor, don HMDs (Head-Mounted Displays) and move into a didactic discussion within a virtual space, interacting through avatars. Following the video, students respond to a questionnaire based on the UTAUT-2 model, designed to measure the acceptance of new information technologies. The results indicate a positive receptivity to VR, highlighting expectations related to academic performance and a significant hedonic motivation. The study provides quantitative evidence that the integration of VR into architecture curricula has the potential to be well received by students, significantly enriching the educational experience.

Keywords: Virtual Reality · History of Architecture · UTAUT

1 Introduction

1.1 Context

The emergence of Virtual Reality (VR) as an educational tool stands out for its ability to provide immersive and interactive experiences, influencing teaching methods across various fields of knowledge [1]. In the realm of architecture and urbanism history, VR offers, among other things, an opportunity to address issues raised nearly a century ago regarding the limitations of materials frequently used in architectural learning, notably teaching through photographs and drawings [2], which are still canonically used today [3].

Zevi [2] argues that instruction based merely on two-dimensional images, constrained by the photographer's perspective, is inadequate for fully understanding architectural

A. Marcus et al. (Eds.): HCII 2024, LNCS 14714, pp. 237–246, 2024.
https://doi.org/10.1007/978-3-031-61356-2_16

space. He emphasizes the critical importance of physical site visits, which allow learners to navigate and explore the space on their own. This direct experience enables students to choose their own viewpoints, revealing the architectural space step by step and allowing them to contemplate the building from within. Unlike the appreciation of artworks, which often occurs through a two-dimensional representation contained within a frame, Zevi proposes a more interactive and spatially engaging approach to understanding buildings, highlighting the need to experience architecture in its three-dimensional entirety, that is, from within.

Given the impracticality of conducting physical visits to the various buildings studied in Architectural History, virtual reality emerges as a feasible alternative, enabling students and teachers to virtually enter buildings and urban spaces. This technology allows for real-scale and collaborative visits, where participants can walk, interact with the place, and with colleagues through avatars, opening a range of possibilities for exploration and learning.

Furthermore, virtual reality offers the capability for students and teachers to visit spaces that no longer exist but have been virtually reconstructed from existing graphic data, such as photos, maps, drawings, and technical plans [4]. This virtual immersion technology enables students to explore, in an immersive manner, places of historical and architectural significance that were, in the past, demolished or have been significantly altered.

However, despite the favorable arguments described above, the effective implementation of VR in architectural and urbanism education is still far from consolidation. The need to access specific VR equipment and develop programming skills to manipulate virtual models are barriers that can considerably limit the adoption of this technology [5]. Moreover, student acceptance of VR is deemed crucial for its successful integration into the educational process.

In this scenario, multiple factors can shape student acceptance, from the perception of its educational value and the ease of use of virtual reality tools to the potential barriers encountered during its implementation. It is within this context that the present study is situated, proposing an investigation into the receptivity towards the use of collaborative virtual reality as a didactic resource in the teaching of architecture and urbanism history. The aim is to map the main impressions and potential obstacles to the adoption of VR, providing insights into student acceptance regarding the integration of this technology into the academic curriculum. To achieve this understanding, a questionnaire based on the Unified Theory of Acceptance and Use of Technology – UTAUT-2 – [6, 7], was adapted, seeking to unveil the nuances influencing VR acceptance in the educational environment of the subject in question.

1.2 UTAUT 2

In this work, the Unified Theory of Acceptance and Use of Technology (UTAUT), developed by Venkatesh, was chosen for use. The authors, at the time, identified the existence of various competing theories to evaluate the acceptance of new information technologies. As a result, they proposed the unification of these theories, leading to a set of constructs designed for this purpose [7].

Almost a decade later, the author and his colleagues refined the model [6], incorporating new concepts and culminating in nine constructs, thus consolidating the second version of the theory, named UTAUT-2. These constructs are a) Performance Expectancy, b) Effort Expectancy, c) Social Influence, d) Facilitating Conditions, e) Hedonic Motivation, f) Price Value, g) Habit, h) Behavioral Intention, and i) Use.

The UTAUT model, by combining various behavioral theories, provides a robust framework for analyzing users' readiness to adopt new technologies. With the addition of new variables in its second version, the elements of the model's evaluation were expanded. Therefore, this research adapted the constructs of UTAUT-2 to the context under discussion, aiming specifically to explore the acceptance of VR in the teaching of architecture and urbanism history. As has occurred in previous research, such as the work of Hidayat [8] and Rebelo [9], the constructs f) Price Value and i) Use were removed from the adapted questionnaire, due to the requirement of prior knowledge and experience with the technology.

2 Method

The methodology adopted in this study consists of two main instruments. The first is a two-minute informative video designed to illustrate the use of Virtual Reality in the educational context, specifically in a teaching session on the history of architecture and urbanism. This video shows a real class, led by a professor, covering topics relevant to the discipline. The recording, made in a classroom with real students and a professor, aims to demonstrate the interaction of students with an immersive virtual environment, representing a historical setting. Initially, this space is introduced to the students by the professor using photos and maps, followed by a demonstration of its exploration through collaborative immersion. The purpose is to stimulate reflection on the applicability and impact of VR in traditional educational environments.

The second instrument, a questionnaire based on the UTAUT-2 model, seeks to evaluate participants' perceptions regarding the adoption of VR as a teaching tool. The development and details of both instruments will be described in the subsequent section.

2.1 Instruments

Video. The video is made available to students through a Google Forms link and starts with reflective questions, such as "Have you ever imagined using the metaverse at your college?". After the introduction, the script addresses the theme of architectural heritage that has been demolished. Then, it illustrates a traditional classroom setting at a college, with students paying attention to a teacher who is lecturing in front of a blackboard. The narrative progresses to the second part of the class, where the students, still in the same room, put on HMDs (Head Mounted Displays) and are thereby virtually transported to the location previously discussed in the teacher's explanations.

In this phase, the video exclusively focuses on the virtual environment, showing students interacting with each other and with the scenario through avatars. The content is displayed via YouTube and highlights various functionalities of the immersive tool, including teleportation, freehand 3D drawing, collaboration, and time travel. The video concludes with a scene of students in the real world, using VR equipment. The following images illustrate the storytelling.

Fig. 1. – Storytelling of the video used to illustrate the use of VR in an architecture history class. In the first part of the class (01 and 02), the teacher explains the subject to the students in a conventional manner. In the second part of the class (03 and 04), everyone immerses in the virtual environment, and there, through avatars, the class continues within VR (05 and 06). Source: Author's own.

In Fig. 1, above, the storytelling is divided into six parts. Parts 01 and 02 observe the beginning of a class, with a teacher presenting a historical setting to their students in a real classroom context. Part 02, still within the same context, shows the teacher pointing to an image projected on a screen, illustrating the conventional didactic approach adopted in the first part of the class. The transition to virtual reality is documented in part 03, where students are depicted equipping themselves with HMDs (Head-Mounted Displays) and VR controllers. Part 04 displays the continuation of the class in the physical room, where the presence of students using the VR devices can be observed.

Part 05 presents the virtual environment experienced by the participants, with avatars (students and the teacher) standing in front of a digital model of a historical building at a 1:20 scale. In part 06, also within the virtual environment, the model of a historical urban space is explored by the students, who interact through their avatars, pointing out and discussing relevant details of the lesson.

The recording was made with a Samsung Note 10 smartphone, and image and sound editing were done in Adobe Premiere software. The three-dimensional modeling of the historical environments was produced in Trimble Sketchup, based on images and drawings from the past [4, 10], and immersive, collaborative navigation was enabled by the VRSketch plugin. The video was made available to participants via YouTube. The VR equipment used included Metaquest 1, Metaquest 2 (three units), and Rift headsets.

The activity was recorded on July 30, 2022, in the city of Belém, with the participation of students from the fifth semester of the Architecture and Urbanism course.

Questionnaire. A questionnaire, structured into two sections—a) acceptance and b) demographic data—was made available to participants. The acceptance section is based on the Unified Theory of Acceptance and Use of Technology (UTAUT-2), with specific adaptations for this study to explore participants' perceptions regarding the use of VR in the subject under analysis. This part includes 14 questions, distributed across 7 constructs in a 2 to 1 ratio, providing a detailed investigation of the respondents' attitudes. As previously mentioned, the constructs "monetary value" and "use" were removed due to the need for specific prior knowledge on the subject, reducing the original model from 9 to 7 constructs. The assessment was conducted using a 7-point Likert scale, ranging from 1 ("Strongly Disagree") to 7 ("Strongly Agree").

The second section, containing 12 items, focuses on collecting demographic information, aiming to identify, among other aspects, participants' affinity with digital technologies, their previous experiences with VR, and their age groups. Google Forms was chosen as the platform for creating and applying the questionnaires. Table 1 displays the adapted questionnaire, in accordance with each construct.

2.2 Sample

The sample for this research consisted exclusively of students enrolled in architecture and urbanism courses at colleges located in the city of Belém do Pará, Brazil. The collection took place predominantly in private institutions. A total of 55 participants, ranging in age from under 20 to 50 years old, contributed to the study. About 85% declared being under 30 years old. All had previously taken courses related to the history of architecture, ensuring a basic understanding of the subject matter.

2.3 Procedures

The data collection methodology adopted in this study involved the researcher's physical visit to classrooms of higher education institutions, motivated by the low effectiveness of previous online collection strategies. Prior experiences with sending links through social networks did not achieve the expected participation, resulting in a response rate of less than 5%. Therefore, a more direct approach was necessary.

Hence, interventions in the classroom were chosen, where teachers were asked to allocate approximately 10 min of class time for conducting the survey. This methodological change significantly increased the response rate to approximately 80%, culminating in the participation of 55 individuals.

Table 1. Questionnaire adapted from Venkatesh [6]. Source: Author's own.

Construct	Question
Performance Expectancy	Virtual reality in architecture classes will allow me to understand content more quickly
	I think that if we used virtual reality in architecture classes, it would increase my chances of getting good grades
Social Influence	People whom I consider good examples support the idea of integrating virtual reality into the architecture curriculum
	I think it would make a good impression among my circle of friends and family if I used virtual reality in my college classes
Hedonic Motivation	I believe that using virtual reality to learn architecture will be a pleasant experience
	I think I will have fun in classes when using virtual reality
Facilitating Conditions	I think virtual reality is compatible with the 3D models and software that I already know how to use at college
	I believe that my college has the necessary conditions (interest of the administrators, financial availability, and qualified technical staff) to implement the use of virtual reality in classes
Effort Expectancy	I believe that using virtual reality in architecture classes will be something intuitive and easy to understand
	I believe that virtual reality equipment will be easy to use in architecture classes
Habit	I believe that using virtual reality in classes would become a habit for me
	I want to use virtual reality
Behavioral Intention	I would like to have classes where I could use virtual reality in the coming months
	I plan to use virtual reality in the coming months

With the teacher's permission, the survey link was shared with the class, beginning a period dedicated to reading the preliminary instructions, viewing the video, and subsequently, answering the questionnaire. The link provided to students included cover sheets that provided initial information about the research and included an informed consent form. This document clarified to participants that their responses would be treated anonymously and that their participation was voluntary, assuring them the freedom to stop filling out the questionnaire at any time, without needing to provide a reason.

The procedure sequence included accessing the questionnaire via the link, a brief introduction to the topic and the informed consent form, followed by the display of a two-minute video, and finally, answering the questions, including demographic questions in the final stage.

Although this approach led to a smaller sample size, it ensured a significantly higher response rate, strengthening the study's feasibility and contributing to more accurate and relevant data collection, capturing the participants' perceptions more faithfully.

3 Results

In this study, student acceptance of using virtual reality as a teaching tool in the history of architecture and urbanism was evaluated. The results were analyzed based on the Unified Theory of Acceptance and Use of Technology (UTAUT-2), adapted to the context of architectural education. Below, we present thc main findings, organized by construct:

- **Performance Expectancy** (79%): This percentage indicates that a large majority of participants perceive VR as an effective tool in aiding learning in architecture and urbanism. The values suggest that respondents expect VR to significantly improve their understanding of the content and potentially have a positive impact on their academic performance.
- **Social Influence** (83%): This percentage highlights the importance of social support in the decision to use VR. The high score indicates that participants view their social environment as favorable and encouraging towards the use of this technology, demonstrating the positive impact of social influence on the acceptance of VR.
- **Hedonic Motivation** (91%): The highest result among the constructs researched, this percentage reflects the pleasure and satisfaction derived from using VR, in addition to educational benefits. The high hedonic motivation suggests that participants see VR not only as a learning tool but also as a source of entertainment and engagement.
- **Facilitating Conditions** (79%): This value indicates that participants perceive the existence of adequate support for the adoption of VR, including the necessary infrastructure and access to technical resources. They believe that the current conditions are suitable for integrating VR into the educational process effectively.
- **Effort Expectancy** (81%): With acceptance slightly higher than Performance Expectancy, this result shows that participants are willing to dedicate the necessary effort to learn and use VR, perceiving it as accessible and not overly challenging.
- **Habit** (82%): This high percentage reveals the willingness and interest of participants to incorporate VR into classroom activities, treating it as a recurrent practice and an integral part of the educational routine. This indicator suggests a consistent adoption of technology, promoting its acceptance and integration into the curriculum.
- **Behavioral Intention** (80%): This percentage shows a strong willingness of participants to use VR in the context of their classes, reflecting a positive acceptance of technology as a valuable tool for learning in architecture and urbanism, especially in the discipline of architecture and urbanism history.

4 Conclusions

This study explored the acceptance of virtual reality as an educational tool related to the curricular component of Architecture and Urbanism History, utilizing the UTAUT-2 model to structure the evaluations.

The analysis of constructs for the adoption of VR in architecture and urbanism education revealed positive acceptance, with Hedonic Motivation standing out by reaching 91%, suggesting that the pleasure derived from the use of immersion is among the main motivators. The influence of social context and daily routine, reflected in the percentages of Social Influence (83%) and Habit (82%), highlight the importance of social relations and the intention regarding the habitual use of technology.

Facilitating Conditions showed a value slightly below 80%, indicating that there is still room for improvement in institutional support and the infrastructure provided so far. The strong Behavioral Intention (80%) and high expectations regarding performance and effort confirm the participants' willingness to adopt the technology discussed here. These results suggest a very favorable reception by the student body to the use of immersive environments in face-to-face classes.

For each construct, the research applied two specific questions, according to the original proposal by Venkatesh et al. In most cases, the variation between the averages of these questions was minimal, with differences not exceeding 10%. However, for the constructs of Habit and Behavioral Intention, the differences between the responses to the two corresponding questions were notably larger, reaching 17% and 20%, respectively.

In the case of Habit, the percentage of 74% indicates positive receptivity but with some degree of reservation, possibly due to unfamiliarity with the technology or uncertainty about costs or how it would be integrated into their existing learning routines. The question that obtained the highest average, 90%, suggests that students see VR not just as an interesting addition, but as a tool of great relevance for the future of teaching in their area, possibly motivated by the presentation in the video that illustrated the benefits of technology.

Regarding Behavioral Intention, the variation in averages points to a duality: on the one hand, there is high enthusiasm (90%) for the idea of having classes with VR, reflecting a robust interest in technology; on the other hand, the concrete intention to use VR in the coming months is considerably lower (70%), suggesting caution possibly due to practical issues like access to resources.

Overall, the expectation of use of the virtual reality tool by students proved to be significantly positive. This result confirms the favorable receptivity to VR, paving the way for future investigations into promising pedagogical methods that incorporate advanced digital technologies, as previously suggested by Ghida [11]. It is believed to be positive for educational institutions to consider these factors when planning the integration of immersive technologies into their curricula, aiming not only to improve academic performance but also to enrich the learning experience for students.

This study aligns with the results presented by researchers like Kowalski [1] and Shanti [12], who emphasize the benefits of using VR in the education of architecture and urbanism history. Thus, it contributes to a deeper understanding of the acceptance level of this technology among the student body, providing quantitative data to academics, educators, and policymakers interested in implementing the educational potential of virtual reality.

5 Limitations

Among the main limitations of this study, it's noted that the sample used, although relatively small (55 students), was restricted to students of architecture and urbanism from predominantly private institutions located in Belém do Pará, Brazil. This geographic and institutional concentration may not reflect different educational contexts.

Furthermore, the assessment of VR acceptance was based solely on responses to a questionnaire and perceptions generated from an informative video, without participants having a direct and prolonged experience with the technology in real learning contexts. This approach may not fully capture the nuances and challenges associated with the effective integration of VR into college educational environments.

Another point to consider is the removal of the "Monetary Value" and "Use" constructs from the UTAUT-2 model adapted for this study, due to the need for prior knowledge and experience with the technology. While this decision is justified by the nature of the research, it may omit important aspects related to the cost and practical implementation of VR, which are relevant for technological adoption on a large scale.

Lastly, future studies could benefit from methodologies that allow for practical experience with VR, in addition to addressing a broader and more diverse sample, to explore in depth the factors that influence the acceptance and integration of VR in the teaching of architecture and urbanism.

Acknowledgments. The authors would like to acknowledge the Portuguese National funds finance this work through FCT - Fundação para a Ciência e a Tecnologia, I.P., under the Strategic Project with the references UIDB/04008/2020 and UIDP/04008/2020 and ITI-LARSyS FCT Pluriannual fundings 2020- 2023 (UIDB/50009/2020).

Disclosure of Interests. The authors have no competing interests to declare that are relevant to the content of this article.

References

1. Kowalski, S., Samól, P., Szczepański, J., Dłubakowski, W.: Teaching architectural history through virtual reality. World Trans. Eng. Technol. Educ. **18**(2), 197–202 (2020)
2. Zevi, B.: Saber ver arquitetura, 5a Edi. São Paulo: Martins Fontes (1996)
3. Wendell, A.: Altin, E.: Learning space - incorporating spatial simulations in design history coursework. In: eCAADe 35, pp. 261–266 (2017). http://papers.cumincad.org/cgi-bin/works/paper/ecaade2017_183
4. de O. Gomes, E.B., Araujo, T.S.L., Ferraz, A.S.P., Aflalo, A.-B.B.: Mapa de confiabilidade: um método quantitativo para análise do grau de confiança nas reconstruções digitais de patrimônios históricos demolidos ou fortemente modificados. Gestão Tecnol. Proj. vol. 17, no. 1, pp. 219–237 (2021). https://doi.org/10.11606/gtp.v17i1.183924
5. de O. Gomes, E.B., Rebelo, F., Vilas Boas, N., Noriega, P., Vilar, E.: A workflow for multi-user VR application within the physical classrooms of architecture and urbanism courses. Ergon. Des. **47** (2022). https://doi.org/10.54941/ahfe1001969

6. Venkatesh, V., Thong, J.Y.L., Xu, X.: Consumer Acceptance and Use of Information Technology: Extending the Unified Theory of Acceptance and Use of Technology. vol. 36, no. 1, pp. 157–178 (2012). https://papers.ssrn.com/sol3/papers.cfm?abstract_id=2002388
7. Venkatesh, V., Morris, M.G., Davis, G.B., Davis, F.D.: User acceptance of information technology: toward a unified view. MIS Q. **27**(3), 425–478 (2003). https://doi.org/10.1016/j.inoche.2016.03.015
8. Hidayat, I.K, Rebelo, F., Noriega, P.: Exploring children's behavioral intention of using the expected game-based learning for protracted waste problem. In: Soares, M.M., Rosenzweig, E., Marcus, A. (eds.) Design, User Experience, and Usability: Design for Emotion, Well-being and Health, Learning, and Culture. HCII 2022. LNCS, vol. 13322. Springer, Cham (2022). https://doi.org/10.1007/978-3-031-05900-1_18
9. Rebelo, F., Santos, D., Noriega, P., Figueiredo, C., Oliveira, T., Vilar, E.: Expected architects acceptance of a BIM tool to optimize the building energetic performance. Adv. Intell. Syst. Comput. (AISC) **1203**, 249–255 (2020). https://doi.org/10.1007/978-3-030-51038-1_35
10. Raiol, K.K.O.: ARQUITETURA, HISTÓRIA E TECNOLOGIA: O GRANDE HOTEL DE BELÉM EM REALIDADE VIRTUAL. Belém- PA, pp. 1–56 (2017)
11. Ben Ghida, D.: Augmented Reality and Virtual Reality: A 360° Immersion into Western History of Architecture. Int. J. Emerg. Trends Eng. Res. **8**(9), 6051–6055 (2020). https://doi.org/10.30534/ijeter/2020/187892020
12. Shanti, Z., Al-tarazi, D.: Virtual Reality Technology in Architectural Theory Learning : An Experiment on the Module of History of Architecture (2023)

Facilitating User Engagement: A Systematic, Survey-Based Approach

Marvin Heuer(✉)

University of Hamburg, Vogt-Kölln-Straße 30, 22527 Hamburg, Germany
marvin.heuer@uni-hamburg.de

Abstract. Organizations are increasingly adopting cloud-based, collaborative IS like Microsoft 365 to enhance collaboration and productivity, which was accelerated by the Covid-19 pandemic. Higher productivity through these systems also offers a solution to potential workforce shortages. However, introducing such IS often faces challenges, including user reluctance to change existing habits and software. For example, low willingness to change and poor communication exacerbate this problem, especially with suites like Microsoft 365, which help transitioning from software to cloud-based, collaborative solutions. The key challenge in integrating new applications is engaging users effectively, as poor engagement leads to unsatisfactory experiences and poor value. Understanding user needs and providing support are crucial for promoting adoption. For collaborative IS, such as conversational agents, their value depends on user interaction. Addressing these challenges requires a structured method focusing on user feedback and requirements during the lifecycle design phase. This study examines the introduction and increased adoption of Microsoft 365 in a multinational organization. Despite expectations for high usage, fostering user engagement remains a significant hurdle. Therefore, we developed a systematic, survey-based approach in a case organization, aiming to stimulate user interaction by repeated fostering of interactions, and, consequently, add value for users.

Keywords: User engagement · approach · collaborative IS

1 Introduction

Increasingly organizations start introducing cloud-based, user-dependent, collaborative information systems (IS), such as Microsoft 365 or conversational agents, in order to facilitate collaboration and increase productivity in their organizations [1]. Especially with the Covid-19 pandemic the introduction of such systems gets even more attention as now even small and medium-sized organizations try to leverage Microsoft 365's power to facilitate collaboration and increasing productivity as more employees want to work from home, which creates a high necessity for these tools [2]. Moreover, a higher productivity can help mitigate shortcomings in the workforce in the years to come [3]. Unfortunately, the introduction of these IS in organization is often unsatisfactory [4, 5]. For instance, user groups are reluctant in changing their existing habits and used

A. Marcus et al. (Eds.): HCII 2024, LNCS 14714, pp. 247–256, 2024.
https://doi.org/10.1007/978-3-031-61356-2_17

software into new ones that better interconnect and help collaborate. This goes hand in hand with the shift of new IS into a cloud model and new innovations posing for user groups a potential barrier to overcome [6]. Also, the temptation for user to simply continue using existing software is very great. The problem lies on several levels, as the willingness to change can be low, e.g., when the change is not well communicated [7, 8]. This becomes especially critical with larger suites such as Microsoft 365, as an example for these transitions from existing standalone software into cloud-based, collaborative combination solutions. For instance, the value of Microsoft Teams becomes particularly clear when it is combined with other Microsoft 365 applications and other users get engaged with it and start using it. Here we do not focus on the technical introduction and migration, but on the actual introduction and increase of the adoption rate of such IS using the example of Microsoft 365 in a multinational organization. As organizations continually introduce new applications that users interact with, organizations expect them to be highly used [9].

One of the key challenges in introducing new applications into high usage is effectively engaging users. In many cases, user engagement falls short and fails to provide satisfactory experiences for individuals who interact with these applications. Users rightfully anticipate meaningful interactions that add value to their work or personal tasks. For instance, employees within a multinational organization may encounter difficulties when adapting to collaborative information systems due to a lack of usability and intuitive design features. Without proper support and an understanding of user needs, it becomes challenging for organizations to foster user engagement and promote widespread adoption of new applications. A structured method can address these challenges by providing a systematic approach that considers users, their feedback, and requirements during the introductory design phase in the lifecycle of this IS class.

Therefore, the design of these applications as well as the appropriate support of the introduction gains special attention. This is particularly challenging with collaborative IS, such as conversational agents, as they only realize their value through the actual use of other users and are dependent on this [10]. In the context of these collaborative IS, the introduction of these is exemplarily accompanied in a multinational case organization and a systematic, survey-based approach is developed and tested to stimulate the users to interact and thus to create value for other users. Here we understand interaction as the regular use of the introduced tool by a user. Increased user engagement should be reflected not only in surveys but also in rising usage rates.

The paper is structured as follows. In the next section, related research and a theoretical background is provided. The third chapter contains the methodology for the conducted research. Subsequently, the results are presented, especially the systematic approach developed as a result of this research. Finally, the results are discussed with their theoretical and practical implications as well as the presentation of limitations and conclusions.

2 Background

To understand the introduction approach, we explain related research and background on the introduction of IS and Microsoft 365.

2.1 General Introduction of IS

The successful integration of IS into organizations leads to increased efficiency and effectiveness in business operations. Several factors need to be taken into account for a successful introduction.

First, the emergence of change management is critical in ensuring that the integration of information systems into businesses is successful. We define change management as "'the process of continually renewing an organization's direction, structure, and capabilities to serve the ever-changing needs of external and internal customers" [11]. In the IS context, change management involves preparing employees for the integration of the new systems into their daily operations. Change management helps to reduce resistance to change, increase buy-in, and ensure that the integration of IS is successful. Typical barriers at the introduction of IS are unfamiliarity, overwhelming demands, helplessness, and degradation [12]. These are overcome through information, qualification, organization, and compensation. Therefore, effective change management involves communication, education, and training of users. Communication involves informing employees of the changes, how it will affect them, and why the change is necessary. Education involves providing employees with knowledge of the new systems and their benefits. Training involves teaching employees how to use the new systems effectively.

In 2004, Markus introduced Technochange Management as an approach to using IT to effectively implement organizational change [13]. While major organizational change can be successful without the use of new IT, also, major organizational change becomes more effective with IT. IT project management and organizational change management alone are not effective in addressing the risks and challenges of these technochange situations, such as the potential misalignment with organizational characteristics [13–15]. Instead, an iterative and incremental approach that combines IT functionality with related organizational changes can produce better results [13], which is particularly relevant for the introduction of collaborative, user-dependent IS as they change work processes by using new technology and adapting to new ways of collaboration by IS.

2.2 Microsoft 365

There are many different cloud-based, collaborative, user-dependent IS. In the context of this work, we used the example of Microsoft 365. Microsoft 365 is a cloud-based service offered by Microsoft that provides users with access to a suite of applications and services, including productivity tools like Word, Excel, and PowerPoint, as well as communication tools like Outlook or Teams [16]. It also includes other services like OneDrive, SharePoint, To-Do, and Yammer, which enable users to collaborate, store, and share files online. Microsoft 365 can be accessed from anywhere with an internet connection and is available for a variety of devices, including PCs, Macs, and mobile devices. The product scope also includes the low-code development platforms Microsoft PowerApps and PowerAutomate.

One of the main benefits of Microsoft 365 is that it provides users with regular updates and new features, ensuring that they always have access to the latest tools and technology. In addition, Microsoft 365 is designed to be highly secure, with built-in protections against malware, phishing, and other cyber threats [16]. In addition, these

IS address other problems that organizations have with, for example, linking to cloud storage so that local network drives become obsolete. The value of this IS comes primarily from the actual use by the end users in the organization, who co-create the value through collaboration.

3 Methodology

Sein et al. (2011) [17] explains that ADR is a research method that aims to co-creatively address specific problems within an organization [17, 18]. It combines action research (AR [19]) with design science research (DSR [20]) to create practical IT artifacts [21]. Because of the organization-driven approach and the situation at which organizations typically find themselves in when introducing these collaborative, user-dependent IS, an ADR-driven procedure was appropriate. The example for these IS, we used, was Microsoft 365. As a first step, we defined what successful interaction and user engagement is.

In a next step, we identified key users from various areas in the organization that were linked to the introduction and who were attributed with a certain set of competence by other experts, also to select a good respondents base [22, 23]. We then conducted a survey [24] with those named key users on the status of the introduction and what challenges they identify in their respective departments. In addition, we conducted a literature search to get an overview of engagement methods from a neutral point of view [25]. Based on these collected insights, we started into an organization-driven BIE cycle [17]. The BIE cycle included the development of the approach rooted in the results of the initial research and the subsequent testing of the developed concept sequence of surveys, which built on each other and combined different approaches from the literature [26–28]. For the creation of those surveys, we used Microsoft Forms which is embedded in the rest of the Microsoft 365 suite [16]. Based on our collected data, gamification approaches in particular were to be combined with classic survey approaches in order to trigger engagement of possible users [29]. Therefore, we defined our goal to accomplish with the surveys. We created concise and unbiased questions and avoided ambiguous phrasing. Further, we combined several types of questions including multiple choice, different scales and also open questions [28, 30]. We based the flow and order of questions in these surveys to ensure a logical progression which helps maintaining respondents' engagement.

4 Results

As a starting point to develop such a proposed concept for improving the adoption and introduction of these IS, an organization should conduct a first survey regarding the status quo of key users within the organization. This step involves conducting an initial survey to understand the current situation, needs or behaviors of key users within the organization. After conducting such a first survey, further steps could be derived based on the tools that are used the most and/or need more support.

In order to build up confidence on these tools, reach a higher adoption rate und get more people involved, a next survey should be offered to form the organization. Key in the creation of such a survey is, to offer some material for people to learn about the tools (as in a one-pager) and a low barrier to participate in the quiz [26, 27]. This is meant on several levels, as the survey should be accessible on a computer as well as on a laptop. Further, the survey shouldn't be too long (max. 10 min) because people will get distracted otherwise [30, 31]. When using Microsoft 365 as an example, the idea is to distribute ten tools of the Microsoft 365 suite in ten days in ten different small surveys with ten different one-pagers on these tools. Furthermore, people need to be assured that the survey is anonymous, and the results cannot be analyzed by their superiors. As an example, for how such a survey could look like on the first day, the survey on Microsoft Teams is shown in Fig. 1.

In the final survey of key users, the statement about when to use which tool was increased from 62.98% to 69.41%, an increase of about 10%, in comparison to the initial survey conducted on the Status Quo within the organization. The percentage of detractors was reduced from 52.88% to 48.24%.

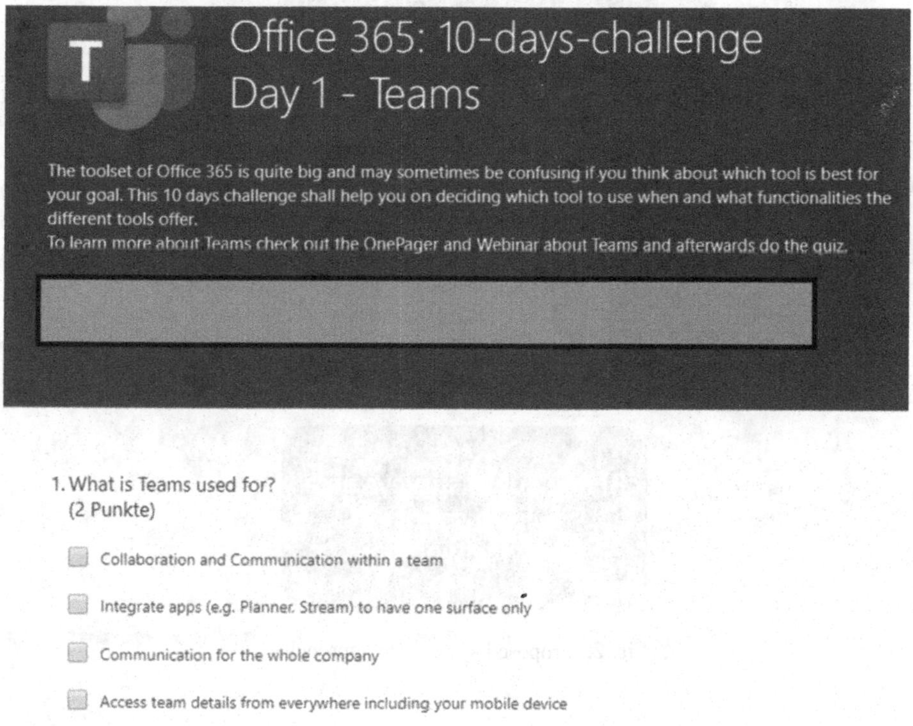

Fig. 1. Survey in the first cycle.

Based on this data, we propose the following concept as shown in Fig. 2. In general, this approach helps facilitating user engagement while introducing collaborative, user-dependent IS in organizations by organizing a systematic, subsequent channel of surveys on users. The results show that this can trigger participation and engagement and foster a value-driven use culture. In a first step, a survey needs to be conducted on the status quo of key users in the business units of an organization that shall be impacted by the introduction. Second, based on the conducted survey, the asked key users will offer as a result what tools are unclear from their perspective or which need the most reshaping. Therefore, such questions need to be included in the first step. For each new function/tool, a distinct survey must be developed for the next step. Further information on this part of survey creation is found on the page before. This lays the groundwork for disseminating the surveys within the organization. Key to a successful approach is the continued distribution of these surveys on following workdays to gain a higher attention and traction within the organization. Afterwards, as a fourth step the usage and response rates can be evaluated, which is an indicator for the success of the approach.

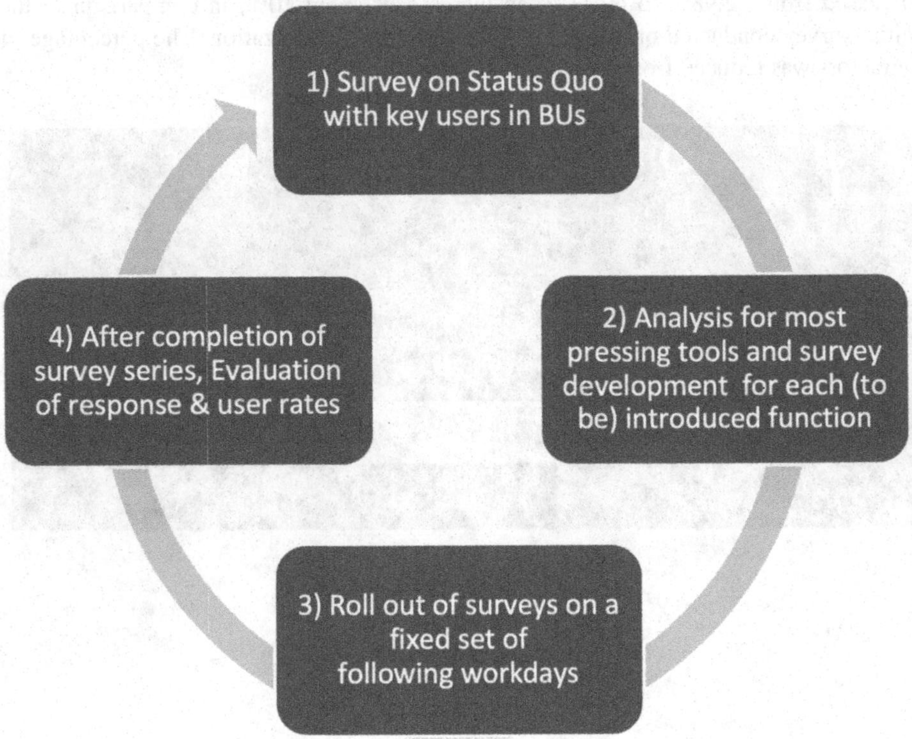

Fig. 2. Proposed systematic approach.

5 Discussion

The adoption of cloud-based, collaborative Information Systems (IS) like Microsoft 365 has been significantly accelerated by the Covid-19 pandemic, aiming to enhance collaboration and productivity across organizations [32]. This transition is particularly relevant as businesses seek solutions to potential workforce shortages by leveraging higher productivity through these systems. Despite the apparent benefits, the introduction of such IS often faces considerable challenges, primarily stemming from user reluctance to change existing habits and software. This discussion delves into the complexities surrounding the adoption of these IS (using Microsoft 365 as an example), focusing on the hurdles of user engagement and the strategies to overcome them.

Our work addresses the scarce field of research on the introduction on IS that are increasingly user-dependent and collaborative and require different approaches. In this work, we show how an introduction concept can be designed and guide its application within an organization and contribute to the emerging field of these knowledge-integrating technologies [33–36].

One key challenge in this field is the user involvement as the interaction of users with the IS is crucial for the IS to establish value within the organization. Therefore, understanding user needs and providing adequate support is essential for promoting adoption and facilitating a smooth transition. This implies that merely introducing new technology is insufficient without a focus on user engagement, satisfaction and expectations [37]. In a first step, users need to be taken care of and motivated for exploring IS if they can't or shall not be forced. User resistance and uncertainty to change is a well-documented barrier in technology adoption [38]. To manage these changes initiated by ISs has been a prominent field of research (e.g., Technochange [13]). Because of the new character of these IS, known approaches have to be evaluated and (sometimes) adapted to stay of value for the introduction of collaborative, user-dependent IS ('knowledge-integrating technologies'). The transition from previously used software to cloud-based, collaborative solutions like Microsoft 365 requires users to alter their workflows, which is often exacerbated by low willingness to change and poor communication within organizations. Addressing these challenges is crucial for the successful integration of new applications, as poor engagement can lead to unsatisfactory experiences and perceived poor value from the introduction.

The study employs a structured, survey-based approach to stimulate user interaction in a multinational organization. Despite expectations for high usage, fostering user engagement with this IS (e.g., Microsoft 365) remains a significant hurdle. This approach aims to understand user feedback and requirements during the IS design phase, acknowledging that successful engagement is critical for the technology to add value. The findings of this study underscore the importance of a systematic method focusing on user feedback and requirements and contributes thereby onto the field of preceding introduction frameworks [13, 37, 39, 40]. This involves not only addressing technical challenges but also ensuring that the organizational culture supports change management processes, which leans in on the Technochange framework [13]. Effective communication strategies and training programs are essential components of this approach, aiming to mitigate resistance by enhancing users' familiarity and comfort with the new system.

In conclusion, the transition to cloud-based, user-dependent, collaborative IS presents both opportunities and challenges for organizations. While the potential for enhanced collaboration and productivity is significant, the success of such systems critically depends on effectively engaging users. Addressing user resistance through structured methods focusing on feedback and requirements is key to overcoming these challenges.

6 Limitations and Conclusion

Increasingly, especially collaborative IS are becoming more user-dependent and intelligent, enabling the facilitation of collaboration, and increasing productivity in organizations. However, successful introduction depends on the use of these IS, which can be facilitated through an appropriately approach on strengthening user engagement and interaction.

The successful introduction and utilization of IS is a complex task that requires careful consideration and planning. One key factor that determines the success of introducing IS is the effective use of these systems by users. This can be achieved through the implementation of an appropriate approach aimed at strengthening user engagement and interaction. For example, in a multinational case organization, fostering collaboration among employees through collaborative IS tools such as virtual workspaces or project management platforms can enhance communication and knowledge sharing between team members located in different geographical locations. Additionally, providing user training programs and comprehensive support services for IS adoption ensures that employees understand how to effectively utilize these systems in their daily tasks. By employing such strategies, organizations can overcome the inherent challenges associated with introducing these IS and successfully integrate them into their operations.

In this work we presented, in an ADR-driven approach, a new method to accompany the introduction of collaborative, user-dependent IS and evaluated this approach. This serves as a starting point for further research in this area. In particular, our approach shows how an organization with a low-resource involvement can lower the barriers to usage for various user groups, thereby increasing adoption and fostering user engagement. Nonetheless has this work some limitations. First, this approach has been conducted in a low-resource effort, so that more resources regarding the problem solution could have let to more thorough outcomes. Nonetheless, the results can be deemed useful, as they were performed within a setting with many actors and users. Second, the concept was developed based on a survey in an organization which by its nature can only show a certain extract of the world. Nonetheless, results show a general value as it has been done in a multinational case organization that is very internationalized which helps establish external validity.

In general, the developed approach could be viewed as useful for further introductions and be part of a starting point for future research conducted on the domain of collaborative, user-dependent IS.

References

1. Veerapandian, S., et al.: Reimagine Remote Working with Microsoft Teams: A Practical Guide to Increasing your Productivity and Enhancing Collaboration in the Remote World. Rogers, S., (ed.), Birmingham, UK: Packt Publishing Ltd. (2021)
2. Lindner, D.: Virtuelle Teams und Homeoffice. Empfehlungen zu Technologien, Arbeitsmethoden und Führung. Wiesbaden: Springer (2020). https://doi.org/10.1007/978-3-658-30893-3
3. Prskawetz, A., Fent, T., Guest, R.: Workforce aging and labor productivity: the role of supply and demand for labor in the G7 countries. Popul. Dev. Rev. **34**, 298–323 (2008)

4. Janssen, A., Grützner, L., Breitner, M.H.: Why do Chatbots fail? A critical success factors analysis. In: International Conference on Information Systems (ICIS). Austin, TX, USA (2021)
5. Schuetzler, R.M., et al.: Deciding whether and how to deploy Chatbots. MIS Q. Executive (MISQE) **20**(1), 4 (2021)
6. König, M., Neumayr, L.: Users' resistance towards radical innovations: the case of the self-driving car. Transport. Res. F: Traffic Psychol. Behav. **44**(1), 42–52 (2017)
7. Kotter, J.P.: Leading change: wie Sie Ihr Unternehmen in acht Schritten erfolgreich verändern. Munich, Germany: Vahlen (2013)
8. Weiner, B.J., Amick, H., Lee, S.-Y.D.: Conceptualization and measurement of organizational readiness for change: a review of the literature in health services research and other fields. Med. Care Res. Rev. **65**(4), 379–436 (2008)
9. Bhattacherjee, A., Premkumar, G.: Understanding changes in belief and attitude toward information technology usage: a theoretical model and longitudinal test. MIS Q. **28**(2), 229–254 (2004)
10. Zierau, N., et al.: The anatomy of user experience with conversational agents: a taxonomy and propositions of service clues. In: International Conference on Information Systems (ICIS). A Virtual Conference (2020)
11. Moran, J.W., Brightman, B.K.: Leading organizational change. Career Dev. Int. **6**(2), 111–119 (2001)
12. Reiß, M.: Wandel im Management des Wandels. in Neue Märkte, neue Medien, neue Methoden—Roadmap zur agilen Organisation: 19. Saarbrücker Arbeitstagung für Industrie, Dienstleistung und Verwaltung 5.–7. Oktober 1998 Saarland University, Saarbrücken, Germany. Springer (1998). https://doi.org/10.1007/978-3-642-58996-6
13. Markus, M.L.: Technochange management: using IT to drive organizational change. J. Inf. Technol. **19**(1), 4–20 (2004)
14. Harison, E., Boonstra, A.: Essential competencies for technochange management: towards an assessment model. Int. J. Inf. Manage. **29**(4), 283–294 (2009)
15. Teubner, R.A.: An exploration into it programs and their management: findings from multiple case study research. Inf. Syst. Manag. **36**(1), 40–56 (2019)
16. Microsoft. Microsoft 365 - Office-Anwendungen, Cloud-Dienste, Sicherheit. [cited 2024 Feb. 26, 2024] (2024). https://www.microsoft.com/de-DE/Microsoft-365
17. Sein, M.K., et al.: Action design research. MIS Q. **35**(1), 37–56 (2011)
18. Cronholm, S., Göbel, H.: Design science research constructs: a conceptual model. In: Pacific-Asian Conference on Information Systems (PACIS). X'ian, China, p. 6 (2019)
19. Susman, G.I., Evered, R.D.: An assessment of the scientific merits of action research. Adm. Sci. Q. **23**(4), 582–603 (1978)
20. Hevner, A.R., et al.: Design science in information systems research. MIS Q. **28**(1), 75–105 (2004)
21. Venable, J., Pries-Heje, J., Baskerville, R.: FEDS: a framework for evaluation in design science research. Eur. J. Inf. Syst. **25**(1), 77–89 (2017)
22. Oppenheim, A.N.: Questionnaire Design, Interviewing and Attitude Measurement. Bloomsbury Publishing, London (2000)
23. Fife-Schaw, C.: Questionnaire design. In: Breakwell, G.M., et al. (eds.) Research Methods in Psychology, pp. 210–231. Sage, Thousand Oaks, CA, USA (2006)
24. Harkness, J., Pennell, B.E., Schoua-Glusberg, A.: Survey questionnaire translation and assessment. Methods Test. Evaluating Surv. Questionnaires 453–473 (2004)
25. Cooper, H.M.: Organizing knowledge syntheses: a taxonomy of literature reviews. Knowl. Soc. **1**(1), 104–126 (1988)
26. Blair, E., et al.: How to ask questions about drinking and sex: response effects in measuring consumer behavior. J. Mark. Res. **14**(3), 316–321 (1977)

27. Andrews, F.M.: Construct validity and error components of survey measures: a structural modeling approach. Public Opin. Q. **48**(2), 409–442 (1984)
28. Lietz, P.: Research into questionnaire design: a summary of the literature. Int. J. Mark. Res. **52**(2), 249–272 (2010)
29. Harms, J., et al.: Gamification of online surveys: Design process, case study, and evaluation. In: Human-Computer Interaction – INTERACT 2015, pp. 219–236. Springer, Bamberg, Germany (2015)
30. Holbrook, A., Cho, Y.I., Johnson, T.: The impact of question and respondent characteristics on comprehension and mapping difficulties. Int. J. Public Opin. Q. **70**(4), 565–595 (2006)
31. White, P.C., et al.: Questionnaires in ecology: a review of past use and recommendations for best practice. J. Appl. Ecol. **42**(3), 421–430 (2005)
32. Wang, W.-T., Wu, S.-Y.: Knowledge management based on information technology in response to COVID-19 crisis. Knowl. Manag. Res. Pract. **19**(4), 468–474 (2021)
33. Heuer, M., Kurtz, C., Böhmann, T.: Towards a governance of low-code development platforms using the example of Microsoft PowerPlatform in a multinational company. In: Hawaii International Conference on System Sciences (HICSS). Hawaii, HI, USA (2022)
34. Heuer, M., et al.: Towards effective conversational agents: a prototype-based approach for facilitating their evaluation and improvement. In: International Conference on Human-Computer Interaction (HCII). Copenhagen, DK: Springer (2023). https://doi.org/10.1007/978-3-031-35708-4_23
35. Heuer, M., et al.: Rethinking interaction with conversational agents: how to create a positive user experience utilizing dialog patterns. In: International Conference on Human-Computer Interaction (HCII). Copenhagen, DK: Springer (2023). https://doi.org/10.1007/978-3-031-35708-4_22
36. Lewandowski, T., et al.: Design knowledge for the lifecycle management of conversational agents. In: International Conference on Wirtschaftsinformatik (WI). A Virtual Conference (2022)
37. Beaudry, A., Pinsonneault, A.: Understanding user responses to information technology: a coping model of user adaptation. MIS Q. **29**(3), 493–524 (2005)
38. Weiler, S., Matt, C., Hess, T.: Understanding user uncertainty during the implementation of self-service business intelligence: a thematic analysis. In: Hawaii International Conference on System Sciences (HICSS). Hawaii, HI, USA (2019)
39. Bider, I., et al.: Design science in action: developing a framework for introducing IT systems into operational practice. In: International Conference on Information Systems (ICIS). Orlando, FL, USA (2012)
40. Andersson, T., Bider, I., Svensson, R.: Aligning people to business processes experience report. Softw. Process: Improv. Pract. **10**(4), 403–413 (2005)

A Study on the Impact of Customer Interactions in Virtual Brand Community on Brand Equity

Bo Liu[1,2](✉), Ethel D. Catamco[2], and Boheng Liu[3]

[1] Guangzhou City University of Technology, No.1 Xuefu Road, Huadu District, Guangzhou, Guangdong, China
liubo@gcu.edu.cn

[2] University of San Carlos, P. del Rosario Street, Cebu, Philippines

[3] Guangzhou City University of Technology, No.1 Xuefu Road, Huadu District, Guangzhou, Guangdong, China

Abstract. The study examines the role of virtual brand communities in brand building and management, particularly for enhancing corporate brand equity. It surveyed 400 Chinese customers in Huawei's official virtual brand community, with the majority being male (51.2%) and aged 59–77 years (21.8%). The majority had a bachelor's degree (35.8%) and had been in the community for 1.2 years (33.3%). The results show that, there is a positive relationship between virtual informational interaction and brand equity. There is a positive relationship between virtual interpersonal interaction and brand equity. Virtual information interaction is not positively and significantly influenced customer perceived value (0.070, $p = 0.334 > 0.05$). The Virtual interpersonal information is positively and significantly influenced customer perceived value. Consumer perceived value mediates the relationship between Virtual interpersonal information and brand equity. But consumer perceived value do not mediates the relationship between Virtual information interaction and brand equity. There is significant differences on the level of virtual information interaction between female and male. There is significant differences on the level of virtual information interaction ($p < 0.000$) and virtual interpersonal interaction (($p < 0.016$) between and within age groups. The study suggests that virtual informational interaction and virtual interpersonal interactions and customer perceived value can be enhanced to enhance the enterprise's brand equity in the virtual brand community.

Keywords: Virtual Community · Customer Interaction · Brand equity · Structural Equation Modelling

1 Introduction

Virtual communities are online social systems consisting of shared interests and experiences that have a very strong social and economic value. This is especially significant for virtual brand communities, as they create a new way of interaction between consumers and brands. Consumers can communicate directly with brands through communities, share their views and opinions, and even help brands design new products and services [1].

A. Marcus et al. (Eds.): HCII 2024, LNCS 14714, pp. 257–277, 2024.
https://doi.org/10.1007/978-3-031-61356-2_18

Virtual brand communities have become an important part of modern marketing and have a significant impact on both companies and consumers. At the same time, virtual brand communities can also provide real-time feedback for companies to help them adjust their products and services in time to improve consumer satisfaction [2]. In terms of consumers, consumers have more access to information and higher quality of information through virtual brand communities, which can provide a more comprehensive understanding of the advantages and disadvantages of products and services [3]. McAlexander, Schouten, and Koenig (2020) define virtual brand communities as self-organized networks of consumers who communicate and share brand information through online channels. These communities not only serve as communication tools but also provide consumer identity, community, and cultural meaning, enhancing brand equity [4]. The main debates among scholars about the impact of customer interactions on brand equity in virtual brand communities is about how to measure the impact of customer interactions on brand equity in virtual brand communities. Some scholars use classical brand equity measures such as brand awareness, brand loyalty, and brand image to measure the impact of customer interactions on brand equity in virtual brand communities [5–7].

However, it has also been suggested that these traditional measures can hardly fully reflect the impact of customer interactions in virtual brand communities and more specific metrics need to be developed to measure them [8]. Given that increasing numbers of customers raise their voices online and Online Customer Engagement remains an under-researched field in the academic literature to date [9], the purpose of this study is to address this gap in the customer engagement literature.

By December 2018, the number of HUAWEI community users (https://club.huawei.com/forum-152-1.html) has exceeded 100 million. Many users express their voices in HUAWEI BVC (brand virtual community), such as feedback about voice assistant and a new design for full screen [10]. In china, many enterprises, such as ZTE, Lenovo, Haier, Huawei, Xiaomi [11–13] and so on, have established brand virtual communities which have the advantage of gathering public wisdom and brainstorming. Although the number of brand virtual communities is still increasing, relevant data shows that about half of brand virtual communities do not work effectively [14].

Although a few companies have made extensive investments in their brand community, and even taken control of interactions within the community, unwanted consequences can also happen [15]. For example, nearly 68% of members leave a virtual brand community after joining it for the first time [16], which makes it very hard to promote brand sustainable development through operating an online brand community [17].

This study focuses on customer interaction in Huawei's virtual brand community due to its significant user base and successful brand communication effects. The current virtual brand community faces challenges in brand sustainability management, but Huawei's interactive community has a large number of users, making it a more representative and valuable research site for other companies. The study highlights the importance of deep customer interaction in managing brand sustainability in virtual brand communities.

2 Literature Review

2.1 Review of the Literature

It is critical to identify the factors influencing brand equity in virtual brand communities to assess how customer interactions affect brand equity and to thoroughly examine the extant literature on the various prerequisites and brand equity. In this chapter, the authors synthesize the relevant literature to improve the theoretical understanding of brand equity and its predecessors in virtual brand communities and to identify gaps in existing research.

Review of Virtual Brand Communities. Virtual brand communities are the result of combining traditional brand communities with electronic networks, where people with common ideas establish stable interpersonal relationships through long-term communication and interaction on the Internet, gradually forming virtual communities, which are formed when members focus on a specific brand [18]. He Aizhong (2019) suggests that virtual brand communities are a valuable platform for customer participation in value co-creation, allowing enterprises to understand market demand, optimize products and services, and enhance brand performance. He suggests that enterprises should focus on establishing long-term relationships with customers to encourage participation in value co-creation [19]. Virtual brand communities offer companies a new communication method for relationship marketing, enabling them to communicate effectively with consumers, obtain continuous market feedback, and build long-term relationships with loyal users, thus improving their marketing model in the Internet era [20]. Muiz et al. (2001) categorized virtual brand communities into company-initiated and consumer-initiated. Company-initiated communities offer detailed product information, but are controlled by companies, preventing negative consumer opinions. Consumer-initiated communities contain valuable information without clear purpose, but their ability to provide detailed product information is limited [21]. Zhang Xinsheng et al. (2017) argue that the Internet economy has given birth to virtual brand communities, and that companies need to build trust between virtual brand communities and community members based on consumer satisfaction in order to motivate consumers to participate in value co-creation [22].

Review of Brand Equity Research. In the 1990s, brand management guru Aaker (1992) defined brand equity as the related assets or liabilities associated with elements such as brand, name, and trademark by constructing a systematic theoretical model [23]. Keller (1993) argued that brand knowledge prevents customers from making negative evaluations and behaviors toward branded products, so the focus of creating brand equity is to increase consumers' brand knowledge [24]. Yoo and Donthu's study explores the relationship between marketing mix elements and brand equity, arguing that dimensions are not equal across cultures. They propose a conceptual framework, revealing that frequent price promotions lead to low brand equity, while high advertising spending, high price, good store image, and high distribution intensity increase it [25].

Regarding the division of brand equity dimensions, Aaker (1991) focused on measuring brand equity from the consumer's perspective, arguing that the meaning of a brand to consumers is the basis of its value [26]. Yoo and Donthu simplified their dimensions based on Aaker's research model and argued that the dimensions are not equal across cultures. Wei Haiying (2009) explored the impact of business-customer and employee-customer interactions on service brand equity. She suggested that business managers should focus on emotional management, improve communication frequency and intensity, address customer needs and feedback, encourage customer participation in brand management, and achieve positive interactions [27].

Users of virtual brand communities are more likely to seek information and purchase products via the Internet, which makes brand loyalty an important component of brand equity. They argue that brand loyalty can promote consumers' purchasing behavior in virtual brand communities and increase brand sales and market share [28]. Bruhn et al. (2014) confirmed that the quality of interactions among customers in virtual brand communities significantly affects brand loyalty, and that consumers with high levels of interaction not only increase their likelihood of purchasing their preferred brand products, but also decrease their likelihood of purchasing products from competing brands [29].

Review of Customer Interactions Research. Bruhn et al. (2014) suggest that the process of collaborative exchange among customers using the same brand products in a virtual brand community using virtual space resources is the process of customer interaction. The process of collaborative exchange between customers using the same brand products in a virtual brand community is inter-customer interaction [29]. Yang R. et al. (2020) argue that the unique experience generated between customers through interaction is the basis for customer value co-creation, and that companies need to accurately identify and understand customer-to-customer interactions and encourage positive consumer interaction behavior through various ways in order to establish good customer relationships [30]. Customer engagement reflects customer interactions with brands, offerings, or firms [31].

There are no clear criteria for classifying the dimensions of customer interactions in virtual brand communities. A study by Nambisan (2009) classified them as member cognitive interactions, product content interactions, and interpersonal interactions [32]. Wu S. et al. (2011) divided customer-to-customer interactions into two categories, one type of information exchange is the information interaction of customers on knowledge acquisition, and the other type of social interaction is mainly the emotional communication between people [33].

Research on the mechanism of interaction between customers of virtual brand communities is divided into two main categories, one is the effect of interaction between customers of virtual brand communities on companies, and the other is the effect of interaction between customers of virtual brand communities on customers. Wang Yong-gui et al. studied the inter-customer interaction behavior of virtual brand communities based on social identity theory and found that product interaction and human-computer interaction had a significant positive effect on community satisfaction, while interpersonal interaction did not have a significant effect on community satisfaction, and finally proposed to use a combination of three kinds of interactions to manage communities and promote inter-customer interaction through various ways [34]. Wang et al. examined the role of customer interaction in virtual brand communities on customers' repetitive purchase behavior from the perspective of value co-creation, and concluded that the interactive behaviors of consumers within the community actively learning about product information and communicating with each other help companies to provide more comprehensive and accurate marketing services, which promote customers' repetitive purchase of brand products [35].

This study draws on the research results of Wang Yonggui (2013) to classify inter-customer interactions into information interactions and interpersonal interactions. Information interactions refer to interactions among customers with information about the use of brand products, technical issues, market development, etc. as the main topics; interpersonal interactions refer to interactions among community members for the purpose of self-actualization and gaining care [34].

Review of Customer Perceived Value Research. Zeithaml (1988) introduced the concept of customer perceived value, which is the loss consumers are willing to bear to obtain a certain benefit. This subjective evaluation of a product or service's utility and satisfaction is multidimensional and includes aspects like economic, emotional, social, and technical value. Customers evaluate the worth of a product or service through its perceived value, which influences their attitudes and behaviors in brand interactions [36]. Sheth et al. (1991) emphasized that companies' products and services can provide significant customer value, which can influence consumers' choices in various ways. Functional value refers to the perceived efficacy of a product or service, while emotional value stems from consumers' emotions and feelings. Social value is related to socioeconomic and cultural ethics, while cognitive value is the novel knowledge gained through the product or service. Conditional value measures the contingency of behavioral choices, with decision conditions playing a crucial role in influencing consumer behavior [37]. Shen Guanglong et al. (2016) used virtual brand communities as a research context to confirm the mediating effect of customer perceived value between interactions among customers and customer participation in value co-creation, and proposed that companies should pay attention to the experience value of interactive members and use various incentive methods to promote customer participation in community interactions [38]. Zhang Min et al. (2021) studied the moderating role of perceived value in e-commerce website opinion leaders' influence on user stickiness from three dimensions: functional value, emotional value and information value, and suggested that e-commerce website opinion leaders should focus on connotation and value in the process of communication, grasp customers' pain points, make customers perceive the sincerity of opinion leaders, and enhance the existence of followers [39].

This paper suggests that consumers can perceive both physical and emotional levels of value in virtual brand communities. Functional perceived value refers to the satisfaction of customers' functional needs, such as product information or decision-making efficiency, while emotional perceived value focuses on customers' social needs, such as trust, personal fulfillment, and self-fulfillment needs.

2.2 Hypotheses Developments

Customer Interactions → Brand Equity. The customer engagement theory model suggests that customer engagement in virtual brand communities (including the level of customer involvement and engagement activeness) has an impact on brand equity.

This model argues that the higher the level of customer engagement in a virtual brand community, the more knowledge, emotion, and loyalty they have towards the brand will increase, thus enhancing brand equity [9].

Zhang et al. (2015) developed a framework to study online brand communities and their impact on brand equity, using psychological sense of community to analyze information exchange among community members. The study explores consumer brand relationships, motivations for participation, value-creation, commitment, brand perception, loyalty, and relationship satisfaction [40]. Yu Zhaoji et al. conducted a study using the Xiaomi cell phone community to investigate the impact of firm-customer interaction on brand equity in virtual brand communities. The results showed a significant correlation between company-customer interaction, brand experience, and brand equity. The study suggests that two-way communication between enterprises and customers, customer feedback, and segmentation can improve brand image and increase purchase conversion rates. The study also found that brand experience is positively correlated with perceived quality, brand association, and brand loyalty [41]. Customer experience refers to the interaction with customers that ensures the derivation of utilitarian and hedonic value [42]. Li Chaohui et al.'s 2014 study revealed that customer engagement in value co-creation can enhance a company's brand equity. The research, using structural equation modeling, found that both initiated and spontaneous value co-creation positively impacted brand equity, emphasizing the significance of brand experience [43]. Wang Yonggui et al. (2013) explored customer interactions in virtual brand communities using utility-hedonic theory. They found that community identity moderates the relationship between interpersonal and product interactions and satisfaction, while human-machine interactions have no significant impact. The study suggests product and interpersonal interactions are the main drivers of satisfaction [34]. Wang Chao Hung et al.'s model reveals that customer interactions directly impact brand equity, while four service encounter factors indirectly influence it. Relationship quality has the largest impact, followed by service staff. Customer similarity and service capes have insignificant direct effects. A positive customer experience and trustworthy connection are crucial for brand equity [44].

Therefore, the following hypotheses are proposed:

H^1: There is a positive significant relationship between virtual informational interaction and brand equity.
H^2: There is a positive significant relationship between virtual interpersonal interaction and brand equity.

Customer Interactions → Customer Perceived Value → Brand Equity. Sweeney and Soutar's study on the Australian telecommunications market found that customer perceived value influences brand equity perception, satisfaction, trust, brand choice, and loyalty. Using multiple value dimensions explained consumer outcomes better than a single value-for-money item, with emotional value predicting willingness to buy [45]. Zhang Lei (2010) defines interaction quality and service brand equity, constructing a model based on multidimensional interaction quality. The model includes resources, value co-creation, brand promise, and message communication, with high Cronbachsa reliability and construct reliability [46]. Vargo and Lusch (2004) introduced Service-Dominant Logic (SDL) to emphasize customer involvement and value creation. They argue that customers are now seen as partners in value creation, with perceived value mediating interactions between customers and companies, influencing brand equity formation [47]. Zeithaml (1988) introduced customer perceived value, a multidimensional concept encompassing economic, emotional, social, and technical aspects. It influences customers' attitudes and behaviors in brand interactions, assessing the product's worth.36.Fan Xiaoping et al. (2009) divided online interactive content into two categories, one is instrumental interaction to obtain product or brand information, and the other is interpersonal interaction for emotional communication, and found that both instrumental utility and psychological utility play a mediating role in the influence of online interactive content on online purchase intention [48].

Based on this, the following hypothesis is proposed:

H^3: Consumer perceived value mediates the relationship between virtual informational interaction and brand equity.
H^4: Consumer perceived value mediates the relationship between virtual interpersonal interaction and brand equity.

2.3 Theoretical Framework

S-O-R Theory. The evolution of stimulus-organism-response (SOR) theory in psychology started with Thorndike's work, that is, stimulus-response (SR) theory. The SOR theory describes how individuals develop behavioral responses to stimuli from the external environment.

Compared with SR theory, SOR theory emphasizes the effect of an external environmental stimulus on individual psychology. Stimulus represents external information, which produces a specific influence on an individual; Organism reflects cognitive and emotion, reflecting the psychological process caused by external information stimulation; Response is the behavior taken by the individual after a series of perception and psychological activities [49].

The S-O-R model suggests that individuals perceive external stimuli and develop a psychological state (internal emotions and cognition) that leads to a subjective attitude or behavioral response. This theory can explain the stimuli and outcomes of consumer behavior in virtual brand communities, where consumers browse information and communicate with each other to trigger stimuli that lead to changes in cognition, attitudes, and emotions, and continue to trigger consumer responses to brand loyalty, brand awareness, and other brand assets (Mehrablan & Russell., 1974). Jing Fengjie et al. (2013) [50] and Tang Fangcheng et al. (2018) [51] used S-O-R theory to construct models of customer interactions, emotions, and post-purchase satisfaction. They found that virtual brand communities provide access to information and emotional resources, generating pleasant emotions that drive consumption evaluations and behavioral responses.

Brand Equity (by Aaker 1991). In the 1990s, brand management guru Aaker defined brand equity as the related assets or liabilities associated with elements such as brand, name, and trademark by constructing a systematic theoretical model [26, 39].

Brand equity is a set of brand assets and liabilities linked to a brand its name and symbol that add to or subtract from the value provided by a product or service to a firm and/or to that firm's customers. For assets or liabilities to underlie brand equity they must be linked to the name and/or symbol of the brand. If the brand's name or symbol should change, some or all of the assets or liabilities could be affected and even lost, although some might be shifted to a new name and symbol. The assets and liabilities on which brand equity is based will differ from context to context. However they can be usefully grouped into five categories: 1. Brand loyalty. 2. Perceived quality. 3. Brand associations in addition to perceived quality. 4. Name awareness. 5. Other proprietary brand assets-patents trademarks, channel relationships, etc.

Social Identity Theory. SIT, a concept introduced by Farfel & Turner (1986), focuses on the distinction between personal and social identity, arguing that social identity is primarily derived from group memberships. It suggests that people strive to achieve or maintain a positive social identity, which boosts self-esteem, through favorable comparisons between in and relevant out groups. If unsatisfactory, people may seek to leave their group or achieve more distinctiveness. Three variables influence intergroup differentiation: subjective identification, evaluative comparisons, and comparability, which increases pressures for distinctiveness.

In the virtual brand community environment, social identity and community identity have the same connotation, and community members' identification with the brand community affects their behaviors and attitudes toward the brand [52]. Based on social identity theory, Hu Bing et al. (2015) argue that customers construct and express a certain social identity motive to others through customized products, so that the relevant groups can identify the unique taste of customers and reflect their relevant preferences, thus gaining group recognition [53].

Social Capital Theory. The resources that are created between people through relationships or social networks are known as social capital. This kind of resource can give people the chance to pursue their passions. "The sum of the actual and potential resources embedded within, available through, and derived from the network of relationships possessed by an individual or social unit" was the definition of social capital [54].Social capital, according to Nahapiet and Ghoshal, has three components: structural capital, relational capital, and cognitive capital. The configuration and pattern of connections among network actors—specifically, the people and frequency with whom they exchange information—are referred to as structural capital [55].The social capital theory model suggests that customer interactions in virtual brand communities can increase social capital among customers, including social relationships, social networks, and social support, which can have an impact on brand equity. This model argues that customer interactions in virtual brand communities can promote mutual understanding, trust and cooperation among customers, which leads to positive brand associations and brand loyalty and enhances brand equity [56].

2.4 Conceptual Framework

Based on brand equity model proposed by Aaker and S-O-R theory and social identity theory and social capital theory are added to the study of brand equity construction in virtual brand communities, and a comprehensive research framework has been established.

This study aims to answer the following question: How do customer interactions in virtual brand communities affect brand equity through perceived value? Are there significant differences in the level of virtual information interactions and virtual interpersonal interactions when grouped by age and sex? Do age and sex play a moderating role between virtual information interactions and CPV and between virtual interpersonal interactions and CPV. Based on the new/revised statement of the problem and hypothesis, the conceptual framework of this study includes 6 variables, where the independent variables are virtual informational interaction and virtual interpersonal interaction, the dependent variable is brand equity, and the mediating variable is customer perceived value, and the modulating variables are generational age and sex (Fig. 1).

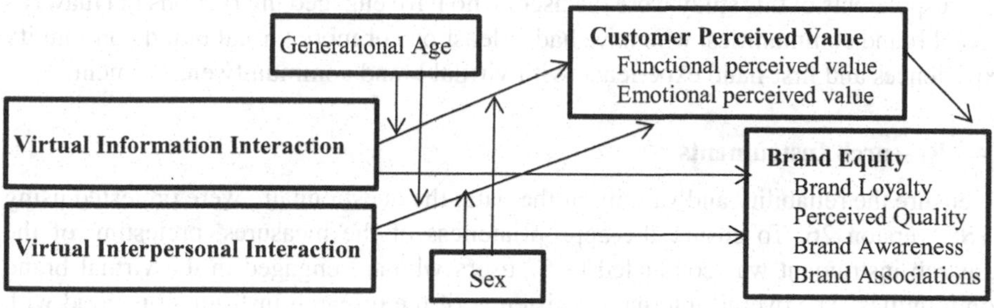

Fig. 1. Conceptual framework of the study

3 Methods

3.1 Research Design

This study was conceptualization in nature. It was descriptive correlational in design and the purpose of this study was to explore how customer interaction affects brand equity in virtual brand communities and to analyze how customer perceived value plays a mediating role between them based on literature review. This dissertation gave a great deal of consideration to the data collection, analysis, and testing of key relationships between constructs of interest. Within quantitative research, researchers utilize major research methodology: survey research [57]. In this dissertation, a survey research methodology was adopted as this approach supports and provides standardized information to define the variables and assess the relationships between variables [58].

This paper used Huawei Community as the research platform for questionnaire survey and data collection, which was a fan exchange community on Huawei's official website, where most of the customers who love Huawei brand were concentrated, which can further ensure that all the interviewees who fill out this research survey were mostly users of Huawei-related products. The research subjects were users in Huawei's virtual brand community, and these users mainly interacted with each other through the Internet. Therefore, this paper created questionnaires through Questionnaire Star, sent questionnaires and collected data by means of online research. The questionnaire was modified and improved according to the characteristics of the virtual brand community, while referring to mature scales at home and abroad, to form the questionnaire in this paper.

3.2 Research Environment

The questionnaire for this study was distributed online. The questionnaire star link was posted on Huawei Community (https://forum.huawei.com/enterprise/zh/index) This community group is managed by the Huawei management.

3.3 Research Respondents

The respondents of this study were the users who have engaged interactions in Huawei's virtual brand communities, who have had at least one or more virtual brand community experiences and first-hand experience with virtual brand community engagement.

3.4 Research Instruments

To ensure the reliability and validity of the data, the questionnaire were pretested using SPSS version 26. To ensure the appropriateness of the measures, pretesting of the research instrument was conducted to 67 users who are engaged in the virtual brand communities. The overall internal consistency of the research instrument is good with Cronbach's alpha of 0.825 and composed of 33 items. This indicates that the construct of the instrument is reliable (Table 1).

Table 1. Pretest Result

Reliability Statistics		
Cronbach's Alpha	N of Items	Interpretation
.825	33	Good

This study developed a structured questionnaire with measurement items using studies from the literature domain as a data collection tool. The questionnaire was divided into two parts, the first part was to describe the gender, age, education, participation time and frequency of visits of virtual brand community users. The second part was to measure the independent variables virtual informational interaction and virtual interpersonal interaction, the mediating variable customer perceived value, and the dependent variable brand equity in this study.

3.5 Research Procedures

The data collected through a structured questionnaire of 33 questions. A total of 522 respondents answered the survey questionnaire. The researcher decided to use 400 random samples using the random function in excel. To ensure that all responses be completed without missing data, respondents are requested to answer all the items in the questionnaire. A total of 400 valid responses were included in the final analysis.

Structural equation modeling (SEM) was a statistical data analysis tool that combines multiple regression analysis, path analysis, and confirmatory factor analysis to test the relationship between observed and latent variables, and latent and latent variables using the collected data based on theoretical assumptions.

In this study, Smart PLS 4.0 software was used to test the model and hypotheses. PLS is a robust statistical method for structural model estimation in greatly multifaceted circumstances [59].

4 Results

4.1 Profile of the Respondents

The respondents of the study were the users who have engaged in Huawei's virtual brand communities. A total of 400 respondents participated in the study.

The study found that 84.3% of men buy online, compared to 77.3% of women. Men tend to search more for products on the internet, with 70% compared to women. Social networks are a useful tool for online commerce, with 62% of men and 50% of women comparing products before making purchases. Men use social media for information, while women use it for connecting with others [60]. The survey data shows that 21.8% of respondents are over 59 years old. This demographic is part of a larger wave of retiring baby boomers in China, who are becoming tech-savvy and ready to spend. With a retirement age of 60 for men and 55 for women, China's silver generation has the money and time to spend [61]. In terms of educational background, the respondents are the respondents are Bachelor's degree (35.8%) and Junior College (34%). To participate in social interactions, you need to have the skills and knowledge to communicate and read information with other customers on social platforms, especially Baby Boomers and Silent Generation, higher education is required to have a better interactive experience with online communities. Among the respondents, the majority of the respondents the survey on the duration of participation in this branded community are participated in the community for one to two years (33.3%). And regarding the respondent's frequency of visits to the community, the majority of the respondents would visit the community 2–3 times a week (26.3%).This means that the majority of respondents have been in the brand community in Huawei for a long time and interact more with other users in Huawei. Users love the virtual brand community and have created loyalty and usage habits (Table 2).

4.2 Estimation of Higher Order Constructs

This research has two higher-order constructs: brand equity with four lower order constructs (brand loyalty, brand awareness, brand association and perceived quality) and the customer perceived value (functional and emotional perceived value).

4.3 First Stage Assessment of Measurement Model (Outer Model)

Reliability and Validity Analysis. The factor loads are all greater than 0.5, which indicates that the factor loads meet the requirements of construct validity. Cronbach's

Table 2. The profile of the respondents

Profile	Characteristics	Frequency	Percent
Gender	Male	205	51.2
	Female	195	48.8
Age	Born 2004–2012 (18–26 years old)	79	19.8
	Born 1981–1996 (27–42 years old)	80	20
	Born 1965–1980 (43–58 years old)	70	17.5
	Born 1946–1964 (59–77 years old)	87	21.8
	Born 1945 and below	84	21
Education background	High school, technical secondary school and below	64	16
	Junior College	136	34
	Bachelor degree	143	35.8
	Master degree or above	57	14.2
Length of participation in the community	Less than six months	102	25.5
	Six months - one year	75	18.8
	1–2 years	133	33.3
	More than two years	90	22.5
Frequency of visits to the community	Once a month or less	57	14.2
	2–3 times a month	80	20
	Once a week	66	16.5
	2–3 times a week	105	26.3
	Once a day or more	92	23

Alpha value between 0.848 – 0.903 which means that measurement used in this study is reliable and consistent. AVE for the lower constructs were above 0.50 which means that the first measurement model exhibits good convergence validity as all factors have substantial shared variance with their associated indicators (Table 3).

Heterotrait Monotrait Ratio (HTMT). According to Henseler et al. [59], if the values are less than the HTMT threshold value of 0.90, this indicates that all constructs are distinguishably unique and distinct from another construct. Based on the findings, all are below the threshold value of 0.90, which validates the discriminant validity of the constructs (Table 4).

Collinearity Statistics (VIF). Smart PLS 4 offers both internal and external models for researchers to analyze. The Variance Inflation Factor (VIF) is examined in PLS-SEM to determine the degree of collinearity. A VIF of more than 5 suggests a possible issue with collinearity [62]. The results indicate that multicollinearity issue does not exist in this model (Table 5).

Table 3. Construct Reliability and Validity in Stage 1

Construct	Item	FL	Cronbach's alpha α	CR	AVE
Virtual Information Interaction (VFI)			0.903	0.904	0.72
	VFI 1	0.899			
	VFI 2	0.819			
	VFI 3	0.846			
	VFI 4	0.833			
	VFI 5	0.845			
Virtual Interpersonal Interaction (VTI)			0.889	0.897	0.694
	VTI 1	0.903			
	VTI 2	0.836			
	VTI 3	0.786			
	VTI 4	0.851			
	VTI 5	0.785			
Functional Perceived Value	FPV1	0.847			
	FPV2	0.852			
	FPV3	0.835			
	FPV4	0.810			
	FPV5	0.833			
Emotional Perceived Value			0.885	0.885	0.684
	EPV1	0.845			
	EPV2	0.817			
	EPV3	0.815			
	EPV4	0.826			
	EPV5	0.832			
Brand Loyalty			0.881	0.881	0.737
	BL1	0.856			
	BL2	0.873			
	BL3	0.850			
	BL4	0.855			

(continued)

Table 3. (*continued*)

Construct	Item	FL	Cronbach's alpha α	CR	AVE
Brand Association			0.788	0.904	0.825
	BA1	0.912			
	BA2	0.905			
Perceived Quality			0.873	0.922	0.797
	PQ1	0.89			
	PQ2	0.891			
	PQ3	0.897			
Brand Awareness			0.857	0.858	0.778
	BR1	0.887			
	BR2	0.885			
	BR3	0.875			

Table 4. Heterotrait Monotrait Ratio (HTMT) in Stage 1 (without moderating effect)

Variable	BA	BL	BR	EPV	FPV	PQ	VFI
BA							
BL	0.724						
BR	0.752	0.756					
EPV	0.574	0.610	0.596				
FPV	0.558	0.578	0.571	0.698			
PQ	0.731	0.764	0.748	0.580	0.609		
VFI	0.567	0.537	0.540	0.503	0.455	0.490	
VTI	0.596	0.550	0.576	0.492	0.533	0.546	0.514

4.4 Second Stage Assessment of Embedded Approach

Based on the table, all variables have at least with cronbach alpha (α) of 0.70 Cronbach's alpha and composite reliability. Moreover, the AVE of all the variables has at least a 0.50 value. Based on the findings, all constructs are below the threshold value of 0.90, which validates the discriminant validity of the constructs (Table 6).

Explanatory Power, Predictive Relevance and Effect Sizes of the Model. According to Chin (1998) [63], R2 values greater than 0.67 indicate a substantial level of explanation, values greater than 0.33 but less than or equal to 0.67 suggest a moderate level of explanation, and values greater than 0.19 but less than or equal to 0.33 represent a weak level of explanation. Based on the table, r2 value 0.553 which indicates a moderate predictive power.

Table 5. Collinearity Statistics in Stage 1

Item	VIF	Item	VIF
BA1	1.731	FPV3	2.217
BA2	2.208	FPV4	1.984
BA3	2.301	FPV5	2.156
BL1	2.215	PQ1	2.579
BL2	2.427	PQ2	2.558
BL3	2.142	PQ3	2.558
BL4	2.421	VFI1	3.289
BR1	2.21	VFI2	2.103
BR2	2.151	VFI3	2.403
BR3	2.086	VFI4	2.16
EPV1	2.306	VFI5	2.414
EPV2	2.027	VTI1	3.208
EPV3	1.985	VTI2	2.333
EPV4	2.093	VTI3	1.841
EPV5	2.168	VTI4	2.363
FPV1	2.415	VTI5	1.884
FPV2	2.358		

Table 6. Construct Reliability and Validity in Stage 2

Construct	Cronbach's alpha α	CR	(AVE)
Brand Equity	0.874	0.874	0.726
Customer Perceived Value	0.766	0.766	0.811
Virtual Information Interaction	0.903	0.904	0.72
Virtual Interpersonal Interaction	0.889	0.897	0.694

The Blindfolding/Prediction procedure in Smartpls 4.0 was employed to obtain the Q2 values. If the value of Q2 is greater than zero, it indicates that the model's outcomes has predictive relevance (Ringle, Sarstedt, and Straub, 2012; Hair et al., 2014).Based on the table below, BE (0.453) and CPV (0.475) have strong predictive relevance.

According to Cohen (1998) [64], f-square or effect size is small when greater than or equal to 0.02, medium if greater than or equal to 0.15, and large when greater than or equal to 0.35. When eliminated from the model, the results revealed that CPV to BE (f2 = 0.268), VFI to BE (f2 = 0.081) and VTI to BE (f2 = 0.105), VTI to CPV (f2 = 0.019) have large effect size while VFI to CPV (f2 = 0.003) have small effect (Table 7 and Fig. 2).

Table 7. Explanatory Power, Predictive Relevance, and Effect Sizes

Constructs	r2		Q^2	f^2	
	R-square	R-square adjusted	Q^2predict	BE	CPV
BE	0.556	0.553	0.453		
CPV	0.521	0.512	0.475	0.268	
VFI				0.081	0.003
VTI				0.105	0.019

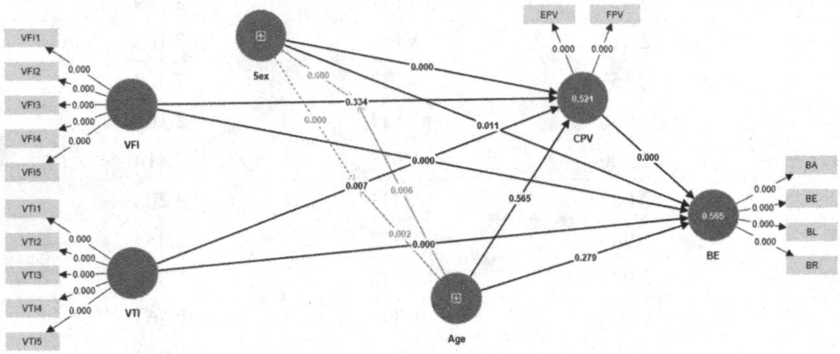

Fig. 2. Structural Model in Stage 2 (with moderating effect of Age and Sex)

4.5 Results of Hypothesis Tests

The study found that virtual information interaction (VFI) has positive and significant effect on brand equity (BE) with ($\beta = 0.256$, $p < 0.000$), supporting H. Moreover, the study found out that virtual interpersonal interaction (VTI) has positive and significant effect on brand equity (BE) with ($\beta = 0.328$, $p < 0.000$), supporting H2.

The path coefficient of virtual information interaction to customer perceived value to brand equity is 0.030, but the P value is 0.334 > 0.05, not supporting H3. The direct path coefficient of virtual interpersonal interation to customer perceived value to brand equity is 0.066, the P value is 0.009 < 0.05, the path relationship is established, supporting H4 (Table 8).

Table 8. Results of hypothesis tests

No.	Path	β	T stat	P values	Decision
H1	VFI -> BE	0.256	4.911	0.00	Supported
H2	VTI -> BE	0.328	7.224	0.00	Supported
H3	VFI -> CPV -> BE	0.03	0.966	0.334*ns	Not Supported
H4	VTI -> CPV -> BE	0.066	2.626	0.009	Supported

4.6 Moderating Effect

The results show that age generation and sex have a significant moderating effect between virtual informational interaction to customer perceived value, and virtual interpersonal interaction to customer perceived value (Table 9).

Table 9. Moderating Effect of Sex and Age

Path	β	T stat	P values	Decision
Sex x VTI -> CPV	0.437	5.347	0.00	Supported
Age x VTI -> CPV	0.128	3.171	0.002	Supported
Age x VFI -> CPV	0.11	2.767	0.006	Supported
Sex x VFI -> CPV	0.387	4.468	0.00	Supported

5 Discussion

This study establishes the relationship between customer interaction and brand equity. This paper provides an important theoretical basis for enterprises to manage customer interaction and brand equity in virtual brand community, and proves that there is a positive correlation between virtual information interaction and brand equity. Virtual interpersonal interaction is positively correlated with brand equity. It provides a new theoretical perspective for the management field and emphasizes the importance of customer interaction in the brand management of virtual brand community.

This study reveals the role of customer perceived value in corporate brand equity in virtual brand communities. This helps enterprises to improve the customer's perception of the value of products or services and enhance the relationship between enterprises and customers to provide an important source of reference. Understand the multidimensional nature of business performance and emphasize the importance of developing employees' creativity and self-efficacy in improving business performance.

This study proposes a theoretical framework for mediating effects. It provides a useful theoretical framework for the study of mediating effects and helps to better understand the correlations between different factors and their effects on performance.

This study reveals the moderating effects of gender and age on virtual interpersonal interaction and customer perceived value, and between virtual information interaction and customer perceived value. This provides an important reference for enterprises to better understand the different gender and age of customer interaction and perceived value.

This research expands the research field of corporate brand equity. This study provides a new research perspective for enterprises in the field of virtual brand community management and brand equity construction, and provides a valuable reference for future research. Based on these structures, researchers can further explore the issues related to customer interaction and brand equity in virtual brand communities.

6 Conclusions

The main purpose of this study is to based on brand equity model and use S-O-R theory and social identity theory and social capital theory to build a model of the relationship between customer interactions and brand equity in virtual brand communities, to further fill the research gap of how customer interactions affect brand equity through customer perceived value, and to reveal the relationship mechanisms between customer interactions, customer perceived value and brand equity in virtual brand communities.

The main finding of this study shows that, there is a positive relationship between virtual informational interaction and brand equity. There is a positive relationship between virtual interpersonal interaction and brand equity. Virtual information interaction is not positively and significantly influenced customer perceived value (0.070, $p = 0.334 > 0.05$). The Virtual interpersonal information is positively and significantly influenced customer perceived value. Consumer perceived value mediates the relationship between Virtual interpersonal information and brand equity. But consumer perceived value do not mediates the relationship between Virtual information interaction and brand equity. There is significant differences on the level of virtual information interaction between female and male. There is significant differences on the level of virtual information interaction ($p < 0.000$) and virtual interpersonal interaction (($p < 0.016$) between and within age groups.

The study suggests that virtual informational interaction and virtual interpersonal interactions and customer perceived value can be enhanced to enhance the enterprise's brand equity in the virtual brand community.

Acknowledgments. We would like to thank all the respondents who participated in this study and helped us to complete the study. We would also like to thank the official Huawei community for providing a very valuable research environment for this study. Thanks to LESLIE-ANNE CHUA for her valuable comments for this study. Finally, thanks to all the friends who helped us to complete the study.

Disclosure of Interests. The authors have no competing interests to declare that are relevant to the content of this article.

References

1. Mollen, A., Wilson, H.: Engagement, telepresence and interactivity in online consumer experience: reconciling scholastic and managerial perspectives. J. Bus. Res. **63**(9–10), 919–925 (2010)
2. Wang, D., Yu, C., Chen, H.: Exploring the effects of different types of interaction on virtual brand community loyalty. Comput. Hum. Behav. **100**, 248–259 (2019)
3. Li, C., Chen, L.: Exploring the antecedents and consequences of virtual brand community identification. J. Bus. Res. **92**, 273–283 (2018)
4. McAlexander, J.H., Schouten, J.W., Koenig, H.F.: Building Brand Community. Sage Publications, Thousand Oaks (2020)

5. Chen, Y., Chen, J., Shang, J.: Social interactions and brand awareness in virtual brand communities: The mediation effect of social presence. J. Bus. Res. **89**, 371–378 (2018)
6. Li, Y., Wang, J., Huang, L.: Virtual brand community interaction: The influence of social and informational interactions on customer loyalty. Int. J. Inf. Manag. **39**, 227–237 (2018)
7. Wu, P.C., Yeh, Y.T., Hsiao, C.R.: The effect of online consumer reviews on brand equity. J. Bus. Res. **64**(3), 329–335 (2011)
8. Zhang, H., Lu, Y., Gupta, S., Zhao, L.: The effects of interaction types on virtual brand community loyalty: an empirical study in China. Internet Res. **28**(2), 366–386 (2018)
9. Brodie, R.J., Ilic, A., Juric, B., Hollebeek, L.: Consumer engagement in a virtual brand community: an exploratory analysis. J. Bus. Res. **66**(1), 105–114 (2013)
10. Sun, Y., Zhao, C., Shen, X.-L., Wang, N.: Perceived firm attributes, social identification, and intrinsic motivation to voice in brand virtual communities: differentiating brand-general and innovation-specific perceptions. In: Proceedings of the 53rd Hawaii International Conference on System Sciences (2020)
11. Li, M.W., Jia, S.L., Du, W.Y.: Fans as a source of extended innovation capabilities: a case study of Xiaomi technology. Int. J. Inf. Manage. **44**, 204–208 (2019)
12. Meng, Q.L., Hang, Y., Chen, X.J.: User roles in virtual community of crowdsourcing for innovation: a case study of Xiaomi MIUI in China. Tehnicki Vjesnik-Technical Gazette **26**, 1392–1399 (2019)
13. Meng, Q., Zhang, Z., Wan, X., et al.: Properties exploring and information mining in consumer community network: a case of Huawei Pollen Club. Complexity **2018**, 1–19 (2018)
14. Porter, C.E., Donthu, N., MacElroy, W.H., et al.: How to foster and sustain engagement in virtual communities. Calif. Manage. Rev. **53**, 80–110 (2011)
15. Lee, J., Park, H., Wise, K.: Brand interactivity and its effects on the outcomes of advergame play. New Media Soc. **16**, 1268–1286 (2014)
16. Ren, Y., et al.: Building member attachment in online communities: applying theories of group identity and interpersonal bonds. Mis Q **36**, 841–864 (2012)
17. Li, M., Hua, Y., Zhu, J.: From interactivity to brand preference: the role of social comparison and perceived value in a virtual brand community. Sustainability **13**(2), 625 (2021)
18. Rheingold, H.: The Virtual Community: Homesteading on the Electronic Frontier. Harper Perennial, New York (1993)
19. Aizhong, H., Jingying, Y.: Research on the impact of virtual brand community-like social interaction on value co-creation interaction behavior. Soft Sci. **33**(09), 108–112 (2019)
20. Andersen, P.H.: Relationship marketing and brand involvement of professionals through Web-enhanced brand communities: the case of coloplast. Ind. Mark. Manage. **34**(3), 39–51 (2005)
21. Muniz Jr, A.M., O'guinn, T.C.: Brand community. J. Consum. Res. **27**(4), 412–432 (2001)
22. Xinsheng, Z., Xianguo, L.: The influence of virtual brand community characteristics on consumers' willingness to co-create value - based on satisfaction and trust explanation of any intermediary model. China Circulation Econ. **31**(07), 70–82 (2017)
23. Aaker, D.A.: The value of brand equity. J. Bus. Strategy **13**(4), 27–32 (1992)
24. Keller, K.L.: Conceptualizing, measuring, and managing customer-based brand equity. J. Mark. **57**(1), 1–22 (1993)
25. Yoo, B., Donthu, N., Lee, S.: An examination of selected marketing mix elements and brand equity. J. Acad. Mark. Sci. **28**(2), 195–211 (2000)
26. Aaker, D.A.: Managing Brand Equity: Capitalizing on the Value of a Brand Name. Free Press, New York (1991)
27. Haiying, W., Liu, G.: An empirical study on the impact of interaction on service brand equity. Soft Sci. **23**(11), 43–47 (2009)
28. Keller, K.L., Lehmann, D.R.: Brands and branding: research findings and future priorities. Mark. Sci. **25**(6), 740–759 (2006)

29. Bruhn, M., Schnebelen, S., Schaefer, D.: Antecedents and consequences of the quality of e-customer-to-customer interactions in B2B brand communities. Ind. Mark. Manage. **43**(1), 164–176 (2014)
30. Yang, R.: Interaction-based construction of inter-customer value co-creation dimension–a virtual brand community as an example. Bus. Econ. **03**, 50–58 (2020)
31. Hollebeek, L.D. Sprott, D.E., Brady, M.K.: Rise of the Machines? Customer engagement in automated service interactions. J. Serv. Res. **24**(1), 3–8 (2021)
32. Nambisan, S., Baron, R.A.: Virtual customer environments: testing a model of voluntary Participation in value co-creation activities. J. Prod. Innov. Manag. **26**(4), 388–406 (2009)
33. Wu, S., Ling, Y.H., Wang, L.: A study of the relationship between interaction, trust and willingness to participate in virtual brand communities. Intell. Miscellaneous J. **30**(10), 100–105 (2011)
34. Yonggui, W., Shuang, M.: An empirical study on the drivers of customer interaction and the impact on customer satisfaction in virtual brand communities. Guan J. Sci. **10**(09), 1375–1383 (2013)
35. Tingting, W., Huijin, L.: Virtual brand community interaction and repeat purchase behavior in the perspective of value co-creation - a brand identity the role of regulation. Bus. Econ. Res. **23**, 80–83 (2020)
36. Zeithaml, V.A.: Consumer perceptions of price, quality, and value: a means-end model and Synthesis of evidence. J. Mark. **52**(3), 2–22 (1988)
37. Sheth, J.N., Newman, B.I., Gross, B.L.: Why we buy what we buy: a theory of consumption values. J. Bus. Res. **22**(2), 159–170 (1991)
38. Guanglong, S., Xiaodong, P., Pengfei, Q.: A study on the impact of inter-customer interaction in virtual brand communities on customer participation in value co-creation–experience value as a mediating variable. J. Manag. **13**(12), 1808–1816 (2016)
39. Zhang Min, L., Fangting, W.Q.: A study on the influence of opinion leaders on user stickiness in e-commerce websites based on trust and perceived value research. China Econ. Trade J. **02**, 100–104 (2021). (in Chinese)
40. Zhang, J., Shabbir, R., Pitsaphol, C., Hassan, W.: Creating brand equity by leveraging value creation and consumer commitment in online brand communities: a conceptual framework. Int. J. Bus. Manag. **10**(1), 80–91 (2014)
41. Zhaoji, Y., Yingzhi, Z.: The impact of firm-customer interaction on brand equity in virtual brand communities. Bus. Econ. **37**(03), 58–65 (2018)
42. Shenga, M.L., Teo, T.S.H.: Product attributes and brand equity in the mobile domain: the mediating role of customer experience. Int. J. Inf. Manag. **32**, 139–146 (2012)
43. Li, C., Jin, Y., Bu, Q.: Study on the impact of customer participation in virtual brand community value co-creation on brand equity - pin the mediating role of brand experience. J. Mark. Sci. **10**(04), 109–124 (2014)
44. Wang, C.-H., Hsu, L.-C., Fang, S.-R.: Constructing a relationship-based brand equity model. Serv. Bus. **3**(3), 275–292 (2009)
45. Sweeney, J.C., Soutar, G.N.: Consumer perceived value: the development of a multiple item scale **77**(2), 203–220 (2001)
46. Lei, Z.: A multidimensional interactive quality basin-based service brand equity management model. PhD thesis, Jinan University (2010)
47. Vargo, S.L., Lusch, R.F.: Evolving to a new dominant logic for marketing. J. Mark. **68**(1), 1–17 (2004)
48. Xiaoping, F., Qingguo, M.: Research on the influence of virtual community-based online interaction on online purchase intention. Zhejiang Univ. J. (Humanities and Social Sciences Edition) **39**(05), 149–157 (2009)

49. Song, Y., Zhang, L., Zhang, M.: Research on the impact of public climate policy cognition on low-carbon travel based on SOR theory-Evidence from China. Energy **261**(Part A), 125192 (2022)
50. Jing, F., Zhao, J., Yu, S.: Analysis of interaction-emotion-post-purchase satisfaction relationship between customers based on online brand communities perspectives. China Distrib. Econ. **27**(09), 86–93 (2013)
51. Tang, F., Jiang, Y.: A study of customer value co-creation behavior in virtual brand communities. Manag. Rev. **30**(12), 131–141 (2018)
52. Bagozzi, R.P., Dholakia, U.M.: Antecedents and purchase consequences of customer Participation in small group brand communities. Int. J. Res. Mark. **23**(1), 45–61 (2006)
53. Bing, H., Xiong, Y., Yu, L.: The influence of identity motivation on consumers' participation in product customization - based on social identity theory perspective. Econ. Manag. **29**(02), 84–90 (2015)
54. Nahapiet, J., Ghoshal, S.: Social capital, intellectual capital, and the organizational advantage. Acad. Manage. Rev. **23**(2), 242–266 (1998)
55. Tsai, W., Ghoshal, S.: Social capital and value creation: the role of intrafirm networks. Acad. Manage. J. **41**(4), 464–476 (1998)
56. Ellison, N.B., Steinfield, C., Lampe, C.: The benefits of Facebook "friends:" social capital and college students' use of online social network sites. J. Comput.-Mediat. Commun. **12**(4), 1143–1168 (2007)
57. Creswell, J.W.: Editorial: mapping the field of mixed methods research. J. Mixed Methods Res. **3**(2), 95–108 (2008)
58. Malhotra, M.K., Grover, V.: An assessment of survey research in POM: from. J. Oper. Manag. **16**(4), 407–425 (1998)
59. Henseler, J., Ringle, C.M., Sinkovics, R.R.: The use of partial least squares path modeling in international marketing. New Challenges Int. Mark. **20**(4), 277–319 (2009). Emerald Group Publishing Limited
60. Aleksandra Atanasova. Gender-Specific Behaviors on Social Media and What They Mean for Online Communications. Freelance Social Media Consultant. Published Nov. 6 (2016)
61. Yuan, M.: China's Silver Generation Has Money and Time to Spend. https://www.eastwestbank.com/ReachFurther/en/News/Article/Chinas-Silver-Generation-Has-Money-and-Time-to-Spend. October 15 (2018)
62. Hair, J. F., Ringle, C.M., Sarstedt, M.: PLS-SEM: indeed, a silver bullet. J. Mark. Theor. Pract. **19**(2), 139–151 (2011)
63. Chin, W.W.: The partial least squares approach to structural equation modeling. Mod. Methods Bus. Res. **295**(2), 295–336 (1998)
64. Cohen, J.: Statistical Power Analysis for the Behavioral Sciences, 2nd edn. Lawrence Erlbaum Associates, Publishers, Hillsdale, NJ (1988)

Insights from User Perceptions Towards the Design of a Proactive Intelligent TV Assistant

Tiffany Marques(✉), Jorge Ferraz de Abreu, and Rita Santos

DigiMedia Research Centre, Department of Communication and Arts, University of Aveiro, Aveiro, Portugal

{tiffanymarques,jfa,rita.santos}@ua.pt

Abstract. Recognising the potential to enhance the television (TV) experience, the integration of proactive behaviours in an intelligent TV assistant is thought to reduce the user's interaction effort and promote a more natural, friendly and empathetic use. However, existing research lacks a comprehensive understanding of the desirable dynamic and features of proactive behaviours in the TV context and their effects on perceived empathy and overall user experience (UX). This paper discusses the appropriateness and usefulness of proactive behaviours in an intelligent TV assistant prototype, seeking insights into their effects on perceived empathy and UX. To operationalise the study, the Wizard-of-OZ (WoZ) method was used to analyse users' perceptions of the design of the proactive scenarios that compose the prototype. The results showed that the prototype provided a good UX and was perceived as being empathetic. However, although all proactive scenarios were seen as useful some issues related to their suitability to the user's context and preferences were identified. The results of this study provide significant contributions to the TV domain, highlighting users' propensity to adopt proactive TV assistants and emphasising the importance of personalisation for better UX and perceived empathy.

Keywords: Proactivity · TV Ecosystem · Intelligent Voice Assistant

1 Introduction

Commonly used to control smart home devices, set reminders [1, 2], make purchases [3], search for information on the web [2] and content on television (TV) [4], intelligent (voice) assistants are advancing in its capabilities.

Faced with an ever-growing market for intelligent assistants [5], the increasing technological progress driven by artificial intelligence, machine learning, recognition technologies and recommendation systems [2, 6] is turning these assistants more sophisticated [7] and anthropomorphic. Increasingly able to understand their environment and the user's context, intelligent assistants have progressed to the point where they can predict the user's preferences, behaviours and intentions, enabling them to act proactively. These behaviours allow the assistant to support and perform tasks contextually, even in the absence of user requests [2], which is useful in different contexts [2, 6, 8, 9]. To

A. Marcus et al. (Eds.): HCII 2024, LNCS 14714, pp. 278–297, 2024.
https://doi.org/10.1007/978-3-031-61356-2_19

integrate this type of (proactive) behaviour, assistants need to access to and process more contextual data about the user and their environment [7] in order to cross-reference this contextual information and use predictive models to anticipate the user's needs [10]. Although proactivity is not yet a widespread feature of intelligent assistants [11], there are some studies that propose proactive intelligent assistants for specific domains, situations, environments and tasks [8, 12], and some commercial solutions that support a limited number of proactive behaviours [13, 14]. For example, Google Assistant (on the smartphones) can send personalised music suggestions and podcasts, as well as notifications about flight delays and nearby activities [14].

In the context of the viewer experience with the TV ecosystem (that involves user interactions with video content across multiple sources and a constellation of media devices: TV, smart TV, media players and set-top boxes (STBs)), most intelligent TV assistants still lack proactivity. However, Google TV has already introduced some features in this direction. The new Google TV user interface (UI) includes a feature that allows users to proactively receive personalised results [15]. The UI includes small widgets at the bottom of the screen that provide personalised information such as local weather, news, sports results, YouTube videos, music playlists and podcasts. Nevertheless, this functionality is not integrated into an intelligent voice assistant. Actually, intelligent TV assistants are still essentially based on reactive behaviours [16], presenting (voice) interactions that lack human, friendly and empathetic qualities. Some of their capabilities include searching for TV content (linear and non-linear) and over-the-top (OTT) content (e.g. content available on Netflix and YouTube), changing channels and volume, and accessing TV applications [4].

With the premise of enhancing the viewer experience, the integration of proactive behaviours into an intelligent TV assistant is expected to reduce the user' interaction effort, favouring a more natural, friendly and empathetic use. However, existing research does not provide a comprehensive understanding of the dynamics and desirable features of proactive behaviours in the TV context, such as the opportune moments to interrupt the user and the system behaviour in a multi-user scenario. There is also a lack of understanding of the effects of this type of behaviour on perceived empathy and overall User eXperience (UX). Therefore, the focus of this work was to explore the appropriateness and usefulness of the proactive behaviours of an intelligent TV assistant prototype, seeking insights on their effects on perceived empathy and UX.

Following this introduction section, the paper is structured as follows: Sect. 2 presents a theoretical background of relevant aspects to consider when designing a proactive intelligent assistant; Sect. 3 presents the methods used; Sect. 4 reveals and discusses the results; and the last section presents the conclusions.

2 Theoretical Background for Designing Proactive Intelligent Assistants

When a user interacts with an intelligent assistant, his/her intention can be explicit when a request is made to the assistant perform a specific action (reactive behaviour), or (depending on its level of proactivity), it can be deduced, whereby the assistant sends notifications, suggestions or, even, makes decisions, after a context analysis [17].

Thus, the way a proactive assistant can cooperate in a mixed-initiative interaction can range from a reactive behaviour to a fully autonomous proactive behaviour, in which the assistant makes decisions and performs tasks without prior confirming with the user, as suggested by the Interface-Proactivity (IP) continuum introduced by Isbell and Pierce [18]. This continuum expresses the combination of possible actions between the system and the user to accomplish a specific task through five **levels of proactivity**, thus demonstrating the possible balances of interaction between the two. In addition to the minimum and maximum levels (from a reactive behaviour – level 0 to a fully autonomous proactive behaviour – level 4), the continuum shows intermediate levels of proactivity, including alerts that the user should pay attention to (level 1), notifications about what he should pay attention to (level 2) and suggestions (level 3). Given this continuum, the more proactive an assistant is, the less control and responsibilities the user has, which increases the risk of failure. For this reason, most assistants now base their proactive behaviours on providing notifications or suggestions [16, 19], as the cost-benefit ratio is more controllable [17]. According to an elicitation study by Kraus et al. [7], users are more likely to **establish a relationship of trust** with **assistants** who have **low and medium levels of proactivity**.

Assistant-initiated interactions resulting from proactive behaviours can imply a loss of privacy and autonomy in task performance, as well as a disruptive interference in the user's social activities, and this may lead to inhibitions in adopting such systems [6]. These factors result in challenges in the **design of proactive behaviours.** To guide the conceptualisation and development of proactive behaviours in intelligent assistants, Yorke-Smith et al. [20] proposed a set of guidelines. According to the authors, a proactive assistant should be: **opportune**, interrupting the user at appropriate moments; **valuable**, providing information that **meets the user's needs and tasks**; **competent** within the context for which it has been trained; **safe**, minimising negative consequences; **transparent** about the data it collects from the user; and **unimposing**, avoiding interfering with the user's activities and attention. It must also follow a process of **continuous learning** and **improvement**, analysing the data it receives about the actions it takes [17].

Several studies [2, 6, 8, 9] have shown that users view proactive behaviours in an intelligent assistant **positively** and find them **useful**. Although proactive assistants can provide useful information to help and engage users, **identifying the convenient timing** and **relevance of proactive interventions** are essential to achieving a good **UX** [21], and can often be challenging to accomplish [8]. The relevance of proactive behaviours depends on the value it adds to the UX [17, 20].

Interruptions at inconvenient or inappropriate times can lead to disruption or irritation, potentially resulting in withdrawal from the use of these systems [8]. Therefore, proactive assistants should **understand the environment** to assess the appropriate moment to intervene without causing discomfort or overloading users with information. This is particular important when users are cognitively engaged, such as during a conversation or task [8]. Proactivity is key, but it must be balanced with sensitivity to the user's needs. Based on a field study with 40 participants, Cha et al. [22] pointed out that the assistant's knowledge of the **user's personal contextual factors**, such as their **current activity** and **state of mind/mood**, as well as elements related to daily routines, such as the **presence of other people**, are key to determining the appropriate time to provide proactive assistance. Following this, several studies [6, 8, 23] show that for proactively initiated interactions to be desirable and successful, it is essential to consider the user's characteristics as well as their social and situational context and **domain of use**.

In a domestic context, an online elicitation study [6] showed that key factors for a desirable proactive intervention include the identification who is present in the same space, the **type of activities taking place**, the **urgency of the task/activity**, the emotional state of the user, and the initiation and formulation of the assistant's proactive intervention. In this respect, the results of a study [2] based on an online questionnaire showed that **interactions** in which **users were alone** were generally rated **more positively** than those in which other people were present. Furthermore, scenarios in which the **assistant intervened** in a **conversation and contextualised previous conversations** were considered **less appropriate**. Another study [9] (of an exploratory nature) set in the domestic domain, more specifically in the **TV context**, showed that users need **more control over the assistan**t when they are watching/using the TV. This control is related to the data accessed by the assistant, the moments/situations in which it can interrupt the user, as well as the way it communicates and the content of that communication, especially when the user is in the company of other people. A possible solution proposed would be to allow the **user to pre-configure the system** to adjust the level of cordiality and formality of the communication, as well as to determine the data that the TV system has access to and the appropriate times to interrupt the user.

Another factor that is gaining relevance in the evaluation of proactivity is the user's perception of the **personality, social** and **emotional intelligence** of intelligent proactive systems. For example, in a study by Tan et al. [24], they explored through a WoZ experiment the relationship between five levels of proactive behaviours integrated into social robots and users' anthropomorphic factors. The results of this study showed that **level 3 proactive interventions** (i.e., proactively initiating interactions with users and recommending service solutions) were perceived as **more caring and polite**, making users feel that the robot was concerned about them. Other studies [9, 16] suggest that the integration of proactive behaviours has the potential to bring an additional "human" layer to intelligent assistants, and consequently promote their **empathy** (insofar as it is appropriate to the user's situation), leading to a **more natural** and **friendly use** of these systems. From this perspective, a study by Brave et al. [25] showed that the integration of empathic emotions in a virtual assistant has a significant **positive effect on the users' perception** of this type of system. The results showed that users perceived the empathic assistant (expressing emotions congruent with the user's situation) as **trustworthy, pleasant** and **caring** compared to the assistant that did not express empathic emotions. Following this, an empirical study [26] showed that when comparing an empathic assistant with an assistant who does not express this type of behaviour, participants have a more positive perception of the first type of assistant. However, they mention that perceptions may **differ depending on the congruence** and **appropriateness** of the **empathic interventions** to the user's situation.

3 Methods

The study was carried out with the aim of understanding the desirable characteristics of proactive behaviours in an intelligent TV assistant, as well as the effects of these behaviours on its perceived empathy and the associated UX. A medium-fidelity prototype was developed, which consisted of visual representations of a set of 6 proactive scenarios relevant to the television context (see Subsect. 3.1 Definition of scenarios).

Considering the potential scenario that participants may not have prior experience with solutions featuring proactive behaviours, and may be unaware of their capabilities and characteristics, there was a risk that their expectations could surpass the actual capabilities of the system [23]. This could potentially affect their overall experience and perception of the system's empathy. To avoid this, the prototype was tested in two separate sessions with the same participants (15) using the Wizard-of-OZ (WoZ) method [27] (see sub-Sect. 3.3 Experimental procedure). The first WoZ session was aimed to familiarize the users with the prototype and its capabilities while soliciting their opinions on the usefulness and appropriateness of each of the scenarios (6) that compose the prototype. Following their exposure to the prototype, the second WoZ session sought to assess their perceptions of the desirable characteristics of proactive behaviours and the effects of these behaviours on perceived empathy and UX (see sub-Sect. 3.3 Experimental procedure). Throughout both sessions, participants were contextualised about the scenarios that compose the prototype before testing it.

3.1 Definition of Scenarios

The scenarios defined according to the results of a previous study [9], were framed in everyday situations in which the assistant (integrated in the TV) can anticipate possible user requests or recommend content available on TV. As users have different preferences and viewing habits, the scenarios were defined to meet the needs of different user profiles and in different contexts of use. Table 1 describes each of the 6 proactive scenarios that compose the prototype.

The scenarios designed do not have the maximum level of proactivity according to Isbell & Pierce's [18] Interface-Proactivity (IP) continuum, so as not to be perceived as too intrusive by the participants. To this end, all idealised scenarios present a level 3 of proactivity (make suggestions). All the scenarios aimed to present a type of proactivity focused on usefulness [20], in which the assistant makes suggestions that may be of interest to the user. To establish and maintain an involvement with the user, as suggested in the study [28], a proximity approach was chosen, using informal and polite speech.

3.2 Prototype Design

Once the scenarios were defined, the Voice User Interface (VUI) for TV was designed and the prototype was developed. The prototype was developed on a Portuguese commercial IPTV infrastructure using the Microsoft Mediaroom middleware, based on the Microsoft Mediaroom Presentation framework. Google's Automatic Speech Recognition (ASR) API was integrated to recognise user voice interactions and display them on

Table 1. Definition of the proactive scenarios that compose the prototype

Scenario descriptions
Scenario 1 - Start watching a missed content Anne usually watches an episode of 'The Mentalist' when she gets home. However, due to an extended meeting, she missed the broadcast of the episode. Faced with this situation, when she turns on the TV, the voice assistant asks if she wants to watch the episode from the automatic recordings (catch-up TV service)
Scenario 2 – Start watching a related content Football players are being interviewed at the end of the 'Benfica vs. Porto' derby! The match ended with the victory of the Porto club and there is plenty to say about it. The voice assistant informs John that an analysis of the match is being done at a TV show on BolaTV (a sport TV channel) and asks if he wants to see that show
Scenario 3 - Recommendation in view of the user's expected departure Joana eats breakfast before going to work and turns on the TV to watch the news. As it is forecast to rain later, the assistant suggests she takes an umbrella before leaving the house
Scenario 4 - Content recommendation Rafael is bored at home on a Saturday night. He decides to watch some TV, but when he zaps the TV (changing channels), he doesn't find any interesting content. The assistant, detecting that the user changes channels frequently, suggests a comedy content from the automatic recordings (or from Netflix) that might be of interest to him
Scenario 5 - Continue watching an interrupted content Peter has fallen asleep in front of the TV set watching 'Game of Thrones'. The voice assistant detects this and asks the user if he is still watching the content. In the absence of a response, it turns off the TV. The next day, when the user turns the TV back on, the assistant reminds him that he fell asleep yesterday and asks if he wants to continue watching
Scenario 6 – Recommendation of content for co-viewing Peter is watching an episode of 'The Simpsons' when Joana enters the room and joins him on the sofa. Sensing Joana's arrival, the assistant suggests they watch the new episode of 'The Walking Dead'

the TV interface. This gives users a better understanding that the system is listening and processing their interactions.

As with existing commercial solutions, the main mode of interaction in the VUI is speech. This is complemented by visual outputs on the TV interface that support the audio feedback resulting from the interactions between the assistant and the user. The VUI consists of a layer at the bottom of the screen, superimposed on the existing interface, which is activated when the user or the assistant interacts by voice (see Fig. 1). This layer supports the general visual elements of the VUI to provide feedback to the user on the voice interactions of both actors (user and proactive intelligent assistant). For the visual elements, typography, colour palette and call-to-action elements (voice interaction icon and its animation) were considered. The voice interaction icon and its animation appear in the bottom left corner. Following these is the textual output of the voice interactions between the assistant and the user. Depending on whether the interaction is coming from the user or the assistant, the colour of the voice interaction icon is different. While in an assistant interaction the icon/animation is orange (RGB: 247, 147, 30) (see image a) in Fig. 1), in a user interaction the icon/animation is displayed in red (RGB: 255, 0, 0) (see image b) in Fig. 1). In addition, sound alerts are triggered when the animations appear to attract the user's attention. These sound alerts differ depending on who is involved in the interaction (user or assistant).

a) Proactive assistant interaction in the VUI **b) User interaction in the VUI**

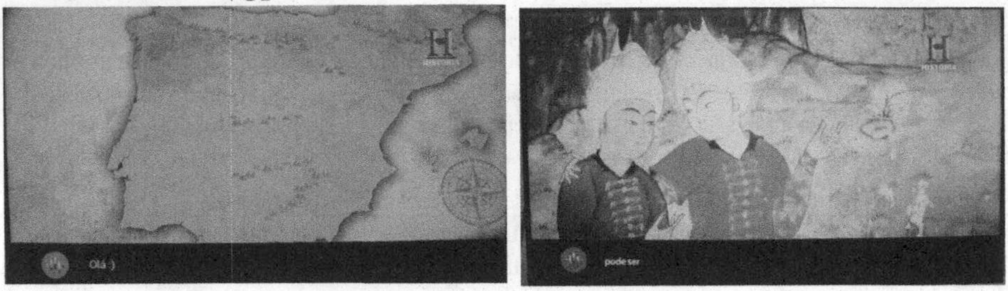

Fig. 1. Examples of the prototype.

Other graphical outputs were also created (see Fig. 2) for situations in which the assistant suggests a set of contents (Scenario 2 - Content recommendation) and for situations in which the assistant suggests resuming interrupted content (Scenario 4 - Continue watching an interrupted content). In the latter case, after positive feedback from the user, the system displays a set of frames of the interrupted content on the TV interface for the user to choose from which point to resume.

a) Graphical output of the suggested contents. **b) Intermediate layer for resuming an interrupted content.**

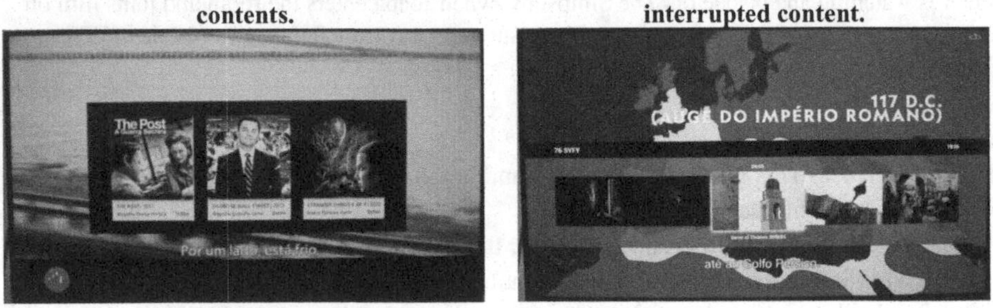

Fig. 2. Graphical output from the prototype on the TV interface.

The layout of these graphical outputs consists of layers overlaid on the existing interface. In the first case (image a) in Fig. 2), this layer is made up of illustrative pictures of the proposed content and some information about it, such as the title of the content, the year of its release, the film genres and the duration of the content. In the second case (image b) in Fig. 2), the layer is made up of several frames of the interrupted content, as well as the name and season (if it's a series) of the content and the minutes to which the selected frame corresponds.

For a better understanding of the prototype, a demonstration video is available here.

3.3 Experimental Procedure

15 participants were selected using convenience sampling to test the prototype. As participants' perception of the proactivity and empathy of an intelligent assistant for TV may be affected by the fact that they have never experienced an assistant with these features and/or are unaware of its potential, they tested the prototype at two different times in a WoZ experiment. The prototype's proactive behaviours were simulated by the researcher using a simple (web) application that enabled the system's suggestions to be triggered and, in turn, acted upon depending on the positive or negative feedback from users. This application also made it possible to trigger Google's Automatic Speech Recognition (ASR), which recognised user interactions and in turn displayed them on the TV interface. The experiment setup scheme is available here.

To ensure the necessary conditions for the study, the sessions took place in a UX laboratory on the university premises. This laboratory features a test room that resembles a living room, ensuring optimal conditions for the study and providing a comfortable and peaceful environment.

The WoZ sessions were conducted two weeks apart. Before the first WoZ session, participants were asked to complete a brief characterisation questionnaire. The strategy followed is illustrated in Fig. 3.

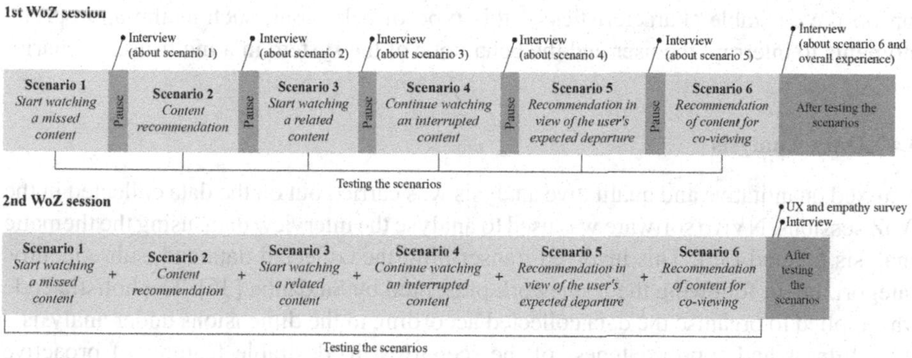

Fig. 3. WoZ sessions procedure strategy

1st session of WoZ. The purpose of this session was to give participants a first contact with the prototype and understand their perception about the proactivity of each of the scenarios, in terms of their usefulness and appropriateness.

When the participants arrived, they were informed about the objectives of the session and the procedures to be followed. An informed consent form was also given to them. After this introduction, the WoZ experiment began in which the participants tested the various scenarios that compose the prototype, after being given a brief description of the context of each of the 6 scenarios. They were asked to interact by voice as naturally as possible, accepting or rejecting the proactive suggestions made by the assistant (prototype). During the tests, the researcher simulated the behaviour of the prototype in the back-office of the laboratory. Between the tests of each scenario, a semi-structured interview was conducted in which the participants were asked for their opinion of the tested scenario in terms of its usefulness and appropriateness. After the tests, the session ended with a coffee break.

2nd session of WoZ. The aim of this session was to analyse the participants' perception of the desirable characteristics of proactive behaviours in the TV context and the effects of these behaviours on the perceived empathy of the prototype and the associated UX. To this end, the participants re-tested the prototype in the same environment and evaluated its empathy and UX, as well as giving their opinion on the proactive behaviours.

As in the previous session, at the beginning of the session, the participants were informed about the aims of the experiment, the procedures they would have to follow and were given an informed consent form. Participants tested the scenarios after being remembered about each one. After testing all the scenarios, participants completed a UX questionnaire following the Components of User Experience (CUE) model [29] to evaluate the UX of the prototype. The questionnaire, based on the methodology of the study [30], consisted of a triangulation of the SAM [31], SUS [32] and AttrakDiff [33] scales to measure users' perceptions of instrumental qualities (effectiveness, efficiency and ease of learning), non-instrumental qualities (stimulation and identification) and emotional impact (emotion and aesthetics). Participants also completed an empathy questionnaire consisting of an adapted version of the RoPE scale [34] to measure perceived empathy of the prototype. Finally, during a short interview, the participants expressed their opinion on the desirable characteristics of this type of behaviour, such as the appropriate moments to interrupt the user and the behaviour of the system in a multi-user scenario.

3.4 Data Analysis

A mixed quantitative and qualitative analysis was carried out on the data collected in the WoZ sessions. NVivo software was used to analyse the interview data, using the thematic analysis method [35]. This involved transcribing the collected data and, subsequently, categorizing it, following the framework presented by Saldanha [36]. The holistic code was applied to organise the data collected according to the dimensions under analysis – i) usefulness and appropriateness of the scenarios; ii) desirable features of proactive behaviours; iii) overall UX; and iv) perceived empathy. Categorising these data allowed it to be divided, analysed and quantified in the respective dimensions. The InVivo code was also used to extract some of the participants' comments. Statistical analysis method was used to analyse the data collected from the characterisation questionnaire and the final questionnaires - UX (SAM, SUS, AttrakDiff scales) and empathy (RoPE scale).

3.5 Sample Characterization

15 participants, 10 women and 5 men, took part in the study. The average age of the participants was around 31 years. In terms of academic qualifications, more than half of the participants ($n = 9$) had a Master's degree, followed by 3 with a PhD and another 3 with a Bachelor's degree.

In terms of TV viewing habits, more than half of the participants (n = 7) said they watched/used TV at least once a day and others said they watched a few times a week. As for voice interaction systems, 6 participants said they used this type of system frequently (several times a week), 2 said they used it less than once a week and 5 said they had tried it but didn't use it in their daily life. The remaining two said they have never used this type of system. Of those who said they used or had experience of voice interaction systems (n = 13), 11 had experience of them in a TV context, but only 3 used them moderately often - a few times a week (n = 1); and less than once a week (n = 2).

4 Results and Discussion

This section presents the results and subsequent discussion of the dimensions analysed in both WoZ sessions. The results of the first session consist of the data analysed on the participants' opinion of each of the proactive scenarios, in terms of their usefulness and appropriateness. The results of the second session consist of the analysis of the desirable characteristics of the proactive behaviours, the overall UX and the perceived empathy of the prototype.

4.1 1st WoZ Session

Usefulness and appropriateness of the scenarios. When analysing the interviews conducted after testing each of the scenarios in the first WoZ session, most participants (n = 14) found Scenario 1 - "Start watching a missed content" useful and appropriate for their routines. For example, 2 participants mentioned that the suggestion was useful because it acted as a reminder. Another mentioned that it was appropriate because it was consistent with their context, as they have routines for watching content. On the other hand, some (n = 4) mentioned that the scenario is useful, but that it is not appropriate according to their daily practices and the type of audio-visual content they usually follow.

In Scenario 2 – "Start watching a related content" all the participants found it useful, but this was not the case regarding the suitability of the proactive behaviours. More than half of the participants (n = 8) felt that the scenario was not suitable because it is not aligned with their audio-visual content preferences. They also mentioned that the usefulness of this scenario depends a lot on the user profile. Another mentioned that although he watches football, he doesn't usually watch programmes that analyse these games. However, he pointed out that he would consider using this type of suggestion in a situation where he hadn't watched a content from the beginning and the assistant suggested he watch a summary of it.

Regarding Scenario 3 – "Recommendation in view of the user's expected departure", the results of the analysis showed that the participants perceive the scenario as practical, relevant and very useful. One of them even mentions that - "It's a simple feature, but it can make all the difference in a person's daily life" (#P.7)[1]. Participants also emphasised that the scenario is useful in situations where the user has a habit of forgetting objects at home, or for people who frequently travel on foot. In general, participants also considered

[1] #P.7 – represents participant #7.

the behaviours to be appropriate to their routines. However, some (n = 3) said that the suggestion wasn't appropriate for them because they don't usually watch TV in the morning. They therefore suggested that the assistant provide the suggestion the night before.

In Scenario 4 – "Content recommendation", participants consider the proactive behaviour to be very useful for the following reasons: i) suggesting recent content; ii) providing the suggestion according to the user's context - in response to a boring and time-consuming action by the user (prolonged zapping); iii) suggesting content from different platforms; iii) reducing the time spent choosing and selecting content; and iv) facilitate the process of choosing content. The results also showed that the behaviour is perceived as appropriate by recognising the user's context (e.g. boredom; prolonged zapping) and adapting the suggested content to the user's preferences. Participants also emphasised that the number of proactive suggestions provided (3) was sufficient because it didn't require too much cognitive load. However, some (n = 4) mentioned the need for an intermediate intervention by the assistant before the suggestions were made available, to validate with the user the type of content desired (e.g. film, series,…). Only 1 participant didn't think it was appropriate for the assistant to mention the user's state of mind (bored).

In the case of Scenario 5 – "Continue watching an interrupted content", all participants recognise the usefulness of the scenario and the proactive behaviours associated with it. However, half of the participants (n = 7) do not consider the behaviour appropriate for their context, as they don't have the habit of falling asleep while watching TV or don't have the necessary devices, such as a smart band/smartwatch. The rest found the scenario appropriate and would be willing to use a smart band/smartwatch to access this proactive behaviour because they identify with the habit of falling asleep while watching TV. However, they also mentioned that receptiveness to this scenario would depend on the user profile. Two participants warned that users might not fall asleep with a smart band/smartwatch on their wrist because it's uncomfortable.

Finally, the results of Scenario 6 - "Recommendation of content for co-viewing" showed that the participants showed interest in the scenario, but didn't find it very useful with the current approach, finding it too intrusive. They found the assistant's behaviour of interrupting the viewing of content when another user enters to be inappropriate and intrusive. One mentioned that "there is no guarantee that the person who has entered the same room will want to watch TV" (#P.10). Another said: "I found it strange that he was directing himself at another user when I was the one using the TV" (#P.8). Following on from this, various insights into adapting proactive behaviours were mentioned. One participant said that in this scenario the initiative for suggestions should come from the user, asking for suggestions of content to watch together. Others mentioned that the system should have a dashboard for configuring proactive behaviours and setting limits, such as enabling and disabling proactive suggestions. There was no consensus on content. While some felt that the assistant should suggest new content that none of the users follow (series) or have already seen (film), others said the opposite. For them, the suggested content should follow what they watch together.

In line with other studies [9, 23, 37], the results show the importance of adapting proactive scenarios to different user profiles according to their preferences and contextual factors. This suggests that personalising proactive behaviours is essential to improve the performance of the intelligent TV assistant, as well as users' perceptions of its usefulness and suitability.

4.2 2nd WoZ Session

Desirable Features of Proactive Behaviours. Regarding the level of proactivity, most participants (n = 11) are not receptive to autonomous proactive behaviours, in which the assistant acts without the user's consent. They indicated that they would prefer the assistant to make an intermediate validation intervention in the form of a suggestion, as presented in the prototype. Consistent with this, other studies [2, 7, 38] show that users tend to favour systems with an intermediate level of proactivity between notifications and suggestions.

The loss of control over the content viewed was the main reason why participants did not want this level of proactivity (level 4). Other reasons, such as a lack of understanding of the assistant's actions and the possibility that they were inappropriate for the user's current context, were also mentioned. The participants (n = 4) who were receptive to this type of behaviour warned that it would depend on the transparency of the system and the user's trust in the assistant and its ability to recognise and learn their behaviours, habits and routines. Another mentioned that it would depend on mood, that if he was very tired and didn't want to think about anything, he would be predisposed to autonomous behaviours.

In terms of opportune moments for the assistant to interrupt the user while they are using the TV (watching or listening), the participants showed a preference for interrupting at times when there is a break/transition in the content, such as during commercials. Some of them (n = 3) were also receptive to being interrupted in a situation of prolonged zapping. In general, participants were not receptive to being interrupted while watching content. However, some of them (n = 2) said that if it was news time and the interventions were relevant and within their routine, they wouldn't mind receiving proactive suggestions. Others (n = 5) said they would be willing to receive proactive suggestions while watching content, if it was done in a non-disruptive way, such as notifications without auditory feedback. Only 2 participants were open to receiving proactive suggestions at any time, if they were relevant.

When asked about their receptiveness to receiving proactive suggestions in the company of other users, more than half of the participants (n = 10) gave positive feedback, especially if it was someone from their household. One of them said that, in these situations, proactivity "would help a lot to reduce conflict and time when choosing content to watch together." (#P.7). However, some (n = 4) warned that in a visitor situation they wouldn't want to receive proactive suggestions because they might contain personal and sensitive information. They also mentioned that in the company of visitors, suggestions would be unnecessary in some situations, as the TV would only serve as background noise. In this sense, one of them suggested a pre-configuration dashboard to disable proactive behaviours or even the assistant itself at certain times, including when accompanied by visitors and/or family.

As for the desirable voice and speech characteristics of a proactive intelligent TV assistant, participants generally favoured a friendly voice and informal speech. Two participants mentioned that they preferred these characteristics to a neutral voice and formal speech because they believe they have the potential to establish a connection between the user and the assistant, leading to a more efficient interaction. To establish this connection, another participant suggested that the assistant's speech should be relational, overcoming any emotional barriers. From this perspective, one participant mentioned that the assistant's voice and speech should show emotions depending on the user's actions. Another, on the other hand, believes that the dialogue should not be too sentimental, preferring a neutral voice and objective speech. One of the participants also emphasised that the speech should not be imposing to avoid a confrontational reaction with the user. Nonetheless, one of the participants said that these characteristics depend on the user's profile.

These findings emphasise the importance of considering user preferences and characteristics, as well as their situational/social context, in the design and development of proactive intelligent assistants. As one study [8] suggests, users' success and desire for proactive behaviours depends on the user's features (such as the personality and mood) and a better understanding of their context (such as surrounding environment and daily activities). Personalisation features, system transparency and a differentiated understanding of user profiles are crucial elements for creating an assistant with these attributes that aligns with user expectations and improves their overall experience.

Overall UX. The UX questionnaire, consisting of the triangulation of the SAM, SUS and AttrakDiff scales, allowed the collection of quantitative indicators on the instrumental (effectiveness, efficiency and ease of learning) and non-instrumental (stimulation and identification) qualities of the prototype and the users' emotional reactions (emotion and aesthetics) – see Table 2.

Regarding the instrumental qualities - efficiency, effectiveness and ease of learning - measured by the SUS scale, we found that the prototype received a score of 90, 83 on a scale of 0 to 100, which means that the usability of the system is "Best Imaginable". The reduced interaction effort with this prototype may have contributed to the high score in the usability aspects. The participants, already familiarised with the prototype, had well-established expectations in line with the prototype's current capabilities, which are still at a conceptual stage. The results, scored using a 5-level Likert scale, showed that the participants expressed a desire to use the prototype frequently (m = 4, 17), found it easy to use (m = 4, 83), realised that its functionalities were relatively well integrated (m = 4, 83) and quickly learned how to use it (m = 4, 5). They also felt confident using the prototype (m = 4, 33), suggesting that participants did not have significant privacy and security concerns.

The data collected on the SAM scale in relation to emotional impact, scored using a 5-level Likert scale, showed that the participants on average gave scores greater than or equal to 4 on the 'Satisfaction' (m = 4.08), 'Motivation' (m = 4) and 'Control' (m = 4.08) components. This shows that the participants were motivated and satisfied when using the prototype, demonstrating their receptiveness to integrating this type of (proactive) behaviour into an intelligent TV (voice) assistant. In terms of control, although the participants had little control over the prototype, they felt that they were in charge and that the decision making was their responsibility.

Table 2. Overall UX results of the WoZ session - triangulation of SUS, SAM and AttrakDiff.

Instrumental Qualities		Non-instrumental Qualities	Emotional Impact			
Effectiveness, Efficiency and Ease of learning		**Stimulation and Identification**	**Emotions**			**Aesthetics**
SUS (0 to 100)	**AttrakDiff** (−3 to 3)		**SAM** (1 to 5)			**AttrakDiff** (−3 to 3)
	PQ	HQ	Satisfaction	Motivation	Control	ATT
90,83	1,90	1,13	4,08	4	4,08	1,58

The data obtained using the AttrakDiff scale (scored on a scale −3 to 3) showed that the hedonic quality (HQ) received the lowest rating (1, 13), while the pragmatic quality (PQ) received the highest rating (1, 90). Attractiveness (ATT) was rated at 1, 58. In terms of HQ, participants didn't think the prototype was very elegant, nor did they think it was a premium solution. However, this was expected given that it was a medium-fidelity visual prototype and not a final solution. The results also show that participants rated the prototype as creative and captivating. In terms of PQ, participants classified the prototype as simple, practical, somewhat predictable and clearly structured. In terms of ATT, they found it good and somewhat attractive, despite its rather simple interface.

Still on the outputs collected from this scale, the prototype was positioned between the "task-oriented" and "desirable" quadrants (see Fig. 4), suggesting that users would like to use this prototype and recognise that it is task-oriented. However, it should be noted that the participants had somewhat dispersed opinions on these qualities, as the respective confidence intervals are less than 60 percent.

In overall, the results revealed positive UX indicators. The analysis showed a very good usability of the prototype, in which users felt motivated and satisfied when experiencing it. However, it should be noted that the participants had already experienced the prototype (1st WoZ session) and were aware of its current capabilities, which may have moulded their expectations of the assistant's usability.

Despite proactively initiated interactions, users also felt in control of decision-making. In addition, the prototype was perceived as desirable and task-oriented, which indicates a predisposition to use it.

Perceived Empathy. The results measured by the RoPE scale, scored using a 5-level Likert scale, showed that the assistant behaves appropriately according to what the user has experienced (m = 4.33), showing that it knows their needs (m = 4) and helps them when they need it (m = 4.08). The prototype was perceived as being natural in its interaction (m = 3.92) and as having an understanding of what the user is doing (m = 4.33) and what the user is saying (m = 4.33). In this sense, the participants gave, on average, a low rating to the assistant's lack of understanding (m = 1.83). The results also revealed that they did not feel anxious when interacting with the assistant (m = 1.08), nor did they perceive their interactions as being constant and automatic (m = 1.92).

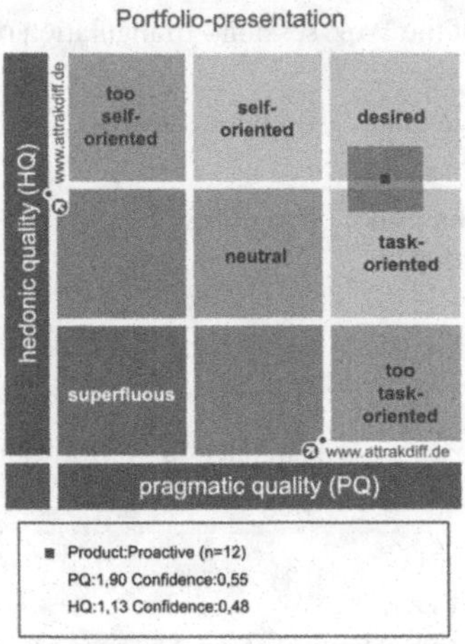

Fig. 4. AttrakDiff outputs - Portfolio-presentation (confidence intervals)

As for the emotional context, the participants gave more intermediate scores on average, between 2.5 and 3.5, to statements such as i) "The assistant reacts to my words but doesn't realise how I feel" (m = 2.67); ii) "The assistant seems to feel bad when I'm sad or disappointed" (m = 3); iii) "Whether the thoughts or feelings I express are 'good' or 'bad' makes no difference to the assistant's actions towards me" (m = 2.75); iv) "The assistant always interacts in the same way, regardless of what I say about myself" (m = 2.67); v) "The assistant comforts me when I'm upset" (m = 3.08); vi) "The assistant encourages me" (m = 3.5); and vii) "The assistant praises me when I do something successful" (m = 2.92). These scores may suggest that the participants already see some indicators that the assistant understands the user's emotional context, but still to a very limited extent.

When asked in the interview about the perceived empathy of the prototype, most of the participants mentioned that the assistant is already empathetic enough for the television context and his approach is appropriate, one of them even mentioning that "the fact that the assistant shows proactive behaviours already makes him more empathetic" (#P.1). Another said that he was "sympathetic and to a certain extent empathetic because he was able to hypothetically meet my needs, for example by recognising that I'm bored because he detected prolonged zapping" (#P.10). Nonetheless, to improve the way in which proactivity is introduced to make the assistant more empathetic, participants suggested that the assistant should greet the user by name to establish a stronger connection between the two. For example, one of them said that 'if the assistant says my name, I feel more available to listen to what it has to say' (#P.1). Some participants also suggested that proactive suggestions should include some contextual clues about the reason for the suggestions, as one pointed out: "I think it's important for the assistant to provide some context in its suggestions. For example, if it asked me if I wanted to watch 'The Game of Thrones' without giving me any context, I'd probably wonder if I'd watched that episode or not". (#P.3). However, one of them warns that some caution is needed in this contextualisation "because users will experience these kinds of scenarios every day" (#P.10).

Others say that it can become more empathetic if the assistant adapts and acts according to the user's context. One of them is even more specific, saying that the assistant should suggest content to cheer up the user when it detects that he or she is sad - emotional context. However, this is not the opinion of 10 participants who found it disturbing, invasive and somewhat creepy for the assistant to recognise their emotions/mood - "For me it would be a bit weird, for the assistant to know how I'm feeling. (#P.14). Those who took the opposite opinion (5) said that if the assistant recognised emotions, it could adjust the conversational features according to the user's mood, avoiding interrupting them in undesirable situations. Another mentioned that the voice and speech of the assistant could be adjusted according to the time of day - "… a more energetic tone in the morning and a softer tone in the evening. This would make the system more natural and the conversation more fluid". (#P.7). According to some participants, voice and speech characteristics are fundamental for the assistant to be perceived as empathetic, one of them even mentioning that "the tone of voice will define the empathy of the machine" (#P.10). In this sense, they emphasise that the voice must be pleasant, calm and friendly, and that the speech must be adapted to the user's context.

In this sense, the results showed that the assistant was perceived as empathetic, understanding the user's needs and providing assistance when necessary and according to what the user had experienced. Although the prototype was perceived with a limited understanding of the emotional context, the participants considered it to be sufficiently empathetic for the TV context. However, they showed mixed feelings about the recognition of the emotional context. While some participants expressed discomfort and felt it was invasive for the assistant to recognise their emotions, others saw potential benefits in adapting interactions accordingly. To optimise proactively initiated interactions to make the assistant more empathetic, participants suggested including personalised greetings to each user, referring to their name and, learning and adapting the assistant's proactive behaviours to the user's context. Some also proposed adapting and configuring the assistant's voice and speech features according to the user's mood or time of day.

Although scarce research relates the proactivity and empathy of an intelligent assistant, a study [39] has revealed that there is no consensus opinion about the empathy of a voice assistant, showing that the participants' opinion was polarized, between those who prefer a personal, empathetic and friendly assistant and those who prefer a neutral task-oriented assistant. In this regard, the authors suggested that users should have the possibility to configure the levels of empathy.

5 Conclusions

The present study provided pertinent insights into the participants' perceptions of the suitability and usefulness of the proactive scenarios, as well as the desirable characteristics of the proactive behaviours of an intelligent TV assistant and how these behaviours affect the perceived empathy of the prototype and its UX.

The results showed that the 6 proactive scenarios that compose the medium-fidelity prototype were generally perceived as useful, but they were not always perceived as suitable for the user's context, either because of their daily practices (scenario 5), the content suggested (scenario 2), the additional devices required (scenario 5), or the inconvenient interruptions (scenario 6). However, as users expressed, the appropriateness of proactive behaviours depends very much on the user's profile (such as behaviours, and preferences) and context (such as activities being performed, presence of users).

Although there is evidence that the desirable characteristics of proactive behaviour vary according to user profile, context and domain of use, the results of this study showed that some characteristics are desirable for all participants. Users preferred intermediate levels of proactivity, where they can validate suggestions before the assistant acts. They were not receptive to fully autonomous proactive behaviour due to concerns about losing control over the system's actions. They also expressed a preference for the assistant to interrupt during pauses or content transitions, particularly during advertisements. However, they expressed some willingness to accept non-disruptive interruptions while viewing content, as long as the assistant's behaviour is not intrusive. For example, providing notifications on the TV interface without voice output. Users were also receptive to proactive suggestions in the presence of other people, particularly in a family context. However, in a social visiting context, this receptivity decreased due to concerns about the possibility of disclosing personal and sensitive information in the presence of people outside the home environment. Regarding the characteristics of the assistant's voice and speech, users were unanimous in their preference for a friendly voice and informal speech.

The evaluation of the prototype of a proactive intelligent TV assistant yielded positive results, highlighting good usability and a favourable UX and empathy. Users felt that maintained a sense of control despite the introduction of proactive behaviours, demonstrating a willingness to engage with the system. However, it is important to emphasise that the positive results may have been influenced by the users' previously established expectations of the prototype's capabilities, shaped during the 1st WoZ session, in which the participants experienced the prototype for the first time.

The assistant was perceived as empathetic and understanding of the user's needs, although opinions differed on the recognition of emotional context. To improve empathy, participants recommended personalised greetings and adaptive behaviours that are aligned with the user's context.

These results suggest a predisposition on the part of users to adopt a proactive TV assistant with these types of characteristics and for these contexts of use, finding the prototype useful and easy to use. However, there is a general need to personalise the assistant, adjusting its proactive behaviour to users' preferences, characteristics and social/situational context. This personalisation is seen as crucial to improving the user experience and perceived empathy. In this sense, in the future we intend to personalise the prototype according to different potential user profiles, adapting the proactive suggestions according to their needs, preferences, routines, situational context and mood. This approach aims to ensure that the assistant effectively meets the diverse needs and expectations of users, paving the way for the future development of proactive TV assistants.

Acknowledgments. The study reported in this publication was supported by FCT– Foundation for Science and Technology nr. 2020.08009. BD and DigiMedia Research Centre, under the project UIDB/05460/2020.

Disclosure of Interests. The authors have no competing interests to declare that are relevant to the content of this article.

References

1. Ammari, T., Kaye, J., Tsai, J.Y., Bentley, F.: Music, search, and IoT: How people (really) use voice assistants. ACM Trans. Comput.-Hum. Interact. **26**(3), 28 (2019)
2. Reicherts, L, Zargham, N., Bonfert, M., Rogers, Y., Malaka, R.: May I Interrupt? Diverging opinions on proactive smart speakers. In Proceedings of the 3rd Conference on Conversational User Interfaces (CUI '21), pp. 10 ACM, New York (2021)
3. McLean, G., Osei-Frimpong, K.: Hey Alexa ... examine the variables influencing the use of artificial intelligent in-home voice assistants. Comput. Hum. Behav. **99**, 28–37 (2019)
4. Fernandes, S., Abreu, J., Almeida, P., Santos, R.: A review of voice user interfaces for interactive TV. Commun. Comput. Infor. Sci. **1004**, 115–128 (2019)
5. Statista. Anzahl der Nutzer Virtueller Digitaler ASsistenten Weltweit in den Jahren von 2015 Bis 2021. https://de.statista.com/statistik/daten/studie/620321/umfrage/nutzungv%on-virtuellen-digitalen-assistenten-weltweit/. Accessed 27 Dec 2023
6. Zargham, N., et al.: Understanding circumstances for desirable proactive behaviour of voice assistants: the proactivity dilemma. In: Proceedings of the 4th Conference on Conversational User Interfaces (CUI'22), Article 3, pp. 1–14. ACM, New York (2022)
7. Kraus, M., Wagner, N., Callejas, Z., Minker, W.: The role of trust in proactive conversational assistants. IEEE Access **9**, 112821–112836 (2021)
8. Miksik, O., et al.: Building Proactive Voice Assistants: When and How (not) to Interact (2020). arXiv:2005.01322
9. Marques, T., Abreu, J., Santos, R.: Proactivity in the TV context: understanding the relevance and characteristics of proactive behaviours in voice assistants. In: Proceedings of the 2023 ACM International Conference on Interactive Media Experiences, pp. 314–319. ACM, New York (2023)
10. Schweitzer, N., Gollnhofer, J. F., Bellis, E.: Exploring the potential of proactive AI-enabled technologies. In: Proceedings of the Conference on AMA Summer Educators, IN18-IN19 (2018)
11. Silva, A.B., et al.: Intelligent personal assistants: a systematic literature review. Expert Syst. Appl. **147**, 113193 (2020)
12. Kraus, M., et al.: "Was that successful?" On integrating proactive meta-dialogue in a DIY-Assistant using multimodal cues. In: Proceedings of the 2020 International Conference on Multimodal Interaction (ICMI '20), pp. 585–594. ACM, New York, NY (2020)
13. Campbell, I.C.: Amazon's Alexa can now act on its own hunches to turn off lights and more. https://www.theverge.com/2021/1/25/22249044/amazon-alexa-update-proactive-hunches-guard-plus-subscription. Accessed 29 Dec 2023
14. Binay, D.: Stay on top of your day with proactive help from your Assistant. https://www.blog.google/products/assistant/stay-top-your-day-proactive-help-your-assistant/. Accessed 29 Dec 2023
15. Romero, J.: Google TV's new Ambient Mode with "proactive personal results" rolling out for some. https://chromeunboxed.com/google-tv-ambient-mode-proactive?utm_content=cmp-true. Accessed 29 Jan 2024

16. Abreu, J., Santos, R., Silva, T., Marques, T., Cardoso, B.: Proactivity: the next step in voice assistants for the TV ecosystem. Commun. Comput. Inf. Sci. **1202**, 103–116 (2020)
17. Sarikaya., R.: The technology behind personal digital assistants: an overview of the system architecture and key components. IEEE Sig. Process. Mag. **34**(1), 67–81 (2017)
18. Isbell, C.L., Pierce, J.S.: An IP continuum for adaptive interface design. In: Proceedings of HCI International (2005)
19. Lopez-Tovar, H., Charalambous, A., Dowell, J.: Managing smartphone interruptions through adaptive modes and modulation of notifications. In: Proceedings of the 20th International Conference of Intelligent User Interface, pp. 296–299 (2015)
20. Yorke-Smith, N., Saadati, S., Myers, K.L., Morley, D.N.: The design of a proactive personal agent for task management. Int. J. Artif. Intell. Tools **21**(1), 30 (2012)
21. Amershi, S., et al.: Guidelines for Human AI Interaction. In: Proceedings of the 2019 CHI Conference on Human Factors in Computing Systems, Article 3, pp. 1–13 (2019)
22. Cha, N., et al.: Hello there! Is now a good time to talk? Opportune moments for proactive interactions with smart speakers. In: Proceeding of the ACM on Interactive Mobile Wearable and Ubiquitous Technologies, vol. 4, no. 3, Article 74, pp. 28 (2020)
23. Meurisch, C., et al.: Exploring user expectations of proactive AI systems. In: Proceedings of the ACM on Interactive, Mobile, Wearable and Ubiquitous Technologies, vol. 4(4), Article 146, pp. 22 (2020)
24. Tan, H., et al.: Relationship between social robot proactive behavior and the human perception of anthropomorphic attributes. Adv. Robot. **34**(20), 1324–1336 (2020)
25. Brave, S., Nass, C., Hutchinson, K.: Computers that care: investigating the effects of orientation of emotion exhibited by an embodied computer agent. Int. J. Hum. Comput. Stud. **62**(2), 161–178 (2005)
26. Ochs, M., Pelachaud, C., Sadek, D.: An empathic virtual dialog agent to improve human-machine interaction. In: Proceedings of the 7th International Joint Conference on Autonomous Agents and Multiagent Systems (AAMAS '08), pp. 89–06. International Foundation for Autonomous Agents and Multiagent Systems, Richland (2008)
27. Martin, B., Hanington, B.: Universal Methods of Design, 1sr edn. Rockport Publishers, Beverly (2013)
28. Bickmore, T., Gruber, A., Picard, R.: Establishing the computer–patient working alliance in automated health behavior change interventions. Patient Educ. Couns. **59**(1), 21–30 (2005)
29. Mahlke, S., Thuring, M.: Studying antecedents of emotional experiences in interactive contexts. In: Proceedings of CHI 2007 - Emotion & Empathy (2007)
30. Abreu, J., Camargo, J., Santos, R., Almeida, P., Beça, P., Silva, T.: UX evaluation methodology for iTV: assessing a natural language interaction system. Commun. Comput. Inf. Sci. **1433**, 149–161 (2021)
31. Bradley, M.M., Lang, P.J.: Measuring emotion: the self-assessment manikin and the semantic differential. J. Behav. Ther. Exp. Psychiatry **25**(1), 49–59 (1994)
32. Brooke, J.: SUS-A quick and dirty usability scale. In: P. W. Jordan, B. Thomas, I. L. McClelland, B. Weerdmeester (Eds.), Usability Evaluation in Industry, pp. 6 (1996)
33. Hassenzahl, M., Burmester, M., Koller, F.: AttrakDiff: Ein Fragebogen zur Messung wahrgenommener hedonischer und pragmatischer Qualität. In: Szwillus, G., Ziegler, J. (eds.) Mensch & Computer 2003. Berichte des German Chapter of the ACM, vol. 57, pp. 187–196. Verlag, Vieweg+Teubner (2003)
34. Charrier, L., Rieger, A., Galdeano, A., Cordier, A., Lefort, M., Hassas, S.: The RoPE scale: a measure of how empathic a robot is perceived. In: Proceedings of the 14th ACM/IEEE International Conference of Human-Robot Interaction (HRI'19), pp. 656–657. IEEE Press (2019)
35. Braun, V., Clarke, V.: Using thematic analysis in psychology. Qual. Res. Psychol. **3**(2), 77–101 (2006)

36. Saldaña, J.: The Coding Manual for Qualitative Researchers. SAGE Publications, London, UK (2016)
37. Nothdurft, F., Ultes, S., Minker, W.: Finding appropriate interaction strategies for proactive dialogue systems—an open quest. In: Proceedings of the 2nd European 5th Nordic Symposium Multimodal Communication, pp. 73–80. Electronic Press, Estonia (2015)
38. Peng, Z., Kwon, Y., Lu, J., Wu, Z., Ma, X.: Design and evaluation of service robot's proactivity in decision-making support process. In: Proceedings of the 2019 CHI Conference on Human Factors in Computing Systems, paper 98, pp. 1–13. ACM, New York (2019)
39. Biermann, M., Schweiger, E., Jentsch, M.: Talking to stupid?!? Improving Voice User Interfaces. Mensch und Computer 2019 - Usability Professionals. Gesellschaft für Informatik (2019)

Design Methods for Catalyzing Co-creation in Community Building: An Evaluating Approach

Duan Wu and Yuhong Ma(✉)

College of Design and Innovation, Tongji University, Shanghai 20092, China
{wuduan,mayuhong}@tongji.edu.cn

Abstract. Community building, an intricate design endeavor integrating place, people, and their interactions, involves the provision of diverse methods by designers to facilitate stakeholder co-creation. Despite this prevalent practice, there needs to be more research on the appropriateness of design methods for community-building projects and assessing their efficacy. Following Hester's (1975) methods evaluation scale, this study orchestrated co-design workshops with target professional designers. The workshops systematically captured preferences and evaluations from designers with different backgrounds addressing the same community building issue. The study presented a descriptive account of the results, conducted through comparisons and reflective analyses, which elucidates that factors of accessibility, usability, flexibility, and communication form influence users' assessments of tools. This finding contributed a strategy for design methods evaluation, thereby establishing foundational principles for methods selection in the intricate realm of community building endeavors.

Keywords: Design Methods Evaluation · Co-creation · Community Building

1 Introduction

The exploration of design practice and theoretical research in community building has garnered significant attention, particularly in the past decade, marked by the emergence of numerous practical cases. Beyond the physical transformation of residential spaces, it encompasses the restructuring of relationships between individuals and among individuals, governments, and institutions, ultimately elevating the overall quality of community life. However, it is imperative to recognize that our communities have transformed in the wake of five years of living with the impact of COVID-19.

In the pursuit of enhancing experiences and optimizing efficiency in long-distance relationships, there has been an inadvertent oversight of our daily lives and the fundamental existence of communities. Ezio Manzini, recognizing the utopian implications of the 'everything at/from home' paradigm, urges resistance to its impact on our lives. Instead, he advocates for reconstructing proximity-based communities [1, P3-4]. However, the current imperative is to construct an idealized community from the ground

A. Marcus et al. (Eds.): HCII 2024, LNCS 14714, pp. 298–313, 2024.
https://doi.org/10.1007/978-3-031-61356-2_20

up rather than carve out spaces within existing communities laden with challenges and delicate balances. Within these spaces, ideas can be exchanged, and opportunities can emerge – a recurrent challenge faced by practitioners in the field.

The main challenges encountered in community development are rooted in the intricate dynamics among stakeholders, constituting a 'wicked problem.' This term denotes issues characterized by uncertainty, stubbornness, and complex factors that defy scientific resolution [2, P165]. Addressing such problems, as posited by Richard Buchanan, necessitates designers to meticulously analyze all elements, with problem-solving emanating from the synthesis of design activities, striving for unity and balance among diverse needs [3]. Accumulating professional skills and knowledge, designers comprehensively analyze problem elements, seeking equilibrium through design activities [4]. Nevertheless, practitioners face nuanced conflicts of interest, particularly when confronted with uncertainty and a clash of value interests during deep project involvement. In such situations, impartial judgment of objective facts becomes challenging due to biases rooted in professionalism, an occurrence termed 'limits of rationality' by Simon [5, P114-117]. Consequently, scholars advocate for co-creation, especially interdisciplinary, as it facilitates the active participation of diverse stakeholders, enhancing comprehension of social systems' complexity and the interaction between human behavior and social relationships [6, 7].

Design methods are pivotal in co-creation by acting as translating and facilitating mechanisms. Primarily, they furnish visual tools that serve as aids in translating ideas between practitioners and co-creators. This proves particularly advantageous for practitioners, as these design methods assist untrained designers in uncovering valuable insights from co-creators and, at times, even solutions to problems [8]. Furthermore, design tools can visualize and guide co-creators in articulating intuitive and subconscious thoughts into conscious expressions that can be communicated externally, fostering innovation.

Evidently, the choice of design methods significantly influences the effectiveness of co-creation. However, this selection often hinges on the personal preferences of practitioners, whether they are expert designers or community members less acquainted with design methods. Limited research has been conducted on the efficacy of various tools at different design stages, with scarce literature evaluating the roles of distinct tools. Through a retrospective study, this study explores the correlation between the roles and choices of tools and methods at different stages, amalgamating practical experience and literature research. Feedback on tool evaluation was collected through expert workshops, and factors influencing the selection of design tools were summarized.

While this paper delves into the construction of physical community spaces and the establishment of interpersonal physical relationships, it is essential to acknowledge that the fusion of the physical and virtual worlds is underway in the current digital age. Our sphere of action gradually transforms into a hybrid society, blending physical and digital realms. Consequently, the insights from this research remain applicable to developing digital communities and endeavors to enhance user experience through co-creation initiatives in digital communities.

2 Organizing and Approaches of Community Building

2.1 Co-creation and Design Methods

Co-creation, encompassing designers, users, and other non-professionals collaborating to find solutions, has emerged as a comprehensive term in the design process [6]. It strives to foster an active dialogue, ensure equal access, promote information transparency, and provide a clear assessment of risk-benefits to users, facilitating the joint creation of mutually valued outcomes [9]. This approach is highly responsive to the interests of diverse groups, recognizing users as a vast hidden resource where everyone possesses the creativity and capability to contribute to design [10, 11].

Meroni & Sangiorgi [12] differentiate between task or goal-oriented systems, such as company-customer service or specific public service systems, and action-oriented or fun-based community-based services. The latter, driven by enjoyment and emotions, requires time to anticipate design. Establishing human relations becomes a prerequisite in these scenarios. Collaborative involvement degree, active involvement, social tie strength, and relational intensity are identified by Baek, Kim, Pahk, and Manzini [13] as vital collaborative elements reinforcing co-creation in the community.

In community building, design challenges necessitate collaborative creation involving participants from various fields, moving beyond reliance solely on practitioners or individual designers' decisions. The multifaceted nature of challenges in community building often requires expertise from multiple professional domains. Designers play a crucial role in activating professional knowledge distributed among participants. Operating under the 'symmetry of ignorance,' design methods facilitate the organization of diverse perspectives and knowledge into problem-solving pathways [14]. Recognizing that participants contribute to and create knowledge at different levels is imperative. Accordingly, designers must tailor co-creation methods to diverse target audiences, whether leading, guiding, providing scaffolds, or offering a clean slate [6].

2.2 Evaluating Design Methods

Confronted with many design methods, practitioners require a systematic approach for selecting and evaluating these methods. In community building, practitioners hail from diverse backgrounds, presenting interdisciplinary and cross-domain collaboration challenges. A comprehensive understanding of the effectiveness of design methods, coupled with consensus on method selection and usage, facilitates the transformation of practical solutions into tangible realities. Evaluation criteria for design methods exhibit variability, with some focusing on characteristics of design outcomes, such as their capacity to foster innovative results [15], facilitate education and cognitive enhancement [16], or contribute to social equity and care [17]. Others delve into the interaction between methods and users during usage, encompassing content, purpose, and designer responses [18]. However, a standardized, evidence-based method for evaluating design methods needs improvement [19].

In 1975, Randolph Hester published "Neighborhood Space," a seminal work examining community environments and neighborly relationships. Within this book, Hester intricately detailed the interactive relationships between individuals and spaces within the small-scale setting of a community. He introduced User-Needs Techniques (UNT) as a subdivision element for evaluating diverse design methods. Hester asserted that these user-needs techniques demand specific standards, including the specification of information types needed and determining the suitability of techniques at various design stages. This encompasses tasks such as analyzing existing situations, defining problems, generating ideas, setting goals, and evaluating alternative solutions or resolving user conflicts. Technical costs, including professional input levels, speed, input intensity, and difficulty, were also considered criteria [20]. Hester's UNT evaluation criteria are deemed valuable for screening and assessing design methods, serving as the primary theoretical foundation for evaluating and validating our methods.

3 Methodology

3.1 Design Methods Selection

To comprehend the facilitating role of design methods in collaborative design for community building, we employed an inductive method rooted in experience and concepts [21]. This systematic research approach expands the understanding of theory and empirical phenomena through a cyclical process of empirical observation and theoretical study [22]. Following the abductive research approach, we identified 120 design methods from 14 theoretical works [20, 23–35], undergoing manual processing to eliminate redundancy. These theoretical sources span diverse fields, including service design, social innovation, business innovation, and urban planning. Six publications focus on design methods tools, three on business innovation, and the remaining five on participatory design methods in community planning. Most sources selected are publicly oriented, aiming for broad applicability among practitioners beyond exclusively professional designers. The selected design methods, coupled with practical experience, were categorized into six design stages: establishing links with the public, extensive background research, information processing, and concept formation, prototype iterative testing, confirming implementation plans, and lean operation management. Specific classifications can be found in the Appendix.

The second author, with eight years of experience in community building and service design, and the first author, a design educator at university, having taught 240 h of design method application courses for graduate students, utilized their practical and theoretical research experience in design methods to select 20 methods (see Fig. 1. Twenty design methods screened based on the authors' practical experience.). These methods are believed to foster co-creation activities in community building across various design stages. Subsequent research and validation will be conducted on these selected design methods.

3.2 Research to Design Approach

To ascertain whether design methods contribute to community building effectively, this study adopted a research-to-design (RtD) approach, conducting scenario-based design experiments that leverage design knowledge for practical application [36]. A structured

Fig. 1. Twenty design methods screened based on the authors' practical experience.

experimental framework (see Fig. 2) was devised, encompassing a community-building design intent, an experiment exploring design intent using design method knowledge, and an evaluation of the methods employed. Twelve designers specializing in environmental design, service design, industrial design, and interaction design, with an average expertise of 9.3 years and three experts possessing over 15 years of practical experience, were invited to participate.

The workshop introduced hypothetical community building issues, prompting experts to rank tools based on their relevance to different design phases. In the first segment of the experiment, we presented six design stages and 20 design methods, inviting participants to supplement any stages or methods they considered valuable but

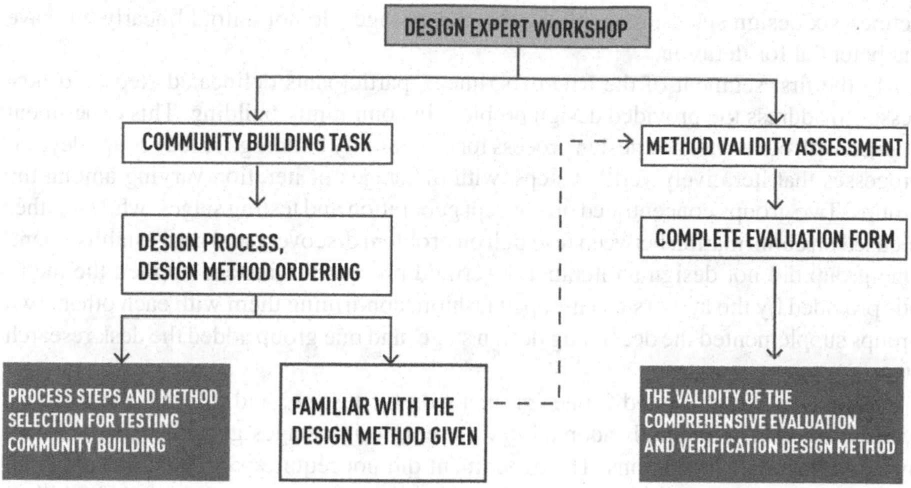

Fig. 2. Process and the goal of expert workshop

may have been overlooked. We employed the User-Needs Techniques (UNT) evaluation scale in the second segment. Participants assessed the 20 design methods by placing stickers on indicators of value. To streamline the original Hester evaluation scale, which had three dimensions: (1) positive value in that consideration, 2) neutral value in that consideration, and 3) negative value in that consideration, we chose only dimensions with positive effects to control for accuracy within the limited time of the experiment.

The inherent logic of the two parts of the RtD experiment is evident. Firstly, the hypothetical design problem in community building inspired participants' thinking. Specific textual explanations of the 20 design methods and visual case cards of tools were provided, prompting participants to employ these methods in addressing community-building problems. In this phase, designers were encouraged to familiarize themselves with the specific characteristics and functions of the 20 design methods. Participants' use of design methods extended beyond expected usage, offering new insights into the logic of method application. The second part, utilizing the Hester scale for evaluation, built on participants' familiarity with the evaluated methods from the first segment, ensuring reliable method evaluation data could be obtained within the 3.5-h workshop timeframe.

4 Results

4.1 Design Methods Selecting and Process of Design

Various researchers employ different approaches to explore design problems, ranging from John Dewey's renowned pattern of inquiry to the prevailing innovation thinking patterns in the design field over the past decade. These approaches seek to visualize and substantiate the design process. Moreover, when confronted with design problems, particularly wicked problems in community building, this process is often considered to necessitate iterative cycles. Thus, in the initial phase of selecting design methods, we defined six design stages, recognizing that these stages do not unfold linearly but have the potential for iteration.

In the first segment of the RtD experiment, participants delineated steps and processes to address the provided design problem in community building. This experiment aligned with our envisaged design process for community building. Three groups devised processes that iteratively verified steps, with the stages of iteration varying among the groups. Two groups concentrated on concept generation and testing stages, while another focused on confirmation between research on problem discovery and goal establishment. One group did not design an iteratively verified process but instead applied the methods provided by the authors in a grouped fashion, confirming them with each other. Two groups supplemented the deepening design stage, and one group added the desk research step.

Moreover, we presented 20 design methods for testing, and all of these methods were selected. The methods adopted in different design stages generally aligned with the experiment's expectations. The experiment did not require participants to apply all 20 design methods in their entirety, and additional explanation cards and method illustrations were provided to assist participants in understanding the usage instructions of each design method. Furthermore, three groups supplemented additional design methods during the exploration process, such as back costing, community workshops, and test feedback. This offers valuable insights for enriching this study's community-building design toolkit. The experiment results are illustrated in Fig. 3.

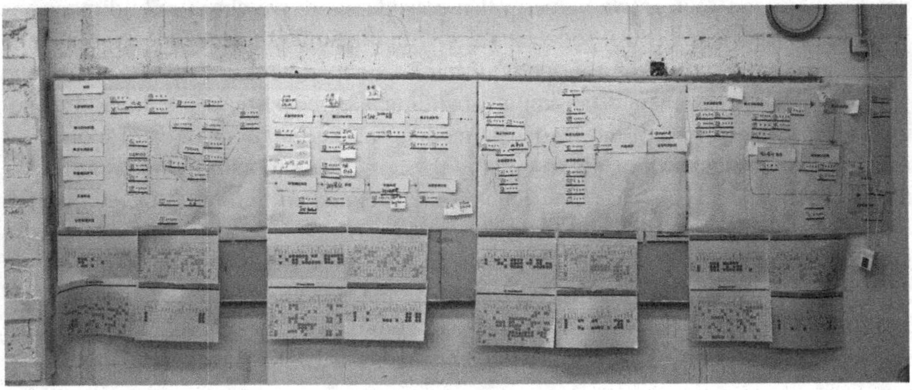

Fig. 3. Four sets of experimental results from the workshop.

4.2 Design Methods Selecting and Process of Design

Before conducting the RtD Experiment, the authors utilized the UNT method evaluation scale to assess 20 design methods based on three levels: positive value, negative value, and neutral value. This assessment reflected their practical experience and understanding of design methods. As the UNT method evaluation scale was simplified in the RtD experiment, with only two dimensions, positive value (selected) and negative value (not selected), the summary results of the experiment were categorized accordingly. To cross-verify the experimental results with the authors' method assessments, a reanalysis of the binary judgments was conducted:

- If three or more groups (including three groups) considered it a positive value, it was categorized as a positive value; otherwise, it was a negative value.
- If two or fewer groups (including two groups) considered it a positive or negative value, it was categorized as a neutral value.

Following this rule, an analysis of the differences between the two datasets was performed, and the comparative analysis is presented in Table 1. Pink dots indicate situations where the judgment results are opposite (i.e., positive value versus negative value). In contrast, yellow dots indicate differentiated judgments (i.e., positive value versus neutral value or negative value versus neutral value).

Table 1. Analysis of comparative evaluation.

	WHAT THE TECHNIQUE DETERMINES			DESIGN PROCESS APPLICABILITY								COST										ACCOMMODATION OF OTHER GOALS					
	What people do in the space?	How people feel about the space?	How people interact in the space?	Analyzing existing situation	Defining a problem	Generating ideas	Projecting a future	Giving alternative choices	Evaluating and making choices	Resolving conflicts	Evaluating post construction	Overall cost (need for professional input)	Speed developing technique	Technique administration	Necessity of repeating	Ease of interpretation (recording and analyzing data)	Accuracy, reliability and validity of sample in predicting real want-needs of total group	Feasibility of off-site administration (does not have to be done on-site)	Ease of self-administration	Flexibility (can be easily duplicated)	Versatility (can be applied to a variety of situations)	Neighborhood education	Neighborhood power (organization, leadership, and control)	Neighborhood communication	●	○	Total number
community communication platform						●		●	○		●		●	○					●			○		○	5	4	9
POEMS		●							●							●	●	●		●					6	0	6
trend matrix	○		○											○		●									1	3	4
initial opportunity map				○										○											0	2	2
survey					○			○			○					○	○			○					0	6	6
interview			○	○	○			○		○						○	○		●						1	7	8
observation			●					○					○		●										2	2	4
six thinking hats					●								●		○	○	○					○	○	○	2	6	8
storyboard				○		●											●				●				3	1	4
scenarios		●		○													●			○					2	2	4
personas			●			●				○															3	1	4
user journey map				○		●				●			●		●					○	●				5	2	7
system map						○							●												1	1	2
stake holders motivation matrix									○			○					○			○					0	4	4
kano analysis		○	○					●		●						●			●						4	2	6
quick prototype						○				○				○			●								1	3	4
co-design			○																	○					0	2	2
community meeting					○			○				●													1	2	3
strategic roadmap					●	●			○		○					●									3	2	5
solution evaluation														●				○							1	1	2
●	0	2	2	0	2	5	0	2	1	2	1	1	4	1	2	4	4	1	3	1	2	0	0	0			
○	1	1	4	5	3	2	0	4	3	3	2	1	1	4	1	3	4	1	0	5	0	2	1	2			
Total number	1	3	6	5	5	7	0	6	4	5	3	2	5	5	3	7	8	2	3	6	2	2	1	2			

● Large difference between before and after
○ Fine tuning

Analysis of Design Method Judgments. A comparison of the data on design method judgments reveals that the methods with a significant number of completely opposing judgments in UNT's four major evaluation subcategories include Community Communication Platform (5), POEMS (6), and User Journey Map (5). Methods with noticeable but not significant discrepancies include Survey (6), Interview (7), and Six Thinking Hats (6). Methods with overall significant discrepancies (including opposition and differentiation) include Community Communication Platform (9), POEMS (6), Survey (6), Interview (8), Six Thinking Hats (8), and User Journey Map (7). Kano Analysis (6) also falls into this category. POEMS is the method most prone to judgment ambiguity (opposition), while the Community Communication Platform is the most prone to misinterpretation (including opposition and differentiation). Conversely, the Initial Opportunity Map, System Map, Co-design, and Solution Evaluation are relatively less prone to misunderstanding.

In analyzing the differences in experimental results, we employ a retrospective research approach and offer the following analysis:

- *Impact of Method Usability.* The 20 design methods tested in the experiment are generally comprehensive, such as POEMS, Kano Analysis, etc. These methods may need improvement for first-time users or novices concerning understanding and usability.
- *Impact of Method Complexity.* Similar to usability, some tested design methods require preliminary research results or involve integrating and synthesizing various information before use, adding complexity to the operational application of the design methods.
- *Impact of Method Flexibility.* Some design methods are applicable in various scenarios and stages of the design process, contributing to increased uncertainty in method evaluation due to their flexible application.
- *Impact of Visualization in Design Methods.* In situations where the usability and complexity of design methods are similar, a visual representation helps evaluators quickly grasp the specific role of the method, enhancing judgment accuracy and speed.

Analysis of UNT Element Judgments. On the other hand, we also compiled comparative data for the four categories and 24 evaluation elements in the UNT evaluation scale. Among the evaluation elements for judging the 20 design methods, those with a significant number of completely opposing judgments include Generating Ideas (5), Speed Developing Technique (4), Ease of Interpretation (4), Accuracy, Reliability, and Validity of Sample in Predicting Real Want-Needs of the Total Group (4).Elements with noticeable but not significant discrepancies include Analyzing Existing Situation (5), Flexibility (5), How People Interact in the Space (4), Give Alternative Choices (4), Technique Administration (4), Accuracy, Reliability, and Validity of Sample in Predicting Real Want-Needs of the Total Group (4). Among these, the element most prone to generating ambiguous judgments (opposition) is Generating Ideas (5). In contrast, those most prone to misunderstanding (including opposition and differentiation) are the Accuracy, Reliability, and Validity of the Sample in Predicting the Real Want-Needs of the Total Group (8) and Generating Ideas (7). Evaluation elements less prone to misunderstanding include Projecting a Future (0), What People Do in the Space (1), and Neighborhood Power (1).

Analyzing the differences in experimental results, we offer the following insights:

- *Influence of Degree Descriptions in Evaluated Elements.* Some of the evaluated elements involve judgments related to degree, such as Speed Developing Technique, Ease of Interpretation, Ease of Carrying Out Technique, etc. If there is no explicit specification regarding the degree of judgment, it can impact the evaluation results.
- *Impact of Descriptive Format of Evaluated Elements.* The UNT evaluation elements are described in short phrases or sentences. While succinct, concise, and descriptive formats may need more details and limit evaluators' imagination of usage scenarios for the methods.

4.3 Influencing Factors and Key Points in the Evaluation of Design Methods

Through the analysis above of design method judgments and UNT element assessments, four key factors influencing the evaluation of design methods have been identified: accessibility, usability, flexibility, and communication form. Additionally, we introduce two pivotal aspects for evaluating design methods: concretization and contextualization. Concretization articulates and elucidates the extent of influential factors, while contextualization is utilized to implement and structure these factors, thereby enhancing the precision of evaluations.

- **Accessibility.** This dimension refers to the effort or external intervention practitioners require when applying design methods. It is delineated with a two-level measure of complexity – simple and complex. This holistic factor encapsulates the temporal dimension's time consumption in completing a design method process. Correspondingly, the depth and breadth of information obtained increase, accompanied by considerations of economic costs such as the involvement of professional and non-professional participants and the input costs of auxiliary materials.
- **Usability.** Usability concerns whether design methods require users or participants to possess specific professional knowledge. This criterion is evaluated on a novice user-expert designer quadrant system. The judgment of usability is applied during the design preparation stage to assess the selection range of involved participants. It profoundly influences the continuity and development of projects in later stages, determining whether on-site non-experts can effectively contribute.

- **Flexibility.** This aspect encompasses the thinking mode during the application of the method, delineated on a linear thinking-non-linear thinking spectrum. Linear thinking entails relying on past experiences and established rules when contemplating solutions. Conversely, non-linear thinking involves breaking free from fixed patterns, emphasizing divergent thinking, and leveraging associative capabilities. This flexibility is also evident in the developmental process of ideas, with linear thinking being purpose-driven and one-time, while non-linear thinking entails multiple iterations and practical experiments.
- **Communication Form.** This dimension refers to the presentation format of the outcomes generated by the design method, illustrated on a visual-non-visual spectrum. Visual presentation encompasses graphical or image-based expression, whereas non-visual presentation involves textual or non-graphical forms, such as organizing activities and executing plans. The visual-non-visual spectrum is a reference standard for method characteristics and guiding considerations, such as using visual means to summarize stage outcomes or attract public attention and engagement.

The above is our analysis and retrospective study of the data from the RtD experiment, resulting in four factors influencing the evaluation of design methods. We have defined these factors with dual-polarity axes to represent the degree of differences: complex-simple, novice user-expert designer, linear thinking-non-linear thinking, and visual-non-visual. Furthermore, to facilitate a more easily understood and communicable context for method judgment and selection, combining the dual-polarity axes of these four influencing factors can create different judgment scenarios.

Compared to professional terminology, contextualization is more accessible for public dissemination and provides a sense of involvement in scenarios. Even for those unfamiliar with design methods, quick responses can be elicited. Creating contextualization not only aids in evaluating design methods but also contributes to the screening and selection of methods.

We illustrate this with the example of usability, as it is a factor that users and evaluators can perceive based on their knowledge levels. Usability can be combined with complexity, flexibility, and communication form to form 2×2 models. Each quadrant represents a usage scenario for a specific design method in these models. For instance, in the combination of usability and complexity, a scenario called "Novice Organizing" represents novice users on a simple axis. This scenario is suitable for non-professional communities to accept project development and advancement, as it requires lower knowledge levels and organizational capabilities. On the other hand, the combination of usability and flexibility in the "Expert Knowledge Contribution" scenario involves expert designers introducing professional design methods or providing guidance in the design process. The illustration in Fig. 4 depicts these scenarios.

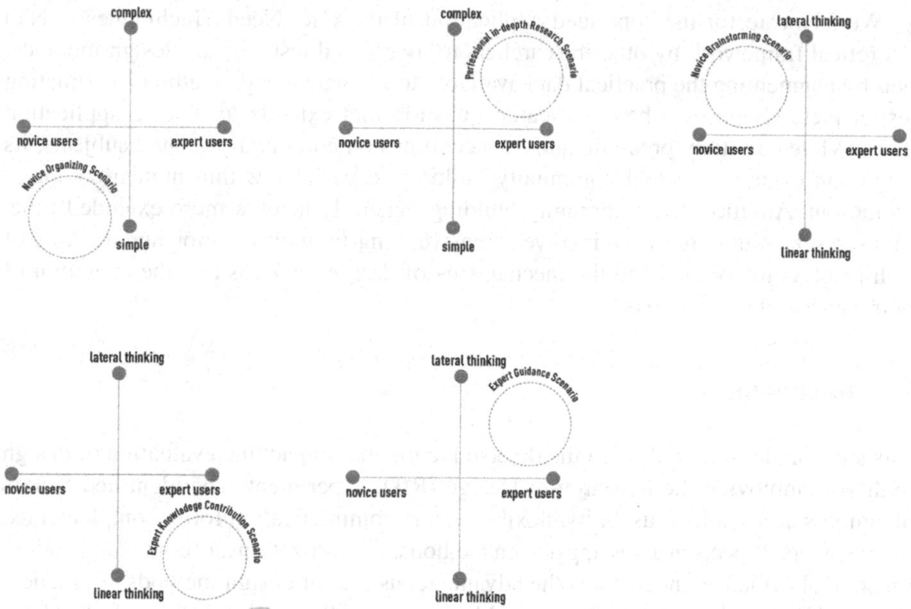

Fig. 4. Scenario-based modelling of design methods.

5 Limitation and Future Research

It is crucial to emphasize that the methods examined in this study do not represent definitive, standardized solutions for community building. Instead, they serve as suggestions for community-building actions at the level of design methods. These tested methods do not offer universal rules applicable to community-building practices, given the evolving and structurally complex nature of the problems at hand. The experiments introduced, along with the influencing factors in evaluating design methods, are intended to spark ongoing research and the development of best practices. Owing to the constraints of research time, we selected 20 design tools for experimentation based on experiential judgment, and our exploration needed to encompass comprehensive experimentation and testing of a broader array of design methods.

Moreover, it is essential to acknowledge that this research is in its initial exploratory stage, with a limited number of experts participating in the experiment. Future research endeavors can progressively broaden the pool of participants, encompassing design experts, community residents, and organizers of community practices to diversify the types of evaluators.

We advocate for the continued application of the User-Needs Techniques (UNT) theoretical framework by other researchers to assess and test various design methods, thereby augmenting the practical data available to evaluate design methods. Evaluating design methods poses a broad research question that extends to diverse application areas. While our study predominantly concentrates on community-related subjects, its scope can extend to virtual community building, especially within human-computer interaction. Additionally, community building generally takes a more extended time. Future research initiatives can involve extensive, long-term observation and tracking of such projects to comprehend the mechanisms of design methods and the evolution of their usage in these contexts.

6 Conclusion

This study endeavors to discern the diverse factors that impact the evaluation of design methods, employing the Research-to-Design (RtD) experiment. The identified factors encompass accessibility, usability, flexibility, and communication form, complemented by two pivotal aspects in assessing design methods: concretization and contextualization. Substantial evidence underscores the advantageous role of design methods in practical contexts [37], particularly in steering and facilitating collaborative design efforts. Community building inherently entails engaging multiple stakeholders with varied interests, whether applied to physical or virtual communities. While our experimental framework is rooted in the context of physical community spaces, the insights garnered are transferable to cultivating relationships within virtual communities within the domain of human-computer interaction.

Through our exploration of the evaluation of design methods, our overarching goal is to heighten the awareness and proficiency of practitioners, empowering them to partake in transformative community building endeavors independently. Envisaging design tools as instrumental in co-creation, we anticipate their role as catalysts in community-building. To instigate sustained social development and meaningful transformations, communities, being integral entities, emerge as pivotal players and catalysts for transformative occurrences. As practitioners engage in ongoing practices and building initiatives, they will consistently evaluate and appraise the efficacy of design methods, unlocking their more profound and refined potential. This iterative process is poised to propel societal transformation and development.

Appendix

	ESTABLISH LINKS WITH THE PUBLIC	EXTENSIVE BACKGROUND RESEARCH	INFORMATION PROCESSING AND CONCEPT FORMATION	PROTOTYPE ITERATIVE TEST	CONFIRM IMPLEMENTATION PLAN	LEAN OPERATION MANAGEMENT
BLUE OCEAN STRATEGY	[illegible]	[illegible]	[illegible]	[illegible]		
HUMAN CENTERED DESIGN		[illegible]	[illegible]	[illegible]		
DESIGN WITH INTENT	[illegible]	[illegible]	[illegible]	[illegible]	[illegible]	[illegible]
UNIVERSAL METHODS OF DESIGN	[illegible]	[illegible]	[illegible]	[illegible]	[illegible]	[illegible]
[illegible]	[illegible]	[illegible]	[illegible]	[illegible]	[illegible]	[illegible]
[illegible]	[illegible]	[illegible]	[illegible]	[illegible]	[illegible]	[illegible]
[illegible]	[illegible]	[illegible]	[illegible]	[illegible]	[illegible]	[illegible]
[illegible]		[illegible]	[illegible]	[illegible]	[illegible]	
[illegible]	[illegible]	[illegible]	[illegible]	[illegible]	[illegible]	
[illegible]	[illegible]	[illegible]	[illegible]	[illegible]	[illegible]	[illegible]
[illegible]	[illegible]	[illegible]	[illegible]	[illegible]		[illegible]
[illegible]	[illegible]	[illegible]		[illegible]		
[illegible]	[illegible]	[illegible]	[illegible]	[illegible]	[illegible]	[illegible]
[illegible]	[illegible]	[illegible]		[illegible]		

References

1. Manzini, E.: Livable proximity: idears for the city that cares. EGEA spa, Milano (2022)
2. Rittel, H.W.J., Webber, M.M.: Dilemmas in a general theory of planning. **4** (1973). https://doi.org/10.1007/BF01405730
3. Buchanan, R.: Wicked Problems in Design Thinking. **8** (1992). https://doi.org/10.2307/1511637
4. Beckett, S.J.: The logic of the design problem: a dialectical approach. **33** (2017). https://doi.org/10.1162/DESI_A_00470
5. Simon, H.A.: Reason in Human Affairs (1983)
6. Sanders, E.B.-N., Stappers, P.J.: Co-creation and the new landscapes of design. **4** (2008). https://doi.org/10.1080/15710880701875068
7. Steen, M.G.D.: Co-design as a process of joint inquiry and imagination. **29** (2013). https://doi.org/10.1162/DESI_A_00207
8. Campbell, A.D.: Lay designers: grassroots innovation for appropriate change. **33** (2017). https://doi.org/10.1162/DESI_A_00424
9. Prahalad, C.K., Ramaswamy, V.: Co-creation experiences: the next practice in value creation. **18** (2004). https://doi.org/10.1002/DIR.20015
10. Boyle, D., Harris, M.: The challenge of co-production. **56** (2009). http://www.camdencen.org.uk/Resources/Public%20services/The_Challenge_of_Co-production.pdf
11. Manzini, E.: A laboratory of ideas. diffused creativity and new ways of doing.,13–15 (2007). https://www.researchgate.net/profile/Anna-Meroni-2/publication/251181009_Emerging_User_Demands_for_Sustainable_Solutions_EMUDE/links/5dcec6eca6fdcc7e1383f1c5/Emerging-User-Demands-for-Sustainable-Solutions-EMUDE.pdf#page=14
12. Meroni, A., Sangiorgi, D.: Design for services: from theory to practice and vice versa. Des. Serv., 9–35 (2011)
13. Baek, J.S., Kim, S., Pahk, Y., Manzini, E.: A sociotechnical framework for the design of collaborative services. **55** (2017). https://doi.org/10.1016/J.DESTUD.2017.01.001
14. Rittel, H.J.: Second-generation Design Methods. Developments in design methodology (1984)
15. Chulvi, V., Mulet, E., Chakrabarti, A., López-Mesa, B., González-Cruz, C.: Comparison of the degree of creativity in the design outcomes using different design methods. **23** (2012). https://doi.org/10.1080/09544828.2011.624501
16. Quinn, S.: Collaborative learning design in the middle school: sculpting 21st century learners. **22** (2015). https://doi.org/10.18848/1447-9494/CGP/V22/48747
17. Akoglu, C., Dankl, K.: Co-creation for empathy and mutual learning: a framework for design in health and social care. **17** (2021). https://doi.org/10.1080/15710882.2019.1633358
18. Cash, P., Daalhuizen, J., Hekkert, P.: Evaluating the efficacy and effectiveness of design methods: a systematic review and assessment framework. **88** (2023). https://doi.org/10.1016/j.destud.2023.101204
19. Cash, P.: Developing theory-driven design research. **56** (2018). https://doi.org/10.1016/J.DESTUD.2018.03.002
20. Hester, R.T.: Neighborhood Space. Hutchinson & Ross, Inc., Dowden (1975)
21. Van Maanen, J., Sørensen, J.B., Mitchell, T.R.: The interplay between theory and method. **32** (2007). https://doi.org/10.5465/AMR.2007.26586080
22. Dubois, A., Gadde, L.-E.: Systematic combining: an abductive approach to case research. **55** (2002). https://doi.org/10.1016/S0148-2963(00)00195-8
23. Kim, W.C., Mauborgne, R.: Blue Ocean Strategy (2004)
24. ORG, IDEO.: Human-Centered Design Toolkit: An Open-Source Toolkit To Inspire New Solutions in the Developing World. Original work published (2011)

25. Lockton, D., Harrison, D., Stanton, N.A.: Design with Intent: 101 Patterns for Influencing Behaviour Through Design. Equifine (2010)
26. Martin, B., Hanington, B.M.: Universal Methods of Design: 100 Ways to Research Complex Problems, Develop Innovative Ideas, and Design Effective Solutions (2012)
27. Kumar, V.: 101 Design Methods: A Structured Approach for Driving Innovation in Your Organization (2012)
28. Osterwalder, A., Pigneur, Y.: Business Model Generation: A Handbook for Visionaries, Game Changers, and Challengers. (2010)
29. Stickdorn, M., Schneider, J.: This is Service Design Thinking: Basics – Tools – Cases (2012)
30. Liedtka, J.: Designing for Growth: A Design Thinking Tool Kit for Managers (2011)
31. Service Design Tools | Communication methods supporting design processes. https://servicedesigntools.org/
32. Lewis, J., Perry Walker, Unsworth, C.: Participation Works! 21 techniques of community participation for the 21st century (1998)
33. Wates, N.: Involving local communities in urban design: promoting good practice. Urban Des. Q. **67**, 16–37 (1998)
34. Wates, N., Knevitt, C.: Community Architecture: How People Are Creating Their Own Environment (2013)
35. 佐藤, 滋.: 社区规划的设计模拟. 浙江大学出版社 (2015)
36. Frayling, C.: Research in Art and Design. **1**, 1–5 (1993)
37. Brown, T., Martin, R.L.: Design for action. **44** (2016). https://doi.org/10.1109/EMR.2016.7559061

A Product Design Strategy that Comprehensively Considers Consumer Behavior and Psychological Emotional Needs

Ning Xie, Jingluan Wang(✉), Jiashuang Fan, and Dengkai Chen

Key Laboratory of Industrial Design and Ergonomics, Ministry of Industry and Information Technology, Northwestern Polytechnical University, Xi'an 710072, China
wangjingluan1@163.com

Abstract. In product design, the consideration of consumers' emotional needs has gained increasing importance. While traditional methods of emotional ergonomics have been widely applied in various areas of product design, they tend to focus more on consumers' intuition rather than their behavior. Consequently, design decisions may not accurately reflect the genuine voice of consumers. This study aims to assist designers in restructuring and upgrading designs by taking into account consumers' psychological and behavioral requirements. To obtain valuable insights into consumers' emotional needs, a comprehensive design approach is proposed. This method comprises three layers: the design element layer, the perceived image vocabulary layer, and the relationship layer between design elements and perceived image vocabulary. In the first layer, design elements are identified. In the second layer, perceived image vocabulary for product design is established. In the third layer, the relationship between design elements and perceived image vocabulary is analyzed using a quantitative theory based on the least squares method. The design features of the target product are discovered based on consumers' emotional needs. Finally, the practicality and effectiveness of this design model are validated through a case study using CNC machine tools. The results of the case study demonstrate the promising application prospects of this method in consumer-emotion-based product designs.

Keywords: Emotional design · Psychological requirements · Behavioral requirements · Kansei engineering · Eye movement analysis

1 Introduction

Product designs is the direct way to reflect the emotional requirements of consumers [1]. In the traditional design, the product design mainly comes from the designer's creative thinking based of personal experience and aesthetic cultivation. Along with the advance of the science and technology, consumer's demand for products has not only focused on functionality and practicality, but also emphasizing the emotional experience and personality differences [2]. This makes it difficult for designers to gain recognition for products due to cognitive limitations in the fierce competition of the product market.

A. Marcus et al. (Eds.): HCII 2024, LNCS 14714, pp. 314–329, 2024.
https://doi.org/10.1007/978-3-031-61356-2_21

The consumers are more concerned with the spiritual feeling brought by the product, that is, "emotional requirements" or "perceptual images"[3]. The perceptual image is the consumer's psychological expectation to the product [4, 5]. It is playing an important role in helping the designer to provide the impetus for design restructuring and upgrading based on consumer's emotional requirements.

Kansei engineering is a traditional method of product emotional design, which has achieved good performance in product design [6], human-machine interface design [7], mechanical products [8], construction products and other fields [9–14]. Notwithstanding involving in broadening fields, the research perspective hardly broke away from those factors contributing to emotional design such as the psychological point of view of aesthetic intuition. As a result, the design decision on Kansei engineering may not be consistent with the true voice in the consumers. In previous studies, there has been relatively little research on emotional design from various aspects such as psychology and behavior. With the development of psychology, cognitive science, computer science and many other related disciplines, how to effective integration of different disciplines into product design will be the hotspot of research.

Therefore, this work proposes a combined design method of the perspective of aesthetics, psychology, ergonomics and behavior based on consumer's emotional requirements. Based on consumers' psychological requirements and behavioral requirements, this paper explores the perceptual images of product design using statistical methods combined with eye movement analysis to capture user behavior requirements. The relationship between the perceptual image vocabularies and the design elements is analysis based on the corresponding mathematical analysis model. And the design engine based on the perceptual image vocabularies is constructed and the design elements which are more in line with the consumer's perceptual requirement are obtained.

2 Literature Review

2.1 Emotional Design

Emotional design is a creative activity aimed at the emotional communication between people and things. Several studies have been conducted on ways to consider the design theory, design method and design model. Um et al. [15] proposed an emotional design framework of multimedia learning. Mayer et al. [16] proposed an emotional design model in multimedia instruction based on the cognitive affective theory. Plass et al. [1] proposed an emotional design framework of design elements of color and shape. Ho et al. [17] explored the basic concepts and definitions of emotion design, emotional design and emotionalize design to help us further understand how these are closely related to human-oriented design activities. Heidig et al. [2] explored the differentiation on relevant design features and their effects on emotions and learning. Park et al. [18] proposed an emotional design model based on an eyetracking study of positive emotions in multimedia learning. Uzun et al. [19] proposed a more direct measure of emotion recognition of emotional design, and results revealed that positive emotions generally increased as the amount of emotional design features increased. Triberti et al. [20] proposed an emotional design framework based on emotions cognitive processes, it differs greatly from the aspects such as user features, personalized service, and interactive technologies.

Based on the above analysis, emotional design is a major component of product design. The theory of emotional design is formed and developed based on the different methods and models (such like expert meeting method, conversation method, questionnaire method, statistical analysis method, experimental investigation method, system emotional design model, conceptual emotional design model, dynamical integration design model, etc.). Based on the different methods and models, emotional design is conducive to satisfy the customers' various types of psychological demands and stimulate their consuming desire.

2.2 Kansei Engineering

Kansei engineering is a combination of sensibility and engineering. It mainly designs products by analyzing consumer's sensibility and makes products according to people's preferences. It is a new branch of engineering. Many experts and scholars have conducted Kansei engineering review through different perspectives. Chen et al. [21] proposed an exemplification on applying Kansei engineering to design service in service industries. The Partial Least Square is used to analyze the relationships between the real feelings of customers and characteristics of home delivery service. Huang et al. [22, 23] identified a method to deal with consumers' Kansei requirements for emotional design in new product development based on a design structure matrix. They also proposed method can be utilized to better classify products of Kansei tags as well as to facilitate decision-making in practical industrial design cases. Huang et al. [24] provided an objective approach to trade to show booth planning based on fuzzy product positioning and Kansei engineering. Lu et al. [25] developed a methodology of Kansei engineering to the integration of emotional qualities of the design of products, which taking into account the cognitive and affective processing of users. Roy et al. [26] explored a method of applying Kansei as part of a product design creative process of web-based pictorial questionnaires. Huang et al. [27] proposed a method to address product attributes with emotional impacts on new product development based on product configuration analysis. Guo et al. [12] developed a systematically emotional design method of products' hard interfaces based on Kansei Engineering, which can be used to design a product that echoes users' emotions. Dolgun et al. [28] explored a product planning with sensory customer requirements based on quality function deployment and kansei engineering.

3 Design Method

This study developed a comprehensive design method aimed at satisfying consumer emotional cognition. On the one hand, the perceptual images of product design based on statistical methods is explored. Perceptual image is an important research hotspot in the field of emotional design, and it belongs to kansei engineering (a discipline that combines perceptual needs and engineering technology). This study is based on Kansei engineering to explore the relationship between the design elements and the emotional semantics of the product, which is used to guide the designer to redesign. On the other hand, the user behavior requirements of product design based on eye movement analysis is explored. The eye movement and gaze direction of the consumer when looking at a particular product design are monitored by the eye tracking technology. The research framework of the design model is shown in Fig. 1.

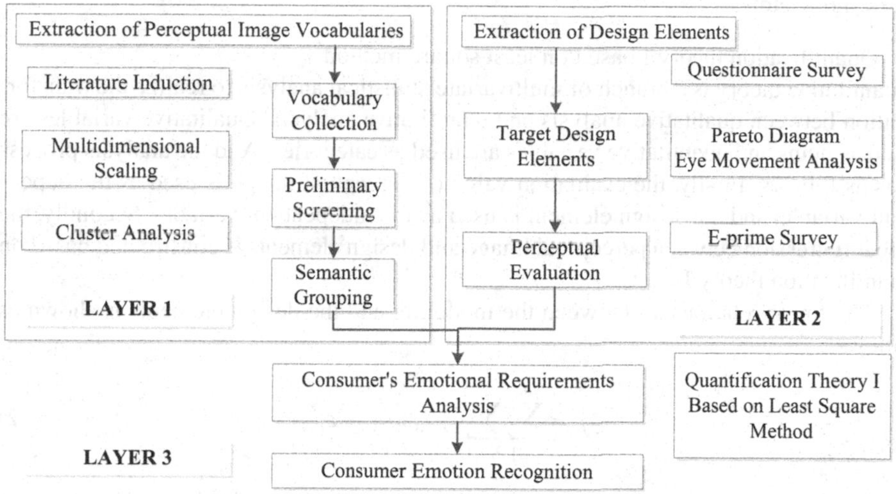

Fig. 1. Research framework of the design model.

1. Multidimensional scaling

Multidimensional scaling is a multivariable analysis method used in the fields of sociology and psychology. And multidimensional scale is used to explore the implicit relation between different perceptual images. The analysis process is as follows: Firstly, Euclidean distance (1) is used to analyze the distance between different users' preference. Secondly, the analysis object of multidimensional space is transformed into low dimensional space. Thirdly, the target object is set to N items. And the distance formula is used to calculate the center coordinates of each item. Fourthly, the distance between various items is analyzed and the perceptual image is adjusted in time.

$$d_{ij} = \sqrt{(X_{i1} - X_{j1})^2 + \cdots + (X_{ir} - X_{jr})^2} \quad (1)$$

2. Cluster analysis

Cluster analysis is a multivariate statistical method for classification, including hierarchical clustering and iterative clustering. In this study, the iterative clustering was adopted. And the analysis process was as follows: Firstly, the implicit relation between perceptual image is explored by using multidimensional scaling. Secondly, the similarity of the perceptual image is judged according to the distance of users' preference. Thirdly, the classification of perceptual image is obtained.

3. Pareto diagram

The pareto principle refers to the social imbalance (20% of the population creates 80% of the wealth, 80% of the profits come from 20% of the goods). The imbalance is the law of the two - eight rule, which emphasizes to get twice the result with half the effort. And the analysis process was as follows: Firstly, the design elements are drawn into histogram based on the relevant frequency of Pareto diagram. Secondly, the modeling elements with high cumulative frequency are selected as the target design factors.

(4) Quantification theory I based on least square method
Quantitative theory is a branch of multivariate statistical analysis to realize the transformation between qualitative analysis and quantitative analysis. Qualitative variables are used as items and quantitative variables are used as categories. And the analysis process was as follows: Firstly, the evaluation value of perceptual image is used as the dependent variable, and the design element is used as the independent variable. Secondly, the linear regression between perceptual image and design elements is constructed based on quantification theory I.

The linear relationship between the modeling and the design elements is shown as follows.

$$y_j = \sum_{i=1}^{m} \sum_{k=1}^{c_i} x_{ik}(j)\alpha_{ik} + \varepsilon_j \tag{2}$$

where, α_{ik} stands for the influence of the k category of i item in the design elements on the product design. α_{ik} is the quantization representation of the qualitative variable $x_{ik}(w)$. ε_j stands for the random error in the j sampling.

The coefficient vector is represented by A. $A = [\alpha_{ik}] = \left[\alpha_{11}, \alpha_{12}, \ldots, \alpha_{mC_m}\right]^T$. The error vector is represented by E. $E = [\varepsilon_w] = [\varepsilon_1, \varepsilon_2, \ldots, \varepsilon_n]^T$. The formula (1) can be further expressed as $Y = XA + E$. Moreover, the solution can be reduced to a linear function that makes the error a minimum $Y = XA^* + E^*$. A^* is obtained based on the least square method. $A^* = \left(X^TX\right)^{-1}X^Ty$. Where A^* stands for the quantification of qualitative categories of design elements. $\hat{Y} = XA^*$. $\hat{Y}$ stands for the predictive value of design elements.

4 Experimental Process of CNC Machine Tool

At present, CNC machine tool technology has been organically combined with computer-aided design and manufacturing technology, and it has gradually moved to the advanced level of the world in terms of technological innovation and functional design. But with the enrichment of material wealth and the intensification of the homogenization of technology and function, the competition of CNC machine tools is not only about the contest of performance, function and price, but more emphasis on the modeling competition. CNC machine tool modeling is the material carrier and spiritual carrier of the product, and it is also an important medium for the communication between the user and the designer. In the era of emotional consumption and experience economy, consumers prefer the CNC machine tool products with individual attributes and emotional identity. This part illustrates the proposed model with a case study of CNC machine tool.

4.1 Design Elements Layer

1. The selection of design elements based on statistical methods

We collected 126 pictures of various kinds of CNC machine tools by consulting literature and expert interview. Twenty users were invited to vote on the sample of CNC machine tools by questionnaire. The sample with the same or similar were removed. Twenty users were selected to score the pictures of CNC machine tools by using the Likert scale. Finally, fifteen representative pictures were taken in Table 1.

Table 1. Representative pictures of CNC machine tools.

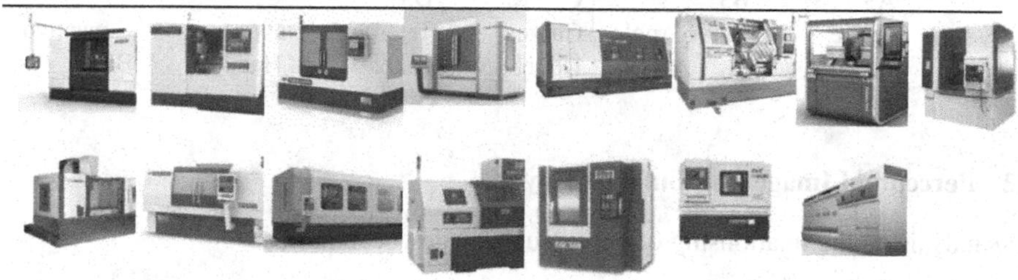

The design elements affecting the modeling of CNC machine tool are analyzed based on expert interview and questionnaire survey. The contribution of the design elements to the modeling of CNC machine tools is obtained based on the Pareto diagram. The design elements include protective cover, door, observation window, handle, control panel, machine base, control key, brand identification, electric control cabinet and water tank.

2. The selection of design elements based on eye movement

The eye movement of the experimenter was tracked based on the ASL EYE-TRAC6 head-mounted eye tracker. Experimenters are required to have good eyesight and no eye diseases such as color blindness and color blindness. Moreover, fifteen representative pictures of CNC machine tool are played by E-prime program. The interest area and design elements of the experimenter are obtained based on measurable indexes such as fixation time, refixation times and blink rate.

Based on the above analysis, the selection of design elements of CNC machine tool is made. The design elements of CNC machine tool that the experimenter is interested in are obtained based on the analysis of each sample, namely, protective cover, door, observation window, handle and control panel. The six design elements, such as protective cover, observation window, door, control panel, handle and machine base, are used as the target elements of CNC machine tool (see Table 2).

Table 2. Analysis of target design elements of CNC machine tool.

Design Elements	A Protective Cover	B Observation Window	C Door	D Control Panel	E Handle	F Machine Base
	A1 Plane	B1 Round Angle	C1 Plane Door	D1 Mobile Panel	E1 Converted Handle	F1 Entity Base
	A2 Converted Plane	B2 Right Angle	C2 Converted Door	D2 Embedded Panel	E2 Elliptical Handle	F2 Plane Base
	A3 Curve	B3 Curve Angle	C3 Curved Door	D3 Telescopic Panel	E3 Plane Handle	F3 Converted Base

4.2 Perceptual Image Vocabularies Layer

1. Analysis on the relationship of perceptual image vocabularies

Consumer's perceptual image vocabularies of CNC machine tool are acquired based on questionnaire survey and brainstorming method. At first, 49 semantic vocabularies of perceptual images which are suitable for describing CNC machine tool are collected as shown in Table 3. After the initial screening process, 17 semantic vocabularies is obtained.

Table 3. The image vocabularies of CNC machine tool.

	Image Vocabularies								
Primary Vocabularies	Contemporary	Solid	Comfortable	Kind	Natural	Safe	Durable	Softly	Harmonious
	Traditional	Stable	Graceful	Rational	Deft	Simple	Practical	Serviceable	Economic
	Accurate	Cozy	Regular	Decent	Advanced	Distinctive	Symmetrical	Steady	Coordinated
	Luscious	Full	Concise	Artistic	Scientific	Fashionable	Cordial	Individual	Precise
	Smooth	Mordern	Technological	Decorous	Rhythmical	High-end	Environmental	Functional	Rounded
	Exquisite	Warm	Succinct	Compact					
Target Vocabularies	V1 Steady	V2 Technological	V3 Contemporary	V4 Precise	V5 Decent	V6 Simple	V7 Concise	V8 Regular	V9 Exquisite
	V10 Economic	V11 Graceful	V12 Distinctive	V13 Smooth	V14 Fashionable	V15 Natural	V16 Safe	V17 Serviceable	

Thirty experts are invited to group the seventeen image vocabularies of CNC machine tool by the questionnaire shown in Appendix A. The experimenter divides the image vocabularies with the same nature into the same group according to the subjective association. Moreover, the statistical results were transformed into similarity matrix Aij. The data are analyzed by multidimensional analysis based on SPSS. The effectiveness of statistical results is inversely proportional to Kruskal, which is proportional to RSQ. If Stress < 0.1, RSQ > 0.7, it indicates that the coordination degree between the statistical objects is good, and the statistical results are feasible. Based on the above analysis, Stress = 0.05326 and RSQ = 0.96392 are obtained through experiments, indicating that the statistical results are valid.

2. Specify a grouping of perceptual image of CNC machine tool

The similarity frequency matrix Aij based on multidimensional analysis is converted to the coordinate value. Based on the clustering analysis, the Kruskal was the minimum and the RSQ was the largest when the group number was 4. Moreover, the seventeen image vocabularies of CNC machine tool are divided into 4 groups, as shown in Table 4.

Table 4. Perceptual vocabularies grouping based on clustering analysis.

First group	Second group	Third group	Fourth group
V7(distance:0.248) V1(distance:0.252) V6(distance:1.122) V10(distance:1.168)	V2(distance:0.068) V9(distance:0.139) V13(distance:0.168) V16(distance:0.192)	V3(distance:0.128) V8(distance:0.182) V14(distance:0.235) V17(distance:0.284)	V5(distance:1.121) V4(distance:1.210) V11(distance:1.280) V12(distance:1.382) V15(distance:1.964)

3. The establishment of the perceptual evaluation matrix of CNC machine tool

A scoring questionnaire was made on the perceptual image of CNC machine tool. Thirty experimenters were invited to score perceptual vocabularies on representative pictures of CNC machine tool based on subjective images. 1, 2, 3, 4, 5 represent the correlation degree between perceptual vocabularies and representative pictures, respectively. 1 indicate that there is no correlation, 2 indicates weak correlation, 3 indicates medium correlation, 4 indicates correlation, and 5 is very relevant. The perceptual evaluation is shown in Table 5.

4.3 Relationship Layer

Regression analysis is made on the relationship between design elements and perceptual vocabularies based on SPSS. The partial correlation coefficient between perceptual vocabularies and design elements is obtained based on quantitative theory I. The relationship between the design elements of CNC machine tool and the perceptual vocabularies of "Technological" in Table 6.

Table 5. The perceptual evaluation of CNC machine tool.

	Perceptual Evaluation				Design Elements																	
	V7	V2	V3	V5	A			B			C			D			E			F		
					A1	A2	A3	B1	B2	B3	C1	C2	C3	D1	D2	D3	E1	E2	E3	F1	F2	F3
1	4.2	4.4	3.1	4.5	1	0	0	1	0	0	1	0	0	0	0	1	0	1	0	1	0	0
2	2.6	4.0	2.3	2.0	1	0	0	0	1	0	0	0	1	1	0	0	0	0	0	0	1	0
3	4.6	4.6	3.6	3.8	1	0	0	1	0	0	0	1	0	0	1	0	0	0	1	0	0	1
4	4.7	4.2	4.2	4.6	0	1	0	1	0	0	0	0	1	0	0	0	1	0	0	0	1	0
5	3.8	3.9	4.2	4.1	0	1	0	0	1	0	0	0	0	1	0	0	0	1	0	1	0	0
6	3.2	4.4	3.3	3.5	1	0	0	0	1	0	0	0	1	1	0	0	0	0	0	0	1	0
7	2.6	3.0	2.3	2.0	0	1	0	1	0	0	0	0	1	0	0	0	1	0	0	0	1	0
8	3.6	4.6	3.3	3.3	0	1	0	0	1	0	0	0	0	1	0	0	0	1	0	1	0	0
9	4.7	3.2	4.2	3.6	1	0	0	0	1	0	0	0	1	1	0	0	1	0	0	1	0	0
10	3.3	3.3	3.2	4.6	1	0	0	0	1	0	0	0	1	1	0	0	0	0	0	0	1	0
11	4.2	4.3	4.3	3.5	1	0	0	1	0	0	0	1	0	0	1	0	0	0	1	0	0	1
12	3.2	4.0	4.3	2.6	0	1	0	1	0	0	0	0	1	0	0	0	1	0	0	0	1	0
13	4.6	4.6	3.2	4.6	0	1	0	0	1	0	0	0	0	1	0	0	0	1	0	1	0	0
14	4.1	3.2	4.5	2.1	1	0	0	0	1	0	0	0	1	1	0	0	1	0	0	1	0	0
15	4.5	3.1	3.8	4.0	0	1	0	1	0	0	1	0	0	1	0	0	0	1	0	0	1	0

Based on the above analysis, the relationship between the perceptual vocabularies "technological" and the design elements of CNC machine tool is different. The partial correlation coefficient of the design elements and the perceptual vocabularies "technology" is listed as follows (see Table 7): protective cover A(0.930 > observation window B(0.843 > machine base F(0.739 > door C(0.572 > handle E(0.429 > control panel D(0.292). Taking the protective cover as an example, the ranking of the utility value of the design elements is represented as follow: Converted Plane (1.619) > Plane (1.327) > Curve (0.491). Moreover, the function relation between "technological" and the design elements of CNC machine tool is expressed. The constant term in the function is automatically calculated by using SPSS software.

$$\begin{aligned} \mathrm{Y}_{\mathrm{technological}} = & 1.327\mathrm{A1} + 1.619\mathrm{A2} + 0.491\mathrm{A3} - 0.033\mathrm{B1} + 0.897\mathrm{B2} + 1.103\mathrm{B3} \\ & + 0.109\mathrm{C1} - 0.474\mathrm{C2} - 0.847\mathrm{C3} + 0.243\mathrm{D1} + 0.047\mathrm{D2} \\ & - 0.013\mathrm{D3} + 1.037\mathrm{E1} - 0.087\mathrm{E2} + 0.126\mathrm{E3} + 2.227 \end{aligned}$$

A new experimental sample was selected to evaluate the design elements of the CNC machine tool, and the validity of the test method was proved. 29 CNC machine tool pictures were selected, and the above experimental steps were repeated. The function relation between the perceptual vocabularies "modern" and the design elements of CNC machine tool is expressed:

$$\begin{aligned} Y_{\mathrm{modern}} = & 0.491A1 + 2.019A2 + 1.329A3 - 0.033B1 + 0.583B2 + 0.109B3 \\ & + 0.472C1 - 0.137C2 - 0.847C3 + 0.433D1 + 0.047D2 \\ & - 0.306D3 + 1.037E1 - 0.138E2 + 0.841E3 + 2.444 \end{aligned}$$

Table 6. Relationship between design elements and perceptual image vocabularies of "Technological".

Design Elements		Partial Correlation Coefficient	Contribution Rate	
			Opposite Directions	Technological
A Protective Cover	A1 Plane	0.930		1.327
	A2 Converted Plane			1.619
	A3 Curve			0.491
B Observation Window	B1 Round Angle	0.843	-0.033	
	B2 Right Angle			0.897
	B3 Curve Angle			1.103
C Door	C1 Plane Door	0.572		0.109
	C2 Converted Door		-0.474	
	C3 Curved Door		-0.847	
D Control Panel	D1 Mobile Panel	0.292		0.243
	D2 Embedded Panel			0.047
	D3 Telescopic Panel		-0.013	
E Handle	E1Converted Handle	0.429		1.037
	E2 Elliptical Handle		-0.087	
	E3 Plane Handle			0.126
F Machine Base	F1 Entity Base	0.739	-0.306	
	F2 Plane Base			1.206
	F3 Converted Base		-0.841	

The T test of the two results of formula (8) and (9) is conducted, and the test results are shown in Table 7. Based on the above analysis, the results of the Levene test of the variance equation are as follows: The variance value (F) is 0.684 and the significant value (Sig) is 0.416. And significant value (0.416) > specified value (0.05). It shows that the variance of the two groups of samples is "not significant", that is, it is consistent with the homogeneity of variance. Moreover, the results of the T test of mean equation are as follows: significant value (0.867) > specified value (0.05). This indicates that there is no significant difference between the two samples.

Table 7. Partial correlation coefficient between perceptual vocabularies and design elements.

Perceptual Vocabularies	Partial Correlation Coefficient					
	A Protective Cover	B Observation Window	C Door	D Control Panel	E Handle	F Machine Base
Technological	0.930	0.843	0.572	0.292	0.429	0.739
Concise	0.529	0.295	0.358	0.382	0.769	0.346
Natural	0.765	0.637	0.620	0.456	0.359	0.721
Decent	0.739	0.672	0.731	0.567	0.683	0.833

Based on the statistical analysis and eye movement analysis, we find that users pay more attention to the design features of the protective cover, observation window and machine base in the design of CNC machines tools, which helps the designers form the design strategy of CNC machine tools to meet users' emotional needs. For example, designers should focus on the protective cover when considering the design of modern CNC machine tools. This enables the designed products to meet the customer's emotional requirements and make the design process more targeted.

5 Discussion

The eye movement of the experimenter were tracked based on the ASL EYE-TRAC6 head-mounted eye tracker. The interest area and design elements of the experimenter are obtained based on measurable indexes such as fixation time, refixation times and blink rate. In order to verify the validity of the experimental results, the same experimenter were invited to experiment with the same sample pictures with Tobii eye tracker (see Table 8).

Based on the above analysis, the selection of design elements of CNC machine tool is made. Eye-tracking visual trajectory reflects the sequence and fixation time of the experimenter when browsing the sample design elements. The area with high brightness and large area indicates the interest area in which the experimenter's eye gaze for a long time. Eye-tracking heat map shows the degree of attention to different design elements of CNC machine tool. Red indicates a high level of attention. Yellow indicates a moderate degree of concern. And green is less concerned. The design elements of CNC machine tool that the experimenter is interested in are obtained based on the analysis of each sample, namely, protective cover, door, observation window, handle and control panel. Design element of protective cover is more concerned than design element of observation window based on the Tobii eye tracker. Design element of controal panel is more concerned than design element of machine base based on the ASL eye tracker. The six design elements, such as protective cover, observation window, door, control panel, handle and machine base, are used as the target elements of CNC machine tool (see Fig. 2 and Fig. 3).

Table 8. Experimental comparison.

		ASL eye tracker	Tobii eye tracker
Experimental process		 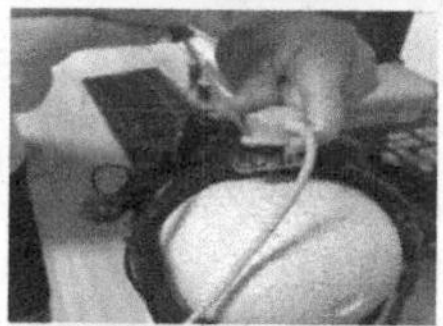 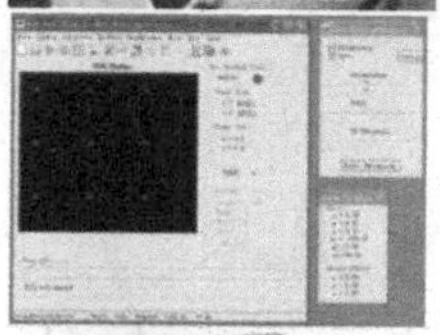 	   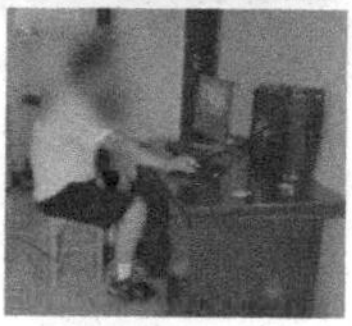
Experi-mental datas	Time to first fix-ation	84.32	35.02
	Dwell time	7381.32	5223.01
	Revist count	3.02	3.23
	Fixation count	4.13	4.30
	Total fixation duration	5562.33	6024.33
	Pupil diameter	3.61	4.02
Experi-mental results	Heat map		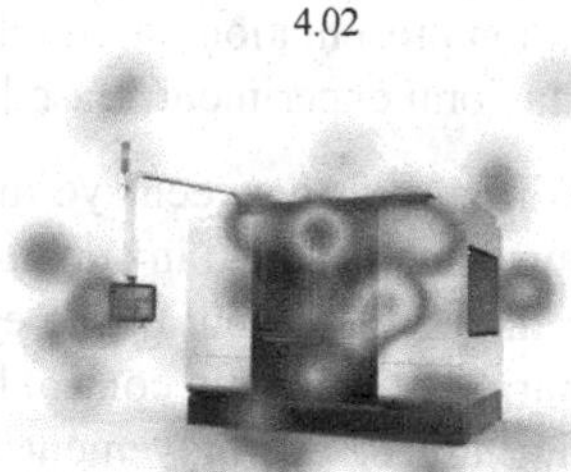
	Visual trajectory	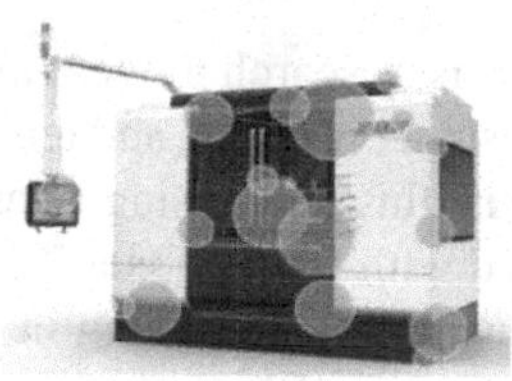	

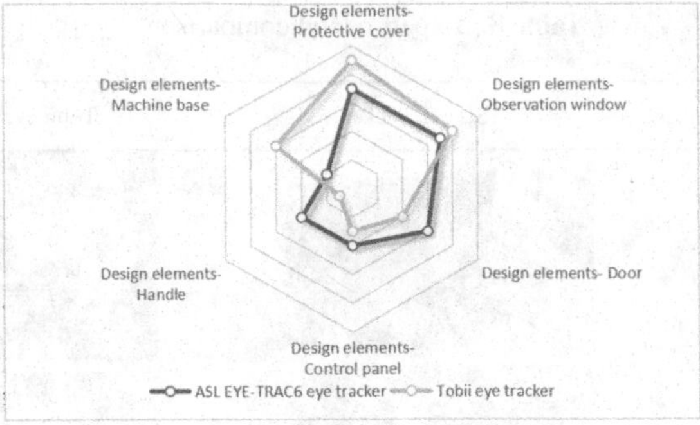

Fig. 2. Experiment comparison of target elements.

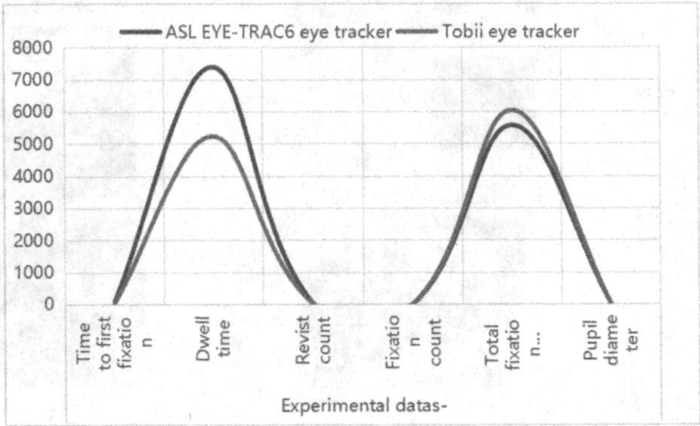

Fig. 3. Experiment data comparison.

This paper studied the efficiency of searching to design elements from the angle of information presentation based on existing research with the method of eye-movement and behavioral experiment. Based on the experimental comparison and analysis,

1. The differences between eye-movement in conditional reasoning mainly exist on the premise interest area; in conclusion interest area, there is no significant differences.
2. By relating the output of the eye-movement experiment, this paper reveals the real scenario of the human control behavior model.
3. Taking use of eye-movement technology, experiment observes the eye-movement indicators of target elements of CNC machine tool.

The proposed method breaks the exist research mode limitation on using traditional methods pay more attention to the consumer intuition and ignore the consumer behavior. The proposed method's performance is illustrated using a case study on CNC machine tools. The results show that, compared with a traditional Kansei engineering approach for emotional design, the proposed method is promising in handing consumer's emotional requirements based on psychology and behavior. The research is to solve the scientific problem of the evaluation of CNC machine tool design scheme, and to provide a theoretical basis for the product identity strategy.

6 Conclusions

A combined design method based on statistical analysis and eye movement is proposed and described in this work. The method takes consumers' psychological requirements and behavioral requirements into consideration for emotional design. The method is divided into three layers: Design elements layer; Perceptual image vocabularies layer; The relationship layer between the design elements and the perceptual image vocabularies. In the first layer, the selection of design elements is made based on statistical methods (Pareto diagram) and eye movement analysis. The design elements are obtained. In the second layer, the evaluation matrix of perceptual image vocabularies is established based on multidimensional scaling and clustering analysis. The perceptual image vocabularies of product design are obtained. In the third layer, the relationship between the design elements and the perceptual image vocabularies is analyzed by using quantitative theory I based on least square method. The design features of the target product are found based on consumer's emotional requirements. This study presents a combined design method based on statistical analysis and eye movement analysis to deal with consumer's emotional requirements for product design based on psychological requirements and behavioral requirements. It appears that the proposed method can be utilized to capture and analyze consumer's emotional requirements as well as to facilitate decision making of design restructuring and upgrading in practical industrial design cases.

However, we still have some limitation factors of this study. On the one hand, although we applied different search terms while selecting references, the searching was carried out only within a limited database and search range, especially we took only English journal articles in consideration, excluding books, conference papers. On the other hand, we classified the combined design method of three layers. This categorization may not represent the method objectively and comprehensively. We would like to address these issues in future research. Future work would focus on improving the effectiveness and accuracy of identifying the design elements. We should improve the construction of the deduction engine based on consumer's emotional requirements, and introduce the interactive evaluation module in the emotional design process to envisioned that a fully consumer's-oriented design method can be realized.

Acknowledgments. This work was supported by the "National Key R&D Program of China, Transparent pressure-resistant structure and development of manned submersible" [grant number: 2021YFC2800600], the "Province Key R&D Program of Shaanxi, Research on dynamic three-dimensional evaluation and adjustment model of manned airtight cabin operation comfort" [grant number: 2022GY-311] and the "Innovation Foundation for Doctor Dissertation of Northwestern Polytechnical University" [grant number: CX2023049].

Disclosure of Interests. The authors have no competing interests to declare that are relevant to the content of this article.

References

1. Plass, J., Heidig, S., Hayward, E., et al.: Emotional design in multimedia learning: effects of shape and color on affect and learning. Learn. Instr. **29**, 128–140 (2014)

2. Heidig, S., Müller, J., Reichelt, M.: Emotional design in multimedia learning: differentiation on relevant design features and their effects on emotions and learning. Comput. Hum. Behav. **44**, 81–95 (2015)
3. Schneider, S., Nebel, S., Rey, G.: Decorative pictures and emotional design in multimedia learning. Learn. Instr. **44**, 65–73 (2016)
4. Kamil, M., Abidin, S.: Unconscious human behavior at visceral level of emotional design. Procedia Soc. Behav. Sci. **105**, 149–161 (2013)
5. Franzak, F., Makarem, S., Jae, H.: Design benefits, emotional responses, and brand engagement. J. Prod. Brand Manage. **23**(1), 16–23 (2014)
6. Saariluoma, P., Jokinen, J.: Emotional dimensions of user experience: a user psychological analysis. Int. J. Hum.-Comput. Interact. **30**(4), 303–320 (2014)
7. Pengnate, S., Antonenko, P.: A multimethod evaluation of online trust and its interaction with metacognitive awareness: an emotional design perspective. Int. J. Hum.-Comput. Interact. **29**(9), 582–593 (2013)
8. Park, B., Jang, E., Chung, M., et al.: Design of prototype-based emotion recognizer using physiological signals. ETRI J. **35**(5), 869–879 (2013)
9. Man, D., Wei, D., Chih-Chieh, Y.: Product color design based on multi-emotion. J. Mech. Sci. Technol. **27**(7), 2079–2084 (2013)
10. Fokkinga, S., Desmet, P.: Ten ways to design for disgust, sadness, and other enjoyments: a design approach to enrich product experiences with negative emotions. Int. J. Des. **7**(1), 19–36 (2013)
11. Michelle, Y., Widen, S., Russell, J.: The within-subjects design in the study of facial expressions. Cogn. Emot. **27**(6), 1062–1072 (2013)
12. Guo, F., Liu, W., Liu, F., et al.: Emotional design method of product presented in multi-dimensional variables based on Kansei Engineering. J. Eng. Des. **25**(4–6), 194–212 (2014)
13. Guo, F., Liu, W., Cao, Y., et al.: Optimization design of a webpage based on Kansei engineering. Hum. Factors Ergon. Manuf. Service Ind. **26**(1), 110–126 (2016)
14. Yang, Y., Chen, D., Gu, R., et al.: Consumers' Kansei needs clustering method for product emotional design based on numerical design structure matrix and genetic algorithms. Computational intelligence and neuroscience (2016)
15. Um, E., Plass, J., Hayward, E., et al.: Emotional design in multimedia learning. J. Educ. Psychol. **104**(2), 485 (2012)
16. Mayer, R., Estrella, G.: Benefits of emotional design in multimedia instruction. Learn. Instr. **33**, 12–18 (2014)
17. Ho, A., Siu, K.: Emotion design, emotional design, emotionalize design: a review on their relationships from a new perspective. Des. J. **15**(1), 9–32 (2012)
18. Park, B., Knörzer, L., Plass, J., et al.: Emotional design and positive emotions in multimedia learning: an eyetracking study on the use of anthropomorphisms. Comput. Educ. **86**, 30–42 (2015)
19. Uzun, A., Yıldırım, Z.: Exploring the effect of using different levels of emotional design features in multimedia science learning. Comput. Educ. **119**, 112–128 (2018)
20. Triberti, S., Chirico, A., La, R., et al.: Developing emotional design: emotions as cognitive processes and their role in the design of interactive technologies. Front. Psychol. **8**, 1773 (2017)
21. Chen, M., Hsu, C., Chang, K., et al.: Applying Kansei engineering to design logistics services–A case of home delivery service. Int. J. Ind. Ergon. **48**, 46–59 (2015)
22. Huang, Y., Chen, C., Khoo, L.: Kansei clustering for emotional design using a combined design structure matrix. Int. J. Ind. Ergon. **42**(5), 416–427 (2012)
23. Huang, Y., Chen, C., Khoo, L.: Products classification in emotional design using a basic-emotion based semantic differential method. Int. J. Ind. Ergon. **42**(6), 569–580 (2012)

24. Huang, M., Tsai, H., Huang, T.: Applying Kansei engineering to industrial machinery trade show booth design. Int. J. Ind. Ergon. **41**(1), 72–78 (2011)
25. Lu, W., Petiot, J.: Affective design of products using an audio-based protocol: application to eyeglass frame. Int. J. Ind. Ergon. **44**(3), 383–394 (2014)
26. Roy, R., Goatman, M., Khangura, K.: User-centric design and Kansei Engineering. CIRP J. Manuf. Sci. Technol. **1**(3), 172–178 (2009)
27. Huang, Y., Chen, C., Wang, I., et al.: A product configuration analysis method for emotional design using a personal construct theory. Int. J. Ind. Ergon. **44**(1), 120–130 (2014)
28. Dolgun, L., Köksal, G. Effective use of quality function deployment and Kansei engineering for product planning with sensory customer requirements: a plain yogurt case. Quality Engineering (2017)

Author Index

A. Marcus et al. (Eds.): HCII 2024, LNCS 14714, pp. 331–332, 2024.
https://doi.org/10.1007/978-3-031-61356-2

Printed in the United States
by Baker & Taylor Publisher Services